THE MESPOT
LETTERS
of a
COTSWOLD SOLDIER

THE MESPOT LETTERS

of a

COTSWOLD SOLDIER

FREDERICK WITTS

EDITED BY JASPER HADMAN

AMBERLEY

First published 2009 by
Amberley Publishing
Cirencester Road
Chalford
Stroud
Gloucestershire
GL6 8PE

ISBN 978-1-84868-041-8

Typesetting and origination by Amberley Publishing
Printed and bound in Great Britain.

CONTENTS

LIST OF APPENDICES

LIST OF ILLUSTRATIONS

Illustrations in the Text:

76. Kazhimain Mosque, Baghdad.
77. Gufars near the North Bridge, Baghdad.
78. A gufar.
79. Official Christmas card to the troops, 1917.
80. General Maude's funeral.
81. Lieutenant-General Sir William Marshall.
82. The bridge at Baghdad.
83. British residency in Baghdad.
84. Bazaar scene, Baghdad.
85. Gufars at Baghdad.
86. Lieutenant General Sir Alexander Cobbe.
87. Bridge of boats over the Tigris, broken up by storm, January 1916.
88. View over Baghdad.
89. Waterwheels at Hit.
90. The Leave Train (The *Bystanders* 'Fragments from France').
91. Postcard looking down to the ford in Upper Slaughter.
92. Hotel Maude, Baghdad.
93. The Manor, Upper Slaughter (from the Vineyards).
94. Armistice proclamation in Baghdad 31/10/18.
95. Fathah Gorge.
96. Craw (or Cray) fishing at Aston Brook August 1915.
97. Sharif Hussein.
98. The Hospital Ship *Erinpura*.
99. View of Baghdad downstream of the British Residency.
100. View of Baghdad upstream of the British Residency.
101. Baghdad Racecourse.
102. The Grand Stand at the Baghdad Races.
103. Sheikh Mahmud.
104. *Cheltenham Chronicle* 13th August 1910: The wedding of Jack Kennard and Frances Witts 9th August 1910 at Lower Guiting (Guiting Power).
105. Hillah from the south-east.
106. Ruins of Ancient Babylon.
107. Hindiyah Barrage.
108. Najaf.
109. Pony. F.V.B.W. written: 'This pony was mine later on'.
110. A Handley-Page aeroplane.
111. Lieutenant-Colonel Sir A. T. Wilson.
112. Mosul.
113. Kurds of the Rowanduz District.
114. Flying over Southern Kurdistan.
115. Rowanduz Gorge.
116. Erbil.
117. Erbil from the south.

118. Zakho camp.
119. Lieutenant-Colonel G. Leachman.
120. Kurdish tribesmen at Rania, 1919.
121. Kurdish scenery near Rayat.
122. The result of a stunt.
123. *Cheltenham Chronicle* 16th July 1910: The wedding of Jack Cheetham and Mabel Witts on July 7th 1910 at Lower Guiting (Guiting Power).
124. Eyford Park (side). Eyford was the home of Jack and Mabel Cheetham; Mabel was F.V.B.W.'s first cousin.
125. *Cheltenham Chronicle* 13th August 1910: The wedding of Jack Kennard and Frances Witts 9th August 1910 at Lower Guiting (Guiting Power).
126. 'The women of Upper Slaughter thank Major E. F. B. Witts (F.V.B.W.'s eldest brother) …' F.V.B.W. received one similar.
127. The bazaar, Baghdad.
128. Floods on Maude Bridge.
129. Major-General G. Leslie.
130. Fortified town of Salihiya.
131. Buckingham Palace Investiture 1920: Frank and Ruth Witts.
132. Tel Afar.
133. General Sir J. Aylmer Haldane.
134. Rumaitha – buildings defended are within white line.
135. Diwaniyah and camp.
136. Mesopotamian scenery.
137. Maude Bridge looking East.
138. Copse Hill Fete 8th August 1920: presentation of medals by Lieutenant-Colonel Edwin Brassey.
139. *Cheltenham Chronicle* 11th September 1920: 'Opening of Parish Hall and Fete at Upper Slaughter'.
140. Baghdad skyline.
141. F.V.B.W. in *War Illustrated*, June 9th 1917.
142. Sir Percy Cox.
143. Upper Slaughter School, 1895.
144. Ruth Witts riding a camel in Algeria on February 4th 1921 (Mrs Witts died two days later).
145. F.V.B.W.
146. Family group in the Manor back garden December 1919: Frank, Ruth, Mrs Witts, Elma, Jack and Edith. (Photo taken by Agnes).

Illustrations in the Colour Section:
1. F.V.B.W. in his mid-twenties.
2. Oil painting of Mrs Margaret Witts (F.V.B.W.'s mother).
3. F.V.B.W.'s Coat of Arms, incorporating the Witts Coat of Arms with

his medals, many awarded in Mesopotamia. It can be seen on the memorial tablet at the Royal Hospital, Chelsea (*see* colour illustration 22 below).

4. Canon Broome Witts (F.V.B.W.'s father); he was sometimes referred to by F.V.B.W., in his letters, as 'Dear old father'.

5. Mrs Margaret Witts (F.V.B.W.'s mother).

6. Oil painting by Agnes Witts (F.V.B.W.'s youngest sister) of the front of the Manor, Upper Slaughter.

7. Oil painting by Agnes Witts of the back of the Manor, Upper Slaughter.

8. Oil painting by Agnes Witts (F.V.B.W.'s youngest sister) of Wyck Hill House (*see* p. 118, note 6).

9. Oil painting of Guiting Grange by Susan Boone. Guiting Grange was the home of F.V.B.W.'s Aunt Maggie (Mrs Waddingham Witts). It was inherited from her, first by her daughter Sophie, and then by her daughter Francie.

10. F.V.B.W. as a Cadet, stepping into the back garden at the Manor.

11. Hand-painted Christmas cards from Mrs Witts to F.V.B.W., 1918

12. Envelopes sent to F.V.B.W. in Mesopotamia, 1920.

13. Coloured print of the crossing of the Tigris at the Shumran bend February 23rd 1917.

14. The Maude Proclamation in Arabic (*see* p. 160, note 2))

15. The Maude Proclamation in English (see p. 160, note 2))

16. Eastern Bank, Baghdad cheque book c. 1920. It is interesting that the bank's name was recorded not only in English and Arabic, but also in Hebrew.

17. X-Ray: 'bullet in my arm 20th December 1916'.

18. The silk Kashan rug which F.V.B.W. sent home to his mother in 1920 with his friend Norrie Fuller. It arrived shortly before she died.

19. Statue of the 'Winged Figure of Victory' commemorating the deeds of the Bengal Sappers and Miners. Please see Appendix XVIII. The plaque on the base depicts the crossing of the Tigris at Shumran, with the minarets of Baghdad and the Spiral Mosque of Samarrah on the horizon (photos by Charles Holman, R.E. Museum, Chatham).

20. Postcard of the Thomas Denny stained glass window at the east end of the chapel in Upper Slaughter church. Please see Appendix XVII (photo by Clive Barda).

21. Photo of the Trefoil stained glass window on the north side of the chapel in Upper Slaughter Church. Please see Appendix XVII (photo by Clive Barda).

22. F.V.B.W.'s memorial tablet at the Royal Hospital, Chelsea. He served there as Lieutenant-Governor from 1944 until 1948 and as a Commissioner from 1948 until 1957.

LIST OF MAPS

ACKNOWLEDGEMENTS

I am very grateful to various people for their help: Graeme Baldwin for his initial work on the Witts/Mesopotamia papers ten years ago (before the letters themselves had been discovered), Simon Moody at the National Army Museum for his expertise, Stephen Lloyd for his research on his forebears in the Woodroffe family, Elizabeth Witts for her very helpful suggestions, the Crew at 2 Barony street for their generosity and support when I was working in Edinburgh, Tom Bowden for his expert suggestions, Alan Sutton for publishing the book, Hattie Peters for all her work, Michael Boone for stepping in as my personal chauffeur, William Hadman for sacrificing his bedroom as my study, my parents, Carol and Bill Hadman, for their immense support, and Emma Rogers for her unfailing patience and encouragement.

The small army of typists and proof readers deserve enormous thanks – Carol Boone (senior typist), Carol Hadman, Louise Boone, Michael Boone (senior proof reader), Grace Hadman and Robert Hadman. (F.V.B.W.'s letters were comparatively easy to read; his mother's were not).

I am also most grateful to all the authors mentioned in the bibliography, some of whom I have quoted briefly in the footnotes or narrative, and from some of whom I have borrowed maps and illustrations.

Last, but not least, I would like to thank Francis Witts, son of Frederick, who gave me this project and has been a truly prodigious support throughout. He has painstakingly read and re-read the manuscript time and again, ruthlessly, but always justly, dissecting my work until I finally produced something which is hopefully comprehensible. His help and generosity have been unbounded and I owe him a great debt of gratitude.

For all the mistakes and omissions I accept full responsibility.

Lower Swell
October 2008

Jasper J. Hadman

FOREWORD

Having spent much of my working life in and about the Middle East, it has long been a sadness for me that I never much had the chance of hearing first hand from my father, who died when I was young, about his military experiences in Mespot (as he called Mesopotamia) during the First World War, and later on in Egypt and Palestine. I am thus particularly grateful to Ruth Gosling, our twentieth century archivist, for discovering these letters, and hugely grateful to Jasper Hadman for taking time out between his global motor bicycling journeys to edit them and to provide a commentary. (I think in time this book will become known as Hadman's Witts). The commentary is necessary as my father's own letters, of course, were subject to the war censor's savage red pen. From time to time he comments to his mother how difficult it is writing a letter, when he is not allowed to say anything interesting.

So we cannot claim that these letters expose any great military secrets, but they do provide revealing insights such as his private cable correspondence with General Maude before the Shumran crossing and also his part is saving his cousin General Lake from drowning. We also learn much about the life and times and attitudes of a Cotswold squarson's youngest son, as he pursues his chosen career in the military, in surroundings so remote from his beloved Slaughter. He speaks in language which his mother would understand. A very early start for a long ride is 'worse than cub-hunting'. And Christmas on board ship in the Arabian sea en route to Basra must be going well, as they have 'all the Slaughter hymns'. He speaks affectionately of his late father: 'how dear old father would have enjoyed these figs'.

His mother is forever sending him parcels, including numerous papers and journals, as though he was still at boarding-school. She is asked not to send jugged hare again, after a disaster in a Fortnum's hamper. Some things she sends, like a safety lifebelt waistcoat, or fly whisks to ward off the flies, one might have thought the War Office would have provided, rather than an elderly widow in the Cotswolds.

The letters are not always politically correct by today's standards. While normally very supportive of his Indian troops there is the occasional lapse, such as describing the drowning of one as rather a nuisance for himself. And his famous (or infamous) telegram 'Very fit. Busy killing Arabs' provokes an immediate response from his mother 'Arabs can kill too, so look out!' His mother's health is declining during the correspondence, but her commentary on Upper Slaughter and family life remains loving and sharp to the end.

There is fascinating background material in these letters for anyone interested in Iraq or the Cotswolds, and I have much filial pleasure in recommending them to you, dear reader.

Upper Slaughter   Francis E. B. Witts
St Peter's Day 2008

PREFACE

Frederick Witts' own letters inevitably were censored, and the intention of the narrative in this work is to complement his letters and to enhance their meaning to the reader who is unfamiliar with this important period of Iraq's history. The narrative is, essentially, a very broad outline, but it does focus in some detail upon the parts of the story in which F.V.B.W. had the most involvement. Material for a more comprehensive study can be found in the bibliography.

A Note on Spelling, Punctuation and Editing.
Throughout the process of transcription, great emphasis has been placed on accuracy. F.V.B.W. had relatively neat handwriting with good punctuation and there was very little need to interfere with his letters. In certain places, however, punctuation has been changed to improve readability, and capitals have been removed where F.V.B.W. was trying to make words, mostly of Arab place-names, absolutely clear for his mother. I have also made certain additions in the text, always within square brackets, to inform the reader about dates or names where F.V.B.W. was either being vague or, more commonly, showing awareness of his obligation to censor his own letters. On rare occasions I have inserted words, again in square brackets, where I thought it necessary to maintain the flow of a sentence, but, on the whole, the typed versions of F.V.B.W.'s letters are exactly the same as the originals.

His mother's letters, on the other hand, were very difficult to read, and often required some application of 'editorial licence' to make them more comprehensible. By this I mean that an educated guess was made for the odd word, although the original meaning of a sentence was never compromised. Margaret Witts continued to write letters to her son to within a month of her death, aged 72, in February 1921; her writing generally declined with her health, but her mind remained sharp. She did, however, become confused or absent-minded when it came to names. For instance, she continually referred to her daughter-in-law, Elma, as Edna or Elena, and only sometimes as Elma; to avoid confusion for the reader, in such-like examples the assumed correct name has been substituted in the text. Her lack of full stops and excessive use of dashes have also been amended somewhat to enhance readability. The other surviving letters to F.V.B.W. during this period, mostly from his brothers, George and Frank, were easily decipherable and did not present any particular problems in transcription.

F.V.B.W.'s spelling provided an interesting dilemma. Most is in line with modern standards, but there are a few exceptions. Where, with words like develope, shew, or kitchin, his spellings are consistent and his meaning obvious, they have been retained as another aspect of historical interest. Where, however, he has clearly made a spelling mistake, a correction has been made. The same rules were applied to his mother's spelling, which was far more erratic.

Generally speaking, the spelling of Arab names varies widely, and accepted transliterations are not necessarily the most accurate. F.V.B.W. was not an Arabist and his own transliterations are sometimes unusual; examples include Kubela (Karbala), Nejf (Najaf), Kurna (Qurna) and Busra (Basra). However, since Arabic transliterations did vary enormously between published works, and F.V.B.W.'s own versions are not difficult to interpret, they have been retained in the text.

At the time, and in later life, F.V.B.W. always referred to Mesopotamia as Mespot. Hence the use of Mespot in the title of this book.

Lastly, I should point out that in the footnotes I have referred to F.V.B.W. by his initials, whereas in the narrative I have generally called him Captain or Major Witts.

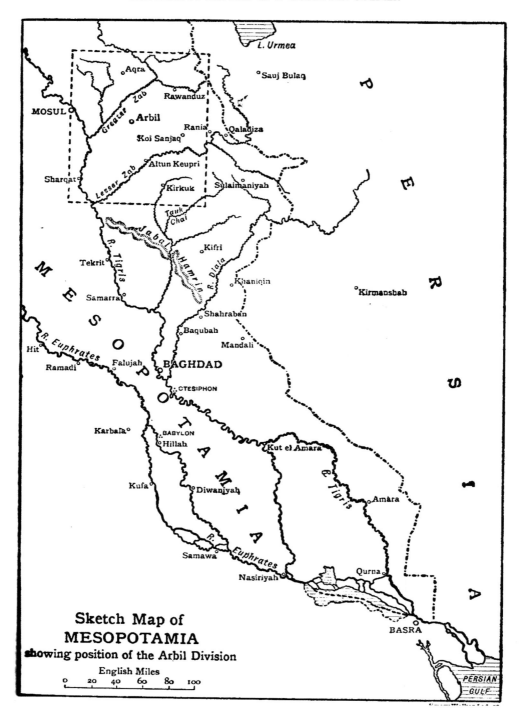

Map 1. Sketch map of Mesopotamia.

INTRODUCTION
The Background to Mesopotamia.

A Short Description of the Country.

Mesopotamia, the pre-1920 name for Iraq, is a Greek word meaning 'land between rivers'. The Tigris and Euphrates are both sourced in the mountains of eastern Turkey; they flow through Mesopotamia from the north and north-west respectively, converging in the south to form the Shatt-al-Arab, a wide muddy channel 110 miles long, the gateway to Mesopotamia from the Persian Gulf.

The country is generally referred to as two separate halves, Lower and Upper, defined by differing climatic and physical features, roughly divided along a latitudinal line parallel with Baghdad. To the north-east of Upper Mesopotamia is the mountainous region of Kurdistan, home to the ethnic Kurds, which extends beyond the country's borders into Turkey and Persia. To the west of Kurdistan, the land subsides into a rocky, undulating plain, the north-eastern extremity of the Syrian Desert. Lower Mesopotamia consists of a flat alluvial plain, bordered in the east by Persia and the expansive Arabian plateau to the west and south. This is the region from which the name of Mesopotamia is derived. The land between the rivers is a vast floodplain intersected with swamps where life is regulated by annual floods. The flood calendar starts in November when water levels are at their lowest. Rainfall through to January initiates a gradual swell. In March, melting snow in the Caucasus and Kurdistan, where the Tigris derives much of its volume from tributaries, causes a sudden and dramatic rise in water levels. The result is widespread flooding across much of Lower Mesopotamia as well as in regions just to the north of Baghdad, lasting through to May.

Mesopotamia's climate is one of extremes. In the summer months between April and September it is exceptionally hot with temperatures often reaching above 120°F in the shade. During this period, the swampy regions of Lower Mesopotamia become especially oppressive. Humidity is high and disease is easily spread. Temperatures drop dramatically in the winter season from November to February, falling as low as 0°F in Kurdistan. In Lower Mesopotamia, heavy winter rains reduce the flat, dusty landscape to a sticky morass, whilst in the spring, depending on flood barriers, the flood renders much of the land completely impassable.

The population at the start of World War I was between two and two and half million. It was predominantly Arab, except in the north-east of the country where the majority were Kurds, and Christian Armenians were also well represented. In the towns, minorities of Jews, Persians and other Christians existed, but rarely in rural areas. Roughly half of the Arabs in

Mesopotamia belonged to nomadic or semi-nomadic tribes, living, to various extents, as pastoral herders or partially settled farmers. The other half of the Arab population were either townsmen or settled cultivators living in village communities. Tribal law and organisation were still maintained in these communities, although to a lesser extent in the towns where the tribal bond was much less profound. In religion, the majority of Kurds and Arabs in Upper Mesopotamia were, like the Turks, Sunni Muslims, and the Persians and Arabs of Lower Mesopotamia were Shi'ites.

Ottoman Mesopotamia.
Civilisation has existed in Mesopotamia since around 4,000BC when the Ubaid people first began using the floods of the Tigris and Euphrates to irrigate their crops. From these humble beginnings emerged the first conception of Empire. For over three thousand years, many great civilisations from the Sumerians to the Sassanids flourished and decayed alongside the banks of the Tigris and Euphrates. Two events, however, occurring at either ends of the Middle Ages, were to change the course of Mesopotamian history forever.

The *hijra*, the migration of the Prophet Mohammad from Mecca to Medina in AD 622, marked the beginning of Islam in the Middle East and the foundation of the Arab Caliphate. Under the Abbasid Caliphs, Mesopotamia enjoyed a golden age; Baghdad became the political and cultural centre of an Islamic Empire stretching from India in the east to Spain and Morocco in the west. Then, in 1258, disaster struck when the Mongol prince, Halagu, grandson of Genghis Khan, swept through the country in a devastating crusade. He was bent on plundering Mesopotamia's wealth, and, in the process, he stripped her of her cultural identity. Baghdad was sacked and its inhabitants were massacred; in the country, the ancient systems of irrigation were destroyed. The damage proved irreparable and the population reverted to a pastoral society of practically Ubaidan times.

The Sunni Ottomans conquered Mesopotamia in 1514 after a long-standing feud with the Shi'ite Safavid Persians who had come to rule the land. Having established themselves as rulers, Ottoman administration was generally apathetic. Three centuries of degeneration since the Mongol invasion had left the country exceptionally poor and underdeveloped. After the arrival of the Turks, persistent animosity between the ruling Sunnis in the towns and the Shi'ite majority hindered any hopes of building a proper economy. The inhospitable climate, tribal population and complete lack of communications discouraged Turkish re-settlement, and made the country extraordinarily difficult to govern, resulting in administrative neglect. Like Siberia in Russia, Mesopotamia was viewed as a remote, pestilential backwater where shunned Turkish officials could be sent in penance.

The Turks only really started to take an interest in Mesopotamia in the mid-19ᵗʰ century. To simplify administration the country was divided into 3 wilayats (provinces): the Basra wilayat, comprising all the land south of Kut-al-Amara on the Tigris and Samawah on the Euphrates; the Mosul wilayat, the northern third of Mesopotamia, comprising the eastern edge of the Syrian desert and the mountainous region of Southern Kurdistan; and the Baghdad wilayat comprising the centre of the country. The incentive for this administrative reorganisation was derived from a desire to convert Mesopotamia's tribal elements into settled agricultural communities, and thereby to increase exports of rice and dates, thus facilitating the collection of taxes.

This scheme to promote agriculture gave rise to Turkish and foreign investment in Mesopotamia, particularly in associated engineering projects such as land reclamation, dam building and canal digging. By the beginning of the 20ᵗʰ century, examples of innovative projects were beginning to emerge. The Hindiyah Barrage, controlling the floods in the Mid-Euphrates basin, was first built in 1891 by French engineers and then rebuilt in 1913 under British supervision. The Berlin-Baghdad railway, financed by Germany and begun in 1903, was an especially enterprising project. Agricultural production had doubled in the 50 years before WWI, and the proportion of nomadic tribesmen in Mesopotamian society had diminished as a result.

Ultimately, however, administrative reorganisation and the advent of foreign investment came too late for Turkey to gain any substantial benefit; Mesopotamia remained exceedingly poor right up to the end of Ottoman rule. But, whilst Turkey had neglected her colony, Britain had noted Mesopotamia's potential as a trade route and agricultural producer, and had recognised her strategic value. By the time oil was added to the list of Mesopotamia's possible resources, Britain had already established herself at the head of the Persian Gulf.

British Involvement in Mesopotamia pre-1914.
The origins of British interest in Mesopotamia are linked inherently to her control of India. Since the early 19ᵗʰ century, schemes to establish new trade-routes across Mesopotamia between India and Europe had been explored, but, although they could have been profitable, investment was never forthcoming. In 1869, such schemes were made redundant by the completion of the Suez Canal, which inevitably soon handled the lion's share of trade with the East. Despite this, British interest in Mesopotamia did not whither; it simply changed its character. The 'Great Game', the original Cold War between Britain and Russia, had been proceeding in Afghanistan since the early 19ᵗʰ century. Britain was convinced that Russia would go to any lengths to gain the upper hand in India, thus pushing the head of the Persian Gulf into the frontline of Britain's strategic defence. To guarantee against the establishment of a warm-

water Russian port, the British strengthened existing ties with the powerful
Arab Sheikhs of Kuwait and Muhammerah, who controlled the small stretch
of coastline either side of the Shatt-al-Arab. These ties had been established
back in the 18th century by the British East India Company; in the interests of
trade, they had pledged to protect the Sheikhs' lucrative pearling industry by
eradicating piracy in the Persian Gulf. In the meantime, any consideration of
Ottoman sovereignty was completely ignored; by the end of the 19th century
British Naval power was the new master of the Persian Gulf.

For some years before that, the great Ottoman Empire had been crumbling.
Gone were the days when she asserted her imperial strength over dominions
in Asia and Africa, and frightened Christendom with the spread of Islam from
the East. Now, her own borders were under threat from Russian expansion
through the Caucasus, a common fear of which had pushed her closer to
Britain. Anglo-Turkish relations reached a peak in the Crimean War of 1854-
56. In the following decades, however, their friendship began to sour as British
imperialists turned a predatory eye towards Turkey's vulnerable empire. In
1878, Britain's cynical diplomatic acquisition of Ottoman controlled Cyprus,
following the Russo-Turkish War, was highly resented in Turkey, adding to the
discontent surrounding the assertion of British supremacy in the Persian Gulf.
In 1882, Turkish bitterness was solidified by the British occupation of Egypt,
which Britain excused as an attempt to help preserve the Ottoman Empire.
Meantime, the Franco-Prussian War of 1870 had established a new military
power in Europe. Feeling mistreated by the British, Turkey began to look for
support elsewhere. She found a willing friend in Germany.

The first major sign of a new commercial partnership between Turkey and
Germany was the promulgation in 1893 of a joint scheme to build the Berlin-
Baghdad railway. In 1898 the Turko-German Anatolian Railway Co. obtained
a concession for a route from Ankara to Baghdad, via Konya, Aleppo and
Mosul. At this early stage, the concession was welcomed by the British; with
German interests now at stake in the Middle East, it was unlikely that Russia
would dare pursue an aggressive foreign policy from the Caucasus. However,
it was not long before Germany herself appeared to be the greater threat.
The development of German expansionism, and her mounting influence over
the Ottoman Empire, created an atmosphere of tension in Europe and the
Middle East at the start of the 20th century. Germany's youth and aggression
made Europe's foremost imperial powers, France and Great Britain nervous.
In 1904, in response to this apprehension, the Entente Cordiale, an alliance
between France and Britain, was signed. Russia, meanwhile, felt isolated.
Having lost prestige in the disastrous Japanese War of 1905-6, the aggressive
turn in German imperialism, ominously named *Drang Nach Osten* ('Drive
to the East'), was seen as a direct threat to her western empire. In 1907, in a

dramatic reaction to this threat, Russia initiated a formal reconciliation with her old enemy, Great Britain, which resulted in the formation of the Triple Entente between Russia, Britain and France.

In Turkey, meanwhile, German influence was growing rapidly in the wake of the 'Young Turk' revolution of 1908 and the rise to power of Enver Pasha, a dynamic pro-German officer in the Turkish Army. As a result of German influence, Turkish foreign policy in the Middle East was beginning to turn distinctively anti-British. At the time, a 'Pan-Islamic' movement was sweeping across the Middle East and Afghanistan, calling for solidarity amongst Muslims and hostility towards Christians. Turko-German intrigue was industrious in its efforts to direct this religious extremism against Britain. In Persia, British relations had already been ruptured by the highly unpopular Anglo-Russian Agreement of 1907, subjecting northern Persia to Russian influence. German agents were particularly relentless in trying to exploit this rift, infiltrating the highest offices in Tehran and offering their friendship and sympathy in the form of subsidies. It had become abundantly clear that German interest in the Middle East, particularly in the Berlin-Baghdad railway, was as much imperial as it was commercial.

While Britain was vulnerable across most regions of the Middle East, her most important diplomatic ties, the Sheikhdoms of Kuwait and Muhammerah, were impervious to Turko-German intrigue. Both Sheikhs were vigorously anti-Sultan and anti-Shah (Muhammerah, although Arab, was a Persian subject), and their loyalty to the British was founded on familial friendships over a century old. In 1900, this loyalty was tested by the arrival of German envoys in Kuwait, offering an extremely lucrative deal to the Sheikh for a concession to build a port on his coastline. Their offer was firmly rejected; the Turkish inability to force the issue demonstrated the extent of the Sheikh's power when backed by British support.

In 1908, British interest in the head of the Persian Gulf increased considerably. Vast oil fields were discovered in the Persian district of Shushtar in Southern Arabistan, roughly 150 miles from the mouth of the Shatt-al-Arab. The area was just beyond the territory of the Sheikh of Muhammerah, but friendships were made with the chiefs of the local Bakhtiari tribes and a concession for the land was applied for and granted by the Persian Government, despite German influence. Before long, the all-British Anglo-Persian Oil Co. was established. A pipeline was built from the oilfields at Shushtar, across land controlled by Sheikh Muhammerah, to Abadan, an island in the Shatt-al-Arab, where the company set up a refinery. In 1913, when the enterprise was in full production, the British Government purchased a controlling share in the company; the fuel used by the British fleet had recently been converted from coal to oil.

By this time, on the European stage, the armament race was well underway. Through the diplomacy of the Turkish War Minister, Enver Pasha, Turkey had been thrust inexorably alongside German foreign policy. Towards the end of 1913, the prestigious German officer, General Liman von Sanders, was sent to Constantinople to help train and reorganise the Turkish army, taking with him hundreds of German staff and regimental officers. Turkey's involvement in the coming conflict was assured, but the extent to which the Middle East would be used as an active theatre for war was still uncertain.

As far as Mesopotamia was concerned, the British Government had considered an invasion on various occasions in the early 20th century, but the idea had been rejected for reasons of cost and climate, not to mention fears of volatile natives and religious antagonism. This judgement was the result of measured contemplation. It follows, therefore, that the British advance up the Tigris in 1915 was opportunist rather than planned: dangerous circumstances for any military campaign.

Condition of the Indian Army.
The British Government in India ('the Indian Government'), along with its responsibilities on the North West Frontier, was to be accountable for military commitments in Mesopotamia. At the turn of the century, the Indian Army was a neglected force, outdated in equipment, training and organisation. The Russian threat on the North West Frontier drew attention to these shortcomings and precipitated a grand scheme of modernisation. In 1902, Lord Kitchener was appointed Commander-in-Chief of the Indian Army; his main aim, whilst updating military equipment and keeping internal peace, was to bolster the defence of the North West Frontier by a process of concentration, reorganisation and redistribution. His reforms, however, clashed with the Government's excessively parsimonious attitude towards military spending. After the signing of the Anglo-Russian Agreement in 1907, and the resultant dispersion of the Russian threat, the economisers gained the upper hand, and the programme for military modernisation ground to a premature halt. By the outbreak of war in 1914, the Indian Army was in a pitiable state. Equipment was 20 years out of date and no adequate training or provision had been made for the possibility of fighting overseas. Nevertheless, in early August, two Indian divisions were given orders to mobilise and set sail for France. Captain Frederick Witts R.E. was among the troops bound for the Western Front. A year later, at the end of 1915, these divisions (7th and 3rd) would be transferred to Mesopotamia.

The Mesopotamian Campaign: November 1914 – December 1915.
The primary reason for sending a British expedition to Mesopotamia was for the protection of its Persian oil assets. The Admiralty was already relying

heavily on oil and, with demand rising due to the war, its security was of paramount importance. A complicating factor, however, was that for the first few months of the war, Turkey did not declare her position. The Indian Government was concerned that an apparently undue show of aggression against the Turks – the self-proclaimed 'protectors of Islam' – before a formal declaration of war, could trigger a *jihad* (holy war) across the Islamic world, including parts of northern India. By early October, however, Turkish intrigue in Southern Arabistan had reached such a pitch that it was threatening the diplomatic ties vital to the security of the oilfields. Britain decided to act. Whitehall ordered a brigade of the Indian 6th (Poona) Division, named the "Indian Expeditionary Force 'D'", to sail into the Shatt-al-Arab, to show solidarity with the Sheikhs of Muhammerah and Kuwait, and defend the 140 miles of pipeline connecting Shushtar with Abadan. The expedition was placed under the control of the Indian Government.

On 5th November, following Turkish attacks on Russian ports in the Black Sea, the Entente powers declared war on Turkey. On the same day, at the head of the Persian Gulf, Force 'D' steamed into the Shatt-al-Arab. Their principal strategic objective was the town of Basra, on the right bank of the Shatt-al-Arab, 60 miles north of its mouth. On the 22nd November, having been reinforced with the rest of the 6th Division under General Barrett, Force 'D' put the Turkish defenders to flight and occupied Basra. The speed and boldness of their advance made a profound impression upon the Arab townspeople and the outlying tribes and raised British prestige in the region. By this stage, Force 'D''s mission had already been accomplished; local Anglo-Arab relations were stronger than ever before, and the oilfields, pipeline and refinery were safe. Restraint, however, or a lack of it, was to be the curse of the Mesopotamian

1. The Quay at Ashar Creek, Basra.

Campaign. With conquering spirit, the modest objectives of November 1914 were soon forgotten.

The notion of an advance on Baghdad was first suggested by Sir Percy Cox, chief political adviser to the expedition. If successful, the effect it could have had on British prestige in the Islamic world was prodigious. With this in mind, the Indian Government seized on the idea, seeing it as the solution to brewing unrest in Islamic India and the latent threat from Afghanistan on the North West Frontier. Political enthusiasm, however, overlooked the military perspective; Baghdad lay 300 miles north of Basra across an alluvial plain of the most inhospitable character. Its strategic position was weak, and it would require many reinforcements to defend and consolidate it. With the unprecedented demands of the war in Europe, Britain could ill afford to allow her troops to be diverted on an expedition for purely political reasons. After lengthy debate, a compromise was settled between G.H.Q. in Simla, Himachal Pradesh, and the Indian Government in Delhi. An advance to Qurna, 50 miles beyond Basra where the Tigris and Euphrates converge to form the Shatt-al-Arab, would bring both strategic and political advantages by boosting British prestige and consolidating her position at the head of the Persian Gulf. For now, idealistic political ambition had been restrained by good sense at Simla. Under the surface, however, sound military judgement was already becoming clouded by visions of a glorious advance on Baghdad.

Qurna was taken on the 9th December after a surprisingly stiff fight; at this remote extremity of the Ottoman Empire, Turkish forces consisted mostly of Arab conscripts.

2. Arab Conscripts.

3. Mesopotamian Marshland.

The British expedition had gone extraordinarily well, but the physical and climatic vagaries of the country had not yet been fully experienced. In March 1915, melting snow in the Caucasus and Kurdistan caused the banks of the Rivers Tigris, Euphrates and Shatt-al-Arab to burst, forcing the British garrison to evacuate Qurna to positions further downstream. All communications were greatly hampered by the flood. In the meantime, the Turks had been plotting a counter-attack. A large Turko-Arab army had concentrated at Nasiriyah, on the Euphrates 80 miles west of Qurna, threatening Basra's security. Meanwhile, in Persia a detachment of Turkish troops was reported to be heading towards the oilfields. Earlier, a recalcitrant tribe of the Bakhtiari had been persuaded by German gold to cut a portion of the pipeline. In response to this threat to the oilfields, General Barrett sent a detachment of troops up the Karun River to occupy Ahwaz. In Basra, at the same time, he prepared his force against the impending Turkish attack from Nasiriyah. The mounting problems convinced the General Staff in India that it was necessary to send another division (the 12th) to Mesopotamia.

On 12th April 1915, the expected Turkish attack was launched on British positions at Shaiba, 10 miles west of Basra, over land under 2 to 3 feet of floodwater. Barrett had not anticipated such an attack and, as a result, he had left Shaiba only sparsely defended. Nevertheless, in what was to become known as 'the miracle of Shaiba', British and Indian troops held out in stifling conditions for three days, fighting to the point of exhaustion. On April 15th the Turks, equally exhausted, finally gave up their assault.

At this point, a decision was made by the General Staff in Simla to replace General Barrett as G.O.C. in Mesopotamia with General Sir John Nixon. Nixon was a practical man, with a positive, optimistic nature and a reputation for dash, though apt to neglect administrative detail. His appointment by the Commander-in-Chief in India, General Sir Beauchamp Duff, was illustrative of Simla's new support for an aggressive policy in Mesopotamia.

4. General Sir John Nixon.

General Nixon, as expected, immediately pressed for an advance to Amara, the next large town on the Tigris, 70 miles north of Qurna. With the support of his political adviser, Sir Percy Cox, he argued that its capture would cut off any possibility of a Turkish advance into Southern Arabistan and further enhance the British reputation amongst the Arabs. These motives were undoubtedly sound, but the problem of communications had been ignored. The administrative side of Force 'D' was already under strain without adding a further 70 miles to its supply lines. The Secretary of State for India, Lord Crewe, had the final word on policy in Mesopotamia; at this stage, he was the only major voice of restraint. Being in London, however, he felt out of touch with the situation on the ground and was heavily reliant on the opinions of General Nixon and the Indian Viceroy, Lord Hardinge. Under their persuasion, he sanctioned the advance on Amara, trusting in what he hoped would be their better judgement.

For Nixon, the capture of Amara was the central element of a tripartite plan intended to close comprehensively all routes to Basra and the oilfields. It would also enable him to inch closer towards Baghdad: his ultimate goal. First, before advancing up the Tigris, Nixon sent a column under Major-General Gorringe into Persian Arabistan to deal decisively with the Turko-Arab force still active in the region. It was late April by this stage and the heat was becoming intolerable; nevertheless, Gorringe's column drove out the Turks and defeated the hostile Arabs. In defiance of the intense heat, Gorringe's force

5. Marching 'in the blue'.

6. A native bellum.

then proceeded westwards across the desert towards Amara to hold down the Turkish left flank, keeping them from joining their main force above Qurna, where the 6th Division launched a separate advance.

Qurna was still encompassed by a vast flood averaging 3 feet in depth with deep irrigation ditches. This greatly restricted any movement of troops or artillery. Turkish positions, meanwhile, to the north of Qurna, consisted of a series of small islands rising above the flood-line, dotted either side of the Tigris channel, each defended by a cluster of troops. In such unusual conditions, the opportunity for improvisation in the attack was great. General Townshend, commanding the 6th Division, organised an amphibious flotilla of boats ranging from gunships in the deep Tigris channel, to light armoured *bellums* (native punts) crammed full of infantry, for easy movement across the floodwaters. On 31st May 1915, 'Townshend's Regatta', as it became known, was launched. Under cover of concentrated artillery bombardments from naval guns and batteries floating on rafts, the mass of 'assault-*bellums*' were punted into the reed banks of the Turkish island defences. Their cargoes of infantry disembarked and rushed the enemy positions, overpowering them one by one. After nightfall, having lost confidence in their positions, the remaining Turks took to their punts and retreated towards Amara. Townshend ordered a pursuit at dawn. On board *H.M.S. Espiegle*, at the head of his flotilla, he chased the Turks all the way up to

7. Major-General Charles Townshend.

Amara, dealing a heavy blow to their rearguard with the help of five other gunboats, the vanguard for the chase. On June 3rd Townshend reached Amara, finding it in a state of complete confusion. With a band of just 30 sailors and soldiers and a handful of officers, he captured the town of 20,000 inhabitants and a Turkish garrison of 850 men. It was not until 6.30p.m. the following day that the first battalion of Townshend's infantry finally caught up with him, much to the relief of his small force at Amara.

With Persian Arabistan and the Tigris, as far as Amara, secured, Nixon turned his attention to the third phase of his consolidation programme: the occupation of Nasiriyah, on the River Euphrates 80 miles west of Qurna. Nixon felt that Nasiriyah's location at the junction of the Shatt-al-Hai, a river connecting the Tigris with the Euphrates, was of great strategic importance. It was also an ideal base from which Nixon could establish control over the powerful Arab tribes of the Lower Euphrates.

At this time, the full weight of the Mesopotamian summer was upon Force 'D' and they were suffering terribly from it. In addition to heatstroke, malnutrition, brought on by a lack of fruit and vegetables, was taking a massive toll. Medical amenities, meanwhile, were sparse. Facilities which had been overstretched at the start of the campaign, when Force 'D' consisted of just one division, were now expected to deal with two infantry divisions, a cavalry brigade and corps troops. Even basic comforts against the heat such as ice, clean water and adequate shelter were not forthcoming. Medical staff were extraordinarily short-handed. The General Staff in India, however, were reluctant to send more trained personnel or equipment. Even when the severity of the situation was fully understood, the efforts made to rectify medical shortages were totally inadequate.

Despite the great hardships already borne by Force 'D', Lord Hardinge and Sir Beauchamp Duff saw little reason to restrict General Nixon in spreading his commitments along the Euphrates. The new Secretary of State for India, Austen Chamberlain (appointed in May 1915), remained quiet on the issue of an offensive against Nasiriyah. In the event, his reticence was taken as a nod of approval.

General Gorringe, fresh from his arduous success in Arabistan, was given command of a column of one brigade, much depleted from sickness, and two artillery batteries for the advance on Nasiriyah. He was also supported by a Naval flotilla for the journey as far as the Hammar Lake, where the Euphrates channel became shallow and tortuous (although the country was still waterlogged, much of the floods had subsided by this stage). Having left Qurna on the 5th July, Gorringe reached the outskirts of Nasiriyah 10 days later. The conditions were suffocating, and not helped by the swarms of biting insects. Nevertheless, with grim resolve, Gorringe's men began making preparations for an amphibious assault on Turkish defences positioned around the town. At dawn on the 24th July the attack was launched; by the end of the day, Nasiriyah was in British hands. With the capture of Nasiriyah, Force 'D' was finally given the chance to rest and focus on simply enduring the discomforts of the Mesopotamian summer.

At this point, British interests in Persian Arabistan and at the head of the Persian Gulf were safe beyond any doubt. British prestige elsewhere, however, was suffering. In Persia, German intrigue had supplanted British influence to such a degree that British diplomats feared she might cast off her neutral status and enter the war on the side of the Central Powers. In India, internal unrest against British rule in the northern Islamic states was becoming unusually violent. In the Dardanelles the British were facing defeat, and on the Western Front Allied offensives were proving inconclusive. The Viceroy believed that the famous 'City of Caliphs' was the key to restoring faith in British supremacy.

Kut-al-Amara, lying 150 miles north of Amara at the junction of the Tigris and its effluent, the Shatt-al-Hai, was the next major stepping-stone in the direction of Baghdad. Unsurprisingly, General Nixon shared the Viceroy's aspirations to continue the advance towards the capital. Back in June, whilst the advance on Nasiriyah had been under discussion, Nixon had also pressed his case for attacking Kut. His main reason had been that Kut's strategic position on the Hai junction gave the Turks scope to counter-attack in two directions: either down the Tigris to Amara, or down the Hai to Nasiriyah. Kut's occupation, argued Nixon, would remove the need to garrison Nasiriyah and enable Force 'D' to concentrate its strength on the Tigris. While Lord Hardinge's support was assured, Sir Beauchamp Duff, responsible for assessing the military perspective, was more sceptical about extending Force 'D''s communications a further 150 miles up the Tigris. Intelligence reports, however, were reaching Simla that a strong detachment of the Russian Caucasus Army was marching on Baghdad. Based on the assumption that they would divert Turkish forces, Sir Beauchamp Duff and the General Staff in India gave their approval for the advance. Once again, the Secretary-of-State for India was the solitary voice of doubt. After deliberation, however, Chamberlain allowed himself to be swayed by Lord Hardinge's persuasive words on the political aspect; the advance on Kut was sanctioned. Remarkably, Force 'D''s glaring deficiencies in river transport, communications and medical arrangements were disregarded by all. A blind eye was also turned to the exhausted condition of the troops, the voluminous sick-lists and the warnings emanating from offices in both London and Simla that no reinforcements were available for Mesopotamia.

On September 16th General Townshend's 6th Division reached Beit Isa, on the right bank of the Tigris, 16 miles below Kut. eight miles further upstream, the Turks, commanded by Nur-Ud-Din, were entrenched in a strong position astride the river at Es Sinn. On the 27th, Townshend launched his attack against the enemy trenches on the right bank. His intention was to wrong-foot Nur-Ud-Din. After two days of fighting on the right bank, Townshend secretly crossed his force over the river under cover of darkness, hoping to surprise the Turks with a dawn attack up the left bank of the Tigris. When dawn came, however, it revealed the Turkish trenches were empty. The previous night, whilst Townshend had been crossing the Tigris, Nur-Ud-Din had quietly abandoned Kut and retreated towards Ctesiphon, a prepared position 80 miles upstream, within a day's march of Baghdad. Townshend launched an immediate pursuit, but the diabolical state of his supply line frustrated any hope of engaging the Turks on open ground. On 5th October, the pursuit reached Aziziyah, 30 miles from Ctesiphon. The men were tired and weak from insufficient food and the piercing cold at night. Most of the 6th Division's casualties had been caused by disease rather than bullets. Medical care was still far from sufficient and Force 'D''s administrative engine was in desperate need of attention. General Nixon, however, was not discouraged. Force 'D''s remarkable success had made them seem invincible, and the Turks had consistently proved themselves to be a weak opponent. Having come so far and fought so bravely, to turn away from the greatest prize of all, the legendary 'City of Caliphs', was, to a man of Nixon's temperament, simply unthinkable.

On October 3rd 1915 General Nixon sent a telegram to the Secretary of State saying 'I consider I am strong enough to open the road to Baghdad, and with this intention I propose to concentrate at Aziziyah.' So began three weeks of convoluted debate between political and military departments in Britain, India and Mesopotamia on the risks and opportunity involved in an advance on Baghdad.

Political approval was already unanimous due to anxiety over India's security regarding Turko-German intrigue in Persia and Afghanistan. The military argument, however, was less convincing. According to Nixon, the military value of occupying Baghdad lay in depriving the Turks of a base from which they could otherwise organise a counter-attack. Nixon had given the same reasons for advancing on Amara, Nasiriyah and Kut, begging the question: where did he intend to stop? In London, the inherent vulnerability of Baghdad as a defensible position and Nixon's lack of sufficient troops to consolidate it discouraged support for the advance. Mesopotamia was considered a secondary theatre; the outcome of the campaign would not be the decisive factor on the wider picture of the war. The War Secretary, Lord Kitchener, was not willing to risk Mesopotamia becoming a drain on troops and resources which were more needed elsewhere.

8. Monitors, paddle-steamers and motor-boats at Basra.

Kitchener was unfamiliar with the details of the campaign and, as a result, his observations were broad. The General Staff at Simla, however, including the Commander-in-Chief, were well aware of the administrative chaos that had befallen Force 'D'; yet, like General Nixon, they were willing to ignore the glaring flaws of an offensive strategy.

Communications presented the greatest problem; by October 1915 Force 'D''s supply line stretched 460 miles from Aziziyah on the Tigris to Bushire in Southern Persia, where Nixon was responsible for a small British force engaged in counteracting German intrigue. The extraordinary span of Nixon's commitments meant that his army of two divisions and two cavalry brigades, depleted by sickness, was very widely dispersed. This deprived General Townshend of any appreciable reserve at the front. Nixon was also unable to concentrate his whole force on the Tigris, as had been hoped for with the capture of Kut, the volatility of the tribes of Southern Arabistan and the Lower Euphrates required garrisons to be kept at Ahwaz and Nasiriyah. The entire British operation, meanwhile, was being crippled by a great lack of river transport. Adequate food and military goods could not be supplied to the front with any degree of reliability or efficiency, and Nixon's repeated requests for more transport had been as good as ignored by the General Staff at Simla.

In the light of the administrative shambles, it seems remarkable that an advance could even have been contemplated from a military perspective. But, in spite of all this, Force 'D' was undefeated. To General Nixon, 'the man on the spot', there was nothing to suggest that Baghdad was not well within the limits of Force 'D''s capability. Whilst Townshend waited for a decision to be made, any notion of a reverse, was barely entertained.

In London, to settle the debate on whether to sanction the advance, the

9. Turkish troops posing with their rifles.

Cabinet appointed a special inter-departmental Committee. A joint Naval and Military appreciation of the situation was made, re-affirming the political benefit of capturing Baghdad and, most significantly, determining that two Indian divisions serving in France could be spared for reinforcements in Mesopotamia. This ended concerns that Baghdad might have to be abandoned soon after its capture and it decided the matter for the Committee. On the 23rd October a telegram was sent by the Secretary of State to the Viceroy: 'Nixon may march on Baghdad if he is satisfied that force he has available is sufficient for the operation … two divisions will be sent as soon as possible.' In the event, Nixon did not have sufficient strength and the reinforcements arrived too late. No thought was spared, meanwhile, for the extra strain that two more divisions would undoubtedly place on administration.

In Mesopotamia, the case against attacking Ctesiphon was becoming more apparent. Since early October Nixon had been receiving intelligence that Turkish reinforcements from Syria and Anatolia were converging on the Mesopotamian front. But he was not to be discouraged, and he chose to ignore the reports. By the 21st November, after the usual delays in transporting men and supplies, Townshend had concentrated the 6th Division at Lajj, 10 miles below Ctesiphon. By this stage, his own enthusiasm for the advance had somewhat waned. At Lajj, the exhausted condition of his troops and the flagrant deficiencies in his transport and medical arrangements were plain to see. Nevertheless, he was committed to follow Nixon's irrepressible confidence.

On the morning of the 22nd November, Townshend ordered his men to attack. The 6th Division sallied forth with tremendous élan, fighting as though

10. The Arch of Ctesiphon.

they were outside the very gates of Baghdad. They drove the Turks back to their second line of defence with bitter resolve, but, by the evening they had reached the very limits of their strength. Mounting casualties and the complete exhaustion of the troops precipitated an urgent need for reinforcements, but Townshend had none. The Turkish lines, meanwhile, were being strengthened by fresh Anatolian troops of a far superior stock to the provincial soldiers that had fought in Mesopotamia up to that point. The following day, Townshend was unable to renew the offensive; that night, Nur-Ud-Din counter-attacked with devastating effect.

Disaster in the field was compounded by the atrocious state of British medical facilities. On the 24th and 25th, a trail of forlorn wounded began drifting into camp at Lajj. Some having limped or crawled across the 10 miles of boggy plain from Ctesiphon, others having been jostled about in agony on springless, mule-driven A.T. carts, designed only for carrying supplies. Many had died en route from their wounds or the bitter cold. For those who reached Lajj, they were welcomed by a scene of utter chaos. The overriding assumption that Baghdad would be taken had, to the generals and staff officers in charge, excused the blatant deficiency in medical amenities and hospital transport. Upon reaching Baghdad it was assumed that extra transport could be commandeered and a hospital established a short distance from the battlefield. As it was, however, there was only accommodation for 1500 casualties aboard transport at Lajj, and by the 25th November, there were 3,600 wounded needing beds. For those who made it on board the hospital ships, the decks were grossly overloaded and soon covered with dysenteric filth. All notion of sanitation was forgotten in the chaos; dressings were left untended for days and open wounds soon became gangrenous. Medical personnel were hopelessly overwhelmed and many wounded were simply left to die alone and uncared for.

On the 25th November, while the 6th Division's hospital transport embarked on a hellish 13-day voyage to Basra, Townshend ordered a general retreat from his forward positions at Ctesiphon, back downriver to Kut-al-Amara. The retreat from Ctesiphon to Kut is one of the greatest examples of discipline and endurance in the face of horrific adversity in the history of the Indian Army. The men of the 6th Division were exhausted beyond description, cold, hungry, and defeated; and yet, for 80 miles of forced marching, they managed to stave off an enemy of far superior numbers and fitness. On the 3rd December, they arrived at Kut with the Turks not far behind them.

Three days later, Captain Witts of the 4th Company Bengal Sappers and Miners boarded the *Ivernia* at Marseilles, bound for Mesopotamia via Egypt. His Company was a part of the 7th (Meerut) Division, chosen to consolidate Baghdad. After Ctesiphon, fortunes in Mesopotamia had been completely reversed; it would take a monumental effort and numerous attempts to restore British prestige in the region.

The Witts Family.

Frederick Vavasour Broome Witts (Fred to his mother and family, and referred to herein as F.V.B.W.) was the youngest of eight children of Canon Broome Witts and his wife Margaret (née Bourne). *See* family tree (Appendix XIX). He was born at home at the Manor, Upper Slaughter in January 1889 and christened at Upper Slaughter church by his father in April that year.

Canon Witts (who was also Rural Dean of Stow) followed his father, his grandfather and his great-great-uncle (the Reverend Ferdinando Tracy Travell) as successive rectors of Upper Slaughter, and they served for a continuous

11. 1907 Photo of F.V.B.W. aged 18 in the back garden.

12. Postcard of the Manor, Upper Slaughter. (from the front).

13. (*Left*) Canon Broome Witts and his five sons. (Edward, George, Jack, Frank and Frederick – at the bottom, aged 8) at the Manor August 1897: 'my crew'.

14. (*Right*) *Cheltenham Graphic* August 1907: 'A Gloucestershire Cadet's Success – Mr F. V. B. Witts'.

period of 149 years from 1764 to 1913. They were squarsons, which, for the uninitiated, means parson and squire all in one. Perhaps it is not surprising that the unfortunate non-family member, the Reverend Thomas Longley, who succeeded Canon Witts and who was rector for the duration of these letters, is not showered with favourable comments either by F.V.B.W. or by his mother.

F.V.B.W.'s great grandfather, the Reverend F. E. Witts, wrote *The Diary of a Cotswold Parson*, which David Verey edited thirty years ago, and which is now being published in its entirety in ten volumes. His maternal grandfather, Canon G.D. Bourne, was another squarson, at Western Subedge, also in Gloucestershire; he rowed five in the famous Oxford boat in 1843 when Oxford, with only seven oars, beat Cambridge at Henley.

So F.V.B.W. came from squarson stock, and was brought up in a large household with seven siblings and many servants. There were various cousins living nearby, notably at Eyford Park and Guiting Grange. They enjoyed normal country pursuits, hunting, shooting and fishing, according to the season. His mother was moved to express her surprise when their cousin Sophie married someone from Sheffield 'who neither hunted nor shot'.

F.V.B.W.'s social circle may have considered themselves a cut above the villagers, but nevertheless F.V.B.W. went to the village school, where he received a good educational grounding. The headmistress was Mrs Collett, and there are references in the letters to her and to her two sons. One of them, George, was also in Mesopotamia. F.V.B.W. went on to Summer Fields in Oxford, and then to Radley College.

At the age of sixteen and a half he passed top into the Royal Military Academy, Woolwich ('the Shop'), where he was awarded the King's Gold Medal and the Pollock Prize. He was commissioned into the Royal Engineers in 1907, when he was eighteen. After training at Chatham and Aldershot he was posted to India in 1912. He served in Kohat and Roorkee. In January 1915 he was sent to France with the Bengal Sappers and Miners, and served there until December that year. The letters begin as he is on his way towards Mesopotamia, or Mespot as he and his contemporaries called it.

F.V.B.W.'s four brothers, and his sister Agnes, all served during the First World War in various theatres of war. His eldest brother, Edward, (heir to the Upper Slaughter estate) who had also fought in the Boer war in South Africa, served in the Gloucestershire regiment; so did George and Jack. F.V.B.W.'s nearest brother Frank was in the Irish Guards.

As well as F.V.B.W.'s own letters to his mother, quite a few survive from his mother to him, mainly after the war, as well as some from his siblings to him. One learns something of the difficulties of life in a large Gloucestershire country house with the inevitable war-time and post war-time shortages. And there is poignancy towards the end, as F.V.B.W. just manages to get back in time to see his mother before she dies.

15. (*Left*) Mrs Margaret Witts. (F.V.B.W.'s mother)

16. (*Below*) Witts family group at the Manor 1898. F.V.B.W., aged 9, is sitting on the ground bottom left, with his parents and seven siblings.

CHAPTER I

THE FALL OF KUT

Letters: Dec 3rd 1915 – April 30th 1916.

For Captain Witts R.E., the Great War started in earnest in January 1915 when, as part of Indian Expeditionary Force 'A', he departed from India to join the 4th Company 1st K.G.O. Bengal Sappers and Miners in Flanders. Stationed in the Béthune region of northern France, his jobs included digging trenches, setting up wire communications, and reconnaissance. The work was dangerous and the mud and rain were persistent depressants, but Captain Witts was always positive about his Indian troops. In a letter to his mother in March 1915 he wrote, 'out night after night, always under fire to some degree, as often as not getting a man hit, it is marvellous how quickly and silently [the men] work.' However, the sickening impasse on the Western Front had begun to wear the troops' morale. In the same letter, Captain Witts added '…but I think those who have been out here since October have had enough; they cannot properly understand why we are apparently no nearer victory than we were four months ago.' As a consequence, when rumours began circulating in October 1915 of an imminent transfer of the Indian divisions to Mesopotamia, the news was greeted with relief and excitement.

In comparison to the endless stalemate on the Western Front, the campaign against the Turks in Mesopotamia had been a runaway success. In November 1914 Indian Expeditionary Force 'D', consisting of a single brigade, had landed in the country to protect British interests in Persian oil in the region near the head of the Persian Gulf. Within a year, Force 'D' had expanded to two divisions and the area of British occupation had extended 300 miles up the River Tigris, precipitating the need for urgent reinforcements. On 2nd November 1915, Prime Minister Asquith addressed the House of Commons: 'General Nixon's[1] force is now within striking distance of Baghdad. I do not think that in the whole war there has been a series of operations more carefully contrived, more brilliantly conducted, and with a better prospect of final success.' It was a tragic misjudgement. Less than a month later, the indomitable 6th Division, the spearhead of Force 'D', found itself in full retreat, fighting a desperate rearguard action against an altogether rejuvenated enemy. Meantime, the reinforcements assembled for the consolidation of Baghdad had a very different task ahead of them.

On 3rd December 1915, whilst 4th Coy. Bengal Sappers and Miners were getting ready to board transport in Marseilles, the harried 6th Division finally

[1] General Nixon was G.O.C. in Mesopotamia.

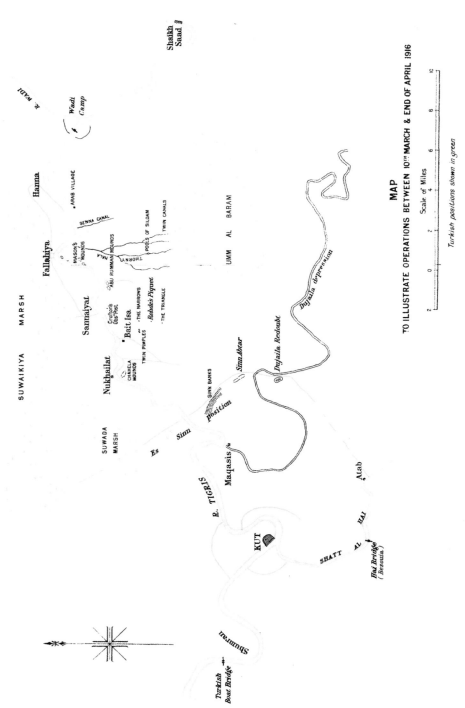

Map 2. The Tigris from Sheikh Saad to Shumran.

17. Kut, looking down-stream.

reached Kut-al-Amara, a town 80 miles down the Tigris from Ctesiphon, scene of the British defeat. eight days earlier, in a disastrous push for Baghdad, Major-General Townshend, the 6th Division's commander, had lost over a third of his combative force. The column's halt at Kut was caused more from exhaustion than as a result of tactical planning, although the town did have strategic advantages. Located within a sharp bend of the Tigris, Kut commanded the river junction with the Shatt-al-Hai, an effluent flowing through the southern marshlands to the River Euphrates. General Nixon was adamant that control of the Hai governed the control of the entire Lower Euphrates; to his mind, Kut was an indispensable position. Shortly after Townshend arrived in the town, Nixon ordered him to prepare for a siege.

By reputation, Townshend was a good man to have in a siege. In 1895 he had made his name by defending Chitral Fort successfully on the North West Frontier of India, earning him the prestigious title, 'Townshend of Chitral'. After initial optimism, however, Townshend became anxious that Nixon's estimation of two months' wait before he could expect relief would be too much for his exhausted garrison. Reports were flooding in that fresh Ottoman reinforcements, flushed by their recent success in repelling the British invasion of Turkey at Gallipoli, were on their way to Mesopotamia. Apart from this worrying information, General Townshend calculated at the beginning of December that with his 7,000 fighting men, 8,000 sick, wounded or non-combatant, and 6,000 domiciled Kut inhabitants,[2] his food stocks could last a maximum of only 2 months. Nixon responded to Townshend's

---

[2] These figures are taken from the *Official History*, Moberly, F. J., *The Mesopotamia Campaign*, vol. II p. 165. The inhabitants of Kut were permitted to remain to avoid antagonising the Arab population.

concerns with characteristic sanguinity. Whilst he reminded Townshend of the strategic importance of the Shatt-al-Hai, he gave assurances that the figure of two months was an outside estimate for the relief of Kut, and that ample reinforcements were already on their way.[3]

Nixon, however, had underestimated the difficulties of coordinating a relief effort. In the Mediterranean, shipping was in very high demand and delays in transporting troops were almost certain. In Mesopotamia, river transport and port facilities at Basra were already in a state of chronic disarray. They could not cope with the present demands on them; doubling those demands with the arrival of two extra divisions from France would ensure disaster. Finally, the extreme nature of Mesopotamia's climate and the Tigris's tendency to flood made it imprudent to rely on a hasty relief. The General Staff at Simla were becoming nervous. On 5th December, Lieutenant-General Sir Percy Lake, the Chief of General Staff, sent a telegram to Nixon expressing doubts about his plans to commit the 6th Division to a siege: 'I am urging on both India and War Office vital necessity of getting reinforcing divisions to Basra at earliest possible moment, but greatly fear there will be delay ... This makes me anxious in regard to Townshend's position at Kut, as his relief will be delayed correspondingly.'[4] Turkish movements, soon put an end to deliberation. On the evening of 7th December, General Townshend informed Nixon that Turkish forces had crossed the Shatt-al-Hai and surrounded Kut, committing the 6th Division to a siege.

As part of the 7th (Meerut) Division, Captain Witts' 4th Company of Bengal Sappers and Miners was one of those selected to travel to Mesopotamia. Although it could not be confirmed, compelling rumours had made them fairly sure of their destination. After nine solid months in the trenches of the Western Front, a change of scenery to an eastern country with a warm climate was a welcome thought, especially to the Indian troops for whom France had seemed so alien. On the train south to Marseilles, away from the hellish memories of Neuve Chapelle, Festubert and Loos, a spirit of adventure hung over the 4th Company of Bengal Sappers and Miners.

To: Mrs Broome Witts

The Manor.

Upper Slaughter.

Glos.

England.

---

[3] The 3rd (Lahore) and 7th (Meerut) Divisions, the latter being F.V.B.W.'s division, had been requested from France. In the light of worrying reports of Turkish reinforcements, Nixon asked for another two divisions, but the War Office could only promise one, and a composite one at that.

[4] Moberly, F. J., *The Mesopotamia Campaign*, vol. II p. 139

F.V.B. Witts.

[Marseilles]
Dec 3rd 1915.

Dearest Mother.

Here we are again in the sunny south: it doesn't seem like nearly nine months since I was last here.

On the 29th I decided to take the Company out for a day in the country, of course, while we were all out, orders came to move.

We started on the 30th and had a very comfortable journey of sixty hours with convenient stops for food.

We are in readiness to embark at once, & rumour mentions tomorrow but I doubt it.

We are under canvas with no flooring, beds, or even straw, luckily it is beautiful weather, and really quite mild.

I am off into the city for a wash & haircut.

No more news.

I got the new walking stick just before starting, very many thanks indeed.

Very best love,
Your ever loving Son,
Fred. V. B. Witts.

F.V.B. Witts.

[Marseilles]
Dec 6th 1915.

Dearest Mother.

Just a line to let you know we are embarking today on the Cunarder 'Ivernia',[5] a magnificent 15,000 ton Atlantic liner. So we are in great luck.

Destination is not known, but is suspected to be the same as Edward's first port of call.

No more news. We have had delightful weather here, and I have done the little business in the city which I wanted to.

We are escorted all the way across the Mediterranean so there is no need to worry about submarines. In fact we shall be across the other side, before you get this.

Very best love,
Your ever loving Son,
Fred. V. B. Witts.

[5] *H.M.T. Ivernia* was originally a passenger ship of the Cunard Line, built in Wallsend-on-Tyne in 1899. Upon the outbreak of war in 1914 she was converted into a troop carrier and operated in the Mediterranean until 1st Jan 1917, when she was torpedoed and sunk by a German UB-47 submarine off Cape Matapan (Greece), claiming 121 lives.

H.M. Transport 'Ivernia'.
At Sea.
Dec 11th 1915.

Dearest Mother.

We are due in at Alexandria about midnight, after an inconceivably perfect passage, which has amply compensated for the rough time I had coming.[6] Without exaggeration the sea has been like a sheet of glass the whole time, and the ship has been so steady, that we might have been lying alongside the quay for all we felt. We left Marseilles on the afternoon of the 7th, passed through the straits of Barifacio on the 8th, and all along the south coast of Sicily on the 9th, getting an excellent view of Mount Etna, who went so far as to smoke in our benefit, much to the surprise of the Indians, most of whom had never heard of a volcano.

We have had no escort, but have got a big gun in our stern, and machine guns mounted all round, in addition to 100 men always ready to open fire. We had a dress rehearsal yesterday afternoon. The ship's crew is not large enough to man even half the boats in case of accident, so our men, who are trained in the handling of boats, have to find crews for the remainder. We have seen very little shipping; a hospital ship, one or two tramps, and a couple of French destroyers. This is quite a big liner over 14,200 tons, designed for an emigrant ship and so eminently suitable for trooping. But she is absolutely full up, 2500 troops on board; and the officers are very closely packed every berth occupied, as the first class accommodation is comparatively limited.

There is little doing on board, some bridge & chess and an impromptu concert the other evening.

I shall try and post this as soon as I get in.

You may hear of our movements from Mrs Bird, my Captain's Mother; he has sent her various addresses of people like you interested in the Company, and any cable he sends home will be circulated to every one.[7]

From what I hear, I think George may follow Edward via France.[8]

They won't accept 'Fred' on cables nowadays, you have to give a surname.

My next letter must be a Christmas Mail.

Very best love,
Your ever loving Son,
Fred. V. B. Witts.

---

[6] In January 1915, en route to the Western Front, F.V.B.W. had had a turbulent voyage from Bombay to Marseilles aboard the *Conconada*.

[7] Captain A. J. Bird R.E. was the commander of F.V.B.W.'s 4th Coy. Bengal Sappers and Miners.

[8] Major Edward Witts (F.V.B.W.'s eldest brother), who had inherited the Upper Slaughter estate on the death of their father in 1913, had served in the Boer War after winning the high jump and long jump cups at Merton College Oxford in 1899 and 1900 respectively. He then farmed in Rhodesia between the Boer War and the WWI During the WWI he served with the Gloucestershire Regiment, winning the DSO.

S.S. Ivernia.
At Sea.
Dec 12th 1915.

Dearest Mother.

We got into Alexandria early this morning. Instead of our getting off, the ship was ordered to go on to Port Said at once en route for our expected destination, without a change of ships.

I am quite disappointed at not getting a chance of seeing this country but you can't expect to combine war and pleasure.

This ship is bigger than any of the P & O by a long way, and will be one of the biggest that has ever been through the Canal. She is built for the cold weather in the Atlantic, and I expect we shall find her terribly hot later on.

We shall get in just about Christmas Day, and in case I don't get another chance, this must be my Christmas letter to you.

I am afraid it will be a very lonely Christmas for you, but you must not get depressed. I expect Jack will be at home, and possibly Frank on leave. Please distribute my good wishes to all the family. I never anticipated that today would be the last mail before Christmas, and it is too late to write all round.

No more news.

With very best love & good wishes.
Your ever loving Son
Fred. V. B. Witts.

Nothing more to fear from submarines, so we shall be able to open our ports and not travel in utter darkness.

In Mesopotamia, General Lake's reservations about committing the 6th Division to a siege in Kut were proving well-founded. Allied shipping was heavily engaged in assisting the Serbian Army on the Adriatic coast. 140,000 Serbian troops had been driven there by a combined German, Austrian and Bulgarian force; this imposed inevitable strains on the availability of shipping elsewhere. As a result, there was a delay in finding transport for the 3rd (Lahore) Division who were still waiting in Marseilles. Meanwhile, in Egypt, numerous field ambulances of the 7th Division were left behind to make more room for troops on board transport. It had been intended that both the 3rd and 7th Divisions should undergo comprehensive reorganisation in Egypt before they set sail for Mesopotamia; but, to compensate for delays, the opportunity to reorganise was abandoned. However, as Captain Witts attests, the short time that was spent in Egypt was clearly a pleasant relief for the troops.

POST OFFICE TELEGRAPHS.   13 12

This Form must accompany any inquiry respecting this Telegram.   15

Office of Origin and Service Instructions.

Portsaid   _Handed in at} 1.15pm. Received here at}   9.58pm._

TO{ _Fco_

Witts Upper Slaughter

Excellent passage proceeding immediately

expected destination

Witts

H.M.T. 'Ivernia.'

Port Said

Dec 15th

Dearest Mother.

You will like a line, though I have little news for you.

This is the only notepaper the ship can produce, having run out of any further notepaper.

We have spent two full days here and are just starting through the canal. I have been doing some shopping, and patronising the various hotels for dinner.

Yesterday we took the men ashore and marched them down to the beach to bathe in the sea. None of them had bathed in the sea before, and all thoroughly enjoyed it. It is a beautiful sandy beach and very safe for bathing.

No more news.

Very best love

Your ever loving Son

Fred. V. B. Witts.

This is written to catch the English mail tonight.

It is a perfect climate here now.

18. Postcard of Upper Slaughter Square, with the church in the background.

H.M.T. Ivernia, at Sea

Christmas Day, 1915.

Dearest Mother.

Very many happy returns of the day, and very best wishes for the new year. I wonder who you have got with you to cheer you up. I have had no family news later than Dec 2nd, so it is rather hard to refer to family matters. Our general news, read in Egypt & picked up at Aden by wireless, has of course been strictly limited to the barest outline, but has been sufficient to show how many important events have occurred,[9] and I yearn for further & fuller news. The Times will be more welcome than ever.

For ourselves, since leaving Suez on the afternoon of the 17th, the voyage has been quite devoid of incident. We had a strong head wind down the Red Sea, and it never even got hot enough for me to wear my thin uniform or to drive us out of our cabins at night inspite of the lack of fans & ventilation. One day it was quite rough for the Red Sea, but this large ship hardly noticed it.

We passed Aden midday on the 22nd quite slowly and quite close in, but we did not stop, and are now (midday) about 850 miles further on just off the Arabian Coast, which we have hugged the whole way from Aden, and for barrenness and inhospitality it quite takes the cake.

The Division Chaplain is on board, so we have been able to keep Christmas complete in every detail. An early service and then morning service with all the Slaughter hymns and No 595 for absent friends in addition. How I longed for later

[9] F.V.B.W. is most likely referring to the start of the Allied withdrawal from Gallipoli and the progress of the Central Powers in the Balkans.

news of every one. We are finishing the day with a dinner and concert, for which there is some excellent talent on board.

There is a Regt on board now, who have spent some time in the Persian Gulf; from them I gather we shall come in for the winter rains, and it is supposed to rain every day for a month, but there should be none of the Flanders mud.[10]

Very best love and good wishes to everyone.

Your ever loving Son
    Fred. V. B. Witts.

At Sea
10 p.m. Dec 28th 1915

Dearest Mother.

We have just dropped anchor at the head of the Gulf, but seventeen miles from the mouth of the river [the Shatt-al-Arab], as this great ship cannot get in any closer.

We are now waiting for news and orders, but don't expect either till morning.

Our Christmas dinner was quite up to standard, turkey, plum pudding and champagne followed by a first rate concert.

On the 26th about tea time we passed Muscat quite close in. It is quite a unique place tucked away in a little cove surrounded by towering rocks, and only accessible from the interior by one small track.

All the nearer peaks are crowned with towers, and there is a very prominent fort.

19. British Transport cart in the mud, January 1916.

[10] F.V.B.W. soon discovered he was very wrong in this supposition.

On the morning of the 27th we passed through the Straits of Ormeez [Hormuz] into the Gulf and got our first distant glimpse of Persia, but never went in close that side.

It has been a most pleasant rest on board, but it is as well it is over as the ship did not start equipped for a long voyage, and today the soda water ran out and everything is at a very low ebb.

I am writing this to send ashore at the first opportunity in order to catch the first mail.

Very best love
    Your ever loving Son
        Fred. V. B. Witts.

Basra, as Captain Witts found it, was in chaos. The existing port infrastructure was completely insufficient to handle the mass influx of troops and supplies flooding into the country, causing delays of up to a month in unloading non-priority goods (anything but troops and ammunition). River transport was also in a state of disarray. Whilst manpower in Mesopotamia had suddenly increased by two divisions, numbers of steamers, tugs and barges had remained the same, creating a considerable backlog of troops waiting to be rushed up to the front at Ali Gharbi, sixty miles downstream of Kut. Disorganisation was rife throughout the entire operation.

Lieutenant-General Sir Fenton Aylmer, an old comrade of Townshend's from the 1895 Chitral siege, was the Corps Commander at the front, and the man responsible for relieving Kut. Based on the food supplies, ammunition and morale of the Kut garrison, Aylmer had concluded that his relief mission must be completed by the 15th January. Speed was his watchword, and amassing troops at the front his main priority. The result was that, from its inception, the relief force (also known as the Tigris Corps) was disorganised. It had an improvised staff and consisted of battalions unfamiliar with their brigades, and commanders unknown to their troops. The strict priority given to soldiers and ammunition on river transport had also meant that doctors,

20. Shipping on the Tigris at Qurna.

medical supplies (those that had made it from Egypt) and pack transport were, for the most part, left waiting in Basra.

On 4th January, Aylmer ordered Major-General Younghusband, commander of the 7th Division, to take all available troops and advance from Ali Gharbi to Sheikh Saad, a Turkish outpost 30 miles upstream, which was thought to be defended only sparsely. Townshend later corrected this assumption, reporting some ten thousand Turks heading towards Sheikh Saad on the 4th. Younghusband, nonetheless, continued his advance, confident that he would be able to flush out any resistance, despite having an incomplete force, the bulk of which was either en route to Ali Gharbi or still awaiting transport in Basra. Over the course of the next three days, Younghusband's division was punished severely for his misjudgement. In miserable conditions, with no prospect of dryness, hot food or the hospital comforts habitual to fighting on the Western Front, British and Indian troops attacked the Turkish trenches repeatedly and with admirable élan, but with little effect. A hollow victory was eventually gained thanks to Turkish transport difficulties, forcing them to withdraw upstream, but only after inflicting over four thousand casualties on British forces. Because of the scandalous medical shortages, a disproportionate number of these casualties would die either of their wounds or of exposure from long nights left helpless in the freezing morass. Arab marauders from outlying tribes were another serious danger. In the aftermath of battle, these scavengers descended onto the battlefield, seizing rifles, stripping clothes and prising out gold teeth. They were merciless in their greed, drowning their wounded victims in the viscous mud if they attempted to resist.

Meanwhile, 200 miles behind the lines, the 4th Coy. Bengal Sappers and Miners had been ordered to remain at Basra for the present, and help in the enormous task of expanding and modifying the port.

[Basra]
Jan 3rd 1916

Dearest Mother.

My last epistle was dated the evening of the 28th waiting for orders. Next morning we were sent back to Koweit Harbour, where we were transhipped into a smaller boat. This occupied till the morning of the 31st when we started again & reached Basra (the base) on the morning of the 1st. Here we are to remain for some indefinite period, working on the general landing arrangements. We have to work in two separate places so I am being separated with half the company, four miles up the river from the others.[11]

We are busily engaged trying to sort ourselves out, as this is the first opportunity

---

[11] F.V.B.W. was sent to Maqil, where there was deeper water along the river bank suitable for constructing berths.

21. Shatt-al-Arab looking downstream.

we have had of opening some of our kit, since we landed in France [12 months before].

It is a very drastic change, trench work in France to real engineering, and we shall all find it very difficult to adapt ourselves to our new circumstances.

There is an unlimited amount to be done, and I foresee I shall be very busy indeed, the hours of work being only limited by the hours of light.

The climate now is perfect, almost too cold at nights: we want all our thick clothes.

The situation at the front seems rather involved, but I mustn't talk about it as the censorship is very strict they say. We are not allowed to censor our own letters. [12] Goodness knows how long we shall be here, it would really be a very good, useful, & pleasant change, but naturally it is hateful not to be in the thick of it [at Kut].

Please pass on all the news I have at the moment, too much to think about to concentrate my thoughts on letter writing.

I have had no letters yet.

Very best love,
Your ever loving Son,
Fred. V. B. Witts.

Remember no news is good news: bad news will arrive far quicker than any of my letters.

---

[12] Censorship was very strict in Mesopotamia, more to conceal bad news than to protect information from reaching the Turks. As F.V.B.W. says, troops were not trusted to censor their own letters; that onerous task fell to the officers of the Censorship Dept.

Maqil near Basra.
Jan 7th 1916.

Dearest Mother.

No letters reached me so far, but I live in hopes of their catching me up.

I am living alone in a tent and am rather overpowered by the amount & nature of the work which has devolved on me. Much heavier & more permanent than I have ever had to think about. I don't yet see my way clear. It is all in connection with the improvement of the berthing facilities for large ships here: I believe the censor will allow me to say this, and also I hear he does not object to Basra being mentioned.

Very cold nights, very hot sun midday, & some showers as the Daily Graphic would say.

I am almost living on dates which appear to be the only product of this country though I manage to get milk & eggs and I have my eyes on a certain chicken.

I hope to post this in Basra tomorrow.

I never told you of the fire the night we arrived, a real good blaze the first I have ever been present at. Not having any kit involved I thoroughly enjoyed it!

No more news.

Very best love
        Your ever loving Son
                Fred. V. B. Witts.

I have never had a chance of cabling, but maybe tomorrow.

No 4 Coy
1st K.G. O.Sappers & Miners.
Meerut Division
I. E. F. 'D'
c/o India Office
London S. W.
Jan 16th 1916

Dearest Mother.

Just got my first mail, a week's Times 2 Bystanders [later absorbed by the Tatler], Truth & your letters of Dec 3rd, enclosing my three photographs, Dec 4th, 8th & 14th. The photographs unfortunately must have just missed me in France. They will be a bit late for Christmas but it can't be helped! Also a letter from Sweet Escott[13] saying he had changed the present for a pair of fish servers and 6 pairs of fish knives & forks, which he wanted. Letters you see take just about a month to reach me here at the base.

---

[13] Sweet Escott was an army colleague of F.V.B.W.'s, crippled in a riding accident in 1911.

I am so sorry to see from your letters how down in your luck you are; Mothers & wives are harder hit than any one in this war, and you particularly suddenly deserted, so to speak, in your old age; but you must cheer up and look forward to the day when you will see us all home again. You can write me off your list of anxieties, living at the base in an almost perfect climate.[14] Always remember no news is good news.

I am gradually getting more settled, but have had a very disturbed fortnight, and you must forgive me if my letters have missed a mail. I send a Post Card to catch it.

I last wrote on the evening of the 7th, I did not go into Basrah as expected next day, but was busy taking soundings in the river for my new work.[15] It is no easy job with a tide running to get accurate results.

The morning of the 9th there was a very heavy fall of rain, and as the draining of the camp had been neglected, we woke to find a foot of water in our tents. We spent the day moving to another part, and draining & drying.

On the 10th we completed our first job of raising existing piers above flood level. The piers are entirely constructed of material collected by the Germans for the famous Baghdad railway.[16]

On the 11th we finished our second job of large settling tanks for the camp watersupply. Purves who had been invalided in France joined me, only to be sent away again next day: a great disappointment as I wanted help & company.

On the 12th we took our first day off, to pay, wash & write letters.

That evening there was a row amongst some of our men on family matters, not unusual amongst Pathans. It took me into Basrah next day, and has been a great worry since. For the time at any rate peace reigns.

On the 13th & 14th we worked on a road to join up our new camp to which we moved yesterday by boat, as it is still inaccessible by land.

Today we have continued work on the road through a steady fall of rain though not heavy. It seems to rain about one day a week. Our new camp is beautifully situated on the bank of the river amongst the date palm trees.

I will get another letter off by this mail later on. But best wishes now for your birthday in case you get no other letter.

---

[14] F.V.B.W. was fortunate to arrive in Mesopotamia in mid-winter. Temperatures around Basra at this time were usually quite mild.

[15] F.V.B.W. was a bridging expert.

[16] Started in 1903, the scheme to build a railway linking Berlin to Baghdad was, at first, welcomed by the British. However, in the years leading up to the war, the scheme began to be viewed as a threat to India and British interests in the Persian Gulf. The railway also demonstrated the alarming extent to which the Ottoman Empire, through skilful German diplomacy, had become economically dependent on Germany.

Very best love

    Your ever loving Son

        Fred. V. B. Witts.

While Captain Witts was kept occupied at Maqil, up at the front it was becoming increasingly apparent that breaking through to Kut was not going to be as easy as expected. The narrow strip of land on the river's left bank leading up to the town between the Tigris and the impassable Suwaikiya marsh was suited inherently to the defenders. But, in a strategic error, the new Turkish commander, Khalil Pasha, had entrenched his men in a relatively weak position at the Wadi River, outside the Tigris/Suwaikiya bottleneck. In so doing he had gifted Aylmer the chance to turn his left flank and swallow the whole Turkish force in a single manoeuvre. In the event, however, a communication breakdown within the Tigris Corps and delays caused by atrocious weather cost Aylmer a consummate victory. With his army still intact, Khalil retreated to the Hanna defile, a formidable position at the opening of the mile-wide corridor between the Tigris and the Suwaikiya marsh. Aylmer firmly believed that his only chance of overpowering such a strong defensive position lay in bridging the Tigris and enfilading the Turkish trenches over the river with artillery fire, thus giving his infantry a chance of success in a frontal assault.

The difficulties faced by the sappers of No. 1 Bridging Train in constructing a bridge over the Tigris were prodigious. Captain Witts would often experience the same difficulties on the Tigris when he assumed command of No. 2 Bridging Train in March 1916. The following account is taken from the *Official History.*

> Work on the Tigris bridge near the Wadi was carried out during the day [16th January] under considerable difficulties, and the bridge was nearing completion when a steamer drifted into it and carried away a considerable portion ... The same inclement weather continued throughout the 17th, but in spite of it the sappers strove strenuously at the bridge across the Tigris. They had just completed it about 7 p.m., when three of its component *danaks* [native barges also known as *bellums*] sank, carrying a portion of the bridge downstream. In spite of the heavy wind and rain, the weary engineers worked on through the night and had almost completed their task when misfortune again overtook them. About 8 a.m. on the 18th, the wind suddenly veered round to the south-west, blowing with still greater force and bringing heavy waves over the boats, with the eventual result that about half the bridge was washed downstream. This portion, fouling several of the ships, had to be dismantled and taken ashore, many of the *danaks* being

[17] Moberly, F. J., *The Mesopotamia Campaign*, vol. II p. 259

sunk and much superstructure lost. All hope of getting a bridge across the Tigris in the immediate future had now to be abandoned.[17]

With bridging the Tigris out of the question, Aylmer saw little point in ordering his men into what he perceived as a suicidal assault against the Hanna defile. He suggested that, with his assistance, Townshend should try breaking out of Kut to save the able-bodied men in his garrison. General Nixon, however, in his final order before his replacement (for health reasons), categorically rejected the idea, demanding that Aylmer should fulfil his original objective and break the siege forcibly.

The subsequent attack on the Hanna defile, launched on 21st January, was a tragic realisation of Aylmer's worst fears. After an ineffectual British artillery bombardment, wave after wave of tightly-packed British and Indian troops ran headlong into a wall of enemy fire, cutting them down in swathes. Come nightfall, the misery continued. Men with limbs shattered by shells, organs punctured by bullets, and bodies paralysed with cold, whimpered and moaned alone in the darkness with no one to tend to them, or protect them from Arab bandits who had gathered like vultures to a kill. The official Eye-Witness to the campaign, Edmund Candler, later reflected 'for collective misery, the night of the 21st is probably unparalleled since the Crimea in the history of sufferings endured by the British Army.'[18]

In Maqil, Captain Witts would have had little idea of the horrors unfolding at the front; at least, not until the hordes of crippled began arriving in Basra to board ships for home. Even if Captain Witts had known of the sufferings befalling the Tigris Corps, the censor would never have allowed him to impart more than a hint of the depressing truth in a letter to his mother.

F. V. B. Witts
    Capt. R.E.

                  [Maqil, near Basra]
                  Jan 25th 1916.

Dearest Mother.

    I think I wrote last on the 20th.[19] The 21st was a dull day, and it rained hard all that night and the next day the 22nd. And this place is reputed to have a rainfall of 6' inches only a year! As a result the mud reminds one of Flanders. The 22nd I spent in Basrah occupied on a Court Martial – the outcome of the trouble I mentioned. I now hope to hear no more of it. I thought we were stranded in the dark coming

---

[18] Candler, E., *The Long Road to Baghdad*, vol. I p. 96

[19] Unless F.V.B.W. is mistaken, his letter of 20th January must have been either lost en route to England or misplaced by his mother. Considering the U-boat threat in the Mediterranean, the postal service was normally remarkably reliable.

22. Khora Creek, near Basra.

back, as our motor launch failed us. Luckily I managed to borrow another. Owing to the wet the roads were out of the question. The last three days have been beautiful and we have got on fast with the work, which now that we have settled down to it is really the most interesting I have ever had to do. Starting with an untouched Palm grove, we have had to make a road full of small bridges and one big one, level & raise the ground, clear the trees and build the piers. On a fine day, one could not want anything nicer, but a wet day is certainly rather trying. I am living in a Government 40 lb tent, which is only 4 foot high. Luckily I have an 80 lb tent as a mess.

Owing to the sinking of the Persia,[20] I am afraid we have lost a mail, and so I have had no news since I last wrote. I am expecting the next mail on my birthday Jan 30th. Just think of it I shall be 27.

As a result of the rain the river at high tide last night was within 18 inches of our tents. The worst floods do not come until March or April, and I hope to be finished of this work before then!

My syce, Indian groom, was very ill on the ship, and has gone to hospital en route for India. It is a nuisance, as I can't replace him here.

We get very little news here, I don't see the Reuter Telegrams and they give us very scanty news of what is happening up river.

I have met several of our old Roorkee Indian Officers, who rejoined a Labour Corps which was raised for work here. They are now occupied raising roads & certain spaces above flood level.

There is no more news,

　　With very best love,

　　　　Your ever loving Son,

　　　　　　Fred. V. B. Witts.

[20] *S.S. Persia* was a P & O passenger liner, built in 1900 in Inverclyde, Scotland. On 30th December 1915 she was torpedoed and sunk off Crete by a German U-38 submarine without warning, killing 334 of the 501 passengers on board. The sinking was especially controversial as it ignored international naval law stipulating that passenger liners should be given adequate warning prior to an attack, to allow passengers to disembark.

On the same day that Captain Witts wrote the above letter, the situation at the front changed dramatically with an important piece of news from General Townshend. After a thorough search throughout Kut, Townshend had discovered a bounteous stock of additional supplies. With these added stocks, on top of the meat to be taken from his 3,000 horses and mules, Townshend estimated that his garrison could hold out for a further 84 days until April 18th. In a relief effort which had been overshadowed by a state of urgency throughout, this revelation came as a saving grace. But why Townshend had not conducted a comprehensive search for food upon his arrival in Kut was,

23. Lieutenant-General
Sir Percy Lake.

quite understandably, baffling, and indeed frustrating for Aylmer.

With his extended deadline, the new G.O.C. in Mesopotamia, Lieutenant-General Sir Percy Lake,[21] was determined to improve the campaign's shambolic administration. Reducing the congestion at Basra port was a main priority, and Lake employed the services of the distinguished port engineer, Sir George Buchanan, to coordinate expansion and improve efficiency. River transport was still an enormous problem; Lake continued to put pressure on Egypt, London and India to send boats to meet the inflated demand in Mesopotamia. He also ordered stone to be imported from India for road building as well as materials for light railways.

F. V. B. Witts.

[Maqil]
Jan 30th 1916.

Dearest Mother.

27 today! I can hardly believe it. This is the first birthday I have spent absolutely alone. I received what was under the circumstances the most acceptable birthday present possible – the first mail for a fortnight. A letter from you dated Dec 23rd, a week's lot of the Times, a Bystander, and a Truth. You say you are stopping Truth,

---

[21] Lake had formerly been the Chief of General Staff in India and thus carried a portion of the blame for the current situation, partly explaining his eagerness to assume command in Mesopotamia. Coincidentally, Lake was also a distant relation of F.V.B.W. through George Woodroffe, husband of F.V.B.W.'s eldest sister, Apphia. Sir Percy and F.V.B.W. were both aware of their connection and would meet in quite extraordinary circumstances in April 1916 (*see* letter April 10th, p. 74-6).

remember that now all form of literature is doubly welcome to what it was in France, where there were the local shops & bookstalls to fall back on.

You must have had Jack & Frank with you for Christmas which was particularly lucky. I am so glad Frank is sticking out the weather conditions so well. I hope Jack is quite all right again. I shall be interested to hear Edith's plans, what is the rumpus? I think she ought to stay at home & help you while Edward & George are away, I wonder where George has gone, he may well roll up here, we want reinforcements! You must cheer up, Mother; the war cannot go on for ever, remember it depresses us to think that you are so down in your luck, though well you may be.

Now to turn to my own doings: Since the 25th work on my piers has gone on continuously and well. The 28th was the only wet day, so I have no complaints against the weather this time. We have been working very hard and long hours 7.30 a.m – 5 p.m, with only half an hour's interval. This has been necessary in order to make the most of the low tide, which has been at an awkward hour.

Today I successfully launched two very heavy trestles [wooden supports] which have been giving me considerable anxiety. A birthday offering from the gods.

The finding & sentence of the Court-Martial, which I promulgated yesterday morning, was most satisfactory; and I don't anticipate any more trouble.

The Indians don't get fed as well here as they were in France and naturally don't like the change and I have to spend quite a lot of time running round after meat, milk, sugar & otta, which is their flour.[22]

No more news.
>With very best love
>Your ever loving Son
>Fred. V. B. Witts

F.V. B. Witts.
>Capt. R. E.

[Maqil]
Feb 2nd 1916.

Dearest Mother.

Although I only wrote on the 30th, I find I can catch a mail tomorrow, and in this short interval I have had another mail with the Times up till Jan 6th, a Bystander, and your letter of New Year's Eve. I am so glad you have news of Edward, I thought he

---

[22] In Kut, General Townshend was having similar difficulties in accommodating the sepoys' abhorrence of horse-flesh.

24. Witts household staff at the Manor *c.* 1900.

might have been mixed up in the retreat.[23] I am glad the two Easts, Butler, & Pittaway have been refused, but I am afraid you will soon lose Fuller, if not already gone.[24]

I have little news; work on the 31st 1st & today has gone on as usual without any noticeable incident. We have been having perfect weather combined with very low tides, which are a great help to my work. The nights are bitterly cold, a frost regularly; I am thankful I brought all my warm things from France. Of course it soon gets pleasantly warm when the sun comes up. We are working long hours and I find it a bit lonely, but I have never had a pleasanter job under pleasanter conditions. An ideal camp in a date grove on the actual site of the work. The rain and the consequent mud is the only drawback and that occasional.

There are a few duck about and I have got hold of a gun and cartridges, but have had my time so fully occupied that I have not been out after them.

I am now working on eight 30 ft gangways, amongst other things, for ships coming alongside.

No more news.

    With very best love

        Your ever loving Son

          Fred. V. B. Witts.

[23] F.V.B.W. is presumably talking about the 'Great Retreat' of Serbian forces to the Adriatic coast in the winter of 1915. In October, a combined Anglo-French force, perhaps including F.V.B.W.'s brother Edward, landed at the Greek port of Salonika to help the Serbs repel the invasion of the Central Powers. They were too late to change the outcome, but, instead of joining the retreat, they fortified their enclave at Salonika.

[24] Pittaway was the Witts' groom; the two Easts, Butler and Fuller were other villagers.

25. No. 5 Wharf,
Maqil.

F. V. B. Witts
        Capt. R. E.

[Maqil]
Feb 7th 1916.

Dearest Mother.

No further mail from home, but I must write to make sure of catching the next mail to home. Since I wrote on the 2nd, the weather has remained perfect except for one small shower – the nights are not quite so cold.

I have finished the piers and am now busy making up landing gangways and then expect to move into Busra.

On the 4th I went into dinner at the big camp, on the 5th Bird paid me a visit in the morning, and the sapper General in the evening. I went out with my gun that evening for the first time and got five duck. I have been out again tonight and collected seven duck and a snipe. It is a pleasant change to ration beef! I have not got my own gun, but we have bought two cheap ones for the company.

26. Shatt-al-Arab at Maqil.

Would you like to send me some solidified Vinolia Brilliantine in a metal case – not bottle or tube – I have seen it advertised, and it is a very convenient form. I want to preserve my locks. Otherwise I think literature is all I want: the Bystander each week would be very welcome and the Round Table when it comes out each quarter.

No more news,

    With very best love,

        Your ever loving Son,

           Fred. V. B. Witts.

F. V. B. Witts

    Capt. R. E.

                             [Busra]

                           Feb 16th 1916.

Dearest Mother.

Since last writing I have got another mail with your letters of the 6th & 12th of Jan. I am very glad indeed Edith is at home especially, now that George has left England: I shouldn't be a bit surprised to meet him here!

I shall be thinking of you the day after tomorrow, your 68th Birthday, and am cabling to welcome you tomorrow, but the wire may take some time. May your next birthday be spent under happier conditions! I hope you will go and see Mrs Bird sometime, I should like you to meet.

No weekly papers in this mail. I appreciate them more than ever out here, especially the Bystander and Truth. Besides they go the round of several other people!

I finished off my gangways on the 12th and moved down to Busra on the 13th. The first ship came alongside my piers that day and I believe did not knock them down which is comforting. I am still living in a tent so as to be near my work, which is a 100 ft bridge to carry 9 ton motor lorries & to open in the centre to let large barges with masts get through.

It involves pulling down 50 yds square of low buildings to make the approaches, and two large retaining walls. It will take me some time which does not look like an early move forward for us. It won't be such a pleasant job as the other, as one end is on a street with quite a continuous stream of traffic, and there is a lot of traffic up and down the river. In short we shall not be left to ourselves with plenty of room to play about in. So far I have been busy collecting material, and settling up details.

The weather has remained fine, which is a blessing, and it was quite hot when we marched in on the 13th.

Send me details from Edward's letters, I should like to hear what he is doing and he is not a good hand at writing letters all round, and won't have the time either.

No more news

With very best love
      Your ever loving Son
          Fred.V B Witts.

F.V. B. Witts
      Capt. R. E.   [Busra]
February 24th 1916

Dearest Mother.

Just a line to catch the mail, which I have nearly missed, though I have little news.

I thought of you on your birthday and sent a cable to cheer you up.

The bridge I am building is getting on well, but it is a slow job. The remainder of the company are going up a bit of the way today to make new bridges on the road up. I hope to follow as soon as I can finish this job. I have just been packing them carts mules & all on to a river steamer.

It is beginning to get quite hot in the middle of the day, but the nights are still quite cold. We have only had one shower of rain and it is getting unpleasantly dusty.

The mail has been very erratic recently, arriving at odd hours and bit by bit.

I have no more news. I am afraid this is a most unsatisfactory letter, but if I now stop to think I shall miss the mail.

Very best love,
      Your ever loving Son,
          Fred.V. B. Witts

Busra.
Feb. 29th 1916.

Dearest Mother.

A mail has just come in with your three letters of Jan 17th 22nd & 25th, a week's supply of The Times and a Sporting Dramatic. All so welcome. Your last letter was from Bath, I am so glad you have gone there, and hope you are all the better for the treatment. I shall be interested to hear where George goes eventually, it doesn't look as if he was coming my way. I am very glad for your sake; and hope France will be the furthest. I am so sorry to hear you are losing Ketteringham [a retainer], Edward will be too.

Don't send me anything from F & M [Fortnum & Mason],[25] it would be either

---

[25] Established as a luxury food emporium in 1707, Fortnum & Mason has a long tradition of supplying preserved foods to British forces at war, particularly in the Napoleonic (1803-1815) and Crimean (1854-1856) Wars. F.V.B.W. makes up for his current abstemiousness by requesting four 'big fat' Christmas hampers in July 1916.

stolen, drowned, or melted by the heat before it reached me!

The Army & Navy Stores have started a branch here, which I am using, also the Bombay Branch.[26] Once we go upstream, it is very difficult for anything following to reach us. I hope you will get over and see Mrs Bird.

I have a letter from Frank by the same mail. He writes very cheerfully.

I think I told you in my last letter that the rest of the company have moved up a bit of the way for Bridging on the road; while I am left behind to finish my bridge, which is progressing well but slowly, which is not surprising in view of its nature. Today it has been pouring with rain, finishing with a violent thunderstorm which has not hastened matters, as we now have the inevitable sea of mud to contend with. It is quite cold again in consequence.

I am still in a tent here, in the usual date grove. At high tide, the water comes within six inches of the level of the tent floor! However I have the local Mohammedan Burial Ground, which are always placed on any high ground,[27] to retire to near at hand in case of floods, which are due this coming month.

There is a regular R. E. Mess here in a well built brick building of German origin, with electric light and fans laid on. But it is a bit far from my work & the men's camp; and I should have to share a room with about six others. I prefer the privacy of a tent.

> There is no more news,
>> With very best love,
>> Your ever loving Son,
>>> Fred. V. B. Witts.

F. V. B. Witts
  Capt. R. E.

                                                              [Busra]
                                                      March 8th 1916.

Dearest Mother.

It is time I wrote again, though I have no news from you, inspite of another week's mail. You must have just missed it. I have a double supply of letters to look forward to next mail!

I am still working on the bridge, which I hope to finish in the next three or four days, and then I hope to move up & rejoin the company, who are gradually working their way up to the front repairing roads & building new bridges as they go.

---

[26] Army and Navy Stores were a co-operative society established in 1871, selling basic goods to servicemen and their families at the lowest affordable rates.

[27] Cemeteries in Lower Mesopotamia were always placed on high ground to avoid bodies being exhumed by the annual floods. Force 'D' was quick to imitate this custom.

I shall not be sorry to get a move on again, though it is not definitely settled yet; and I may get stuck for another job here.

The bridge promises to be a great success, which is encouraging, though it still remains to be seen if the opening arrangement works satisfactorily, and that it doesn't collapse under the steam roller which has now arrived on the scene.

Rain has been threatening again every day for the last week but has held off, and it has been unpleasantly warm and muggy once or twice. But the evenings and nights are still quite cool.

I have made good use of my time here, and fitted myself up with thin clothing, and laid in a large stock of stuff to take up with me, if I can find room in the boat.

Oswald Bazeley's Battalion is I believe arriving here, but I doubt if we shall meet.[28] We certainly should not recognise each other. I wonder if Fred Bateman is still with them.

My one and only Christmas and New Year's card arrived the other day. I am sending it along to you to keep for me. With it came an imitation bullet pencil case with the Princess's Monogram on it. It was all sent in a brass tin box marked Christmas 1914 – an excellent example in the economy line.

I am sorry to see another P & O liner has been sunk,[29] though I hope there were no mails on board. If you would like to send me a small present, which won't melt, I should like another pair of those imitation knitted puttees;[30] you sent me a khaki pair in France, but I should now like a dark blue pair, which I have seen advertised. They are our Regimental pattern.

No more news,

> With very best love,
> Your ever loving Son,
> Fred. V. B. Witts

Up at the front, after nearly six weeks of preparation, the Tigris Corps was ready for another attempt to recapture Kut. This time the troops were rested, reorganised and well supplied. General Aylmer's plan was complicated but clever; by dawn on March 8th the difficult part had already been completed with remarkable success. Overnight, a column, measuring two miles in length, had marched silently into forward positions on the right bank of the Tigris, surrounding the Dujaila Redoubt, the strategic cornerstone of the Turkish position. When dawn rose, the Turks were completely oblivious to

---

[28] Oswald Bazeley was the son of Canon Bazeley, a great friend of F.V.B.W.'s parents.

[29] The S.S. *Maloja*, a 12,350 ton steamship, struck a mine off Dover on 27 February 1916, claiming 122 lives.

[30] The *Hobson-Jobson Anglo-Indian Glossary* defines a *puttee* as, 'A piece or strip of cloth, bandage; especially used in the sense of a ligature round the lower part of the leg used in lieu of a gaiter.' (Burnell, A. & Yule, H.)

the presence of a large British force lying in wait just beyond their trenches. Fortunately for them, however, the precious element of surprise was squandered by the attackers. Aylmer had prohibited his generals from using any initiative, insisting that his orders were followed to the letter. He had also asserted particularly that the attack should not begin until every unit was in place. Whilst delayed British artillery trundled into position, the British and Indian troops looked on in despair as the Turks realised their mistake and rushed thousands of reinforcements into their defences around the Dujaila Redoubt. By the time the attack was finally launched, the Turks were ready for it. British onslaughts were beaten off throughout the day until, by the evening, a shortage of drinking water forced the Tigris Corps to withdraw back to their camp at the Wadi River.

Failure to break through at Dujaila was a great shock to the British; with ample time to prepare, success had been deemed almost inevitable. Seasonal floodwaters were now beginning to encroach on the land around Kut, narrowing enemy lines of defence and increasing the difficulty of breaking through. A sense of urgency had returned to the relief effort. In Kut, meanwhile, the faith that the garrison had placed in their liberation was dwindling fast.

General Aylmer, widely known as 'Failmer' to his British troops, had finally lost the confidence of his men. He was replaced as Corps Commander by Lieutenant-General Gorringe, the man who had achieved notable success in Southern Arabistan and Nasiriyah the year before. General Lake, meanwhile, preferred to focus his attention on the administrative side of the campaign in Basra, although he was frequently steaming up the Tigris to check on the situation at the front. As the senior officer in Mesopotamia, the weight of the campaign rested predominantly on his shoulders; but his disposition was such that, amid all the tension, he found the time to write to his cousin George Woodroffe, on the subject of Captain Witts.

March 10th 1916.
INDIAN EXPEDITIONARY FORCE 'D'
Basra via Karachi.

My dear George,

Many thanks to the family and yourself for your congratulations on my command – which is going to keep my head and hands pretty busily employed!

I will certainly look up your young brother-in-law if I get the chance – which of course cannot be certain. In any case I should try to do so, for he must be a relation of dear old 'Daddy' Witts?[31]

Curiously enough I had a letter from Broome Witts[32] from Melbourne the day

---

[31] Thought to be F.V.B.W.'s father, Canon Broome Witts who died in 1913.

I received yours.

> With love to all the family
> > Yours very sincerely
> > > Percy Lake

Captain Witts, meanwhile, was on the threshold of his first command; he would soon be sent upriver to the front.

F.V. B. Witts.
    Capt. R. E.

> No 2 Bridging Train.
> 1st. K. G. O. Sappers & Miners.
> I. E. F. 'D'.
> c/o India Office.
> [Busra]
> March 15th 1916.

Dearest Mother.

As anticipated in my last letter, I have received a shower of letters from you in the last week dated Feb 4th 8th 10th & 16th two copies of the Bystander & regular copies of the Times. Also your little parcel of soap, & tea, sugar & milk tabloids; it is so good of you to send them. I have never seen these tabloids before, they are an excellent idea: I am keeping them against the day of scarcity. Now a tin of Turkey and Tongue Paté has rolled up: I am wondering if it has all melted, I must eat it quickly.

I have not met General Lake though I have been living for the last month within a quarter of a mile of his abode. But he has or ought to have more important work to do than looking up his poor relations. But please thank George Woodroffe for writing.

As you will see by the address I give, I have left the fourth company. This morning I was offered the command of a new Bridging Train which has just arrived from Roorkee. Though I am very sorry to leave the Company which I had hoped to command some day, I am naturally very pleased to get my own command. Moreover I made certain it would not prejudice my chance of returning to command No 4 Coy, should Bird get a better billet. I join tomorrow, and remain in Busra for the present fitting out. I may go up stream any time, but you will be glad to realize that it is a job, which does not involve daily trenchwork and other dangerous amusements incidental to my former job when the Company is at the Front.

I am so glad Mrs Farley[33] has been writing to you & sending you information. You must ask her to Slaughter, while Edith & Agnes are available to look after her.

---

[32] Broome Witts was a common Witts family name, and this Broome Witts was a cousin.

[33] Wife of Capt. E. L. Farley R.E., F.V.B.W.'s fellow subaltern in No. 4 Coy. Bengal Sappers & Miners.

27. Wedding group at the Manor 1899: Apphia Witts (F.V.B.W.'s eldest sister) and George Woodroffe. F.V.B.W. is on the left on the ground, aged ten; his mother is standing, third from the right.

I am sorry to hear Jack has been so bad, I hope he has pulled up again by this time.

Now I have got my own show, & am leaving our present mess, I shall not see either Punch or Blackwood. If you would like to send them out with the Bystander & the Times, they would be the most acceptable things you could possibly send me. I can't sit down to a book these days, & food won't travel this distance in this climate. Moreover they will be always passed on to some one else to see & be much appreciated.

I am so glad you are having a silver band made for my old watch at my expense. To make us quits I have bought a patent clockwork Japanese flycatcher local price £1.[34]

28. Copse Hill Hospital Group July 1915: Commandant Agnes Witts (F.V.B.W.'s youngest sister) is in the centre.

It is very ingenious & apparently effective; the flies are already becoming a pest.

I must go to bed now, it is 12 o'clock, I have had a busy day & shall have another tomorrow.

For the first time since I left Flanders I am sleeping in a house, in quite a decent room too though empty.

Very best love.

        Your ever loving Son
            Fred. V. B. Witts.

Before posting I must chronicle my own doings during the week. I finished the bridge on the 12th after just a month's work, it looks very nice and I am very pleased with it, the opening span works excellently. It has been named Pathan Bridge, as most of my men are Pathans.

On the 13th we had a day off. My anticipated move up to join Bird fell through and we were given a new job in the form of a pier for river boats in the main stream. The 14th we were collecting the material & today we shifted camp to the site of the work. And as already related, here ends my history of my time in the 4th Company.

Very best love

        from Fred.

F. V. B. Witts.
    Capt. R. E.

                        No 2 Bridging Train.
                1st. K. G. O. Sappers & Miners.
                              I. E. F. 'D'.
                          c/o India Office.
                              [Busra]
                          March 23rd 1916.

Dearest Mother.

No mail has come in since I last wrote. I sent you a 'week-end' cable a few days ago, to tell you of my new command, and to let you know how to address letters, so that I may get them straight and quickly.

I have had a very busy week fitting out the Bridging Train with the hundred and one things a unit in the field requires. It came from India with nothing at all bar the men themselves,[35] I have had to get together a mess, and office, besides all the

---

[34] 'A box with a triangular piece of wood revolving on a clockwork-operated spindle ... Through a cut-away opening in the box, unsuspecting flies settled on the revolving wood triangle which was made sticky with fly-catching material, and were slowly revolved into the box where they were scraped off' (Barker, A. J., *The Neglected War*, p. 233). The machines were adequate for catching flies but more accomplished in relieving boredom.

29. Flooding in Lower Mesopotamia.

Engineering Stores. It has meant very busy days & long hours, as I have had no one to help me, my subaltern being already at the front, and there is at present no British Non Commissioned Officer or any clerk, though I have asked for and hope to get both. I have had to do all the writing and draw all the stores myself.

We are embarking tonight or tomorrow morning and are going straight up, which means a complete rest of from 5 to 10 days on the way.

I am very pleased indeed at getting a show to myself, not to mention the increase of pay it brings in its train. I have mostly recruits, bar the N.C.O.s & Indian Officers, but I like the look of them, though they have a lot to learn.

We had a terrible storm of wind, thunder & hail yesterday evening. It came almost as suddenly as a shell, and the hail stones were quite an inch in diameter. I was in my tent and thought they were going to come through, so put my topi on as a precaution. Rain poured through my tent, and there was an inch of water on my bed, which was luckily protected by the waterproof valise. My tent was on low ground, and there had been a very high flood tide just before, and I had made a protecting bank all round to keep the tide out. In the suddenness of the storm this was forgotten, and the bank successfully kept all the rain water from getting away. Result another flood under foot. All the men were soaked through. However nothing takes long to dry in this sun, and we have already forgotten all about it.

No more news.

With very best love,

Your ever loving Son.

Fred. V. B. Witts.

[35] F.V.B.W.'s bridging train initially consisted of 80 Indian sappers and was later expanded to 100.

30. Paddle Steamer S.1.

F.V.B. Witts.
   Capt. R. E.

On the Tigris.
March 26th 1916.

Dearest Mother.

I find that by posting this at the half way house I shall catch the next mail home, which I should otherwise miss altogether. I am afraid my letters will become more erratic, as it is very difficult to know when to write to catch the mail, as it starts down at odd times as steamers are available; further I imagine the conditions will not always let me write when I want to. So you mustn't be disturbed if some mails no letters come, the next mail should bring a double supply to make up for it. Always remember bad news travels fast enough, and no news is invariably good news.

We left Busra on the evening of the 24th in a river steamer boasting of the name S. 1, S denoting that she is a Stern-wheeler – that is a paddle steamer with one single paddle at the stern, 1 is of course her number. She has a hold which is incidentally full of bombs & shells for the front, & a main deck, where my twenty tons of kit & stores are stacked, together with many other stores, and His Majesty's mails, which we drop at the different points as we go up: on the upper deck all my men live & sleep & cook, and there are half a dozen cabins, or canvas boxes about 7 feet square, in one of which I have taken up my abode, after rigging up my camp bed etc in it. It is really extraordinarily comfortable, infinitely more so than the troop train journey between Marseilles and the front.

We have had to tie up alongside the bank each night so far, as the river has become quite narrow and tortuous, & going on in the dark only means getting stuck. In the narrower places if we meet another steamer coming down with the stream, we tie up to let it pass, just the same as in the Suez Canal.

The whole aspect of the country has completely changed. It is as flat as water as far as the eye can see. No palms at all except occasionally by a big village. Half the

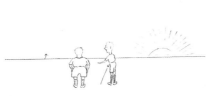

Thomas Atkins (empathetically):-
"Well if that is the garden of Eden, no wonder the
Twelve Apostles 'opped' it."

31. 'Musings from Mespot'

32. Ezra's tomb.

country marsh or under water, as the river is now nearly at its highest owing to the snows melting on the hills to the North and East. Grass, some crops & long high reeds – no bare stretches of sand or desert to be seen. Vast herds of cattle (buffaloes & cows) and flocks of sheep. From the bridge, there is nothing to obstruct the view to the horizon.

Yesterday morning we passed Bird, Farley & Roche working on the road up along the bank. We exchanged a few shouts, but of course could not stop. The men I was with at Busra are rejoining him now. I had an excellent view of the bridges – miles of them – which they have built.[36] We passed Ezra's tomb[37] midday yesterday not extremely exciting!

No more news.

Very best love

Your ever loving Son.

Fred. V. B. Witts.

F. V. B. Witts
Capt. R. E.

No 2 Bridging Train
1st. K. G. O. Sappers & Miners
I. E. F. 'D'.
[Wadi Camp]
April 3rd 1916.

[36] Eleven bridges were built by Bird's company along the Basra-Amara road, over terrain deeply scarred by the remnants of ancient canals. The road was part of General Lake's plan to improve the country's infrastructure to reduce congestion at Basra and free space on river transport.

[37] Purported tomb of the 5th century BC biblical scribe who reaffirmed the Law as a central theme in the Jewish religion after the exile in Babylon. The historian Josephus claims that Ezra was buried in Jerusalem.

33. The Camp at Wadi.

Dearest Mother.

I have had a very busy time the last few days and may have missed a mail. We arrived at Wadi Camp, the headquarters of the relief force on the evening of the 28th, disembarked our kit that night and ourselves next morning. We immediately took over the existing floating bridge of boats over the Tigris about a quarter of a mile long. I was up all the night of the 29th exchanging 22 boats for 11 others double the size, large enough to take 60 tons of cargo. About a fortnight ago the bridge broke in the middle and traffic was interrupted for six days. Hence the change. In midstream there is a very strong current and it is very deep: when there is a strong wind from the south, quite a sea gets up, and the small boats jump about so much that they throw off the roadway. The alteration had to be made at night in the dark as the bridge is wanted for traffic all day. On the night of the 30th, five pontoons were replaced by country boats [bellums]; on the night of the 31st we intended to put in another 7 mahelas [sailing boats] as the larger boats are called, but about 3.30 p.m., a regular gale sprang up from the south. An ammunition wagon was rolled into one of the boats, and then the bridge was closed to traffic. To save it from being smashed up we dismantled about 100 yards where the motion was worst just as it was getting dark. It was an exciting half hour. The wind aggravated by rain, which makes the planks very slippery, kept up all night.[38] About 9 a.m. on the 1st it dropped sufficiently to let us put in the other 7 mahelas. The wind got up again before we had finished & gave us a very rough time. We have been very busy the last two days, but the censor would object to my description.[39] It was a beautiful morning today, but it blew hard this afternoon, though now we have the new boats in, I don't think

---

[38] In *Light Floating Bridges*, F.V.B.W. asserts that the storm was so strong that 'crawling on all fours was the only safe method of progression' (Appendix I, p. 428).

[39] The bridge would have seen a lot of traffic in preparation for the Tigris Corps' next attack.

there is anything to fear.

I have been round to see all fifty sappers of the Meerut Division and have met many friends from France.

So glad to get your letter of Feb 21st and a Bystander. Glad you got my birthday cable, but it seems that you are not getting all my letters.

Many thanks for sending me the photo of the cross, I am glad it is up.

Very best love,

Your ever loving Son,

Fred. V. B. Witts

By now, Kut had been under siege for over three months. Behind its walls disease and famine were endemic, and desertion amongst the Indian troops was on the increase. Meanwhile, melting snow in the Caucasus and Kurdistan swelled the banks of the Tigris, piling the odds against the relief effort. By the beginning of April, General Gorringe was ready to resume the attack, acutely aware that failure at this stage would most likely spell the end for Kut.

On the 5th April 1916, in the dawn twilight, the 13th Division,[40] commanded by Lieutenant-General Maude, cascaded into the Hanna defile. They had been braced for the deafening roar of bursting shells and the rattle of machinegun fire, but, apart from the odd pop of a rifle, nothing transpired. The encroaching waters of the Tigris and Suwaikiya marsh had made the Turkish trenches at Hanna untenable; Khalil had evacuated the position, withdrawing his force to the Fallahiya bend, 2 miles further upriver. With their blood up, the 13th Division charged onwards to Fallahiya, driving the Turks out of their trenches by the end of the day. The next and final position along the Tigris/Suwaikiya bottleneck was at Sannaiyat, three miles closer to Kut. Gorringe was eager to keep up the momentum of the attack; he ordered the 7th Division, commanded by General Younghusband, to relieve Maude's troops and attack Sannaiyat that night (the 5th April); but, in the event, the advance became so delayed in the myriad of Turkish communication trenches, that the 7th Division did not reach Sannaiyat until dawn. As the sun rose, the British and Indian troops were caught in the open and within range of enemy rifle and artillery-fire. The Official Eye-Witness, Edmund Candler, describes the subsequent Turkish bombardment as a 'torrent of death'[41]; any further British movements were abruptly halted until after nightfall, when expanding floodwaters forced the 7th Division to evacuate their make-shift trenches and retire downstream.

---

[40] General Maude's all-British 13th Division arrived at the front in early March, too late to take part in the battle of the Dujaila Redoubt. The Division had suffered heavy losses at Gallipoli in 1915 and was therefore largely made up of new recruits by the time it reached Mesopotamia.

[41] Candler, E., *The Long Road to Baghdad*, vol. I p. 180

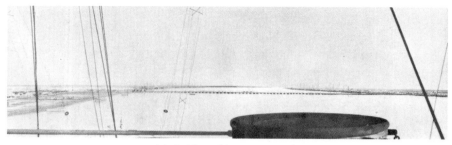

34. Bridge of boats at Wadi.

Meanwhile, on the right bank, the 3rd Division had advanced with some success, capturing Abu Rumman, opposite a point between Fallahiya and Sannaiyat. The expanding Tigris, however, helped by Turkish engineers breaching flood-barriers, had cut communications with the Wadi camp, thwarting any hope of continuing the advance.

At Sannaiyat, Gorringe was faced with little in the way of tactical choice: another frontal assault was the only option for an offensive. By this stage, the British were relying on sheer guts and determination to break Turkish tenacity; their efforts, however, would be tragically in vain. Before dawn on the 9th April, the 13th Division, back in the front-line, began its advance, but the Turks were aware of what was afoot. Flares were released into the night-sky, shining a deadly screen of light onto the advancing lines, disorientating and spreading panic amongst them. Having suffered heavy losses, the 13th Division retreated in disorder back to their trenches.

Despite the outcome, Captain Witts had been disappointed that No. 2 Bridging Train was not selected to accompany the Tigris Corps' advance on April 5th. In their stead, two field companies of Madras Sappers and Miners had erected a bridge at Sandy Ridge, closer to the Hanna defile. Nevertheless, back behind the lines at the Wadi camp, Captain Witts and his unit had certainly not been idle.

F.V.B. Witts
    Capt. R. E.

[Wadi Camp]
April 10th 1916.

Dearest Mother.

I am afraid you will think I am getting a very bad correspondent, but the last few days I think I have lived through more exciting incidents of an unwarlike nature than I am ever likely to experience again in the same interval. I have twice sat down to write & something unusual has occurred each time.

On the 2nd, 3rd & 4th we had days of comparative peace though enormous traffic mostly by night over the bridge. It was an anxious time for me but luckily there

35. Mahailas on the Tigris.

were no accidents. On the 5th our attack resulted in a six mile advance upstream. This meant opening a portion of the bridge for river traffic & then our fun began. In the evening one steamer collided with the end of the bridge & smashed up the end boat. This meant a daylight start next morning to repair it. On the 6th a steam pinnace in tow behind a monitor broke loose and was swept by the strong current across the boats, we rescued the occupants and with difficulty the boat, also a small boat which they foolishly sent after it to the rescue. A small country boat with Arabs in it got foul of one of our anchor cables, and was rescued with difficulty. As a finale about sunset two mahelas, large country sailing boats, had got above the bridge when the wind dropped and they were swept helplessly on to the bridge; it took three hours work with axes & saws in the dark and about forty men pulling to get one of them off. On the afternoon of the 7th, a steamer entangled her paddle and her anchor in a hopeless mess amongst our anchor cables in the Bridge opening. We were very fortunate to get out of this mess without any actual loss or damage.

On the afternoon of the 8th a motor launch steering foolishly near the bridge was swept across the bows of one of our big boats & cut in two one half being swept down each side. The occupants seized various ropes & cables and were all pulled out by my men. They turned out to be Sir Percy Lake and his staff! I introduced myself to him. It was curious our meeting in this manner. He asked me to dine with him on his boat, but that was impossible for me, so he then asked me to lunch next day. However luck was out. That evening soon after dark, a small tug, ignoring the existence of the bridge charged straight into it in midstream. The tug was successfully pulled off by a steamer,[42] but my poor old bridge was sadly the worse for wear. Before we could get the tug necessary to repair it a regular gale sprang up, and to save the rest of the bridge we had to cut the damaged portion adrift. It blew hard all day yesterday, much too rough to do any repairs much less

---

[42] The Lynch Bros.' *Mejidieh*, commanded by Lieut.-Commander C. H. Cowley. (Witts, F. V. B., *Light Floating Bridges*, (Appendix I, p. 428).

36. An Arab sniper taken prisoner by Indian troops.

lunch with Sir Percy Lake with my bridge in pieces! If he is still here, when the bridge is rebuilt I must pay him a visit.

Today it has been calmer, but by no means calm, and we have recovered 16 out of the 20 boats cast adrift. I am fighting the elements now, and they seem to be about as tough as the Germans. Though we are not absolutely free from the perils of war; early this morning some Arabs fired a few shots into camp, and one unfortunately picked off my orderly, who came with me from No 4 Company a rotten piece of luck.

I have a most useful Subaltern, Atkinson; he belongs to the Indian Army Reserve of Officers, and in private life has about twenty years experience as a salvage contractor and general port and harbour work: his experience and advice is invaluable to me in the present circumstances. He is only about 12 to 15 years older than I am, but he plays up awfully well.

No more news, I must to bed.
    Very best love.
            Your ever loving Son,
                    Fred. V. B. Witts.

F.V.B.Witts
   Capt. R. E.

[Wadi Camp]
April 16th 1916.
Easter Day.

Dearest Mother.

Just got a fortnight's mails with your letters of Feb 29th, March 7th & 8th, a fortnight's supply of the Times a Bystander & Truth. All so welcome as we have nothing to read. What a tremendous fall of snow you must have had. I am so glad the foal is doing so well. I hope your new chauffeur is a success.

This last week has been comparatively free of incident. The 9th to the 12th was occupied with the repair of the bridge. It took a long time as we could not afford to throw away any material & had to save everything possible. We were also dependent on tugs to help us, and we could only raise one, which fouled its propeller & had to stop work.

On the 13th, having put the bridge straight I invited myself to lunch on the 'Malamir' with Sir Percy Lake. He was most affable and calling me into his cabin, seating me on his bed, discussed with me all our mutual connections. I only wished I knew more about them; what relation is Fred Witts of Uppingham, who was his school master, and a Broome Witts now out in Australia, whom he had recently heard from? With all his responsibility and anxiety, which at the present moment under the present conditions must be terrible, it seemed wonderful to me how he could apparently forget all about them & bring his mind to bear on such trivial matters. Needless to say, he gave me an excellent lunch. His boat is now anchored off the shore quite close to our camp. On the 14th the worst gale we have had so far came on, and I thought the bridge would be smashed up and swamped. It was very trying standing by helpless wondering when it would go. The waves were quite 6 foot high coming at varying angles & twisting the bridge into all sorts of contortions. However it stuck it out and only slight damage was done. Yesterday it calmed down about midday and since has been like a duck pond, making it impossible to believe it could ever have been so rough. However without the wind it has warmed up considerably bringing out flies in their millions, everything from one's tent to one's hat becomes black with them. I have also heard the first mosquitoes, and I foresee an unpleasant time ahead. So far it has been far cooler than India.

On the 12th a floating mine was sent down on the bridge: one of my men seeing a harmless bit of fire wood floating down pulled it in, when this mine hanging beneath, partly exploded, doing for him, but not hurting the bridge.

The Chief Engineer up here is leaving, & Col Swiney whom I worked under at Busra is coming. He is an awfully nice man.

Very best love,

    Your ever loving Son,

      Fred.V. B.Witts.

While Captain Witts was fortunate to be given an 'excellent lunch', 20 miles away in Kut, the beleaguered garrison were onto their last morsels of mule-flesh, and dangerously close to starvation. The final deadline given by Townshend for his relief (April 18th) had arrived, but aerial food drops were buying Gorringe time for one last chance to break through.

On the 17th April, after a prolonged thunderstorm, Gorringe made his move. Under cover of a heavy British bombardment, the 3rd Division,[43] commanded by Major-General Keary, climbed out of their trenches at Abu Rumman and splashed across the flooded plain towards Beit Isa, the Turkish forward position on the right bank. While British shells were still flying overhead, Keary's men jumped boldly into the Turkish trenches, surprising the occupants who were busy sheltering from the bombardment. After a quick and bloody battle fought with bayonets and kukris,[44] the position was captured with few casualties.

It was an optimistic start for Gorringe, but that was to be as far as it went. Determined to stifle any further progress, Khalil summoned a massive force of 10,000 men and launched a devastating counter-attack; the nerve of the British and Indian troops on the front line was quickly broken, and their lines disintegrated into a ragged retreat. By the time order had been restored to the British lines and the Turkish advance had been halted, the opportunity for a breakthrough on the right bank of the Tigris had been engulfed by the expanding floods. In desperation, Gorringe turned his attention back to Sannaiyat, hopeful that the numbers of Turkish defenders had been reduced to supplement Khalil's counter-attack on the right bank. Further storms delayed an assault on Sannaiyat until the 22nd April; by this stage, the surrounding water-levels were so high that the strip of land between the Tigris and Suwaikiya marsh was barely passable. Nevertheless, at dawn on the 22nd, the enduring 7th Division climbed over the parapet for one final attempt to free the Kut garrison. The conditions, however, were hopeless. Half the attacking force was unable even to begin the assault as their frontage was under a few feet of water. The other half plodded forward defiantly, but the glutinous mud clogged up rifles immediately and slowed the attack to an exhausting crawl. Few men made it to the Turkish lines and those who did were soon killed or captured; by nightfall, Kut was as good as lost.

Back at the Wadi camp, the mood was dejected, but for the sake of the censor, Captain Witts could give his mother little idea of what was happening.

---

[43] The men of the 3rd Division were especially weak as problems with their supply line, caused by the floods, had forced them to subsist on half rations.

[44] The 3rd Division's Gurkhas, famous for their deadly skills with their native kukri knives, distinguished themselves in this attack.

F.V.B. Witts

[Wadi Camp]
Easter Sunday April 23rd 1916.

Dearest Mother.

I discovered afterwards I was a week previous in labelling my last letter Easter Day. Today has produced most beautiful Easter weather, so often enjoyed on the banks of the Aston Brook instead of the turbulent Tigris.[45] I have had no mail since I last wrote, so am confined to my own news.

On the 19th it blew a gale from the South and we only just managed to keep the bridge from breaking up; the waves were quite six feet high. The bridge was behaving like a wriggling eel. This reminds me, would you like to send me a 'Credem' life saving waistcoat suitable to wear in a very hot climate; I run much more risk in my present job from the water than from bullets or shells. I have seen the 'Credem' waistcoat advertised in the Times, but it must be as light as possible suitable for this hot climate. I don't like those inflatable waistcoats such as the Gieve and others. On the 20th cleaning one of the bridge boats nearly resulted in its sinking altogether, it was only its thick layer of dirt which made it watertight. On the 21st & since we have had some Turkish prisoners moving stores for us; they work very willingly and show no animosity. The opening portion of the bridge broke adrift, causing me a lot of anxiety but nothing worse.

Today six pontoons being towed upstream broke away & crashed down on to bridge, only one being saved. One of our bridge boats was badly holed, but we have repaired it temporarily: A search downstream for wreckage proved fruitless.

In addition to my proper job, I am now the senior sapper left here, and consequently get stuck with all sorts of jobs. This is now the flood season, owing to the snow melting on the mountains; the water in the river is above the level of the surrounding country and is only kept out by the banks built along the edges; they require constant attention or will give way and actually flood us all out. The Turks are taking advantage of this to delay our advance, and, I am afraid, with considerable success.

No more news.

Very best love,
Your ever loving Son,
Fred. V. B. Witts.

---

[45] It is a Witts family tradition, continued to this day, to search for the pasque flower (pulsatilla vulgaris) by Aston brook, at Easter time. The surviving siblings of Canon Diana Witts O.B.E. (F.V.B.W.'s youngest daughter 1936–2006) gave a pasque flower seed to the Kew seed bank in 2007 in her memory. F.V.B.W.'s family also enjoyed cray fishing in the Aston brook (see F.V.B.W.'s letter of 23rd November 1918, Chapter VII, p. 260)

37. The *Julna* ready to start for the relief of Kut.

Both Lake and Gorringe knew that Townshend's garrison would starve before another attack could be coordinated. They were desperate for more time, and anything which offered a remote chance of giving it seemed worth a shot.[46] The idea of sending an armoured ship laden with food up the Tigris to Kut had already been considered, but rejected as impractical. However, under the current circumstances, Lake was willing to try anything.

The hospital ship, *Julnar*, had been steel plated and loaded with 270 tonnes of supplies in the utmost secrecy at Amara. A specially chosen crew of unmarried sailors was selected from the long list of volunteers, each one aware that the mission in hand was potentially suicidal. Amongst the crew was Captain Witts' friend, Lieutenant-Commander C. H. Cowley, commander of the Lynch steamer *Mejidieh,* that had saved Witts' bridge not long before by towing away a wayward tug (see April 10th). Having worked along the Tigris for 30 odd years for Lynch Bros. Steam Navigation Co., Cowley had an unparalleled knowledge of the river and was eager to offer his expertise.

On the night of the 24th April, while Gorringe conducted a diversionary bombardment against Turkish positions on the right bank, the *Julnar* started upstream from Fallahiya. Despite a moonless night, the ship was soon spotted by the Turks, and with a maximum speed of six knots, she was an easy target for artillery. After a number of the crew had been killed by bullets and shrapnel, she ran aground on the right bank of the Tigris at Maqasis fort and was forced to surrender.[47]

The failure of the heroic *Julnar* mission sealed the fate of the Kut garrison. Negotiations were already in progress for Townshend's surrender; on April 29th, Kut fell to the Turks.

---

[46] Although they were still being conducted, aerial food drops were almost futile as the quantities of food being dropped were not enough to sustain the garrison for even a few more days.

[47] Only slightly wounded when captured by the Turks, Cowley was separated from the other *Julnar* prisoners and, according to Arab reports, executed by his captors. In the eyes of the Turks, his long career in Mesopotamia had made him an Ottoman subject, and they were deeply resentful of the invaluable assistance he had given Force 'D' since the start of the campaign. The Turks denied murder, but could not give an adequate explanation for his death. Cowley was awarded a posthumous Victoria Cross.

38. After the Fall of Kut: General Townshend (centre) with Khalil Pasha (right).

F. V. B. Witts
    Capt. R. E.

[Wadi Camp]
April 30ᵗʰ 1916.

Dearest Mother.

In the last three days I have had two mails with your letters of March 14ᵗʰ & 21ˢᵗ, two letters from Agnes & one from Jack. I will try and thank them individually in due course; but the weather conditions – especially the flies which have become a regular plague, and the heat which is oppressive in a tent – are not conducive to letter writing. Besides the letters I have had a perfect deluge of papers from you – two Bystanders, a Punch, two Tatlers, a Sketch, an Illustrated London News, English Review, and a novel by Ian Hay, my favourite author. You can't think how I appreciate them; they have come at a moment when there is not much doing for me and they are consequently doubly welcome. When I have done with them, I pass them on to the Hospitals and you should see how eagerly they are seized by the wounded.

Yesterday evening we heard rumours, which I am afraid are only too true, that Kut had fallen. I don't think it has come as a surprise to any one here. It is of course a great misfortune, but not I think as bad as I am sure it will be painted in some papers at home. Whatever you may hear or see in print, you may take it from me that it is not the fault of any Regiments, British or Indian, that we have failed to break our way through. During the month I have been up here I know we have been up against as tough a nut as anywhere in France or the Dardanelles with the added disadvantage of a most indifferent line of supply behind us. We have all been almost reduced to half rations in order to make room on the river boats for ammunition and shells.

We are all very curious to know what is going to happen now. The most reassuring thought is that if the Turks now try to attack us, they will be up against the same difficulties as we have been up against for the last month.

I have today moved my camp back to the original site as we were in imminent danger of being flattened out by erratic aeroplanes going up heavily laden with food to drop into Kut. We were just by the aerodrome.

I got the Turkey & Tongue you sent from Bath, also the chocolate, soup & socks have just come. Thanks awfully for sending them. Thanks also for the Cheltenham Chronicle.

> Very best love,
> Your ever loving Son,
> Fred. V. B. Witts.

As I finish I hear shouts & rush out to see ¼ of my bridge swept away by the incompetency of the transport ships. I am in for a hard time!

In their efforts to relieve Townshend's garrison of 15,000 men, the Tigris Corps had suffered over 23,000 casualties in the space of four months.[48] Kut's capitulation was, at the time, the greatest surrender of troops in the history of the British Army. All the same, despite feelings of shame and bewilderment spreading across Britain, the men at the scene were in no doubt that, as far as courage, resolve and sacrifice were concerned, nothing had been absent from the Tigris Corps' persistent efforts to liberate Kut.

For Force 'D', now was the time for recuperation: to bury the bitter disappointment of failure and to look ahead towards reaffirming British superiority in Mesopotamia. For the sick, emaciated souls of the once proud 6th Division, their trail of inhuman suffering had only just begun.

---

[48] Moberly, F. J., *The Mesopotamia Campaign*, vol. II p. 437

CHAPTER II

DOG DAYS

Letters: May 14ᵗʰ – Sept 22ⁿᵈ 1916

The fate of the Kut garrison was, for the most part, kept a mystery to the men of the Tigris Corps. When, for example, in an exchange of prisoners in mid-August, 340 British and Indian captives arrived at Basra hospital en route to India for convalescence, strict orders were given to them to keep silent about their experiences in Turkish captivity. General Lake wanted to maintain the gentlemanly respect his men felt towards the Turk, encouraging the belief that Germany was the true enemy behind a vulnerable Turkish pawn. However, in her brutal treatment of the wretched 6ᵗʰ Division, Turkey was acting on none other than her own compulsion.

Withered and malnourished after five months under siege, the men of the Kut garrison were given no chance to regain their strength. In the first gruelling stage of what would be an eight month forced-march into central Anatolia, the captives were driven across the blistering Syrian Desert in mid-summer, to labour camps in the Aleppo wilayat. From the outset, the men were treated like animals; deprived of food and water, stripped of their clothes and boots, denied any medical attention and continually beaten and sexually abused. Out of the 12,000 men handed over to Turkish authorities on 29ᵗʰ April 1916,[1] over 4,000 of them died in captivity. In the sober words of the *Official History*, the disgraceful treatment of these prisoners 'must forever form a blot on the Turkish reputation.'[2]

On the Tigris, meanwhile, a sultry stalemate had been ushered in by the hot weather; the next few months promised to be dreary and uncomfortable with plenty of time to reflect on the wasted efforts to relieve Kut. A withdrawal to Amara at this stage may have been advisable for consolidation and transport purposes, but every step backwards further damaged British prestige, adding strain to tenuous links with the Arab tribes of the Lower Euphrates. By maintaining forward positions, Lake was also holding Turkish forces to

---

[1] 15,000 men were in Kut when it was put under siege on 7ᵗʰ December 1915. Of that number, 3,000 troops and followers either had died in battle or from disease, or had deserted, or had been sent back to British lines by the Turks on the basis of severe ill-health. General Townshend, meanwhile, was separated from his men and despatched by luxury transport to the summer residence of the British Consul at Prinikipo, an island in the Sea of Marmara, near Constantinople, where he lived out the war in comfort. In Britain, Townshend received much criticism for not doing enough to help the plight of his men, although his influence was, in fact, very limited.

[2] Moberly, F. J., *The Mesopotamia Campaign*, p. 460

the Tigris; this assisted the Russian Caucasus Army which was advancing westwards through Persia and the Caucasus, threatening Turkey's left flank.

For Captain Witts, the hot season began in a flurry of activity. The destruction of his bridge at the Wadi by a snoozing steamer Captain from the Yukon[3] precipitated its complete transposition 8 miles downriver to Sheikh Saad, where the river was narrower but the current stronger.

F.V.B. Witts
  Capt. R. E.

[Sheikh Saad]
May 14th 1916.

Dearest Mother

I am awfully sorry to have clean missed a mail, as I know how you look forward to our letters. But I have been shifting about, and generally having a restless time since I last wrote on the 30th, the day the steamer crashed through my bridge. We were kept very busy repairing the damaged boats, and I was very glad to get a new draft of skilled workmen from India with a British Sergeant on the 2nd. Their arrival has made me a quite respectable unit, capable of turning out some decent work, when materials to do it with are forthcoming. But it is very difficult to get anything up here, except earth & water, wind & heat. Not that it has been really hot up here yet, in fact it is much cooler than India at this time, and we have been having delightful nights, which make all the difference.

We were ordered not to rebuild the bridge in the old site, and in due course [to build it at] another site about ten miles off to which we duly moved on the 7th & 8th after a strenuous time packing up and trying to raise the bridge anchors. Inspite of all our efforts we could only shift 25 per cent of them and the remainder were lost.

Much to our disgust and inconvenience just as we were settling down to work, the site was again changed [to Sheikh Saad] two miles back in the direction we had come.

We spent the 9th getting ready to move again, the 10th in moving back with the aid of five steam boats of sorts. The 11th & 12th was occupied in building the bridge quite at our leisure, and I was quite surprised on the 13th to get a wire from the Corps Commander, Gen Gorringe, congratulating us on the pace with which we had rebuilt the bridge. It is on a narrow bend in the river, only 2/3rds the width of the old site, but the current is correspondingly stronger and strongest where we have to make the opening for ships to pass. As a result it takes a lot of time and work reforming the bridge for road traffic. Yesterday we experimented with two or three methods.

Every one up here is utterly fed up with the whole show owing to the inefficiency and mismanagement of the river transport, which keeps us short of food, clothes, and engineering material. The transport is run by a service known as the Royal Indian Marine and they are utterly incapable of doing it.[4]

---

[3] *See* Witts, F. V. B., *Light Floating Bridges* (Appendix I, p. 428) for a detailed description of the accident.

39. Boat bridge at Sheikh Saad.

Goodness knows what is going to happen now, but we seem to be settling down for the hot weather, which is a dreary prospect. But it is wonderful how it has kept off.[5]

Owing no doubt to my own erratic movements and to equally erratic moves on the part of the 4th Coy to which my letters are I expect addressed I have had no mails since I last wrote.

If I ever cable any news such as all's well please send it on to the families of my two Company Sergeant Majors:-

Mrs P. Lehané. (wife)
No 6 Oakburn Road.
Tooting, London S.W.
Mrs Deverell.
46 Kingsley Villas.
South Wimbledon.

No more news
Very best love
Your ever loving Son
Fred V B Witts

[4] Shortages of river transport were still critical, but the problem was finally being addressed with appropriate urgency. However, the onset of the monsoon season was bound to delay the influx of river craft from India.

[5] F.V.B.W.'s optimism about the weather differs from other contemporary reports, notably Candler. It is possible that he was trying to paint a more appealing picture for the sake of his mother.

The policy General Lake had been given by the Secretary of State was strictly defensive; however, he was entitled to capitalise on any advantage that might emerge, provided casualties were kept to a minimum. Khalil Pasha, meantime, having assumed supreme command in Mesopotamia from the German General Von der Goltz, turned his attention to the Russian threat, particularly General Baratoff's advance on Khaniqin, on the north-eastern road from Baghdad.[6] While he was concerned by Baratoff's movements, Khalil considered the British threat to be spent, anticipating a withdrawal in the wake of Kut's surrender. Basing his strategy on this assumption, Khalil transferred a division and cavalry brigade from the Tigris to the Persian front, leaving just three divisions surrounding Kut.

With his depleted force, Kiazim Karabekir, the new commander of the Turkish XVIII Corps based at Kut, was unable to maintain the same breadth of defences initially established around the town. On 19th May, British aerial reconnaissance reported a large-scale Turkish withdrawal from the Es Sinn embankment on the right bank of the Tigris. In response, General Keary's 3rd Division advanced forward to occupy the abandoned trenches. Further progress was inhibited by the tremendous heat,[7] not to mention the prospect of attracting Turkish shells. In these conditions, however, General Gorringe was not looking for a fight; it was time to sit out the hot weather and concentrate on keeping fit for the revival of the campaign in the autumn.

The prospect of simply stewing in the great heat for the entire summer was detestable to all in Mesopotamia, no less to Captain Witts and his men.

F. V. B. Witts
> Capt. R. E.

> > > No 2 Bridging Train
> > > 1st. K. G. O. Sappers & Miners
> > > I. E. F. 'D'
> > > [Sheikh Saad]
> > > May 22nd 1916.

---

[6] In a remarkable and daring feat of endurance, a detachment of one hundred of Baratoff's Cossacks travelled 200 miles across hostile terrain in searing temperatures to link up with the British at Ali Gharbi, 60 miles downstream of Kut. Their arrival on the night of the 20th May, after a twelve day journey from their base at Mahidasht in Persia, was completely unexpected but came as an invaluable morale boost to the British and Indian troops. Although they had no particular message to deliver, the presence of the Cossacks evaporated any doubts that there was a Russian army out there somewhere, pressing the Turkish left flank. After a few days rest, the Cossacks returned to their base across the Pusht-i-Kuh hills without losing a single man.

[7] General Keary had already lost several hundred casualties to heatstroke.

Dearest Mother.

I am again behind the time with my mail; I find
the climate conditions are not conducive to letter
writing. My present daily round commences at 4
a.m. working till 11 a.m. with a break for breakfast.
From 11 a.m. to 4 p.m. orders are to lie up and do
nothing owing to the heat. And then at it again from
four to dark. During the midday break I am reduced
too much to a liquid mass to put pencil to paper: after
dark to write by lamplight involves being worried to
death by insects unless you are under a mosquito net,
as I am now lying on my camp bed in pyjamas.

You will gather that the conditions of life are no
longer pleasant out here to say the least of it. By far

40. A Mahaila

the worst trouble at present is the plague of flies. They swarm everywhere and each
meal is a fight as to who is to devour the contents of the plate.[8] The fly trap I got
as a present from you has been doing good work, but it cannot catch them by the
million. At certain times, such as when shaving or trying to write, they nearly drive
one mad. We have rigged up a delightfully cool mess hut out of bridging material,
but the cool spots attract the flies and it is almost impossible to exclude them without
excluding light and air too. A roll of fly proof wire netting and a dozen yards of
muslin would be a godsend now.

I have been having a series of mails recently. I don't think any of your letters or
papers have gone astray: I know I have not missed a single copy of the Times since
the Persia went down. They save one's life during the heat of the day.

I have written my address again, as you have been adding Meerut Division. I am
no longer Divisional but Corps troops

Nothing much been doing since I last wrote, and we have been busy settling in
and making ourselves comfortable for the hot weather. But the developments of the
last few days may upset all our calculations.[9]

We had a lot of traffic over the bridge one morning including 760 vehicles of
sorts. [We] only once got into difficulties getting one mule and both outside wheels
over the edge. But we successfully pulled it back. The remains of No 1 Bridging
Train – half were taken in Kut – who have been with me for the last two months,
left two days ago to take over another existing bridge.

---

[8] On flies, Candler writes 'to describe them is to hazard one's reputation for truth.' (*The Long Road to Baghdad*, vol. I p. 235).

[9] F.V.B.W. was worried that the advance of the front line to the Es Sinn embankment might require the bridge to be moved upstream.

No more news.

    Very best love,

        Your ever loving Son,

           Fred. V. B. Witts.

F. V. B. Witts

    Capt. R. E.

                           [Sheikh Saad]

                           May 28th 1916.

Dearest Mother.

Since last writing I have had a most welcome mail. Your three letters of April 13th 16th & 17th, the blue stocking puttees, which are just the thing I wanted, and will be a great relief this hot weather, Punch, Tatler, Truth, Bystander & Illustrated London News – in fact a tremendous haul, and letters from Agnes & Frank: please explain to them how the conditions militate against letter writing out here, as I pointed out in my last letter.

We have had an uneventful week in fact nothing doing beyond opening & closing the bridge – a monitor [small boat] nearly ran into it one night inspite of her searchlight, and today a waterlogged boat from a Turk bridge came down on to us, but we got her clear without any damage being done.

Did I tell you of our delightful mess hut in my last letter. We have dug a hole in the ground three feet deep by sixteen feet by twelve feet. A roof of spare bridging timbers 4 inches thick with another 4 inches of mud on the top to help keep out the heat, is carried on two bridging trestles, eight feet above the floor level and thus five feet above ground level. The Southern face is banked up with boarding & earth, the other three faces have moveable panels made of two thicknesses of a kind of straw matting stuffed with grass. The entrance with steps down is closed by a mosquito net hanging like a curtain. Our abode is the envy of the whole camp, and we escape from the worst effects of both the flies and heat.

For myself starting with a Government Double 40 lb Tent 6' x 6' x 4' high, I bought myself a respectable 80 lb tent from the kit of some poor fellow killed, and now I have obtained as an act of favour a large tent weighing half a ton, but unfortunately I may have to part with it at any moment. However while I have it I can rest in comfort during the day though I find it hard to sleep.

The official hours for work are now 5 a.m. – 9 a.m. and 6 p.m. – 10 p.m. though our job entails starting at 4 a.m. No work at all, except under military necessity, is supposed to be done between 9 a.m. & 6 p.m.

Our food is monotonous, and mostly tinned. For a long time we managed to get a regular supply of eggs, but now unfortunately they have run dry. We have gradually collected some goats, and get some fresh milk from them, but tinned milk is our only reliable source, and the same with everything else. Fresh meat – sheep or goat, – potatoes, and onions, tea, sugar salt, sometimes rum or limejuice, fresh bread, jam, pepper, bacon (very good) constitute our Government Ration, but very often everything doesn't turn up. Owing to the difficulties of transport they cut everything down very fine: luckily in this hot weather there is an unlimited supply of good drinking water, if the river water is properly treated.

No more news today,

> Very best love,
> Your ever loving Son,
> Fred. V. B. Witts.

F.V.B. Witts
    Capt. R. E.

[Amara]
June 6th 1916.

Dearest Mother.

No mail since I last wrote and nothing in the way of news from my side – this is a hopeful start, I am afraid!

After one oppressively hot day 110 in the shade, which made us all think that the bad hot weather had come it has really been almost pleasantly cool. A strong north wind, known as the 'shimāl', is blowing with consistent regularity all day long. It comes across a large flooded area before catching us, and is consequently delightfully cool and invigorating. It is when this wind dies down that one feels the heat.

However the nights I believe keep cool all the time. This is everything, as you can get in a good sleep, & pick up strength to face another day. The night following the day it was 110 in the shade, the temperature fell to 66 – a tremendous drop and I slept comfortably under two blankets.

I am at the moment engaged on a joy ride, and am writing this at Amara half way down to Busra. I have come down to inspect the boat bridge over the Tigris here, and am going on to see yet another bridge half way between here and Kurna. Combined with this not very arduous duty, I am replenishing our mess stores here as far as possible, and shall return laden with as many cases as I can smuggle on boardship.

This spot [Amara], if the censor permits me to say so, is the big hospital centre of the force.[10] It is situated where the Tigris breaks up into two branches; the main branch taking only 1/3rd of the water whilst 2/3rds goes down the other branch, and spreads itself out over vast marshes, rejoining the Tigris proper again 100 miles lower down. There are quite a lot of date palm groves about, which form a welcome relief to the eye after the treeless plains further up. And some quite respectable houses too

---

[10] F.V.B.W. would spend Christmas 1916 here, recovering from a bullet wound to the arm.

41. Amara Quayside.

– In fact last night I had the use of a room for the first time since I left France; I can't say I slept with a roof over my head as, in order to get the cool breeze, I slept on the roof.

Did I tell you of our regular supply of fresh fish. We have got an Arab fishing net, taught one of our men to use it, and have a guaranteed supply of fresh fish for each week. It is a tremendous boon.

No more news.

Very best love,

Your ever loving Son.

Fred. V. B. Witts.

F. V. B. Witts

Capt. R. E.

[Sheikh Saad]
June 13th 1916.

Dearest Mother.

I got back from my jaunt yesterday and found two complete mails awaiting me. Your letters of April 24th, 27th & May 2nd with all the Blackwoods and other papers you mention in your letters. I am sure all letters and newspapers reach me, but parcels take time. Thanks for the little photo of the cross, I like it very much.

How is Pittaway [the groom] affected by the Universal Service Bill.[11] Yes, the garden must be rather untidy inspite of Edith and Agnes's great efforts. Another

---

[11] The Universal Service Bill (also known as the Military Service Act) was introduced by Prime Minister Asquith in January 1916, compelling all men aged 18-41 to enlist into the armed forces unless specifically exempted.

42. Sketch of the riverfront at Qalat Salih.

nephew is great news, men will be badly wanted after this war.[12]

No sign of the Brilliantine yet. I expect it has melted in the post and run to waste!

I had a great loaf down river. My duty must have occupied six hours at the outside, my own efforts to collect mess Stores another four and the remainder of the time I spent on board ship or waiting for a ship to take me. From Amara to Qalat Salih and back, I had to go in a motor lighter, one of those which have come round here after being used in Gallipoli. Going down was not bad – only a 4 hour run – but coming up on a hot day with no breeze, eight hours of it, with nowhere to sit, no shelter from the sun and only an iron deck, which became nearly red hot, it was a bit thick and I was nearly baked alive.

At Amara you get right out of the war except for the great number of wounded, and people grouse when the supply of ice occasionally runs out – so you can imagine under what luxurious conditions they live there. Qalat Salih is the nearest approach to the garden of Eden I have yet discovered.[13] It is picturesquely situated on quite a pretty reach of the river. It has some excellent gardens where vegetables are grown and I also saw plenty of first rate looking figs, melons, & grapes ripening rapidly, but none unfortunately yet ripe.

I returned laden with stores including 3 hens for egg laying purposes, and wire gauze for keeping flies out of our palace.

[12] This is an especially poignant remark as Apphia's baby son, Maurice, in fact had cerebral palsy and died in 1932, aged only 16.

[13] Lower Mesopotamia, particularly the neighbourhood of Qurna, 40 miles downriver from Qalat Salih, was one of the reputed archaeological sites of the Garden of Eden. The irony of Mesopotamia, a land so closely resembling many people's idea of hell, being a place of divine paradise was often bitterly expounded by the British troops.

43. Qalat Salih.

Our farm yard now numbers 37 head of sheep & goats (giving quite a good supply of milk), 8 head of poultry and one large fat goose — ready for Michaelmas. Did I ever tell you how we caught it. It settled on the river above the bridge: a well aimed clod of earth stunned it, and it floated down on to the bridge where we caught it. It recovered completely and now spends the day tied up by one leg.

No more news.

Very best love,

Your ever loving Son,

Fred. V. B. Witts.

Should I cable for my extra kit★ to be sent to India, unless anywhere else specifically mentioned, send to

The Quarter Master.

1st K. G. O. Sappers & Miners

Roorkee, India

through Cox's Shipping Agency.

★(1)   Tents in bag

(2)   Tin case in a box.

(3)   Two suit cases in a box.   F.V.B.W.

F. V. B. Witts

Capt. R. E.

[Sheikh Saad]

June 17th 1916.

Dearest Mother.

Another mail with your letter of May 9th, Blackwoods, Punch, Truth & Bystander arrived on 14th. I think everything comes regularly and I get all you send. The literature is an absolute godsend during the hot hours of the day 12 – 4, when it is

44. Eyford Park (front). Eyford was the home of Jack and Mabel Cheetham; Mabel was F.V.B.W.'s first cousin.

too hot to sleep or work and one simply exists and tries to pass the time as quickly as possible.

I am not sorry to hear, all things considered, that Edward is not likely to return to France. I am afraid the possibility of Longley moving is too good to be true.[14] I heard from both Frank & George; it is curious he should have gone to the bit of the line I got to know so well. Jack is a long time getting well?

How does Jack Cheetham fare under the new Universal Service Bill?[15] I suppose – if he is still within the age – he is now indispensible to the working of the farm.

We have recently been getting our ration supply of tinned milk and cigarettes – which is an improvement: – but as a counter-blast, fresh meat, bread and sugar have been irregular arrivals.

While I was away, my subaltern Atkinson departed to take up a good job at Basra, which we had been expecting for some time: he has not been replaced yet, and two other sappers, who have been living with me sharing my palace, have left, so I am for the time being alone, which is rather dull. Of course, there are a lot of people here now, so one can get as much society as one wants, though they have not started a club yet!

We have had some hot trying days, as there has been a break in the Shimāl (the North wind) and what little wind there has been has come from the south off the dry dusty plains – a scorching breeze.

We have our daily round on the bridge,[16] varied last night by a dose of work by the light of the full June moon. It was almost as easy to see as day, and beautifully cool.

---

[14] The Revd Thomas Longley was Rector of Upper Slaughter, successor to Canon Broome Witts, F.V.B.W.'s father. He was not thought of favourably by Mrs Witts and the rest of the family.

[15] The names of those who did not serve in WWI without good reason were not forgotten in subsequent years.

[16] See *Light Floating Bridges* (Appendix I) for a detailed description of the 'daily round' for No. 2 Bridging Train.

I also dabble in other jobs as time and materials admit, making sandbag piers for the river steamers, observatories for look outs, breaking up derelict boats, making decent water arrangements. I have completed six nice huts for my men and am starting on three more. They are extraordinarily cool and a great relief during the heat of the day, when the single fly tent – their normal abode – becomes unbearable.

I have just done a good deal with an obliging Supply Officer, exchanged forty tins of bully beef for a real live goat. The bully beef had not been required thanks to our own stock, which we draw on when fresh meat is not issued.

Very best love.
> Your ever loving Son,
>> Fred. V. B. Witts.

F.V.B. Witts
> Capt. R E.

> [Sheikh Saad]
> June 25th 1916

Dearest Mother.

No mail has come in since I last wrote, so I have no acknowledgements for papers or replies to questions to help me fill the paper! What with no change here this is rather difficult! I have dealt in detail with the food and housing problem not to mention the weather, so I don't know where to look for something to interest or amuse you.

The flies, thank goodness, have practically disappeared [killed off by the heat] – only to return again later I expect. The heat is increasing, and it is getting warmer at nights: not that it is too hot to sleep comfortably – I have not yet found it advisable to take my bed up on to the roof of my house. The wind, instead of blowing from the North across the marsh and river making it cool and clear, has been blowing from the South, smothering us all and everything in inches of fine dust, which hangs about in the air – if the wind is not too strong – like a thick London fog, getting into your hair and ears and nearly choking you. I suppose we are blessed with this in order to make up for the absence of flies. Acquaintance with this country makes it easier to understand the Biblical stories of the Flood, plagues of locusts and all the other abominations mentioned.

Midsummer's day past and the days already closing in! Just think of it. Another three months will see us safely out of this inferno. And how quickly the time goes – to me it is one of the most extraordinary experiences of the war. Another week and I shall have been six months in this country.

A lot of fellows are going sick, and it is not surprising. Personally I am feeling extraordinarily fit – fitter than I ever felt in India at this time of year. It is probably

45. A drinking water cart at a chlorination tank.

due to the great care which I take of myself – this I know will please you – but I have every opportunity of doing so and should be a fool if I didn't. To start with my house – complete protection & escape from heat, flies & dust, not to mention the cool roof to sleep on if the nights get warmer. Then I am very careful about water. The river is our only source of course, and it is very muddy; this is taken out and left to stand in large sheltered canvas tanks where with the aid of some alum the mud soon settles and beautifully clear water is the result. This is then put in another tank, where chlorine is added which effectually kills the germs. The last problem is to cool it; this is done in a large tin surrounded by straw which is kept damp. The water is then poured into old lime juice bottles which are brought to the mess, and placed in a large leaky canvas bucket, which remains beautifully cool. Finally I keep the place scrupulously clean, and have built an incinerator to burn things. This all forms part of the duties of the Indian Medical subordinate attached to us.

I hope this will interest you. I really have no news.

       With very best love
         Your ever loving Son
           Fred. V. B. Witts

p.s. I should like you to send me a book 'Between the Lines' by Boyd Cable Publishers Smith, Elder & Co. 15 Waterloo Place. S.W.

While Captain Witts was able to take good care of his health, many were less fortunate. The sick-list for Force 'D' exploded over the summer months with a staggering 34,000 men having to be invalided to India between June and August, not including the thousands crammed into hospitals within Mesopotamia. Despite General Lake's best efforts, river transport was partly to blame as it was still unable to keep up with demands for supplies. At the front there were not enough hot weather helmets and tents to go round, and rations remained deficient. Scurvy and intestinal disease were rife due to a complete lack of vegetables; for many of the Indian troops, the sacred status of the cow in the Hindu religion denied them of their only source of protein in canned bully beef.

The effects of malnourishment were exacerbated by the heat, but for many of the new drafts, especially those from Britain, the climate alone was enough to have them invalided straight out of the country. As early as May a newly arrived draft of Highland Light Infantry lost 111 out of an original 139 just on the journey from Basra to the front; in July the three Indian battalions of the 19th Brigade went into the trenches with only five British officers between them; between June and August a collection of ninety new doctors was reduced to forty.[17] Once again, the only consolation was that the Turks were in the same position.

[Sheikh Saad]
July 3rd 1916.

Dearest Mother,

Two mails in since I last wrote, with a full complement of Times, Bystanders Truths and Punches, letters from Agnes and Frank and yours of May 9th and 17th.

There is again no news from this end. The weather remains the same, it doesn't seem to have got any worse though it certainly hasn't got any better. The river continues to fall at the average rate of 1½ inches a day. It is now nearly six feet lower than when we moved to the present site. I am still alone and finding it very dull, but the presence 'en passant' during a portion of the last week of another of our companies fresh out from India brightened things up considerably, we had so much to talk about.

I am very sorry for the British troops out here. I don't think many of them will see the summer through.

I have had the misfortune to lose my goose. I think lack of society must have been the cause of its death. On the other hand my flock has received the addition of a lamb, and one of my hens is supplying a daily egg for my breakfast.

They have changed my hours again. I now start at 5 a.m. which is just the right time; but I am not allowed to close for the night until 8.30 p.m. This means I have to start my five course dinner at 7.30 p.m. – too early for the season and climate – and am unable to sit over my coffee as I should like.

I am glad to say the subaltern I asked for has been ordered to join me, but I don't know when he will arrive, as he himself has got to be relieved first.

How do you like the Summer Time business?[18] Do you find any difficulty about

---

[17] Candler, E., *The Long Road to Baghdad*, vol. I p. 288

[18] The idea of setting the clocks forward an hour over the summer months was first proposed by the English builder, William Willet, in 1905, but first adopted by Germany and her allies on 30th April 1916. Britain and most of her allies followed suit shortly afterwards.

getting up in the morning.

Yes the Gloucestershire Yeomanry seem to have caught it in the neck – half the élite of the county captured.[19]

My pony was nearly stolen three nights ago; an Arab had cut it loose and was endeavouring to make it step over some barbed wire, when he was spotted and left it and bolted, getting clear away.[20]

Very best love,
> Your ever loving Son,
>> Fred. V. B. Witts.

An enormous melon arrived with rations a few days ago. The first fresh fruit I have tasted since last November; and it was very good too.

> No 2 Bridging Train.
> 1st K.G.O. Sappers + Miners.
> Mesopotamia Expeditionary Force.
> [Sheikh Saad]
> July 10th 1916.

Dearest Mother.

First of all please note my revised address given in full which we are directed to bring to the notice of all our correspondents.

Many thanks for your two letters of May 30th + 31st from Mrs Charnock's. Many thanks for getting the waistcoat:[21] it is sure to turn up in due course but parcels always take some time longer owing to the difficulty of finding transport for them up the river from Basra. The Times and the three weeklies all arrived.

Everything goes on much the same as usual, and I have no comments even to make on the weather.

I was very pleased the other day, when a Tommy was nearly drowned in midstream, our lifeboat was manned with great expedition and got to him just in time.

---

[19] In 1916, the Gloucestershire Yeomanry (also known as the Royal Gloucestershire Hussars), a cavalry squadron of the 5th Mounted Brigade, was posted at Qatia, in the Sinai desert, helping to defend the Suez Canal. On 23rd April, they were overwhelmed in a sudden raid by a detachment of a Turkish force under the German General Kress von Kressenstein. The Gloucesters lost a total of 113 men and the front line of defence fell back to the Suez canal.

[20] Theft was endemic in Lower Mesopotamia; the Arabs themselves shackled their animals at night. More serious, however, was the increase in ambushes and harassments by Arab marauders on the 17 mile supply line from Sheikh Saad to the British front line at Es Sinn.

[21] F.V.B.W. is talking about the Credem lifejacket he had asked his mother for in his letter of 23rd April 1916, p. 79.

I had a touch of fever on the 5th, and as the temperature remained high went to bed, where I remained till the 8th, living on Bovril and milk. I was very lucky to have such a comfortable house to lie up in, but I should have liked some one to look after me and make me rice puddings. However I am out and about again and none the worse.

I heard from Edward last mail, he seems to be fed up with the whole show; and he is not the only one either. There is little of the sporting element left in modern warfare.

I shall rely on you to send me a nice big fat hamper for Christmas. A properly packed box from some shop will travel best, but it must be sent off September 1st or soon after as it will take a long time coming. Send two over for me and one for the two sergeants.

Nothing more

> Very best love,
>> Your ever loving Son,
>>> Fred. V. B. Witts.

[Sheikh Saad]

July 16th 1916.

Dearest Mother.

Many thanks for your letter of June 7th from your club. No Bystander or Truth came this week only Punch: I expect they will roll up next mail.

The waistcoat has arrived. Thanks very much for sending it. It will be invaluable if we have any more accidents to the bridge. But nowdays thanks to the river falling and to the more careful navigation of the shipping there have been no collisions at all.

You say there is a bill for me from the stores. Please send it on to me; I can't remember what it can be for. Whatever you do, don't pay it, until I have seen whether it is correct.

I am very fit again. Not a bit the worse for my touch of fever.

I might possibly go off to India on a month's leave. I was offered it and my name has gone in, but it doesn't follow that I shall get it, and I am not particularly keen either way. Though a change of surroundings and diet would always be welcome. I certainly find the heat less trying out here. It may be hotter, but it is so absolutely dry that you get none of the discomforts of prickly heat, and the nights are far cooler than you ever get in India. I have never once found it difficult to sleep.[22]

The flies have all died away, there is hardly a mosquitoe about, and only a few sandflies.

---

[22] This is contrary to what F.V.B.W. has said in previous letters. He may be trying to assuage his mother's fears concerning his health and well-being.

We have just had another change in the local command.[23] It seems to be a three monthly appointment. I don't think any one up here will be sorry for this last change.

I have had a great disaster. We caught such an enormous fish in my net the other day, that the fish broke away and took half the net with it. I am now without my regular supply of fresh fish. To make up for it, I have at last succeeded in getting a dozen soda water bottles: these I can get filled at the hospital here every day. It is a tremendous luxury. All that is wanted now is some ice to reduce it to a drinkable temperature.

I have had another reinforcement and am consequently well above strength, as my men have been keeping much fitter than most. I am also expecting my new subaltern Nicolle any day. He has got his orders to join me, so I shall not be so lonely. However I have been dining out in society a lot lately. But it is the long hot spell in the middle of the day when I get fed up with my own company.

> Very best love,
>   Your ever loving Son,
>   Fred. V. B. Witts.

F. V. B. Witts
     Capt. R. E.

[Sheikh Saad]
July 25th 1916.

Dearest Mother.

I am afraid I am behind hand again with my letter, but I have been putting it off in the hopes of getting a mail, and it only arrived this morning – your two letters of June 9th & 14th one from Jack, a book from you, & all the usual papers with the Sphere as an extra. Very many thanks for everything.

So sorry to hear of your rheumatic gout in the knee. I hope it has disappeared. What with the foals & pigs you are collecting quite a menagerie at Slaughter!

I hope Jack passed his Board and has gone back to work. He has had a very long trying time of it.

I am really afraid that the Brilliantine must have melted and run out en route.

I had a wire yesterday that my leave has been sanctioned, but I have to wait until my new subaltern (I am now to get one Eastmond of the Indian Army Reserve) arrives to carry on in my absence, so I do not know when I shall start and it leaves plenty of time and opportunity for my leave to be cancelled, which is not at all improbable as so many fellows are going sick, whereas I feel as fit as a fiddle and am rather ashamed

---

[23] General Maude was appointed Commander of the Tigris Corps on 11th July in place of General Gorringe.

of running away from the heat and discomfits. However I believe in taking any leave that comes ones way. It seems very strange to be going on leave <u>to</u> <u>India</u> and I expect to find the climate more trying than it is here. I hope to go via Bombay to Roorkee, where I have several things I should like to straighten out; and from there get some one to come up to the hills with me for a fortnight or ten days.

I am supposed to get a clear month in India, and, as it takes about a fortnight either way, it means an absence of about two months from here. I shall not be sorry to get back to a decent diet & home comforts for a bit. The real hot weather will be over by the time I get back, and things may be beginning to move.

Continue to send all letters & papers here as usual. It is no use trying to switch them off to India for such a short time.

It has been very hot the last ten days – 122° in the shade one day & 120° another – but still always bearable at night, though the sandflies have been worrying more lately. One of my hens died of heatstroke! But yesterday they were supplemented by a new draft of seven hens and three cocks, so my subaltern ought to have an assured supply of eggs. Two days violent gale & sandstorm were rather unpleasant but brought the temperature down with a bump.

A steamer with Lake on board ran down one of my boats on the 20th; the eight occupants were extraordinary lucky to <u>all</u> escape. It is rather curious that he should again be involved in an accident to the bridge.

> Very best love,
> > Your ever loving Son,
> > > Fred. V. B. Witts.

F. V. B. Witts
    Capt. R. E.

> [Sheikh Saad]
> August 1st 1916.

Dearest Mother.

Here I still am, but am expecting to start at any moment. Eastmond arrived on the 30th and everything has been fixed up. The first crowd of fellows went off on the 26th, and I was very disappointed not to be with them, as there were two friends from Roorkee, whose company I should have enjoyed, and whom I shall probably join in the hills, after doing my shopping in Bombay and any necessary work in Roorkee.

I have had a very dull week, nothing to report at all. The 'shimal' – north wind – has been blowing with great persistence frequently rising into a gale. Result has been to keep the temperature down, as a counterblast, the dust up, and it is some dust too – gets into everything everywhere. It has also made the passage of the bridge rather difficult for steamers, so I have had to make the opening wider. The river continues to fall, and is now ten feet lower than when we put the bridge up and about 12 feet below the highest flood level. It is still however very deep in parts – over 50 feet in one place.

No mail since I last wrote and I am afraid I shall not get another one till I get back in about a couple of months time. It is no good your trying to write to me in India – I shall be starting back by the time you get this. I am sending you a week end cable to let you know of my trip.

Just got a wire with orders to proceed, and have fixed up to start by steamer leaving at daylight tomorrow morning. I am due to leave Basra on 6th.

No more news, and I must pack

> Very best love,
> > Your ever loving Son,
> > > Fred. V. B. Witts.

> > > > > S.S. Chakdara.
> > > > > At Sea.
> > > > > 13-8-16.

Dearest Mother.

We are due in Bombay early tomorrow, so I will write to port on landing.

I started down river at daylight on the 2nd in a very comfortable steamer, but in starting we wound a rope round our paddle wheel, and broke it, laying the steamer out for at least a month. After a nine hour delay we got going again this time on an iron barge tied alongside a steamer with no accommodation on her. However with our camp kit we made ourselves comfortable, and luckily a double roof had been built over it. It is a unique journey down: in some places very wide with shifting shoals, on which you stick – we got hung up for twelve hours on one, and there were two other steamers in a similar plight within two hundred yards of us – ; in others so narrow and so tortuous, that you bump from side to side, and at the worst bend known as the Devil's Elbow we got jammed right across the river, our bows up against one bank and our stern up against the other. We took some shifting. But for the absence of stones & rocks, the river would be unnavigable; as it is a large number of boats are always laid up for repair.[24] We eventually reached Busra midday on the 5th, here I put up with the Staff Officer of the Sapper General at G.H.Q. and spent two days in an atmosphere of Generals and ice. I also inspected my piers and bridges, which I am glad to say I still found standing, and saw two or three friends. I came on board this boat on the 7th and we sailed on the morning of the 8th. We made for Bushire, where we arrived at daylight on the 9th and tied up alongside the Juno an old cruiser doing Guard Ship there; we had come to give her a 100 tons of fresh Tigris water as fresh water in any quantity is unobtainable apparently at Bushire; the crew

---

[24] This experience may have given F.V.B.W. some sympathy for those charged with managing river transport.

46. A hair-pin
bend on the Tigris
narrows.

must have a pretty rotten time of it tied down in such a ship in such a climate. We
started away fairly on our voyage about 3 that afternoon. While stationary at Bushire
it was most unpleasant – hot and damp. We passed out of the Gulf through the Straits
of Ouncez [Hormuz], better known now as 'Hell's Gates', midnight of the 10th/11th
and immediately came in for a groundswell, which we hoped was the last remnant of
the monsoon; but luck was out and for the last thirty six hours we have been taking
it in the neck in the thick of a bad monsoon, and she is a small boat too with empty
holds, so she rolls a bit, though not to equal the Conconada[25] in the Mediterranean
last January year.

My plans are still very unsettled. I shall probably go straight on to Roorkee,
and leave my principal shopping till returning when it will be cooler & pleasanter.
Afterwards somewhere to the hills where it will be pleasanter, but the trouble is all
my best clothes are with you at Slaughter, and it is not worth buying a new outfit for
a month in India.

By the way if I ever wire for them send everything along at once through Cox &
Co. I don't see much of a chance of leave for us regulars until long after the war is
over whenever that may be.

        Very best love,
                Your ever loving Son,
                        Fred. V. B. Witts.

                                                ROORKEE, U.P.
                                                INDIA
                                                August 20th 1916.
Dearest Mother.

Here I am back at Roorkee. I disembarked on the afternoon of the 14th and put
up that night at the Royal Bombay Yacht Club. A most comfortable spot where

---

[25] F.V.B.W. sailed on the *Conconada*, a small troop ship, from Bombay to Marseilles en route to the
Western Front. In a letter written on 27th January 1915, he described the ship as 'rolling and pitching
as I never imagined possible'.

everything is awfully well done and is more like England than any other place I have yet struck in India. Needless to say I thoroughly appreciated things.

Next morning I did some shopping, cabled to you and came on here by the evening mail, arriving at daylight on the 17th. Since then I have been looking up all my friends, British & Indian, here, sorting out and repacking my clothes.

Everywhere in the hills is full up – there are so many wounded & convalescent fellows up there, and so it is very hard to get in. I have secured a dressing room in the United Services Club at Simla, and am moving up there tomorrow for three weeks.

The mess here has been immensely improved in the last two years. Electric light and electric fans have been put in, and it makes all the difference this hot weather. The sitting room has been panelled in oak & teak and looks awfully well.

There is no more news.
> Very best love,
>> Your ever loving Son,
>>> Fred. V. B. Witts.

> UNITED SERVICE CLUB,
> SIMLA
> August 25th 1916.

Dearest Mother.

I left Roorkee at 10 p.m. on the 21st and got up here in time for lunch on the 22nd after a very broken journey – two changes in the middle of the night with two hours wait at each. The journey up the hill is quite an experience the first time. There is a 2'6' guage railway all the way up, twisting in and out like a snake, often doubling back on itself two or three times, now in a tunnel, now along the face of the cliff. Simla is of course perched on the top of a hill and the railway has to climb up. It is not a mountain railway – I mean there are no cog wheels. Besides the trains, they run a sort of motor charabanc on the line, and it was this I came up in. It is much quicker and you get a much better view. But it is rather a curious sensation being whizzed through close fitting tunnels in an open motor car and over high viaducts with no hand rails.

I have got a very small room here, but it has a comfortable bed which is all that matters. The club rooms are most comfortably furnished and the messing is very good. It is by far the most comfortable place to stay at in the hills in India. I have met several friends up here, so time is not hanging heavily on my hands, and there is an excellent library too. All the generals, and big I.C.S gentlemen, who have no wife or family up here with them, live here. There is a good deal of excitement over the change in Commander-in-chief just announced.[26] I expect several generals & colonels are wondering what their fate will be in consequence of the change.

---

[26] General Maude succeeded Lake as Commander-in-Chief of Force 'D' on 28th August.

We have been in the clouds ever since I got up, and had rain most days. It is not as cold as I had hoped.

My chief occupation – outside the club – has been going round signing the book at Viceregal Lodge & the C–in–C's, and a little shopping.

> Very best love,
> Your ever loving Son,
> Fred. V. B. Witts.

UNITED SERVICE CLUB,
SIMLA
Sept 1st 1916.

Dearest Mother.

It is a great hardship, resulting from coming on leave, to get no mail. My last news from you was dated about June 20th and I shall not get another letter till I get back in another month's time. It is a month today since I started, and the time has slipped by faster than ever.

There has been rain and cloud most days, since I last wrote, and so I have been chiefly revelling in the library here and at the United Service Institution near by, of which also I am a member. One appreciates a library and quiet reading after nearly two years unrest, during which I have hardly ever opened a book. The billiard tables too have been claiming much of my spare time, which, if you come to think of it, consists of the whole 24 hours of the day.

On Monday I dined with some friends, recently moved up here from Roorkee. Yesterday I went to a most interesting lecture given by a doctor, who had been taken prisoner at Mons and kept for ten months in Germany.

I have also done my duty by the dentist, and I am glad to say that this time I got let down light. I have been very lucky and have never had a touch of tooth–ache since the war: inspite of hard food and distance from dentists. I only hope it will continue.

Great news this week – Roumaine's entry into the war.[27] I really believe it is the beginning of the end; and am expecting to see great changes by Christmas, though

---

[27] Romania was traditionally linked to the Central Powers but relations had soured leading up to the war. Disputes with Austria-Hungary over its treatment of the 3 million Romanian nationals living in Transylvania, a Hungarian state, had turned Romanian public opinion against their alliance with Austria-Hungary, forcing the pro-German King Carol I to declare Romania's neutrality in 1914. Shortly afterwards Carol died and his successor, his nephew Ferdinand, was more inclined to side with the Allies, especially after Russia's success in the Brusilov offensive in mid-1916. With the promise of Transylvania after the war, Romania joined the Allies at the Treaty of Bucharest on 27th August 1916. The treaty was publicised as hugely significant, but, in the event, Romania's entrance into the war failed to have any great impact.

it is bad to be too optimistic. Our own show in Mesopotamia has come to an end I think. We shall hold what we've got, take Kut if they give us the chance, and perhaps follow them up if they have to fall back from Baghdad owing to Russian pressure. I don't anticipate any hard pushing on our part: there seems so little to gain by it and the difficulties are so great. So you need have no anxiety on my account.

> Very best love,
> Your ever loving Son,
> Fred. V. B. Witts.

> UNITED SERVICE CLUB,
> SIMLA
> Saturday Sept 9th 1916

Dearest Mother.

My time is nearly up. I start down on Monday to Roorkee where I shall stay a couple of nights, remobilising and making full arrangements for another two years in Mesopotamia as I don't foresee any leave, bar sick leave, next year, for those of us who got away this year. I am due at Bombay on the 15th and embark on the 16th.

This last week I have been leading a more strenuous life. Tuesday evening I dined out and afterwards went to the 'Gaiety Theatre', where the Amateur Dramatic Society were performing. Thursday I dined out again, and last night I again went to the theatre to see the cinematograph when 'Britain Prepared' was shown: Our own Company in France appeared – we were taken just before leaving.

Tonight I have Foster, of the Frontier Constabulary, whom I lived with in the old days at Hangu, dining with me. He is up here on a month's leave.

Sir Percy Lake has just returned from Mesopotamia, and has just rung me up on the telephone asking me to lunch tomorrow. I left cards on Lady Lake soon after getting up here.

The rains seem to have stopped and we are getting some beautiful weather up here. It is also colder with a healthy bite in the air morning and evenings.

I know you like doing some shopping for me. I want a 'Heppell's Fly Spray, Army Outfit, medium size at 36/-', obtainable from Heppel & Co, 2 Eden Street, London N.W. I think it may be a most invaluable boon, when the fly plague comes on again.

No more news. I have written to all the family since I have been up here.

> Very best love,
> Your ever loving Son,
> Fred. V. B. Witts.

Taj Mahal Palace Hotel
Telegraphic Address
'PALACE – BOMBAY.'
Bombay
Sept 15th 1916.

Dearest Mother.

I embark tomorrow on the Ekma[28] on my return to Mesopotamia. I am afraid I am not experiencing the same feelings of excitement & anticipation as possessed me two years ago. Familiarity breeds not contempt in this case but dislike. With, in my own opinion, no prospect of seeing any serious fighting out there, one great element is lacking. However the climate should now be bearable inspite of the inevitable flies, and with sport plentiful I mustn't grouse.

This hotel – the biggest in the East – has recently been taken over by the Army. Half is used as an Officer's hospital – or rather as much as is required, and the remainder is available for officers like myself passing through Bombay.

I had a very pleasant lunch with Sir Percy Lake & Lady Lake. He was very cheerful and showed no signs of being down in his luck at losing his job in Mesopotamia – reason unknown to me. If you get a chance meet them in England where I believe they are returning at an early date.

I spent two days at Roorkee and did all I wanted to, and am very pleased to find there is at least one officer on board tomorrow, whom I especially wished to see again.

No more news. I must get to bed,

Very best love,
Your ever loving Son,
Fred. V. B. Witts

British India Steam Navigation Co., Ltd.
(Incorporated in England.)
S.S. Egra[28]
Sept 22nd 1916

Dearest Mother.

Just a line to post at Busra, though I have little news. We got off midday on the 16th, and came very slowly across the Arabian Sea, not doing more than 9 or 10 knots. Weather was good though the monsoon was still noticeable in the shape of a swell.

---

[28] The *Ekma* and *Egra* were both troopships of the British India Steam Navigation Co. and built in 1911. They each survived both world wars to be scrapped in 1948 and 1950 respectively. They both operated out of Bombay to Basra and elsewhere so it is quite possible that F.V.B.W. was not wrong when he said he was scheduled to travel on *S.S. Ekma* (see letter of Sept 15th).

47. Mahaila & palms, near Basra.

We passed through Hell's Gates on the evening of the 20th and have been getting a move on since. We reach the bar tonight, and Busra midday tomorrow. How long I shall have to wait for a boat upstream remains to be seen.

The voyage has been as uneventful as most. I have distinguished myself by winning the sweep on the day's run on two successive days.

Four young generals are on board, sent out by the War Office to put this show on its legs. But if they carry on as they have been doing on board, things will end in sudden disaster. They show complete ignorance of the customs and prejudices of the Indian troops, and think that they can be ignored. This was the cause of the Mutiny in '57. However things are not as bad as all that.[29]

I am quite looking forward to getting back and finding eight week's mails from you.

No more news.

> Very best love,
> Your ever loving Son,
> Fred. V. B. Witts.

Disembarking from the *S.S. Egra* at Basra, Captain Witts would have been unable to ignore the improvements made to the port since his last arrival there ten months before. General Lake had understood the vital importance of strengthening the campaign's foundations, and had thus concentrated his efforts on improving efficiency at the base and on lines of

---

[29] Prejudice and a lack of respect towards Indian troops was a problem within the British Army as a whole. As this letter clearly illustrates, however, F.V.B.W. had a sincere respect for his men and a keen appreciation of their customs.

communication. The disaster at Kut, meanwhile, had inclined the powers that be to shift responsibility for Mesopotamia from India to London, ending the parsimonious management of the Indian Government.

Under the expert guidance of Sir George Buchanan, chief port administrator, Basra had been transformed into a modern port, capable of dealing with the prodigious amount of shipping arriving daily in Mesopotamia to supply Force 'D'. New wharves, suitable for ocean-going steamers, had been constructed at Basra and Maqil, and roads had been built connecting them to warehouses, offices, camps and hospitals. A 48 square mile plot of land had been reclaimed from the annual floods by the construction of an embankment. Accommodation for 15,000 troops and 7,000 sick was built on this dry land and space was provided for animals, dramatically reducing congestion.

The problem of river transport was tackled with the same drive, expertise, and ultimate success. Two committees led by experts had been commissioned to undertake a rigorous reorganisation of the river fleet. Despite setbacks – the most expensive being the loss of two thirds of river craft en route to Basra between March and August – the progress had been considerable. By the end of August, 460 tonnes of supplies were reaching the front each day (compared with a maximum of 300 in March) and this total was increasing, especially with the end of the monsoon, enabling more river craft to reach Basra. Railways were also on the increase. There were tracks from Basra to Nasiriyah, from Qurna to Amara and from Sheikh Saad to Es Sinn, alleviating pressure on other land and river transport.

48. River Transport on the Tigris.

Medical facilities were another aspect of vast improvement under General Lake. From their scandalous condition at the start of 1916, there were 20,000 beds available in hospitals and the waiting period for evacuees had been greatly reduced.

In his capacity as Commander-in-Chief in Mesopotamia, Lake had acted more as an administrator than a general, but, in so doing, he had recovered Force 'D' from their defeat at Kut and set them on the path to success. The War Office had discharged Lake on account of his age (61) and wavering health, and replaced him with the young and vibrant General Maude. It would be logical to assume that, in appointing an aggressive G.O.C. such as Maude, the War Office intended to resume the offensive. In truth, however, they were more inclined to sanction a withdrawal from positions surrounding Kut, than an advance towards Baghdad.

Captain Witts arrived back in Mesopotamia frustrated at being on the outskirts of the war. The current policy maintained by the War Office offered little prospect of satisfying the ambitions of an aspiring professional soldier. General Maude, however, had the energy and strength of character to change that defensive policy. In September 1916, Captain Witts can have had little idea of the challenges the forthcoming months would bring, and the important role he, himself, would play in pushing the Turk back up the Tigris and out of Mesopotamia for good.

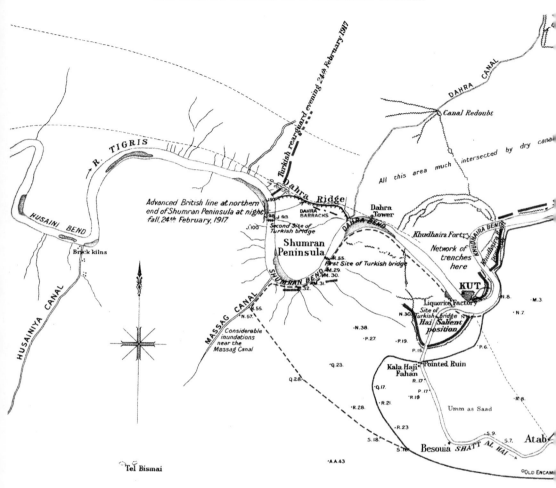

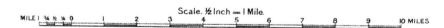

Map 3. The Tigris from Kut to Brick Kilns: Operations from
13th December 1916 – 25th February 1917.

CHAPTER III

MAUDE'S ADVANCE

Letters: Oct 13ᵗʰ 1916 –Feb 3ʳᵈ 1917.

49. Lieutenant-General Sir Stanley Maude.

The Chief of Imperial General Staff in London, Sir William Robertson, made no effort to disguise the fact that the War Office considered Mesopotamia to be a 'secondary theatre' which would engender 'no appreciable effect on the war.'[1] In September 1916, British manpower and resources were stretched to their limits in other, more decisive arenas. In light of this, Robertson reaffirmed the suggestion that Force 'D' should withdraw to Amara and be satisfied with the fulfilment of its original objective: the protection of the oil wells in Southern Arabistan. General Maude, however, was of a very different disposition. He responded by reminding the War Office that maintaining British prestige was essential not only to keeping the Arab tribes of Lower Mesopotamia in line, but also to keeping the troops' morale uplifted in a country where unrelenting forces of nature contrived to dampen even the hardiest spirits. In terms of salubrity, too, Maude argued that every mile closer to the humidity of the Persian Gulf increased health risks – a very serious matter considering the extent of the summer's sick-lists. Russian interests, meantime, in Persia and the Caucasus, were being served by holding Turkish divisions to Kut. On one item, at least, both Robertson and Maude were adamant: the continuation of a passive policy without a clearly defined objective was costly and pointless. Maude's counter-suggestion, therefore, was to attack the Turkish position on the Shatt-al-Hai.

---

[1] Moberly, F. J., *The Mesopotamia Campaign*, vol. III p. 43

General Maude had conceded that attempting another advance on Baghdad was injudicious at this stage, but, as a compromise, gaining a foothold on the Hai promised significant strategic advantages with little risk. Control of the Hai/Tigris junction would cut Kiazim's (the Turkish Corps Commander) supplies from Hai town, 30 miles downriver from Kut; threaten Turkish communications on the Tigris, perhaps forcing an evacuation from Sannaiyat; and strengthen the British position on the Euphrates by isolating the Turkish stronghold of Samawah. Most importantly, however, it would give the Tigris Corps another chance to fight and beat the Turks after a long and restless summer spent savouring the bitterness of defeat. The War Office responded initially with reluctance; after the disasters at Ctesiphon and Kut, assertive action of any sort in Mesopotamia was to be treated with caution. However, General Maude's persuasive reasoning and careful methods soon inspired support for his scheme. By mid-October, the assault on Turkish positions on the Hai was sanctioned and Maude began his preparations.

Like his predecessor, General Lake, Maude recognised that military success depended largely on efficient administration, especially in a country like Mesopotamia. Whilst he continued implementing the reforms initiated by General Lake, he also began to make changes of his own in preparation for the upcoming advance.

Maude attributed past failures largely to an inexperienced staff and set out to lighten their burden. He reorganised the Tigris Corps into two separate corps: the Ist comprising the 3rd and 7th Divisions under Lieutenant-General Cobbe, and the IIIrd comprising the 13th and 14th Divisions under Lieutenant-General Marshall. At G.H.Q., Maude preferred to deal personally with most staff matters rather than to delegate, quickly earning him the reputation of a workaholic.

One of Maude's most enterprising changes was to convert Captain Witts' bridging train into a 'mobile' unit. Up to this point, bridging trains had relied on river transport to carry their material to a site, meaning that bridges could only be built downriver of enemy positions. In making the bridge transportable over land, Maude granted himself the exciting prospect of outflanking Turkish positions by bridging the Tigris beyond Kut. Various modifications, overseen by Captain Witts, had to be made to make transport of the cumbersome bridging material possible over the difficult Mesopotamian terrain. The heavy Indian pattern pontoon and superstructure were replaced with lighter, better crafted English varieties, and the standard pontoon wagons were abandoned for modified A.T. carts, more suitable for coping with the thick mud and dust. The superstructure was carried on ordinary G.S wagons. With 200 A.T. carts and 56 G.S. wagons, Witts' mobile bridging train was capable of laying 500 yards of bridge, employed over 600 driving personnel and 900 mules, and formed a marching column of 2 miles in length.

With the change in the weather and the renewed buzz of activity, the melancholic atmosphere had just about evaporated from the front, as had Captain Witts' own dejected mood.

F. V. B. Witts
    Capt. R E.

[Arab Village]
Oct 13th 1916.

Dearest Mother.

No letters since writing last week.

I have been very busy changing our quarters. I moved on the 8th with half our crowd and Eastmond followed on the 10th.[2]

It was quite a wrench leaving our old quarters where we have been five months. Our new camp is not so comfortable but nothing to grouse about. We took over a first class dug out but unfortunately it is infested with sandflies, and we have just decided to abandon it as Eastmond has got a touch of sandfly fever. We are now attached to the division I was with in France,[3] and it is very nice being back amongst old friends; I went up yesterday and saw our two Field Companies and the C. R. E. [Chief Royal Engineer] whom I was under in France.[4]

We are above the limits of normal river traffic here so only have motor boats etc to pass through our standing bridge; this gives us plenty of time to play about with the mobile bridge which we have now taken over and which is the reason of our move.

I had a disaster yesterday as I collided in our motor launch with a sunken wreckage belonging to ammunition barges blown up in the spring.[5] Our propeller was smashed, and this is not a country where you can replace things. It is very sad as the boat has only just been done up and is now perhaps permanently hors de combat.

There are a lot of sand grouse in the neighbourhood, but what with learning our new job and settling down I have not had time to go after them yet.

We have added a tame jack snipe to our menagerie; he comes and feeds on the foreshore and I gave him some bread today. There are a lot of rats and mice about too, so you see we have plenty of company!

No more news,

Very best love,

     Your ever loving Son,

       Fred. V. B. Witts

---

[2] No. 2 Mobile Bridging Train moved to 'Arab Village', 7 miles up the Tigris from Sheikh Saad.

[3] The 7th (Meerut) Division.

[4] Major-General G. A. Leslie R.E.

[5] On July 11th 1916 Turkish artillery had sunk three British ammunition barges moored at the Fallahiya bend, exploding their cargo of 800 tonnes of shells. Fortunately, there were no casualties, but unfortunately, sunken wreckage remained.

[Arab Village]
Mesopotamia
Sept. 19th 1916.

Dearest Mother.

Thanks awfully for selecting my Christmas dinner: I hope it won't be submarined en route!

I am sorry to hear the Byass' are leaving the neighbourhood.[6]

I have heard from Agnes at Alexandria, and from Jack at Cairo. He tells me he has got a billet out there, and writes very cheerfully. The climate should quite set him on his legs again.

You must feel lonely with only Edith left, but you must bear up and cheer up.

We were lucky enough to get a spare propeller for our motor launch at once: so I am very pleased.

No incident has occurred during the week. A pair of mules and cart fell off the bridge yesterday, but we are expert at salvage now, and they were soon out.

Tomorrow there is a Gymkhana including a steeplechase for ponies. I have entered mine. The jumps are very easy, all remains of Turkish trenches with a small shrub fence. The course is dotted with shell holes and the remains of shell cases.

Very best love,
Your ever loving Son,
Fred. V. B. Witts

F. V.B. Witts
Capt. R E.

[Arab Village]
Thursday Oct 26th 1916.

Dearest Mother.

Many thanks for your letter of Sept 19th with all the usual papers.

The pony chase last Friday was quite amusing and I had a very pleasant ride though my pony wasn't fast enough to do any good. Sunday we intended to have a quiet day and I tried to slaughter some sandgrouse, I got 5½ brace in an hour, but was not shooting up to form. On getting back I found the bridge had been broken by a grossly overloaded wagon, which had gone right through the bridge, and we were busily engaged for the rest of the day pulling it and its load out of the river and remaking the bridge.

---

[6] Captain Jack Kennard's grandfather was a Byass and it was through his visits to Wyck Hill, where the Byass family lived at the time, that Jack met his future wife Frances Witts (*See* family tree appendix. XIX). By coincidence, it was also through Wyck Hill that F.V.B.W. was to meet his own wife, Alice Wrigley, whose father Major Arthur Wrigley bought the Wyck Hill estate in 1920 (see Illustration 8 in the Colour Section).

50. Supply dump at Arab Village.

Tuesday I went up to our No 1 Company [Bengal Sappers & Miners] and Gray, their O.C., took me all round the Sannaiyat trenches. They were extraordinarily clean, tidy and peaceful. I heard one Turkish bullet, two rifle grenades, and not a single shell! I was very interested to see them and compare them with France.

This morning two German aeroplanes were over the bridge but dropped no bombs, although flying fairly low.

The climate here is now almost ideal, though the range of temperature is very great. The other day it rose to 101° and fell to 55°. The flies are not noticeably bad, and the dust is really the only legitimate grouse. It will be another matter next month when the rains come. Moreover the feeding is much better now and we occasionally get a potato.

I have also heard from Edward and George.

Sergt Lehane suddenly reappeared the other day en route to join our No 3 Company. He was looking very fit.[7] You understand that any cables of mine no longer have any reference to him.

No more news

Very best love,
Your ever loving Son,
Fred. V. B. Witts

I am amused to hear that Pittaway is refused on account of his knee hurt on Billy![8]

F. V. B. Witts
Capt. R E.

[Arab Village]
Thursday Nov 2nd 1916.

Dearest Mother.

No mail since I last wrote.

Friday I was out after sandgrouse for a couple of hours and got 15½ brace. You can

---

[7] On 6th October F.V.B.W. had telegrammed his mother saying that Sergt. Lehane had been invalided to India and to pass the news on to Lehane's wife.

[8] F.V.B.W. is talking about Pittaway's exemption from conscription. He was the Witts' groom.

get as much shooting as the time and cartridges available permit. You have to walk out about a mile, and then sit in one of the old trenches of the April fighting. You get every form of shot, birds beating up against the wind, flighting over like duck, kinking like snipe, or flashing past like driven partridges. You may miss six shots running, and then a perfect swarm of them will swing past, and one shot will down six of them (this is my best so far.) A story goes that one fellow got 84 birds with two barrels!!! I was out again in the same place yesterday and brought in 18 brace in under two hours. Both days I only took out fifty cartridges, and didn't finish them. They are not particularly good eating, as far as game goes, though a very pleasant change in our diet.

We had a curious accident a day or two ago, a wheel mule fell into a boat, and was strangled or hung before we could cut him free.

Sunday morning I took my men round the scene of the first fight in April.[9] Everything is rapidly resuming a normal appearance, which is perhaps not hard in this country.

I am very busy, getting things into working order after the hot weather halt. The Turks may fall back, and we should have to follow.

Today I have been out mooring buoys to mark three wrecks. The river is at its absolute lowest now, but we are expecting a rise any day and a fall of rain probably too – the first it will be since May 10th.

It is rapidly getting colder and I am now using three blankets at night. The morning parade is a very chilly show! More flies about but not really bad.

No more news,

      Your ever loving Son,

        Fred. V. B. Witts

F. V. B. Witts

    Capt. R E.

                       [Near Wadi Camp]

                         Nov 9th 1916.

Dearest Mother.

Many thanks for yours of Oct 4th and all the usual papers. I see Frank has been gazetted Captain; he has got on very fast.

On the 4th the wind went round to the south, and blew a gale, the dust was terrible: it is necessary to see and feel it to realize how bad it can be. The 5th was much the same, but later on it turned to rain, the first rain we have had since May 10th. We didn't get much, but it rained hard with thunder up in the hills, and although the Tigris was hardly affected, the Wadi, a small stream running into it, rose six feet in five minutes and washed away all traces of the trestle road bridge. I am now collecting and making up material for a suspension bridge to take its place. I think it will be the

---

[9] Battle of the Fallahiya bend, fought by the 13th Division on April 5th 1916.

51. Mesopotamian dust.

first suspension bridge built in the country, and it's an interesting and pleasant change from our normal routine.[10]

A large reinforcement joined me yesterday, but they know nothing about boats or pontoons as India has been cleared of them in order to supply this country. So I have had to start teaching them from the very beginning.

I went out after the sandgrouse yesterday, but, whether it is due to the arrival of the rain or what, I only got a few shots and brought back three brace. I was very disappointed.

A Bosch aeroplane dropped a bomb just by our camp yesterday, having a shot at the bridge I expect. But he never hits anything.

I shall be alone for a few days, as Eastmond is going along to erect the suspension bridge. My old company with Bird are expected up shortly: Farley[11] blew in yesterday much to my surprise; he's come on ahead. I have not seen him since March. He is looking very fit.

No more news

With very best love,
        Your ever loving Son,
                Fred. V. B. Witts

Next mail will be my Christmas letter.

---

[10] In *Light Floating Bridges*, F.V.B.W. writes, 'A floating bridge was obviously out of the question [because of a lack of material at hand and the unstable water levels], but we had available a large amount of 3-in. steel cable, intended for use with anchors. The span was 105 or 120 ft. and I rigged up a tension bridge, using pontoon superstructure for the roadway. Material for the piers and anchorages were obtained by breaking up a wrecked *mahaila*. It was calculated to carry a 12-pdr. man-handled across. A year or so later I was asked by wire how it could best be strengthened to take lorries; I was gratified to hear it was still standing but felt perfectly justified in replying 'Pull it down and build another" (Appendix I, p. 430).

[11] Captain E. L. Farley R.E. was F.V.B.W.'s fellow subaltern at 4th Company Bengal Sappers & Miners.

We're slicing "Him" up
And hope You are doing the same.

'Ave you read a'bart the perils
Of this 'ere salubrious spot,
Where the flies are big as spar'ers
And the 'ens lay eggs red 'ot,
Or a'bart the creepy crawly things
Which bite us day and night,
'Ow spite of all we're going strong
And eager for the fight?
But Xmas-tide is here once more
And though so far away,
We wish you all the best of cheer
And a Happy Xmas Day.

1916·17

From Fred

To Mother

Mesopotamia.

52. Christmas card, 1916. Issued to the troops to send home.

F.V.B.Witts

Capt. R. E.

[Arab Village]
Nov 18th 1916.

Dearest Mother.

This is my Christmas letter, so very many happy returns of the day to you and all the family (I am afraid I cannot write to them all – times are too strenuous). I hope some male members of the family will be at home to cheer you up, as I am afraid it cannot be a cheerful time for you. There is not much opportunity for selecting a Christmas present from here: a handful of dust weighs a lot and is not much use, a sandgrouse or Tigris fish would I am afraid go bad en route! I am sending a few stamps, obtained from the Field Post Office, they are ordinary Indian issue, but their interest is enhanced by their being surcharged with the letters I.E.F. (Indian Expeditionary Force). I have had postmarks put on, as an expert informed me that this would increase their eventual value.

Very many thanks for your letter of Oct 8th. All the papers come regularly every week. I am very pleased to hear Edith has learnt to drive the Ford. Please thank her for her letter – full of interesting news. I also had a very long yarn from Frank.

The river has risen slowly the last week 2 ft 3 inches in all, not much, but it has given us a lot of extra work on the bridge, especially in view of Eastmond's absence with a party putting up the Suspension bridge. He came back today, having successfully completed the job. It looks very nice and I only hope it will stand! I went down to see it yesterday (my third visit) with the Engineer-in-Chief – the Major General R.E. on G.H.Q. Staff [Leslie]. He is a dear old fellow, and I am now directly under G.H.Q. from which you will gather there have been changes, which the censor might object to my detailing.[12] Got a second bridge to look after now, we put it across today. It is a bad look out for us if floods come with two bridges on our hands.

I had a game of bridge last night at G.H.Q. in very select Company. It was the first I have had in this country.

I was inoculated against enteric, Paratyphoid A & Paratyphoid B a week ago, all three of them together both doses at once. It fairly knocked me over for 24 hours,

---

[12] General Maude moved his headquarters up from Basra to Arab Village at the end of October.

but I am very glad now I was done. All the men are being done too, but they have it in two doses.

I was very pleased to see that my former subaltern Atkinson, and senior Indian Officer had been mentioned in Lake's despatches. The Engineer-in-Chief was kind enough to say that he was very annoyed my name had not appeared too, as he had sent it in. This is the second time I have been beaten on the post as Bird recommended me for the M.C. in France. My turn will come some day. Very best love & Christmas wishes,

Your ever loving Son Fred.

F.V.B. Witts
    Capt. R. E.

No 2 Bridging Train
Meospotamia Ex: Force
[Arab Village]
Nov. 24th 1916.

Dearest Mother.

No mail since I last wrote and very little news.

Our suspension bridge is still standing and every one is very pleased with it, so I hope it won't collapse.

The river has been falling again instead of rising which is an awful nuisance, as we had made special arrangements for a rise; much of this work has now to be undone. We have two bridges over the river to look after now, so all the work is doubled.

The sand grouse are getting much wilder and more wary from the continual shooting, and the large bags are a thing of the past. I expect they will shift to a healthier and quieter locality.

I went out in one of the motor cars, which have found their way up here, this morning, and they are not the pleasant form of travel they appear to be, over these rough tracks often a foot deep in dust. A launch is the only pleasant form of locomotion and I am very lucky to have the use of one.

This is my new year letter, so very many happy returns of the day, very best wishes for the New Year and may it bring us peace.

It is getting really cold at nights now and one is quite glad to get to bed after dinner; we have also given up the midday rest in the heat of the day and work straight on and finish off earlier.

It is very hard to find news, when no mail has come in to answer, when you cannot talk about your most interesting doings and prospects and when you have no recreation to talk about.

My pony is very fit, and I occasionally ride up to see the two Field Companies of ours. I think I told you Farley had arrived, looking very fit and as full of energy as ever.

My unit is now considerably overstrength through new arrivals; unfortunately they know nothing at all about this particular job, and many of them have never seen a boat or handled an oar before, so I have to start classes and teach them from the very beginning.

Very best love, and very best wishes to every one for the New Year.

Your ever loving Son.

Fred. V. B. Witts

At the start of winter 1916, an excited sense of anticipation pervaded Force 'D'. The situation at the front was as follows: the Ist Corps, under General Cobbe, was aligned either side of the Tigris facing the Turkish defences at Sannaiyat; the IIIrd Corps, under General Marshall, was occupying the Es Sinn trenches on a line stretching from Maqasis fort to the Dujaila Redoubt; the sappers of No. 2 Mobile Bridging Train were manning the two bridges at Arab Village where they were accompanied by two brigades of Cavalry; and General Maude had now established G.H.Q at Sheikh Saad. Turkish strength was focused at their bridgehead on the Shatt-al-Hai near its junction with the Tigris, and at the Sannaiyat position on the left bank.

General Maude believed that his main advantage over the Turks lay in his mobile bridging train and the secrecy therein. For Captain Witts, this necessity for absolute secrecy was extremely tiresome. Any form of practical rehearsal to train his novice sappers in the fundamental methods of packing, transporting or unpacking the bridging materials was strictly forbidden. In fact, the materials for his mobile unit had been brought to the front by steamer and stored separately from their specially designed transports until the very day that operations commenced.

[Arab Village]

Dec 2nd 1916.

Dearest Mother.

Many thanks for your letters of Oct 11th & 18th also for all the papers which come regularly, and the Christmas parcels which have arrived intact and undamaged. Many thanks indeed for them. I gave the two to C.S.M. Devent and Sergt Balshaw (Lehane's successor), I gather they have already eaten the contents as we happened to be on a biscuit and tinned beef ration at the time. A Devonshire youth, who drives my motor launch, also shared in the contents.

I am and have been frightfully busy for the last few days, and am wondering what is going to happen.

We have put in 13 hours work today, so I am feeling more like bed than anything else.

No more rain and the river has been falling again gradually, but it is getting very cold at night. The temperature rises to over 80 by day & falls below 40 at night, a tremendous drop, involving a large wardrobe to cope with it successfully. I am glad to say I am feeling very fit.

No more news or time,
    Very best love,
        Your ever loving Son,
            Fred. V. B. Witts

F. V.B. Witts
    Capt. R E.

                    [Imam al Mansur]
                Saturday Dec 9th 1916.

Dearest Mother.

No letters since I last wrote. But the fly spray has arrived. Very many thanks for sending it off. It arrived yesterday, the day after all the flies were washed away by a heavy fall of rain, the first heavy fall but immediately succeeded by another, and the ground has turned from a sea of dust to a quagmire.

I think I told you all the Christmas parcels had arrived?

I am sending you a local Christmas card, which I have only just managed to get. And also a three anna surcharged stamp, which was missing from the set which I sent previously.

I have been very busy the last week, as we have recently been fitted out with new material which has just been arriving, and we have been checking & cleaning it all.

We have also had to shift camp,[13] and were very lucky to have a fine day as it was sandwiched in between two absolute drenchers – not that it ever rained very hard but it was very continuous.

The German aeroplanes have been over more just recently, but they don't get much of a look in, as we are much better off both in aeroplanes and anti-aircraft guns.

No time for any shooting lately, and with the arrival of the rain, the sandgrouse are all fast disappearing as they no longer <u>have</u> to come down to the river to water.

There is no more news, and I am feeling weary, though very fit indeed, I am glad to say. So good–night & very best love,
    Your ever loving Son,
        Fred. V. B. Witts

[13] No. 2 Mobile Bridging Train had crossed over to the right bank in preparation for the attack on the Hai bridgehead.

On 10th December General Maude issued the following despatch listing his objectives: 'First to secure possession of the Hai; secondly, to clear the Turkish trench systems still remaining on the right bank of the Tigris; thirdly, to sap the enemy's strength by constant attacks and give him no rest; fourthly, to compel him to give up the Sannaiyat position; and lastly, to cross the Tigris at the weakest part of his line as far west as possible, and to sever his communications.'[14] The execution of this final element – the bridging of the Tigris – would fall to Captain Witts and his unit. Maude's plan to cross the Tigris beyond Kut was clearly overstepping the restrictions laid down by the War Office, but he soothed their apprehensions by reaffirming that he had no intention of following up any success with an advance on Baghdad.[15]

On the 12th December, an intense bombardment rained down on Sannaiyat from the batteries of the Ist Corps; Maude's aim was to deceive Kiazim into believing that the main British assault was going to be directed against his defences on the left bank. The Turkish commander responded obligingly, flooding reinforcements into Sannaiyat. Having successfully made his bluff, General Maude ordered his genuine advance to go ahead. On the night of the 13th, Captain Witts' bridging train, accompanied by the 13th Division, marched south from Imam al Mansur to Atab, on the muddy banks of the Shatt-al-Hai. The following are extracts from Captain Witts' own account of the events, written in 1923:

> The Hai was seized without any opposition, and, much to the disgust of the newly formed and enthusiastic bridging train, was found to consist of a succession of dry crossings and pools. However, the going was heavy for wheels, and a pool large enough and deep enough to float pontoons was found at Atab and two bridges built. Unfortunately it was also deep enough to engulf a messcart, which went over the edge.[16]

Over the course of the next week, the IIIrd Corps advanced steadily upriver, pinning the Turks back to the Khudhaira bend of the Tigris and their bridgehead across the mouth of the Hai. With the Turks contained and amply distracted at these positions, Maude sensed the opportunity to bring his trump card, the Mobile Bridging Train, into play. On the night of 20th December, Captain Witts' unit, accompanied by a Cavalry Division and Infantry Brigade, crossed the Hai and marched 11 miles through the desert to a reconnoitred spot named 'Brick Kilns', on the Hussaini bend of the Tigris, where the river had been measured as '300 cubits' in width.

---

[14] Callwell, C. E., *Life of Sir Stanley Maude*, p. 254.

[15] Moberly, F. J., *The Mesopotamia Campaign*, vol. III p. 87.

[16] Witts, F.V. B., *The Passage of the Tigris at Shumran*, (Appendix II, p. 136-7).

On arrival at the spot selected…a body of Turks, including machine guns and artillery, were found in occupation of the far bank. Orders were however received to launch a pontoon and row a party of British Infantry across [to establish a bridgehead on the other side of the river].

There was a good covered approach to within 50 yards of the bank, but over this distance the pontoon would have to be carried and launched into the water in full view of the Turks 300 yards across. It had then to be rowed across, still under the concentrated artillery, machine gun and rifle fire of the Turks.

The pontoon was picked up and carried towards the water's edge. The ground was rough and progress slow, so the order was given to shoulder.

Our infantry, who should have been keeping down the Turkish fire with covering fire, seemed more interested in watching the launching of the pontoon. Fortunately, the Turkish aim was bad, and, although bullets were kicking up dust all round only one man was hit at this stage- No. 2607 Sapper Haidar Zaman – who was hit in the leg and hopped back to cover.

The pontoon was launched, and men of the South Wales Borderers dashed forward and leapt in to be rowed across. This was a signal for a concentrated burst of Turkish fire, and in the next few moments most of the men of the South Wales Borderers were hit, and the following men of the Corps.

The Officer Commanding, slightly.

3125 Sapper Raja Khan,

2803 Sapper Rala Singh, seriously, losing an eye.

2783 Sapper Sher Singh, dangerously. He died of his wounds later.

At this moment an order was received to come back. One of the pontoons was abandoned in the river.

Captain C. A. Wood, M.C., I.M.S., the medical officer of No. 2 Mobile Bridging Train, now performed a very gallant act in going out and bringing back one of the wounded men.

The attempt to cross was abandoned shortly afterwards, but not before all arrangements had been cheerfully made to make a second attempt at another place nearby.[17]

General Maude's real intentions regarding the attempted crossing at Brick Kilns are far from transparent. In the event of a successful crossing, there would only have been a single Infantry and Cavalry Brigade available to round up Kiazim's force of 20,000 men. This considered, Maude's aims may, in fact, have been restricted to disrupting Turkish communications along the Tigris to compel Kiazim to withdraw from Sannaiyat. Whatever the case, surprise was clearly considered to be paramount; without it, Maude was not prepared to forgo the casualties involved in a bridging attempt. To some of Maude's

---

[17] Witts, F.V. B., *Attempted Crossing of the Tigris* (Extract from a lecture given in 1923).

staff, the tentative nature of the enterprise had made it entirely pointless from start to finish, but to Captain Witts, despite getting shot and losing a man, the experience was to prove invaluable.

> The attempt had apparently been a dismal failure, but actually it was a blessing in disguise, and contributed in a very large degree to the success of the final effort [at Shumran]. It confirmed the Turks in their belief that a crossing was impossible and also gave them false notions of what would be done if any further attempt were made; this will be seen later. It also gave us a very good idea of what not to do, and of what extensive preparations were necessary. We profited by the experience.[18]

With a bullet lodged in his arm, Captain Witts was sent down to hospital at Amara. The following telegram sent by the War Office was the first news Mrs Witts would have received regarding her son's wound. For this reason, it has been inserted slightly out of sequence with the letters.

POST OFFICE TELEGRAPHS.   05 JA
This Form must accompany any inquiry respecting this Telegram.   17

Office of Origin and Service Instructions.

PHMS: War Office London   *Handed in at}* 4pm *Received here at}* 5.30pm

TO{ Mrs Witts Manor. Upper Slaughter,
        Gloucestershire

Capt. F.V.B. Witts R. E. Admitted No. 2 British General Hospital Amara Dec twenty fourth with Gun Shot wound forearm slight

Sec. War Office

Three days after being shot, Captain Witts was relaxing in relative luxury in Rawal Pindi Hospital, Amara.

---

[18] Witts, F.V. B., *The Passage of the Tigris at Shumran*, (Appendix II, p. 437)

53. Rawal Pindi Hospital, Amara.

POST CARD
On Active Service.

F.V.B. Witts
   Capt. R. E.

Rawal Pindi Hospital,
Amara.
Christmas Eve 1916.

Dearest Mother.

I am afraid what with being on the move and full of work I have not written for quite a fortnight. And now I have got a bullet in my right arm, and as you can see, can only write with difficulty. So you will have to wait a week or so for all my news and full details as to how it happened. Moreover the Censor would object to details which later on I shall be able to give. I have a very gentlemanly wound in the right forearm, no apparent damage to bone, but the bullet is still in and will have to be cut out in a day or two. It gives me no pain, and I am now writing with my right hand. I got back to Amara this morning, and shall remain here until fit to return. I am feeling extraordinary fit otherwise, and am very annoyed at being out of it when things are moving a bit out here. This hospital is very comfortable, beautifully situated & completely equipped – including nurses.

Best love, Your ever loving Son, Fred.V.B. Witts

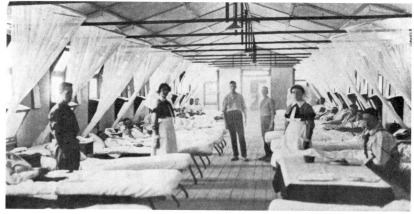

54. Interior of a Hospital Ward in Mesopotamia.

F. V. B. Witts
    Capt. R. E.

Rawal Pindi Hospital
Amara
Dec 26ᵗʰ 1916.

Dearest Mother.

I wrote a post card immediately on arrival here, thinking the mail was going out, but now find there is time for a decent letter.

I went round to the telegraph office on the evening of the 24ᵗʰ, and cabled to let you know how I was. I hope you got it fairly soon, and that you were not unnecessarily anxious on receipt of the official wire.

It was particularly thoughtless of me, as far as you were concerned, to get hit just at Christmas time; but as far as I am concerned personally, it was rather well arranged, as instead of spending Christmas in the open without a tent or indeed anything beyond one's minimum fighting kit, I have spent it with the maximum of comfort and luxury obtainable in this country.

On Christmas Eve we were each provided with a sock of the largest size obtainable, which we duly hung up at the foot of our beds. I awoke next morning to find mine crammed full with the following articles. A piece of large scented soap and washing glove, a pair of woollen socks, a pair of woollen mittens (most valuable of everything as I lost mine on this last show), writing paper, envelopes and pencil, matches, 3 khaki handkerchiefs 3 white handkerchiefs, a packet of Edinburgh Rock, and (what made me think of you) a little bag of lavender. It was all contained in a cretonne bag with my name on it.

At lunch they gave us Sherry and Port and a good old plum pudding, blazing away merrily. Tea was a great function what with endless sweets, and a very large & rich plum cake. In the evening a troupe of carol singers (nurses and others) gave us a selection including our old friend 'Good King Wencelas.' I chucked them a penny, but unfortunately the ground was too soft for it to ring, and they never heard it fall.

55. A Hospital Ship on the Tigris.

At dinner we were each supplied with a small bottle of Champagne – 1911 Bollinger in my case. So you see we fared pretty well, and I wasn't sorry we had nothing more strenuous to do than sleep between meals.

This morning I have been Xrayed again and the position of the bullet, or rather piece of bullet – as it was a ricochet – has been accurately fixed ready for extraction tomorrow. It is deep in just between the bones which have luckily escaped and once out it should not be long healing as the wound is quite clean.[19]

I got hit about midday on the 20th during a reconnaissance of the Tigris about 12 miles above Kut. Four of my men got hit at the same time, and I am very distressed to hear today, that one of them has died; another I am sorry to say has had an eye shot out; the other two escaped lightly like myself. Seven Britishers were hit at the same time in the same place so you will gather it was a pretty hot corner. I had another bullet high up between my legs; it passed through my riding breeches and drawers and just grazed my left thigh. I am glad to say that my men, who are all young sappers, who were under fire for the first time, behaved magnificently, and the General commanding the show [General Crocker], who witnessed the incident, asked for a list of all their names, said he had never seen anything finer, and never let anyone again run down the Indian Army in his presence. This has naturally bucked me up enormously, and I only hope they get something out of it, as they well deserve.

For various good reasons, there was not sufficient ambulance accommodation to go round, and light cases, like myself, had to make our own way. That day I travelled on one of my own wagons – one that was full of sandbags & very comfortable. The jolting was pretty bad, and next day I rode my pony in, until we met the motor ambulances. We finished our journey to Sheikh Saad by train in open goods trucks, spent the night there, and started down here in one of the new steamers next day. I had a cabin and there were two nurses to look after us.

Very best love,
Your ever loving Son,
Fred. V. B. Witts

[19] See Illustration 17 in the Colour Section for the X-ray of F.V.B.W.'s arm, taken at Rawal Pindi Hospital.

F.V.B. Witts
        Capt. R E.

Rawal Pindi Hospital
Amara.
Jan 3rd 1917

Dearest Mother.

I was delighted to get yesterday my first mail since Dec 10th. It had been diverted at Basra direct here, and included your letter of Nov 27th from Bath, one from Frank and all the usual papers which are needless to say doubly welcome here both to me and many other sick and wounded officers. Three or four mails are following me about and will presumably fetch up sometime.

Boxing Day a performance of 'When Knights were bold' was given by the local garrison; I went to it, and enjoyed a thoroughly good show. The 27th & 28th I went to bed again with slight fever, aches & pains, and a most irritating rash all over me. All the result of the injection of Serum, given as a precautionary measure against Tetanus. The 29th I had sufficiently recovered to have chloroform; And the bullet was duly dug out. It was a hit from a ricochet, as I had told them all along, but they were rather surprised to find the pointed half of the empty nickel shell of the bullet embedded in the bone of my forearm. It says something for the toughness of my bones, that it wasn't broken or even fractured; merely a big dent made in it! What happened to the rest of the nickel case or to the lead filling, goodness only knows! Or how it got broken up without the point showing any mark at all!

I remained in bed on the 30th and have since been up and about exploring all the hospitals here, in search of any of my men or other friends. I was very pleased to run to ground the young sapper who was with me and had his eye shot out. He was a perfect model of cheerfulness and his wound had already healed up – leaving him one eye short poor fellow. I also found George Collett's name in the books.[20] He had been in twice for periods of 5 to 10 days with a short interval. He was marked 'Sandfly fever' and inquiry proved that he had never been really bad. He was shewn as a Lance Corporal.

Any further news must keep till my arm is stronger.

The stitches are to be taken out tomorrow, and it should heal rapidly. Unfortunately the nerve of my thumb was touched and temporarily I have not full use of it, but this is nothing seriously inconvenient and will gradually get right.

Very best love,
        Your ever loving Son,
            Fred.V. B. Witts

---

[20] George Collett was from a very old Upper Slaughter family who had been in the village since the sixteenth century. He served with the Gloucestershire Regiment during WWI His mother was headmistress of Upper Slaughter School. (*see* also reference to George's brother Fred in Chapter VII, p. 238, note 23).

56. The Collett Family of Upper Slaughter.

Meanwhile, in Upper Slaughter, Mrs Witts had only received the War Office's telegram that her son had been wounded. She contacted the Enquiry Department at the British Red Cross, anxious for more information.

BRITISH RED CROSS
--AND--
ORDER OF ST. JOHN.

ENQUIRY DEPARTMENT
FOR
WOUNDED AND MISSING

January 5th 1917

18, Carlton House Terrace, S.W.

Dear Madam,

We have received your letter asking us to make enquiries for your son, Captain F.V. B. Witts, R.E., 1st King George's Own Sappers and Miners, who was reported to have been wounded in Mesopotamia.

Before cabling to our Office in Basra for news we must inform the War Office as it is not thought desirable that we should duplicate their cables. We have therefore telephoned and have been told that a cable has been received there stating that Captain Witts has been admitted to the 2nd British General Hospital, Amara, suffering a slight gunshot wound to the forearm. This news has, we believe, been sent on to you by the War Office, who will, no doubt, get a further report shortly.

We feel sure you will consider it re-assuring and that in the meantime nothing further could be gained by our cabling to our Office at Basra. If, however, you should continue to feel anxious please let us know and we will do our best then to get news for you…

Yours faithfully,

K. C. W.

For the Earl of Lucan

Although the British Red Cross could not help Mrs Witts much more at this stage, two cables from her son were soon forthcoming, allaying any serious fears for his condition. Each took a week to arrive.

6th JAN 17

THE EASTERN TELEGRAPH CO., LTD.: GIBRALTAR
LONDON STATION.
RECEIVED BY POST FROM GIBRALTAR

From Basra
Via Eastern
Foreign No.   *No of Words.* 25   *Dated* 30   *Time* 2.20 pm
TO   *Witts The Manor Upper Slaughter Gloucester*

Simple bullet wound right forearm no complications everyone very fit best wishes for Xmas and new year
= *Fred Witts* =

Doubtful Words should be OFFICIALLY repeated. See Rule Book.
No inquiry respecting this Telegram can be attended to without the production of this Copy.

9 JAN 17

THE EASTERN TELEGRAPH CO., LTD.: GIBRALTAR
LONDON STATION.
RECEIVED BY POST FROM GIBRALTAR

From Basra
Via Eastern
Foreign No.   *No of Words.* 11   *Dated* 2
Time 7.55 pm
TO   *Witts Upper Slaughter*

Bullet extracted bone undamaged
   getting well quickly
                  Fred Witts

Doubtful Words should be OFFICIALLY repeated. See Rule Book.
No inquiry respecting this Telegram can be attended to without the production of this Copy.

F. V. B. Witts
    Capt. R. E.

Amara
Jan 10th 1917.

Dearest Mother.

Very many thanks for your delightful long letter of Dec 5th from Bath. Three mails which went upriver while the operations were on are still following me about; as I am returning up river today or tomorrow, I am afraid they will miss me here, and perhaps I shall never see them.

This letter ought to reach you on or about your birthday, so let me wish you many happy returns of the day under happier conditions with us all home to help you celebrate it. I am enclosing a small present, which I want you to spend on yourself just as you like. I tried to buy a present here, such as a Persian rug, but a good one is now very hard to obtain here, and you get done in the eye unless you are an absolute expert. Further to it is impossible to get it sent to you at present!

They looked at my arm again on the 4th – it hadn't been touched since the cutting on the 29th Dec – and to my immense surprise and satisfaction found it had practically healed up, and so took the stitches out at once. By the 7th it had quite healed, and they took everything off and turned me out of hospital. It was of course still pretty stiff, and I nominally went to the Officer's Convalescent camp, but actually got permission to put up with a friend in a comfortable house here, which besides being much more comfortable is far more entertaining in every way.

I got permission to apply for a passage up today or later, and am now only waiting for the first of the new comfortable boats (which I have particularly bargained for) to take me up back to my own unit, for which I am glad to say I have received definite orders to rejoin – thus definitely dispersing some fears of losing the job through going away.

The hand is still stiff in places, and I find some difficultly in doing certain things, but can write and ride and so there is nothing to prevent me going back to duty. The small muscle of the thumb, which has struck work, still refuses to show any signs of life. But this is only a matter of time.

There has been some very wet and windy weather since I got down here and I have not been sorry to have a decent roof over my head, and I am not altogether looking forward to going back to the wet and muddy camps. Now the river has come down in flood and I expect they have been having some exciting times with the bridges up stream, reminiscent of my experiences last April, and I am quite relieved not to have a bridge over the Tigris on my hands. The Hai won't be anything like as bad, and there will be no river traffic just at present.

I have just had definite orders to go on board today on one of the newest boats. So I shall have a comfortable journey up.

I have also just been shewn a wire from G.H.Q. which reads 'Please inform Capt. F. V. B. Witts R.E. that Army Commander has awarded him Military Cross and same time offers his congratulations'.[21] You can imagine how pleased I am, and I know how pleased you will be too, and I only wish that dear old Father was here to share it with us.

I must confess that I was getting rather down in my luck, after two solid years of it without a wound or mention or anything, and felt that I was getting left, so this sudden news has bucked me up and cheered me up enormously. But we must remember to thank God that I came out of it alive.

Well I must stop or I shall miss my boat and mail as well.

Very best love and good wishes,

Your ever loving Son,

Fred.V. B. Witts

I have another bit of good news which I have been meaning to tell you for some time. Namely that the spots on my face have apparently finally and I hope definitely disappeared.[22] It has always rather depressed me, so here's another reason for my feeling particularly pleased with myself, and you must imagine me starting the New Year full of refreshed hopes and ambitions and bubbling over with 'joie de vivre'.

While Captain Witts had been convalescing in Amara, operations at the front had progressed slowly due to War Office strictures on acceptable casualties. At the Hai Salient and Khudhaira bend, the Turks had embedded themselves strongly in deep trenches, so as not to be overrun without persistent, determined attacks which would inevitably bring casualty rates beyond the limits outlined in London. Once again, General Maude was able to convince the War Office to adapt their policy to fit the changing situation; at the end of December, he was granted an acceptable casualty rate of 25%.

For the next three weeks, the narrow Turkish enclave on the Khudhaira bend was bombarded with devastating shellfire, raining down in torrents both day and night between bursts of infantry assaults. The tenacity of the Turkish defenders was remarkable; they fought and died for every inch of churned earth, inflicting heavy casualties on the British attacks. Eventually, however, superior British artillery and relentless assaults drove the defenders into the Tigris. Afterwards, in the decomposing wreckage of mud, shrapnel and corpses, a field telegram was found on one of the Turkish dead; on it

[21] The *London Gazette* of 23rd March 1917 posted the following announcement detailing the award of F.V.B.W.'s Military Cross: 'For conspicuous gallantry and coolness. Under heavy rifle and machine gun fire he made a personal reconnaissance of the river bank, and subsequently led a party of his men carrying a pontoon across the open and down the bank. Although wounded himself, and in spite of casualties among his party, which made the task increasingly difficult, he succeeded, in full view of the enemy, in launching the pontoon.'

[22] F.V.B.W. may have had a case of the 'Baghdad Boil': 'a most dispiriting and undecorative affliction' according to Major Evans, author of *A Brief Outline of the Campaign in Mesopotamia* (p. 8).

was written in Turkish, 'The Corps Commander kisses the eyes of all ranks and thanks them.' As General Maude turned his attention to the Hai Salient, the Turks braced themselves to defend it with equal resolve, despite the same negligible chances of success.

On his return to his unit at Atab, on the Shatt-al-Hai, Captain Witts was relieved to discover that little had been done in his absence. It was unlikely that General Maude would consider another attempt to bridge the Tigris until the Hai Salient had been cleared of all Turkish forces. In the meantime, No. 2 Mobile Bridging Train was busily employed in maintaining the bridge on the Shatt-al-Hai, which, by this stage, had swelled to a respectable size.

F.V.B. Witts
    Capt. R. E.

No 2 Bridging Train
Mesopotamia Exp: Force
[Atab]
16-1-17

Dearest Mother.

Here I am back again, and Farley, who came over in my absence, has returned to No 4 Coy with Bird, who are now up in these parts.

I left Amara on the evening of the 10th, had a very comfortable journey, reached Sheikh Saad on the morning of the 12th, & spent the day there, staying with friends. I came on next morning by train to G.H.Q. where I lunched with the Engineer-in-Chief and afterwards the Army Commander pinned the Military Cross ribbon on, and gave me the printed Order of the Day, which I am sending you for your private use only. Please keep it for me. From there they sent me on here in a motor car, and now I am gradually getting in to the swing of things again.

They have been very busy in my absence, and have had a very trying time, although actually they have done very little, and I have missed nothing which pleases me.

I found here all the missing mails, but have hardly had time to open the papers: how I wish I could have got them in hospital.

I am very annoyed, as, through my being taken away to hospital, my men have hitherto got no reward for their bravery, and I am afraid they will now have to wait a long time, if they ever get, the recognition they deserve. I am quite ashamed to be wearing a ribbon, while they have nothing to show for it.

I have missed some very wet unpleasant days, but unfortunately we have not yet had anything like our full share of rain, and so we have to expect some more rotten times.

The river came down in very heavy flood, but in spite of some difficulties, no actual damage was done to our bridges.

57. Hospital Barges.

No more news.
    Very best love,
        Your ever loving Son,
            Fred.V. B.Witts

F.V.B.Witts
    Capt. R. E.

                         No 2 Bridging Train
                               [Atab]
                             Jan 24th 1917.

Dearest Mother.

    No news since I last wrote and no other mail has reached me yet. But I think it is time for a letter.

    We have remained in our same camp [at Atab, on the Hai], and now have got up the heavy bit which we left behind when operations started and so are much more comfortable. Our work is now all on the Hai, which has been falling rapidly since the recent flood, involving constant changes to the bridges. Half our lot accompanied the Cavalry on their visit to Hai town the other day, and returned just after I got back.[23]

    We have had very good weather for the time of the year, compared with this time last year, though a heavy thunderstorm broke the night before last and rain continued for ten hours, but it is drying very rapidly.

    My arm is better, but it will be a long time before the thumb is all right again. I live

---

[23] The sappers of No. 2 Mobile Bridging Train had accompanied a cavalry detachment on a routine expedition to buy stocks of grain from the residents of Hai town, 20 miles down the Shatt-al-Hai. Upon arrival, they were greeted amicably and were given no trouble in carrying out their task. Three days later, however, when the column began its return journey, the character of the local Arabs completely changed. For reasons unknown, they pursued and attacked the detachment for several miles, incurring roughly 150 casualties upon themselves and 24 on the British and Indian troops (Moberly, F. J., *The Mesopotamia Campaign*, vol. III p. 103). As a punishment, General Maude later sent an aerial bombardment on Hai town. The episode demonstrated the capricious nature of the Arabs in Mesopotamia – a trait which would cause many problems for the British after the war.

in daily peril of dropping a plate at meals, as I cannot lift the thumb over the edge; the only other trouble I have is opening a tightly fastened envelope. Neither point much to worry about!

The doctor massages it for me every evening, which is very comforting!

We have been giving the Turks a tremendous dose of Artillery lately, and they are not in a position to reply to it.[24]

They have already circulated a paper talking about leave next hot weather. But as I went last year, I am afraid I shall not get a look in, unless I go sick which I have no reason to expect.

No more news.
Very best love,
    Your ever loving Son,
      Fred. V. B. Witts

[Atab]
Feb 3rd 1917.

Dearest Mother.

I have been putting off writing three or four days in the hope of getting an English mail. At last one has come in with all the usual papers and your letter of Dec 19th; one mail came in a few days ago with the previous week's papers but no letters: I am afraid they must have sent them to Amara.

Like you I write every week, but posts down river are irregular and one never knows which day to post, so that frequently one's letters miss the mail. I expect it is the same with you, and accounts for the long breaks without letters.

I see you talk about snow. There is snow now within sight of our camps on the higher parts of the Pusht-i-Kuh – the mountains on the Persian border. We had a very cold snap at the end of January and for two mornings there was ¼ inch of ice on the water in the buckets. We seized our opportunity and had iced fruit for lunch! It is most unusual in this country.

The night before my birthday we were out all night rafting heavy guns across. Next night there was a thunderstorm, followed by a S.E. gale which developed into a hurricane, blowing our bridges into a curve upstream. No damage was suffered, but the most exposed was out of action for a few hours as it was rocking about so much that it was impossible to stand up on it.

On the 1st they turned us out at short notice to put another bridge across the Hai; we were shorthanded and it kept us fully employed.

[24] Whereas Kiazim had a total of 66 guns to defend Kut, Maude had 174 guns at his disposal,.

Yesterday they gave us still shorter notice to send out a detachment elsewhere.[25] So you see that we don't know for five minutes on end, what is going to turn up next.

Every one very fit and pleased with themselves.

No more news
   Very best love,
      Your ever loving Son,
         Fred. V. B. Witts

On the 4th February 1917, the Turks were finally prised from their trenches on the Hai Salient. They retreated to a weaker position spread across the shallow curve of the Tigris known as the Dahra bend, just upstream of Kut.

Monumental improvements to river communications, infrastructure, port efficiency and medical facilities had breathed new life into Force 'D'; under the capable, measured leadership of General Maude, they had already regained much of the prestige lost at Ctesiphon and Kut. Nothing, however, could be taken for granted. Kiazim Karabekir was still sheltered behind the formidable defences of Sannaiyat and the Tigris; to succeed where the Tigris Corps had repeatedly failed, despite their unshakeable commitment, was going to take something extraordinary.

At Brick Kilns, No. 2 Mobile Bridging Train had, if little else, proved their courage and dedication beyond any doubt. Their true moment of glory, however, was yet to come.

---

[25] A detachment of sappers with six pontoons was sent with the Cavalry Division to ferry them across the Husainiya canal on their way to shell Imam Mahdi, a Turkish supply base, 17 miles upstream of Kut. As it happened, the canal was dry, but the sappers put their pontoons to good use nonetheless, filling them with two dozen sheep (from an unknown source) to provide the bridging train with quite a feast on their return. (Witts, F. V. B., *Light Floating Bridges*, Appendix I, p. 431).

CHAPTER IV

THE SHUMRAN CROSSING

Letters: Feb 11th –Mar 4th 1917

'Enigmatic' is probably the most commonly used adjective describing General Maude's approach to commanding Force 'D'; there is no better example of this characteristic than in his dealings with Captain Witts in the run-up to the Shumran crossing. On the 5th February, Captain Witts was summoned by the Army Commander for a private interview at G.H.Q.

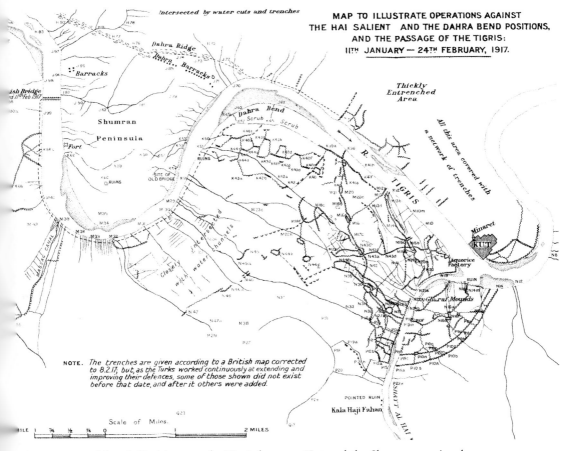

MAP TO ILLUSTRATE OPERATIONS AGAINST THE HAI SALIENT AND THE DAHRA BEND POSITIONS, AND THE PASSAGE OF THE TIGRIS: 11TH JANUARY — 24TH FEBRUARY, 1917.

NOTE. The trenches are given according to a British map corrected to 8.2.17, but, as the Turks worked continuously at extending and improving their defences, some of those shown did not exist before that date, and after it others were added.

Map 4. Positions on the Tigris between Kut and the Shumran peninsula.

---

[1] Even Brigadier Beach R.E., head of the Intelligence Branch in Mesopotamia, was kept in the dark.

I was much surprised at being sent for, and still more so at being sworn to absolute secrecy, being particularly warned against whispering a word of what he was going to say to even the most senior members of his staff.[1] He told me what he wanted and added that my reports were to be made in private letters addressed to him personally by name.[2]

Maude's overall plan at this stage is not certain as his attention to secrecy and predilection for handling matters personally have led to wide gaps in official records. His instructions to Captain Witts, however, were to take soundings (depth measurements) of the Shatt al Hai at its junction with the Tigris to establish whether landing parties could be loaded onto motor launches within the mouth of the Hai, and then rushed across the Tigris in an assault on the Kut peninsula. Remarkably, Captain Witts' original reconnaissance reports have survived, as have General Maude's private field telegrams.[3]

FIRST SECRET RECONNAISANCE REPORT FROM CAPTAIN WITTS TO GENERAL MAUDE, 5TH FEBRUARY 1917:

I reconnoitred the TIGRIS last night from the mouth of the HAI down to below N12, sounding the channel skimming near the right bank. The sandbank opposite the Ruin was shewing above water in patches. The channel here is very narrow and it is not safe to count on more than 3ft of water with the TIGRIS gauge at 106, which is practically the same level as when I made my first reconnaissance of the HAI. The channel gradually improves and below N14a [half a mile west of the Hai mouth] there is ample depth and width. If the river rises another 2'6', there should be no peculiar difficulty in navigating this channel upstream, as all you have to do is keep as near the bank as the depth admits. Coming downstream would be less reliable as a slight mistake and you might be carried round broadside across the channel and jam across it. It is quite possible that further floods may shift the sandbanks nearer to the right bank and otherwise alter the channel.

I think that there is very little chance of navigating round the north of this sandbank, because it is impossible to mark the channel and there would be nothing to steer by, and because when taking the two sharp turns to make the mouth of the HAI there is very grave risk of being carried by the stream broadside on to the bank. I did not attempt to find a sound [in] this channel. Although dark it was a very still night and one sniper apparently heard us and fired a few shots in our direction near the RUIN: otherwise it was absolutely quiet.

---

[1] Even Brigadier Beach R.E., head of the Intelligence Branch in Mesopotamia, was kept in the dark.

[2] Witts, F. V. B., *Light Floating Bridges* (Appendix I, p. 431).

[3] Copies of the original documents can be found in Appendix VI.

GENERAL MAUDE'S REPLY TO CAPTAIN WITTS' REPORT OF NIGHT OF 5ᵀᴴ FEBRUARY 1917:

<u>SECRET</u>

General Headquarters,
I. E. F. 'D'.
6ᵗʰ February, 1917.

My dear *Witts*

Many thanks for your report received late last night.

I have been busy with many other things this morning, and so have not had the time to answer it before this.

I shall be glad if you will go on with the soundings of the HAI between the points mentioned.

The river has gone up 2½-feet during the last 24 hours and this will materially affect the plans which I have in mind. As long as I know the date on which you carry out your reconnaissance I can always add on the extra rise of the river in making calculations later. As regards the portion of the TIGRIS where I want you to take soundings, that is between the mouth of the HAI and, say, N.12 [roughly ¾s of a mile west of the Hai mouth, on the Tigris]. This will be easier possibly in a day or two when we have further developed our positions west of the HAI,[4] and I can let you know further about this when I receive your notes as regards the HAI.

Yrs sincerely
F. S. Maude

To:

Captain F.V. B. Witts, M.C.,
O.C., No. 2 Bridging Train.

SECOND SECRET RECONNAISANCE REPORT FROM CAPTAIN WITTS TO GENERAL MAUDE, EARLY HOURS OF 7ᵀᴴ FEBRUARY 1917:

I went out yesterday afternoon on receipt of your instructions. I had hoped to be able to work by daylight, but found that, with the rise in the river level, the banks no longer afforded cover from view to a boat moving about in midstream, and that we should be easily seen by an observer either in the Liquorice Factory and Bazaar alongside, or from the palm trees N.W. of KUT, so I judged it was desirable to wait till dark. While waiting at P14,3 [on the Hai], during our intense bombardment at 6 p.m. a Turkish shell scored a direct hit on my pontoon; luckily we were all under cover at the time and only one half of the pontoon was smashed up. Half a pontoon

---

[4] The Turks were still firmly established on the right bank of the Tigris at the Dahra bend.

is awkward to work with, and this subsequently greatly delayed my work, and I did not get back till 1a.m. this morning. The pontoon was seen but I think the shell was meant for neighbouring batteries, though several more shells fell within 50yds of the pontoon. I was afterwards informed that the same had been shelled in the morning.

After consulting the local regimental head quarters I eventually got up to a point midway between N21b and N21d [at the mouth of the Hai] and sounded the channel down to P10f. The minimum depth of channel I found in this reach wide enough for the purpose, was 9 feet at about 10 p.m. It follows the channel as shown in T.C.75(A) from N21b to N23a, but between N23a and P10f it is a little further back towards the centre of the river.

After the experience gained last night I hope to complete the HAI in better time as soon as I hear that we are established on its right bank up to the junction with the TIGRIS.

GENERAL MAUDE'S REPLY TO CAPTAIN WITTS' REPORT OF 7TH FEBRUARY 1917:[5]

> General Headquarters,
> I. E. F. 'D'.
> 7th February, 1917.

My dear *Witts*

Many thanks for your letter dated 7th.

I am very sorry to hear of your unpleasant experience, but pleased that the results were no worse.

I do not want you to run any unnecessary risks in carrying out further reconnaissance, and so do not hurry about it till you are quite satisfied that the conditions locally render your movements in that area tolerably safe.

If any doubtful point arises, drop me a line.

> *Yrs sincerely*
> F. S. Maude

To:
Captain F. V. B. Witts, M.C.,
    O.C., No. 2 Bridging Train.

Captain Witts later wrote 'paddling about in a pontoon for two or three nights, with the Turks on one bank and our troops on the other, was no joke, and though the river was 400 to 600 yards wide, I was not sorry when I was in a

---

[5] *See* appendix VI.

position to report the scheme impracticable.'[6] Obstructive sandbanks and the strength of the Tigris current had scuppered Maude's idea for an amphibious assault to be launched from the mouth of the Hai. Captain Witts was now directed to begin searching for a suitable bridge site on the 10 mile stretch of river between Kut and Maqasis fort.

On the 9th February, whilst out reconnoitring the river bank, Captain Witts received urgent orders from General Marshall, commander of the IIIrd Corps, to prepare his sappers to row an assault party across the Tigris in a raid on the Kut peninsula that very night. Marshall had intended the amphibious assault, involving only one battalion of infantry, to divert attention from his main attack on Turkish positions at the Dahra bend. The scheme, however, had not been devised carefully; most of the bridging train's sappers had never even picked up an oar before and the prospect of them rowing a cumbersome pontoon overloaded with infantry across a wide, fast flowing channel under intense enemy fire was horrendous. In desperation, Captain Witts urged General Marshall to give him more time to train his men. To his intense relief, however, an intervention by General Maude, subtly suggesting to Marshall that investigations into crossing the Tigris were already underway, put paid to the whole scheme. Slightly bewildered by the extent of Maude's furtiveness, General Marshall turned his full attention back to the IIIrd Corps' bombardment of the Dahra bend. Captain Witts, meanwhile, resumed his reconnaissance downstream of Kut.

F.V.B.Witts
    Capt. R.E.

[Atab]
Feb 11th 1917.

Dearest Mother.

Just got your letter of Christmas Day. I am so very sorry to hear I was the cause of such an anxious and unhappy Christmas for you. It was most unfortunate that no particulars got through with the original news.

I sent you a cable on Dec 24th as soon as I got down to Amara, which was my first opportunity, but I am afraid it got hung up a day or two at Basra. Did I ever thank you for your cable wishing me a speedy recovery? I have now lost all the stiffness out of my arm, but have not yet recovered complete use of my thumb and forefinger, and I am afraid this will be a very long process, however it doesn't really matter as it doesn't make any serious difference in any important respect.

I have also had another mail with papers up to Jan 4th, but no letters with them. I am very pleased indeed to see in the Times that Frank has got the Military Cross,

---

[6] Witts, F. V. B., *Light Floating Bridges* (Appendix I, p. 431).

58. A Turkish cannon.

as he has had the worst time of any of us.[7] He beat me by a short head! Also Percy Henderson, who was killed, and many other of my friends.

Did I tell you that your missing letter of Dec 12th had arrived after doing a circular tour round this country! So now I have had everything and nothing is missing.

We have been having a restless time since I last wrote, with various wild schemes flying round[8] and ourselves under orders of instant readiness, but nothing has come of it all so far.

I have been doing some reconnaissances, and one evening had my pontoon knocked out by a direct hit from a Turkish Shell; luckily we were all under cover at the time, and the shell also knocked out a 38lb Tigris salmon, which we managed to catch before it had time to recover from the shock of the explosion.[9]

The weather has kept fine and the last two days, there has been a regular dust storm, but this evening it has turned to rain, which will be welcome in moderation, but moderation is a thing unknown in this country.

> With very best love,
>   Your ever loving Son,
>   Fred.V.B.Witts.

[7] Frank Witts (F.V.B.W.'s youngest brother), of the Irish Guards, had been in some of the thickest fighting on the Western Front since the start of the war. He had been wounded in December 1914 and would be wounded twice again before the war had ended. He was awarded his M.C. for valour on 2nd October 1916, fighting on the Somme.

[8] On the 8th February, Maude had proposed crossing two infantry battalions on four motor-launches just above the Sannaiyat position. General Cobbe, however, commander of the Ist Corps entrenched opposite Sannaiyat, had advised against the scheme, reporting that portion of the river to be too strongly defended to suit a crossing. It was widely believed that Maude never actually intended to go through with his idea, it simply being one of his numerous schemes to mislead the Turks, although F.V.B.W. later describes him as sometimes having 'mad ideas' (Nov 25th 1917, p. 202).

[9] F.V.B.W. neglected to mention this in his official report to General Maude on February 7th.

Captain Witts was able to keep only three of his mother's letters during wartime, but many more after the armistice. Those that have survived have been inserted in chronological order. The three letters below were received on the 14ᵗʰ April 1917 at Sinija, on the Tigris, 45 miles north of Baghdad. After these, the next surviving letter is dated August 12ᵗʰ 1919.

59. Mrs Margaret Witts (F.V.B.W.'s mother).

Captain F.V.B. Witts R.E.
No. 2. Bridging Train
I.K.G.O. Sappers & Miners
Mesopotamia Ex. Force.

THE MANOR,
UPPER SLAUGHTER,
GLOS.

Feb 13.1917

Dearest Fred –

Your letters & P.C. were so precious to me as I said last. I wonder if the mails will ever reach you now. There seems a lot of fighting & I am anxious for news: shall be glad when the censor lets some through. I told Collett about George[10] – he was working at carpentry all thru but now has 'joined up'. George [Witts] came unexpectedly on Sunday for 2 nights & has gone. He looks so much better & is quite himself[11] not passed for Foreign Service but now attached to Service training Batt & may move his Camp so came on. The roof of his hut was blown off one night & no water for his men – all frozen. We have had 26 ½ degrees –it has been bitter. Frank is going his rounds of informations and may be back any day – it is thawing at last. Edward has lost several ewes, they are all tired out. Agnes & Jack seem to get a ride on the hills every now & again when off duty.[12] Are you going for Bagdad? Or what?

---

[10] F.V.B.W. had spotted George Collett's name on the books at hospital in Amara (Jan 3ʳᵈ 1917, p. 128).

[11] George Witts had been gassed and suffered shell shock in the trenches on the Western Front. Their effects sadly lingered on throughout his life.

[12] At this point Agnes was in Salonika, working as an ambulance driver. Jack was clearly there also, but details are unknown.

Things are in a mess & the Devil is certainly loose in the Kaiser. Longley[13] is ill & we had no services all Sunday – Alice still unable to move Dr Moore will get her to Bath as soon as he can. Edith & I grumbling along. Dick Hamilton's cos a lad of 17 is here helping Edith he is a good shot & has killed 10 pidgeons in the garden they have deserted Eyford for us! Dick goes to Sandhurst next year. The yearling stands 15 hands Pittaway says it will be 17 before he has done – How I wish I could see you dearest love

      Your loving Mother
      MHB Witts

60. Agnes Witts (F.V.B.W.'s youngest sister). France 1918.

Telegrams: Upper Slaughter.
Station: Bourton-on-the-Water. G.W.R.

THE MANOR,
UPPER SLAUGHTER,
GLOS.

Feb:15.1917

Dearest Fred,

Your dear letter of Jan 10th with your birthday present has just arrived, it is far more than you ought to give me. God bless you. What an escape you had. Thank God for it indeed & may he guard you through it all & bring you safe back to me. Your letters of Dec 26th came yesterday Feb 14th after I had posted mine to you, & evidently written the same time as the P.C. which I had a fortnight ago![14] All particulars are so interesting. You certainly managed Xmas Day well & fancy a stocking & cake!! Edith & I were quite dull with the war office wire & no other news till Jan[y] 6 I went to bed before then [Dr] Moore said Flue I say anxiety as I have never felt bad. However I am well and been twice to Chelt: to Aunt Sybil for 2 or 3 days. Alice is still here to add to ones worries poor thing too weak to move in this severe cold. We have had snow & frost 26 ½ degrees & now a billowing N.E. wind- it was nice on Tuesday and I took George to Dowdeswell as he came for 48 hours in a friend's car with a chain on – too much snow to get mine back from Chelt yet – no petrol after April so I shall not run

<hr>

[13] *See* Chapter II, p. 93, note 14.

[14] Evidently, the postal service going from Mesopotamia to England was as haphazard as it was coming the other way, although it is remarkable that, with the sheer volume of correspondence and the constant threat of U-boats in the Mediterranean, so many letters did finally reach their destination.

mine but use the Ford which Edith can drive. I had a P.C. from your 2 men thanking for Galattes[15] addressed to BW Esq – I am glad you get them all, only wish I could send mittens & anything else – Yes I <u>am</u> so glad about the M.C. you have earned it right well & as to your dear face I am thankful you never had a mark on your skin so it must have been some poison somewhere. I hope you may get all the letters & paper in time as there are lots of them. Pittaway is just going to put a new mouthing bit I have bought into the yearling's mouth for the first time I pity him!!

You were plucky to ride down to Amara & that jolting must have been horrid. I hope the new boat is a good one – & really comfortable – you will be in Kut I suppose I see the Liquorice Factory is there. The picture in the Bystander of Feby 14 about the Kaiser is splendid – even Hell wont have the truth. I ordered a new Dressing Case box at Chelt: & I shall buy it with your money & spend a little more on it mine was really shabby – I use your fur muff every day at my writing table & that shall come out of it! God bless you for your goodness to your old Mother. Longley is very ill & in bed – no services on Sunday the same at Iccomb, the weather knocks everyone up. I am sorry you are in for floods – did you ever get the waistcoat I sent out?[16] The mails are not put in the paper so I don't know when they go but I always write on a Tuesday & this is extra. Your letters of Jany 3 reached me Feb 6th before the Dec 26th just come I am glad you found some friends at Amara – Did I tell you Sweet Escott wrote me a nice letter,[17] but he was <u>not</u> the happy Father – he was glad of your address & said he should write to you. I am sorry about your thumb – rub it sometimes as that is massage & will do it good – rub it quietly up & down. Frank writes leave is stopped & the cold intense he is going back to H.Q. no news yet of Edward Jack or Agnes. I fear all mails may be stopped thanks to the Huns. Dearest love & God preserve you

      Yr loving old Mother
      M.H. Broome Witts

Have you had a Xmas card from me? Or birthday letter?

THE MANOR,
UPPER SLAUGHTER,
GLOS.

Feb 20.1917
Dearest Fred,

I answered your long & delightful letter & good wishes & all, but Tuesday is my day & I cannot miss. Thank you for all your love & goodness to your old Mother – God will bless you for it & preserve you for me.

---

[15] F.V.B.W. had requested four F & M Christmas hampers in his letter of 10th July 1916 (p. 97-8)– two for himself and one for each of his sergeants.

[16] F.V.B.W. had acknowledged his receipt of the Credem lifejacket in his letter of 10th July 1916, p. 97-8.

[17] See Appendix V.

Did you ever get a cable I sent to you at Amara, it was only 'Best wishes for speedy recovery' & the Red X in London sent it for me. Do send me a cable if you ever can after a fight as the papers say much is doing up your ways. Here we have at last a thaw & rain – so I got to Bourton yesterday the first time since Nov: Apphie asked me to have Geoffrey [F.V.B.W.'s nephew] – Winchester is shut down for Pneumonia & mumps – no nurses to be had – so he came. Marlborough is also shut down for measles & what next will happen! We are all on rations – Aunt Maggie dines off bread & cheese oatcakes & gingerbread & eats her meat in the middle of the day! I have little news. Archdeacon Scohill's death is a great loss – a old friend of 50 years. He passed away in his sleep just like Father – I expect he knows & his

61. Geoffrey Woodroffe (F.V.B.W.'s nephew) at Winchester.

guardian Angel watches over you – I will post you a local paper as there is a good picture of Archdeacon Scohill in it: your God Father. The yearling has had the bit in his mouth & was quite quiet he is a fine young animal 15 hands already. I hope you may get home by Xmas or next year – will not your 5 years of Indian service be up? Shall I get your magazines bound if I can? dearest love God bless you

      Yr loving Mother
      MHB Witts

Back in Mesopotamia, the strength of Turkish resistance was beginning to wither. After days of relentless artillery bombardment, a full scale infantry assault on the Dahra bend on the 15th February triggered a mass surrender, finally clearing the right bank of Turkish forces. General Maude now wanted to drive his advantage home; on the morning of the 16th, he issued orders for the 7th Division, entrenched at Sannaiyat, to prepare for an assault for the following day. On the right bank, meanwhile, he telegraphed Captain Witts.

MESSAGES, SIGNALS AND FIELD TELEGRAPHS.

To   No 2 Bridging Train 16/2/17

    AAA Bridging Train commander will reconnoitre suitable sites for bridge over TIGRIS between K51 and M29 [the eastern side of the Shumran peninsula] reference TC62B .K55 approaches thereto. aaa He will take with him someone he can send back to lead Train forward when required aaa acknowledge

From   3rd Corps 8.40 a.m

General Maude's specification that Captain Witts should take a runner on his reconnaissance suggested that he was expecting a bridge to be built immediately. For Captain Witts, the greatest lesson to come out of the debacle at Brick Kilns was that meticulous preparation would be essential to the success of any future bridging attempt. It was with a good deal of apprehension that Captain Witts carried out his orders.

MESSAGES, SIGNALS AND FIELD TELEGRAPHS.

To 3ʳᵈ Corps   16/2/17

AAA Reconnaissance of bridging sites between M29 and K51 *AAA* Good partly covered approach to M29 where guns now action only minor improvements needed *AAA* Opposite front M31 to 300 yards North of K55 Turks have new loopholed bunds and sniping prevents proper inspection of foreshore *AAA* At K51 banks are vertical and river broad but no sniping and possible to go down to water *AAA* No covered approaches here and little work is needed to make road across open *AAA* Am staying out till dusk to make a more complete reconnaissance in neighbour hood of M29 and K55[18]

From O.C. Bridging Train 2.30p.m.

Having conceded that the eastern side of the Shumran bend offered feasible bridging sites, Captain Witts was dreading the order to move into position. For once, however, the weather came as a blessing; a torrential rainfall scuppered any plans for an immediate crossing, 'undoubtedly playing,' according to Witts, 'an important part in the [eventual] success of the crossing, as the time was utilised to organise every detail and practice on the Hai.'[19] While his men got on with their rehearsals, Captain Witts continued his careful reconnaissance of the Shumran bend.

MESSAGES, SIGNALS AND FIELD TELEGRAPHS.

To 3ʳᵈ Corps   17/2/17

AAA Continuation my X of 16ᵗʰ *AAA* Suitable places for launching pontoons exist

[18] K55 was the site of the old Turkish boat bridge.

[19] Witts, F. V. B., *The Passage of the Tigris at Shumran*, (Appendix II, p. 440).

just North of M29 and just South of K55 *AAA* In each case considerable preparation cutting through bunds and filling trenches required *AAA* Ramp of old Turkish bridge 200 yards North of K55 also available but steep and constricted trenches require filling here too *AAA* Yesterday evening's rain converted sunken approach to M29 into stream *AAA* Road from N40 to sites would have to be selected and filled *AAA* Both nullahs [steep narrow valleys] near Q15 require considerable improvement and were quite impassable for us last night

---

From O.C. Bridging Train 9a.m.

On the left bank, meanwhile, despite the weather delaying any chance of a crossing at Shumran, the planned assault on Sannaiyat was ordered to go ahead. For the fourth time, British and Indian troops, this time the 7th Division, charged headlong over the narrow patch of no man's land and into the spray of Turkish bullets and cascading shellfire. For the fourth time, they were repulsed. Turkish grit had held, and their faith in their defences had not subsided with the downturn in morale following the surrender at the Dahra bend. For the British, however, the attack had not been a complete failure. It persuaded Kiazim that Sannaiyat would be the principal target in General Maude's effort to push through to Kut. As Turkish troops were hurried away from Shumran to reinforce Sannaiyat, Maude ordered intermittent bombardments on the position to strengthen Kiazim's mistaken resolve; meanwhile, in eagerness to launch the true attack, he urged Captain Witts to conclude his reconnaissance at Shumran.[20]

MESSAGES, SIGNALS AND FIELD TELEGRAPHS.

To No 2 Bridging Train 18/2/17   *SECRET*

AAA Please report early today whether M34 is suitable as site for Bridge aaa please reconnoitre attracting as little attention as possible aaa the river bank is held by us up to M39 and thence our line follows NAHR-AL-MASSAG [an ancient canal running south from the Tigris] aaa acknowledge and confirm appropriate earliest hour report will be expected today

---

From 3rd Corps   6.22a.m.

Later that day, Captain Witts sent a report of his findings to Maude, confirming his discovery of a suitable bridging site.

---

[20] Copies of the original telegraphs are in Appendix VII.

MESSAGES, SIGNALS AND FIELD TELEGRAPHS.

To 3rd Corps   18/2/17

AAA Suitable site exists about two hundred yards downstream of point mentioned *AAA* Work on ramps and immediate approaches about average *AAA* Road marked to vicinity but at present very heavy going *AAA* From Q13 to N47a road requires remarking in places as some original nullah crossings are impassable *AAA* S13 direct road to Q13 runs through Lake for half a mile

---

From No 2 Bridging Train 2.45p.m.

The site selected by Captain Witts was on the apex of the Shumran bend (*see* map at the beginning of the chapter) where the Tigris was estimated to be roughly 340 yards wide and the far bank consisted of a gentle mud slope, ideal for bridging. As Captain Witts intimated in his report, the near bank, consisting of a small cliff, would have to be cut into ramps to facilitate the launching of pontoons. From a military aspect, the site allowed for converging artillery fire to be concentrated on the loopholed trenches and enemy machine gun emplacements across the river.

Before the bridging train could begin construction, a bridgehead had to be established on the opposite bank. Three points were selected (M.32, M.31 & M.30) downstream of the bridging site as launches for assaulting parties to be ferried across to secure the bridgehead. A battalion of infantry was selected to cross at each point on ferries consisting of 13 pontoons, manned by a total of 825 volunteer rowers, providing four reliefs to allow for casualties and exhaustion.

Vigorous rehearsals by the bridging train and assault parties had been conducted on the Shatt-al-Hai throughout the bad weather, while, in the vicinity of the Shumran bend, General Maude had prohibited all daytime activity after the 19th February. Work on the artillery emplacements and bridging site was only performed after dark.

In the meantime, General Maude continued diligently with his schemes to mislead the Turk. From the 19th February, the muffled clunking of planks being unloaded and the faint creaking of heavy axles echoed across the Tigris from the Liquorice Factory, alerting the Turks to the possibility that preparations were being made for a bridge. By day, pontoons were left partially concealed, noticeable to the perceptive eye of a pilot, and lines of pontoons were towed down the Hai, inducing Turkish lookouts to draw natural conclusions.

Back at Shumran, night-time preparations at the bridge site had been continuing with alacrity. On the 21st February, rising river levels finally abated and Captain Witts sent the following report:

MESSAGES, SIGNALS AND FIELD TELEGRAPHS.

To   3rd Corps   21/2/17

AAA Reconnaissance report *AAA* Road to bridge site in good condition and well marked *AAA* Position of bridge fixed as reported in my 765 of 18th *AAA* With present river level very little work needed on ramps *AAA* Arrangements for launching motor boats decided on and may be successful[21] *AAA* River running very strong making bridge work slow and unreliable *AAA* Turks heard talking on bank opposite

From   No 2 Bridging Train   8.30a.m.

The crossing was fixed for the early hours of the 23rd February, by which time the water levels on the Tigris would have had a chance to fall. Maude's diversions, meanwhile, became even more elaborate, deceiving not only the Turks, but also some of his own most senior officers.

On the 19th February, General Cobbe, commander of the Ist Corps, received orders to attack Sannaiyat once again, stipulating that his assault was to be the decisive blow against the Turks while operations around Shumran were only aimed as a diversion. The opposite, in fact, was the truth, but Maude reasoned that the most convincing way to make a feint was to treat it as the real thing. The assault on Sannaiyat went ahead after three days of 'Chinese bombing', whereby the Turks continually braced themselves for an infantry assault which never transpired, depriving them of sleep and wearing down their nerves. Finally, on the morning of the 22nd February, the bombardments were followed through with a vigorous assault by the 7th Division, driving the Turks back from their first and second lines of defence and repelling all attempts to counter-attack. After so many bloody attempts, Sannaiyat's spell of invincibility had finally been broken.

That same night, another feint, a raid across the Tigris at the Maqasis bend, 10 miles downstream of Kut, also met with extraordinary success. Under cover of British artillery on the right bank, a small band of 100 Punjabis rowed across the Tigris and routed nearby Turkish posts, capturing a trench mortar, before returning to their pontoons and rowing back across the Tigris. To compound the Turks' confusion, the first light of dawn on the 23rd revealed

---

[21] Two armoured motor boats had been given to No .2 Mobile Bridging Train to tow anchoring pontoons into position against the strong current. The motor boats were to be hauled into launching positions on two heavy bullock-drawn wagons.

artillery towers, erected overnight, standing in the vicinity of the Liquorice Factory. Meanwhile, 7 miles upriver of Kut, at the Shumran bend, the main British attack had already begun.

An hour before sunset on the evening of 22nd February, the three ferrying columns and No. 2 Mobile Bridging Train set out from Besouia, on the Shatt-al-Hai, on a 5 mile night-march to their respective positions on the Shumran bend. There was a brief moment of despair when two hostile aeroplanes were spotted overhead in the fading light, but fortunately, they either failed to see the columns, or assumed them to be heading to the Liquorice Factory. Navigating by way of marked mounds of earth, the bridging train and the three infantry battalions all reached their launching sites unnoticed and without further incident. Ramps were dug into the bund at the bridge site to facilitate the launch of pontoons and motor-boats, but otherwise there was nothing more to do but wait, in nervous anticipation, for dawn.

At around 5.30a.m., the three assaulting parties quietly lowered their pontoons into the water and began their crossing. The 2nd Norfolks, the ferry closest to the bridge site, achieved absolute surprise. They immediately captured 300 Turks and five machine guns and successfully secured their drop-off point, allowing their rowers to go back and gather reinforcements. The 2/9th and 1/2nd Gurkha battalions of the other two ferries were less fortunate. The first was caught midstream in a maelstrom of enemy fire, while the second made it across to the left bank, but became isolated immediately with no prospect of reinforcements. Of the 26 pontoons composing these two ferries, only 5 managed a second trip across the river, arriving on the left bank with pontoons full of dead and wounded. With so many pontoons lost, reinforcements for these two ferries joined the Norfolks at M.32 where safe passage across the river had been secured.

At the bridge site, Captain Witts had been ready to start construction since about 6.30a.m. An hour later, despite the far bank still being in Turkish hands and crawling with snipers, he was ordered to begin building the bridge. The following is Captain Witts' own account of the event, written in 1923:

> Orders were given for the bridging train material to come up – the *personnel* had moved up earlier in the day. As previously arranged, the wagons and carts came up at full gallop at three hundred yards interval; they were rapidly unloaded and galloped off again. There was a deep dry canal at M32, two hundred yards or so below the bridge, similar to the one used by the bridging train at the Brick Kilns in December, and evidently the Turks thought we were going to use this one this time, as they kept up a steady stream of 5.9s on it all day. The bridging wagons had, therefore, only to run the gauntlet of the overs and none of them were hit. This is the more remarkable as the country was as flat as the rest of Mesopotamia, and devoid of cover except for the small river bund about three feet high, which,

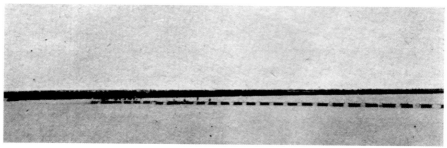

62. The Shumran Bridge.

of course, gave no cover whatever to wagons. The only assumption is that their arrangements for artillery observation were completely upset in the first few minutes.

The shore transom was placed in position and land anchorage fixed, while experiments were made as to rowing pontoons against the current; this was found impracticable. The first motor-boat was, therefore, ordered up, and it was a wonderful sight; towering as it did quite eleven feet in the air and visible for miles around, and drawn by sedate siege train bullocks, who ambled along as if nothing out of the ordinary was happening; it was a marvel to everyone present that they were never hit. The British field company undertook the launching and did it most successfully, though they had never had the opportunity of practising. As soon as the first motor-boat was in the water the second was ordered up and launched equally successfully.[22] All this time accurate sniping was kept up from the other bank and a number of casualties to man and mule suffered. But from now onwards the far bank was sufficiently cleared, and no more sniping occurred. The construction of the bridge went on in earnest.[23]

All further Turkish attempts to disrupt the bridge's steady construction came to no avail. High-explosive shells were launched but fell harmlessly into the water either side of the bridge; floating mines were sent downstream but never struck any cables or pontoons; warnings that a Turkish ship was steaming downstream on course for the bridge never materialised. Under Captain Witts' direction, the sappers of No. 2 Mobile Bridging Train worked at a feverish pace and the bridge quickly took shape. By the time construction was nearing an end, Turkish artillery had been pushed out of range of the bridge by the Norfolks and Gurkhas, who had been continually flooding onto the left bank via the ferry at M.32. At 4.30p.m., after 9 hours of bracing work by the Bridging Train, the Shumran Bridge, measuring 295 yards long, was opened for traffic. The 14th and 13th Divisions began pouring onto the

---

[22] The launching of the motor-boats was successful but handling them in the five knot current was a precarious task. On one occasion one of the motor-boats fouled the bridge, nearly causing a disaster.

[23] Witts, F. V. B., *The Passage of the Tigris at Shumran*, (Appendix II, p. 443-4).

left bank at once, and, by nightfall, a line a mile north of the bridge on the Shumran peninsula was held by General Marshall's men.

That evening, Captain Witts received the following wires, congratulating him and his unit on their great success:[24]

MESSAGES, SIGNALS AND FIELD TELEGRAPHS.

To   O C No 2 Bdg Train   23.2.17

AAA Gen Marshall wires hearty congratulations to you and all troops concerned on most successful crossing

From   Adv 14 Div

MESSAGES AND SIGNALS.

To   No 2 Bdg Train   23rd Feb 17   .

AAA Following wire from General Maude to General Marshall begins Tell your Corps how much I admire + thank them for their splendid work today aaa to cross River in flood in face of Enemy in position is feat to be really proud of ends

From   3rd Corps   9.40p.m.

In bridging the Tigris upstream of Kut, General Maude had haemorrhaged mortally the Turkish position. The next day, Khalil ordered a full scale retreat upriver. With characteristic tenacity, the Turks managed to hold the IIIrd Corps on an improvised line at the base of the Shumran peninsula, long enough for Kiazim to extricate the bulk of his force from Sannaiyat. During the night of the 24th February, the last of the Turks withdrew. General Maude was eager to mount an immediate pursuit all the way to Baghdad, but he was restrained by the expedient concerns of his staff, who were anxious that he would outrun communications and risk repeating the disaster of Ctesiphon. In compromise, Maude agreed to halt at Aziziyah, 65 miles up the Tigris by road, to allow communications to reorganise and catch up. In the meantime, a naval flotilla of five gunships (*Tarantula, Mantis, Moth, Gadfly* and *Butterfly*), under Captain W. Nunn, passed through the Shumran bridge at

---

[24] Copies of the original documents can be found in Appendix VIII.

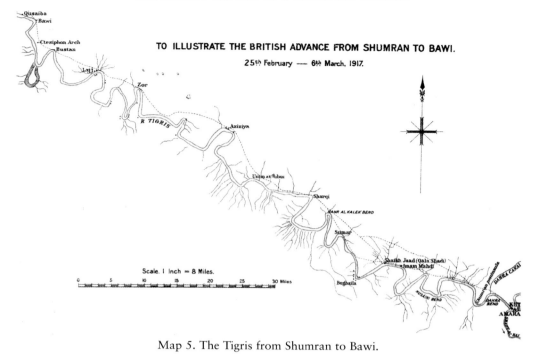

Map 5. The Tigris from Shumran to Bawi.

8a.m on the 25th (requiring Captain Witts and his unit to dismantle a portion of the bridge), and caught up with the Turkish rearguard at the Nahr Al Kalek bend, wreaking havoc amongst them with their guns.

Although he was very busy manning the bridge, the only crossing point for three divisions, a degree of normality had returned to Captain Witts' life; a week or so later, he finally found the time to write to his anxious mother.

F.V.B. Witts
     Capt.

No 2 Bridging Train
Mesopotamia Exp: Force
[Shumran]
March 4th 1917.

Dearest Mother.

It is, I am sorry to say, weeks since I last wrote; to try and make up for it I cabled to you on your birthday and again today to say we were all very fit and pleased with ourselves. The reason is we have been so busy playing a leading part in putting the Turk to flight, that we have been out of touch of any postal facilities: for the same reason it is weeks since we had any English mail.

I now quite forget when I last wrote and where I should take up the tale. However the phase I have to tell you about commenced on February 15th, when, following on our capture of the Dahra Bend with its 2000 prisoners, we were ordered out of our standing camp into bivouac on the far side of the Hai. Of course it rained very hard that evening and without tents it was most miserable. The whole of the next day and evening I was out reconnoitring various sites for a bridge on the newly occupied ground. That evening it hailed and rained even harder than on the previous night; I got soaked and returned to find our bivouac flooded out. Next day saw the whole country under water and all the roads impassable: we did our best to get dry and drain the ground.

The next few days were devoted to further reconnaissances and all necessary preparations for forcing the passage of the Tigris. As a result of the heavy rain the river came down in high flood on the 20th, and bridging prospects did not look hopeful. Operations were postponed one day until it had stopped rising, and finally on the night of Feb 22nd, we marched up close to the river bank and waited till morning. As soon as a covering party had rowed itself across and established itself, we started to build our bridge and got it done in 9 hours. To start with there was considerable sniping and six of my men were wounded, and later on they got on to us with their guns, but our luck was in and though shells were falling each side of the bridge nothing hit us. The very strong current running made it all slow work and we should never have got it done but for two motorboats which we brought up on wagons. Every one was very pleased with our performance, and we were the centre of congratulations and thanks from all the generals and every one else. The men worked extraordinarily well and getting it through certainly put the lid on the Turks. For the next three days, troops, guns and transport poured across, and the bridge carried more traffic than all the other Tigris bridges put together since the beginning of the war. Accidents were inevitable, but nothing serious occurred though several wagons were lost overboard.

On February 27th the Army Commander (General Maude) arrived on his steamer,[25] and next evening I was summoned to dine with him, when he personally thanked and congratulated us on our work. He gave me a very good dinner, and was evidently very pleased with us.

March 1st I was ordered to send on a detachment at once, so Eastmond has gone on ahead,[26] and I am sitting alone on the bridge we built with half my men opening and shutting it in endeavours to meet the conflicting claims of road and river traffic. Quite a reversion to the manner in which I spent the last hot weather, but this time I have our Doctor [Captain C. A. Wood, M.C., I.M.S] and one of my transport officers to keep me company. The Army has passed on,[27] and after having been living in the

[25] Advanced G.H.Q. was moved up to Shumran.

[26] Eastmond's detachment went to join the IIIrd Corps at Aziziyah and from there continue to Zor, a further 20 miles up the Tigris by road.

[27] The Naval flotilla, Cavalry Division and IIIrd Corps were concentrated at Aziziyah, while the Ist Corps were camped around the Nahr al Kalek bend, 30 miles upstream of Shumran by road.

limelight for the last ten weeks, culminating in a show peculiar to ourselves, we have now fallen back forgotten into the background. I have now no excuse for not writing, but the post offices have not been reorganised yet, so there will be delays.

I am very fit, and it is a great load off my mind that we have successfully accomplished the special task for which we were organised at the beginning of last December – to bridge the Tigris behind the Turkish positions on the left bank. After our misfire in December, when I got hit, and the absence of any material progress for the next two months; I had begun to doubt if we should ever get across, and the anticipation and waiting was beginning to tell.[28]

Very best love and good wishes
　　Your ever loving Son
　　　　Fred. V. B. Witts.

In a campaign that had fluctuated between extremes of success and disaster, the point at which the tables were swung irrevocably in favour of the British can be pinned down to one operation: the Shumran crossing. It was the culmination, on the one hand, of a year's intensive labour and vast expense to readdress and rebuild the very foundations of the campaign, and on the other, of great leadership, unquestionable commitment and exceptional skill. In the words of Lieutenant-Colonel E. W. Sandes R.E., the Shumran crossing was a 'carefully planned and boldly executed operation which deserves a prominent place in military history.'[29] In the context of the Mesopotamian Campaign, it was the beginning of the end for the Turks.

64. Baghdad looking upstream.

[28] See appendices IX, X & XI for letters to Mrs Witts congratulating her on F.V.B.W.'s success at Shumran.

[29] Sandes, E. W., *The Indian Sappers and Miners*, p. 487.

CHAPTER V

THE CAPTURE OF BAGHDAD

Letters: March 9th – Sept. 16th 1917

Khalil Pasha, the Turkish Commander-in-Chief, was ill-prepared for a reversal of any sort on the Tigris. While his faith in Kut's natural defences had been absolute, he had ignored Kiazim's warnings about the revival of British strength and his need for reinforcements. Now, in the face of General Maude's advancing army, he was gripped by panic and indecision. Three precious days were wasted while Khalil deliberated on whether to try and save Baghdad, or to retreat to a stronger strategic position. In the end, a sense of obligation, rather than strategy, swayed his decision; after 350 years of continuous Ottoman rule, the humiliation of surrendering Baghdad without a fight would be insufferable.

On the Shumran bend, Captain Witts had been instructed to supervise the bridge while his subaltern, Lieutenant Eastmond, marched north with a detachment of the bridging train, at the head of the IIIrd Corps' advance up the left bank. The first obstruction encountered en route to Baghdad was the Diyala River, a tributary of the Tigris stretching north-north-east into Southern Kurdistan. Brigadier-General O'Dowda, commanding the IIIrd Corps advanced party, gave orders for an immediate crossing on pontoons of the 120yd channel; but Turkish riflemen lined up on the opposite bank, made short work of the attackers who were completely vulnerable in their pontoons. Two crossing attempts were made, sustaining heavy casualties in each, with little to show for it. Eventually, the threat of being cut off by British forces advancing up the right bank of the Tigris precipitated a Turkish withdrawal. With a bridgehead secured, Eastmond and his men began work on a pontoon bridge; by 11.30a.m. on the 10th March, the IIIrd Corps were able to continue their advance to Baghdad.

Meanwhile, back at the Shumran bend, Captain Witts had received orders to take up his bridge and march north with the rest of his unit towards Baghdad.

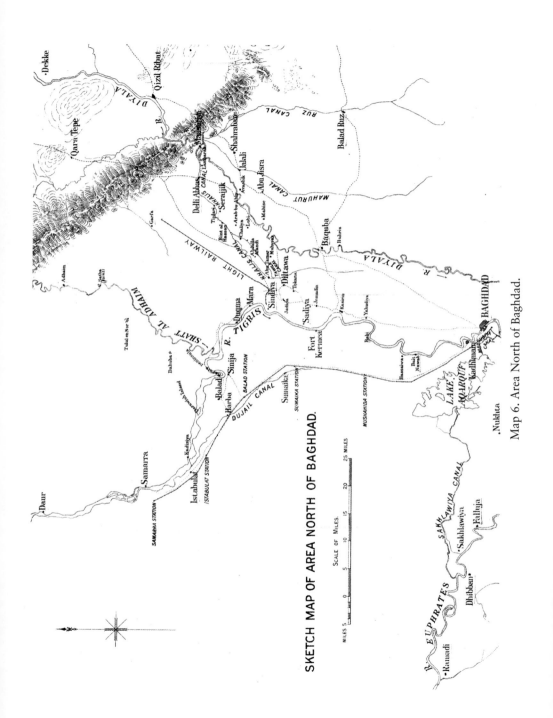

Map 6. Area North of Baghdad.

63. Bridge across the Diyala, March 1917.

F.V.B.Witts
    Capt.

No 2 Bridging Train
Mesopotamia Exp: Force.
[Shumran]
March 9th 1917.

Dearest Mother.

No mails as yet, but this is hardly to be wondered at considering the total disorganisation of the postal services, bound to follow a big advance.

In my last letter of the 4th, I wrote anticipating we should be left here forgotten. However yesterday evening we got orders to take up our bridge and move today to rejoin the army in front.[1] This is sooner than I hoped for at the best of times and is most satisfactory. Looking after a bridge once it is up is not a pleasant job: it has its anxieties without any compensating features. We have from 60 to 100 miles march before us depending on where we go to. It is quite an undertaking as we have a very large amount of transport, and the roads are not too good. I am consequently very busy getting everything ready, as we march at daylight tomorrow, having found it quite impossible to get off today.

This will be handed to some downgoing steamer and will, I hope, be posted somewhere. We have no Post Office here.

We are all very fit.

    I must stop and work,
        Very best love,
        Your ever loving Son,
           Fred.V. B.Witts.

---

[1] No.1 Bridging Train, had constructed a bridge at Bawi, 7 miles below the Diyala; there was thus another crossing over the Tigris when F.V.B.W. was asked to dismantle his bridge at Shumran.

65. British troops enter Baghdad, 1917.

On the right bank, the Ist Corps was advancing through hastily dug Turkish lines surrounding Baghdad. Even at this stage, on the cusp of defeat, the Turks fought bravely and with resolution, refusing to surrender the city without taking a heavy toll of British and Indian casualties. Their efforts, however, soon yielded to the inevitable; by 10a.m. on the 11th March 1917, the Union Jack was flying triumphantly over Baghdad.

In the footsteps of Nebuchadnezzar, Cyrus the Great and Haroun-al-Rashid, General Maude joined an illustrious line of conquerors in Mesopotamia.[2] Maude, however, was not one to be distracted by romantic notions of his own significance; defensively, Baghdad was a liability. An attack could be launched on the city down the Diyala, Tigris or Euphrates, and the Turks could flood its environs by breaching the river and canals to the north and west.

Maude immediately sent columns along these three arteries. First, on the Tigris, Cobbe's Ist Corps drove the Turks out of their trenches at Mushahida, 28 miles north of Baghdad, before the banks could be breached. Secondly, on the Euphrates, a column was sent to Falluja, 40 miles west of Baghdad, but arrived too late to stop the banks of the Sakhlawiya canal from being

---

[2] Whitehall was eager to exploit the historical significance of Maude's triumph by reminding the Baghdad population of their noble heritage and the degradation they had suffered under three and a half centuries of Turkish oppression. In a quite bizarre proclamation, drafted in London without any consultation with political representatives in Mesopotamia, the Government promised the people of Baghdad a revival of their country's former glory under the Caliphate. Published in Arabic and English and distributed throughout Baghdad, the proclamation contained flowery language promoting Arab freedom and independence from Turkish despotism. It was greeted with bewilderment by Arabs and British alike, but, as the British Administration would discover in the turbulent years after the war, its focus on independence would not be forgotten by the intelligentsia. See Illustrations 14 & 15 in the Colour Section for copies of the original Maude Proclamation in Arabic and English.

broken. Fortunately, however, the floods of 1917 were unusually low, and with the help of railway and flood embankments, Baghdad was protected from inundation. Thirdly, on the Diyala, a composite force of the Ist and IIIrd Corps, under General Keary, marched upstream towards Khaniqin, on the Persian border, where the Turkish XIII Corps, commanded by Ali Ihsan, was reportedly retiring in face of General Baratoff's detachment of 20,000 Cossacks. Keary's aim was to coordinate movements with Baratoff in order to engage Ali Ihsan on two opposing flanks, frustrating his efforts to join the Turkish XVIII Corps on the Tigris, which was now under the command of Shefket Pasha.[3] Eastmond's detachment of No. 2 Mobile Bridging Train accompanied Keary's column as far as Baquba, where they built another pontoon bridge over the Diyala. Having crossed the river, General Keary continued his advance upstream to the Jabal Hamrin Hills, and on the 25th March, he finally caught up with Ali Ihsan, although he had still failed to make any contact with Baratoff. Keary attacked nonetheless, but was shocked to be repulsed resoundingly by a force which, by all accounts, was meant to have suffered already at the hands of the Russians. While Keary's column recovered from the unexpected blow, Ali Ihsan's Corps fled the trap, heading west in search of Shefket.

The stark deterioration in the effectiveness and discipline of Russian forces had been a source of anxiety amongst the Allies for some time. Insufficient supplies, horrendous casualty rates and successive defeats had sapped Russian morale in her armies and spread political dissension across the country. In March 1917, interior unrest reached a climax in Petrograd when industrial strikes and food shortages developed into the 'February Revolution' (Russia used the Julian calendar), provoking the abdication of Tsar Nicholas II. Out of the wreckage emerged socialist Soviets (democratic councils formed by workers) throughout Russia, championing the workers' demands for peace and competing with the hastily established Provisional Government. Allied interests were further threatened when, on the 15th March, the newly formed Petrograd Soviet issued the notorious 'Order Number One', demanding 'peace without annexations or indemnities', which lead to mass mutinies throughout Russian forces. In the Middle East, General Baratoff was feeling the effects. Discipline was beginning to waver amongst his rank and file and his officers were becoming nervous for their safety. With such inherent problems, the likelihood that Baratoff, or, for that matter, General Chernozuboff in the Caucasus, could be of any real assistance to Maude was fading fast.

---

[3] A clash of opinions over the defence of Baghdad had induced Khalil to relieve Kiazim Karabekir of his command of the XVIII Corps. Whilst Khalil had opted to make a stand, Kiazim strongly believed that Baghdad should be abandoned in favour of Istabulat, a formidable defensive position on the right bank of the Tigris, 70 miles north of the city, where, he argued the Turks could concentrate in strength.

66. Indian Infantry, Baghdad.

Back in Baghdad, Captain Witts had arrived with his detachment of the bridging train. The Turks had destroyed their floating bridge in the city before their evacuation and Witts and his unit began work on a new one immediately.

Baghdad.
March 22nd 1917.

Dearest Mother.

Here we are at last; we have been a long time about it – it is nearly 15 months since we left the trenches in France en route to Baghdad as we then thought. I don't think they can object to my telling you we are here.

I last wrote on the 9th the evening before starting to march up from Shumran, where we successfully put up our bridge in the face of the enemy. Seven successive days marching and we got up here after covering 102 miles – not at all bad going considering the transport we have. We were not troubled by the Arabs[4] and the weather was kind to us all things considered, though we had some very bad duststorms.[5] Half way up we picked up three weeks of mails – our first letters since early in February. They included all letters and papers up to the end of January, including one from Aunt Maggie.[6] We used to march across the desert cutting off the bends, but camped each night by the river both for water's sake and for safety.

---

[4] The capture of Baghdad had provoked a widespread swapping of allegiance amongst many formerly pro-Turk Arab tribes.

[5] In the fighting on the right bank leading up to the capture of Baghdad, dust storms had often reduced visibility to 150yds or less, causing great confusion to both sides.

[6] F.V.B.W.'s Aunt Maggie was Mrs Waddingham Witts, the widow of F.V.B.W.'s paternal uncle Frederick Witts. She lived at Guiting Grange. See Illustration 9 in the Colour Section.

67. Pontoon bridge, Baghdad

As soon as we got here they wanted our bridge put across, so we had to get to work at once. There were no incidents but with only half our men it was very hard work, and long hours too. Today Eastmond has rejoined us and we are now all together again, and, I suppose settling down for a quiet hot weather.

Baghdad is not an exciting place to see;[7] it was not improved by the Turks burning out the bazaar and otherwise doing as much damage as possible.[8] But there are some very nice houses, and even we are in a new brick house of four rooms, which will be a great improvement on the tents of last year, if we stay here. The immediate result of my coming into rather a draughty house after so many months in the open, is that I have caught rather a nasty cold in the head.

The best point of the place is the oranges. They were 3 a penny when we arrived; they are already 2d each! Finding luscious fresh fruit in Mesopotamia seemed a contradiction in itself. It is also a pleasure to be in a place with trees again.

The news from all round is very good, but I want some more mails from home. I suppose things will settle down shortly.

Very best love
    Your ever loving Son
        Fred. V. B. Witts.

[7] Having endured so much to reach it, many of the British troops had fantasised that Baghdad was a mystical city, promising all the delights of *The Thousand and One Nights*. The reality, for the few troops actually allowed into the city, was disappointing and smelly.

[8] The Turks had also destroyed their newly constructed German wireless station and as much stocked war materials as they could. They had also tried to blow up the citadel, but it was narrowly saved by the arrival of British troops. In the end, despite their best efforts, the haste of the Turkish evacuation meant that an enormous quantity of military, engineering and medical stores was left intact and fell into British hands.

[Baghdad]

March 29th 1917

Dearest Mother.

It is a year today since I got up to this front with my Bridging Train, and I am very proud to think that we have not only done our job satisfactorily, but through the successful crossing of the Tigris have made quite a name for ourselves. I must confess that when I returned from leave last year, I hardly expected such a big move, with so much luck for ourselves. What is going to happen next remains to be seen; it is already beginning to get hot, so perhaps we shall spend the hot weather here.

Another mail has come in bringing your letter of January 30th and all the usual papers. Very many thanks for your birthday wishes. It was my third birthday on service, I wonder how many more there are going to be. I am afraid I rather mistrust the German retirement in France;[9] but of course we only get very partial news of what is happening.

I have had a very peaceful week, and have quite settled down to a routine existence. If we don't move soon, I suppose we shall be starting polo!

The heavy flood, due to the melting of the snow is daily, almost hourly, expected. At present the river is nothing like as high as it was this time last year. But my recollections of the Tigris last April are, as you will realize, not of the pleasantest: and I only hope we shall not have the same trouble this year.

I have not been into the city again – we are about two miles below. But I must go shopping sometime, I wish I was an expert in Persian carpets. They are practically the only thing worth buying bar the oranges.

…You ask about a Capt. Hogg R.E. son of Aunt Sybil's friend. He is out here, and I have seen him several times. He was with me at Woolwich and Chatham.[10]

No more news,

        Very best love,

           Your ever loving Son,

             Fred. V. B. Witts.

---

[9] F.V.B.W. was right to be suspicious. Known as 'Operation Alberich', the retirement of German forces to the Hindenberg Line, a system of trenches and fortifications stretching 100 miles from Arras to Soissons, was engineered to disrupt Allied preparations for the Nivelle Offensive. The Germans adopted a 'scorched earth' policy as they retired, laying booby traps and destroying all resources, presenting the Allied advance with enormous supply and transport difficulties. The operation was a great success for the Germans and the Nivelle Offensive ended in catastrophe for the Anglo-French forces.

[10] The Royal Military Academy Woolwich (also known as 'the Shop') and Royal Engineers H.Q. Chatham.

Despite the advancing hot season, General Maude was adamant that Force 'D' should not relax until a permanent wedge had been driven between the two Turkish Corps. A scheme, however, was already afoot between Shefket and Ali Ihsan to thwart Maude's design.

By the 25th March, Shefket had secretly transferred part of his XVIII Corps onto the left bank and was marching south towards Sindiya, the advanced post for British forces on the Tigris. His

ALSO RAN
Wilhelm: "Are you luring them on, like me?"
Mehmed: "I'm afraid I am!"

68. Punch cartoon, March 1917.

plan was to hold the British at Sindiya whilst Ali Ihsan, in the Jabal Hamrin hills to the east, marched across the desert to link up with the main portion of Shefket's force, located on the Tigris 20 miles above Sindiya. Fortunately for Maude, British intelligence picked up on the scheme and a Cavalry Division was sent urgently to intercept Ali Ihsan at Delli Abbas, in the foothills of the Jabal Hamrin. At Sindiya, meanwhile, the 13th Division drove Shefket's detachment back up the Tigris to the Shatt-al-Adhaim tributary.

F.V. B. Witts
    Capt. R.E.

[Baghdad]
April 4th 1917.

Dearest Mother.

Since I last wrote I have only had an odd letter from you of date Feb 6th, which had evidently gone astray out here.

We have had quite a peaceful time, but our hopes of a quiet time are shattered and we are on the move again at once. It will be rather trying this time as it has suddenly got unusually hot for the time of the year.

I spent another day in the city, but the more I see of it the less I like it.

The river has been rising steadily but slowly, and has not come down in sudden flood as it did this time last year. Let us hope it won't.

One funny thing I saw in the city was a notice 'TOOTH BUILDER' over the local dentist's house!

The French nuns, the owners of the house we have been living in during our sojourn here, paid us another visit yesterday afternoon and had tea with us. They say that if we had been another two or three days in getting here, they would have all been massacred.[11]

Once again we are in touch with the Russians, this time I hope permanently: if only they could settle up their domestic affairs satisfactorily, they might be in a position to do something.[12]

I must get to bed, as I have a long day before me.

Very best love,
>   Your ever loving Son,
>   Fred. V. B. Witts.

Much to their displeasure, No. 2 Mobile Bridging Train had been summoned to join the Ist Corps in their sweltering advance on Samarrah, 75 miles north of Baghdad. In General Maude's view, the capture of Samarrah was the cornerstone of Baghdad's consolidation, and the key to frustrating Khalil's hopes of uniting his force. Despite the oppressive heat already pervading the country, he was determined that the city should be secured before any thought could be given to settling down for the hot season.

On the 8th April, the Ist Corps column on the right bank, including the Bridging Train in its rear, captured Balad, 50 miles above Baghdad. While they pushed on to Istabulat, just south of Samarrah ,where the Turks were entrenched in a strong position, Captain Witts and his men stayed behind to bridge the Tigris at Balad. Meanwhile, on the left bank, progress of the British advance had been hindered by reports that Ali Ihsan had counter-attacked the Cavalry Division at Delli Abbas, precipitating an urgent need for reinforcements. General Marshall, commanding the IIIrd Corps column on the left bank, immediately diverted two infantry brigades to go to the Cavalry Division's aid; by the 15th April the combined British force had driven the Turkish XIII Corps back into the refuge of the Jabal Hamrin hills.

Back at Balad, No. 2 Mobile Bridging Train was waiting patiently for Marshall to clear the left bank of Turkish forces to allow them to begin construction of a bridge, free from enemy interference.

---

[11] After the Turkish evacuation, Baghdad devolved into anarchy as there was there was no existing authority to keep the peace. On the 11th March, a deputation of wealthy inhabitants (both Arabs and Jews) welcomed the British outside the Southern Gate with a petition, also signed by the American Consul, urging them to take control of the city at once to restore law and order.

[12] On 1st April a detachment of General Keary's column met a sotnia of Cossacks at Qizil Ribat, on the Diyala River 20 miles south-west of Khaniqin. Maude sent Baratoff a message requesting him to pursue Ali Ihsan whilst Keary returned to the Tigris to face Shefket. Two days later, the British liaison officer to General Baratoff came to Baghdad to report the dire state of Russian supply, transport and equipment, and Baratoff's flat refusal to engage in any operations taking him further into Mesopotamia.

69. South Bridge, Baghdad.

F.V.B. Witts

[Balad]
April 14th 1917.

Dearest Mother.

Just got a mail bag with three mails in it, including all the usual papers and your letters of Feb 13th, 15th & 20th.[13] All so welcome. Yes I got your cable, but not till after I had rejoined; also the Christmas card and birthday letters.

I see the Times is now 2d, I think they might make an exception in favour of copies sent to the troops. You must send me the bills for these papers, it is too much to expect you to go on for ever sending them to me.

We had a very strenuous 48 hours, during which we removed the bridge from its previous site,[14] loaded it up on to carts, and marched 40 miles. Not so bad for 48 hours. Since then we have been hanging about waiting, with nothing to do; so the mail was doubly welcome.

Luckily we have our tents with us, as it has been unusually hot in the middle of the day. Today we have been blessed or cursed with a duststorm of the worst, all-pervading, character.

So far the river has not played us its last year's tricks. After rising steadily for about 10 days it has started falling again, equally steadily. But we can't consider ourselves safe till the end of this month.

It is very pleasant being in a country again which has some local resources. Eggs and oranges are 2 a penny. Chickens, sheep, beans and milk are also obtainable, not to

---

[13] These are the only wartime letters from F.V.B.W.'s mother that have survived (see Chapter IV, p. 143-6).

[14] F.V.B.W.'s bridge was replaced by a more permanent structure with dredger pontoons and named 'South Bridge'. In 1923 it was destroyed in a typhoon and rebuilt as 'Maude Bridge'.

mention the usual dates.

You suggest binding my magazines: I don't think they are worth it, and think I should like them sent on to me each month. I have been meaning to ask you for them for some time. One rarely finds oneself with too much to read out here.

I am so glad to hear the colts are getting on so well. Edward ought to be very pleased. Will Pittaway be allowed to stay on after all, or will he be caught.[15]

No more news,

> Very best love
>> Your ever loving Son,
>>> Fred. V. B. Witts.

Back on the left bank of the Tigris, having sent a detachment to deal with Ali Ihsan at Delli Abbas, General Marshall crossed the Shatt-al-Adhaim and drove the Turkish defenders north in a disorderly retreat. With the bridgehead thus secured, Captain Witts and his men were able to begin construction of a pontoon bridge across a narrow bend in the Tigris at Sinija, just south of Balad.

> No 2 Bridging Train
> Mesopotamia Exp: Force
> [Sinija]
> April 22nd 1917.

Dearest Mother.

I last wrote on the 14th. We have been on the move again since, and so have had no more mails.

We marched again early on the 16th and were caught by one of the heaviest downfalls of rain and hail, I think I have ever seen. It only lasted an hour, but before the end we were able to water the mules as they stood on the track, which just previously had been a waterless desert. Many of our carts got bogged, and we didn't get everything into camp till dark.

The next two days were spent in reconnaissance, roadmaking and rampbuilding. By the end of them, there was no trace left of the recent heavy rain.

On the 19th we moved down to the river again and put up the bridge, without any incident,[16] though we only just had enough stuff to reach across.[17] We have since

---

[15] F.V.B.W. is referring to the Universal Service Bill – Pittaway had escaped conscription once before through injury in a riding accident. Jack Cheetham, F.V.B.W.'s cousin by marriage, was also endeavouring to avoid the call-up by claiming that he was indispensable on his farm.

been settling down comfortably for the hot weather, but it remains to be seen if we are going to be left here.

Working upstream from the Persian Gulf, this is the first place where any form of stone is found in the river bed. The bridge ends on one side on a bank of shingle. What with this and the higher ground and small hills, we are getting into quite a different type of country. But it is getting very hot in the middle of the day, and I hope we shall soon settle down for the hot weather. Leave is being opened but I am afraid, having had it last year, it won't be my turn this. However with infinitely better transport facilities, and a fertile country in the neighbourhood, conditions ought to be a vast improvement on last year.

Very best love,

Your ever loving Son,

Fred. V. B. Witts.

On 21st April, 20 miles upriver of Sinija, General Cobbe's Ist Corps attacked the redoubtable Turkish position at Istabulat. After two days of intense fighting in almost unbearable heat, there had been little progress to warrant the number of British and Indian casualties. Shefket Pasha, meanwhile, was acutely aware of his vulnerability on the left bank. After the Turkish defeat on the Shatt-al-Adhaim, the path to Samarrah had been left open to the British, giving General Marshall the opportunity to cross the Tigris upriver of Shefket and trap his force at Istabulat. Certain that this was going to happen, Shefket withdrew on the 23rd April to Tekrit, 45 miles up the Tigris, abandoning Samarrah to the British.

Back on the Shatt-al-Adhaim, General Marshall had, in fact, been far too preoccupied by the Turkish XIII Corps to think of closing in on Shefket. The indefatigable Ali Ihsan had driven his men on an arduous march round behind the Jabal Hamrin hills and down the Shatt-al-Adhaim to Adhaim town, 30 miles from the river's junction with the Tigris. Having marched upriver to meet the threat, Marshall attacked the Turkish position on the 30th April. Fighting in terrific heat over difficult rocky terrain, the IIIrd Corps drove the Turks,

---

[16] Contrary to what he told his mother, in *Light Floating Bridges* (Appendix I, p. 435) F.V.B.W. mentions that on the night the Sinija bridge was built, he received warning that the Turks had set fire to two ammunition barges and released them to drift downstream. A tug was sent up to obstruct the barges but ran aground on the shingle almost immediately. Fortunately, the ammunition barges met the same fate and never reached the bridge.

[17] Having absolutely no extra materials meant that every load ready to come across the bridge had to be scrutinised. In *Light Floating Bridges* F.V.B.W. recalls the indignance felt by gunners when told that they had to discard their tents and extra grain from their ammunition wagons before they could be allowed to cross (Appendix I, p. 435).

once again, back into the safety of the Jabal Hamrin hills. The casualties had been heavy on both sides, but finally, Ali Ihsan was forced to accept that all hope of linking up with Shefket before the start of the hot season was lost.

Having been firmly established on the Tigris, Euphrates, Diyala and Shatt-al-Adhaim, Force 'D' had succeeded in building a formidable buffer around Baghdad. 1917 boasted the hottest summer on record in Mesopotamia and it was not without relief that the troops were ordered to halt all strenuous activity. Captain Witts, meanwhile, had moved up to Samarrah where his unit was to spend the summer.

F.V.B.Witts
   Capt. R.E.

Samarrah
May 4th 1917.

Dearest Mother.

Since last writing, we have taken up the bridge and moved higher up, and have rebuilt it at Samarrah,[18] which is in many ways the most interesting place I have yet seen out here. It is a regular walled city, with its wall towers and gates in perfect preservation, situated in the middle of the ruins of a gigantic city, now represented by endless mounds – absolutely desolate.[19]

In the city there is one of the finest mosques in the world, with mosaic minarets, and a gold covered dome which glitters in the sun and can be seen for miles. Just outside there is a large tomb with a quaint spiral tower.[20] At present it is nearly empty, and as there is very little cultivation round about, there are not many local supplies to be obtained.

[18] A site 500yds wide was selected in the hope that the bridge would be able to deal with the dramatic 23ft annual rise in water levels at Samarrah. In peak floods, however, a steamer ferry had to be used as it was found impossible to keep a pontoon bridge afloat.

[19] The earliest records of Samarrah date back to around 5500 BC when the region, then known as Tel Sawwan, was first irrigated significantly. From AD 836, under al-Mutasim, until 892, the city enjoyed a short-lived period as capital of the Abbasid Caliphate.

[20] The Al-Askari mosque, containing the mausoleums of the 10th and 11th Shi'ite Imams, was built in AD 944. Its golden dome was a relatively new addition when F.V.B.W. saw it, having only been built in 1905. The spiral minaret is part of the Great Mosque complex, once the largest mosque in the world, built by the Abbasids in AD 852.

70. Samarrah.   71. Spiral Minaret, Samarrah.

As usual when we do move, they expect us to move very quickly,[21] but this time we were very fortunate in our weather. Leave is now being given broadcast, so, unless the Turk decides otherwise, we may expect to remain more or less where we are. It is getting too hot to fight without a lot of sickness, so we are settling down to make ourselves comfortable for the hot weather. Since moving last December we have given the Turks a good beating, chased him over 200 miles and beaten him thoroughly again, so it is unlikely that he will be keen to try conclusions with us just at present of his own seeking. It has been a very successful show and the difference in people's tempers between now and a year ago when Kut had just fallen is most striking and pleasing. Further the river has not risen in flood as it did last year, giving everyone endless trouble, and the flies have not seemed to worry us so much. In fact Providence has been smiling on us all round. It was certainly our turn for him to do so.

We nearly got flooded out the night before last. We had pitched our tents on the water's edge in order to get out of the dust, and the river started rising rapidly, luckily it was only a local rise due to rain, and it stopped at the very doors of our tents. The real flood season has passed.

Very best love
Your ever loving Son
Fred. V. B. Witts.

[21] In *Light Floating Bridges* (Appendix I), F.V.B.W. complains about the general lack of understanding of the time and effort involved in assembling and dismantling a bridge. A further illustration of F.V.B.W.'s frustration is in his closing words of *The Passage of the Tigris at Shumran*: 'Lastly, a word of warning against the expression 'throwing a bridge.' It tends to give the idea that there is nothing more in it than throwing a cricket ball, whereas actually, as it is hoped has been pointed out, it is a very complicated and delicate process.' (Appendix II, p. 445)

[Samarrah]
May 13th 1917.

Dearest Mother.

Very many thanks for your letter of March 13th, which has taken just two months to get here, but we are lucky to get mails at all, what with the long distance they have to come and the submarines they have to dodge.

Very many thanks for the handkerchief you sent: it has a distinctly classic pattern, quite in keeping with the classic ruins, which abound round here.

You ask about my thumb; I am glad to say it has gradually got quite all right again. It was not till I got your letter, and looked at my thumb, that I realized the fact. I was indeed lucky to get off so lightly.

Nothing doing here at all now; they are giving us an ample supply of large tents this year, and we are busy making ourselves comfortable. We are camped on the edge of the river immediately opposite Samarrah, which stands back about 400 yards from the river.

The river practically forms a rapid for two or three miles above us, and there is plenty of conglomerate rock and shingle about, as we are now out of the Tigris delta. We are now beyond reach of the river steamer, and are using the Baghdad railway to feed us; I hope the German Emperor knows, as it will annoy him so.

This is a very bad place for wind devils, the whole sky gets black with them, and quite a number of tents have disappeared heavenwards, and some say have never returned.

My old division is camped close alongside, with its complement of Roorkee Sappers, including my old company, so we see quite a lot of each other, which helps to pass the time, which will be our chief object in life for the next four months.

Very best love,
        Your ever loving Son,
            Fred. V. B. Witts.

[Samarrah]
May 20th 1917

Dearest Mother.

Many thanks for your letters of March 20th and 21st just arrived. Didn't I ever thank you for your cable, when I was wounded? I got it just after rejoining the unit.

By the way, you must put the M. C. before the R. E. on the envelopes not after.

You ask where the scene of the episode of Dec 20th was: it was at the bottom of the second loop above Kut [the Hussaini bend].

…It has not been as hot recently as last year,[22] but we have had duststorms of varying degrees of nastiness daily, and they are not at all pleasant. One day it blew a

---

[22] Candler attests that 'according to Baghdadis,' the summer of 1917 'was the hottest season in the memory of man' (*The Long Road to Baghdad*, vol. II p. 179) – F.V.B.W. would soon find himself having to agree.

hurricane and was as dark as a thick London Fog.

We are profiting by our possession of Baghdad, and two days ago had a ration of ice! Just think of it, ice on active service – what a contrast to last year.

…Eastmond has gone off on leave to India for one month, but it means his being away from here for 10 weeks or more. However I shall not be alone this year.

I have just been inoculated again against cholera. The doctors are for ever puncturing us against something, as soon as they get some respite from repairing the punctures caused by bullets and shells.[23]

I wish they could inoculate us against being worried by flies. However duststorms tend to scatter them and reduce their numbers.

No more news.

Very best love,
Your ever loving Son,
Fred. V. B. Witts.

[Samarrah]
May 27th 1917.

Dearest Mother.

No mail come in since I last wrote, and nothing of interest to report from this end.

We have settled down to a regular quiet routine existence, and it was quite strange this afternoon to hear a gun poop off just behind our camp strafing some patrol or Arabs who had wandered within range.

It is getting warmer, but is still quite bearable, and the terrible duststorms – far worse than any we had last year – are the worst trials. Apart from the minor storms and winddevils, which however are quite enough to cover everything inches deep in sand and dust, we seem to get a real bad one every third or fourth day with the utmost regularity. However it gives us something to grouse at!

With nothing particular to do, one starts thinking what is going to happen after the war, and longing for that event. Unfortunately there seems no immediate prospect of it, especially now that Russia seems a broken reed. The chief thing is how soon and how much leave home we shall get, and who will be the unfortunate people condemned to remain here with the army of occupation which presumably there must necessarily be. Luckily after the war they probably won't have much use for Bridging Trains, which have been practically raised for the occasion, so perhaps our chances are brighter than some.

Very best love,
Your ever loving Son,
Fred. V. B. Witts.

---

[23] After their scandalous condition earlier in the campaign, medical care and facilities in Mesopotamia were now of an exemplary standard.

72. New Street Baghdad.

F.V.B.Witts
Capt. R.E.

[Baghdad]
June 6th 1917.

Dearest Mother.

I am writing from Baghdad where I have been called in on duty and am living in the lap of comfort for a few days.

The place has changed beyond recognition since I was here two months ago. Electric light and fans in the houses, all the main streets lighted, cleaned and remade: the bazaar, which was burnt out, all rebuilt again and a blaze of colour and crowded with representatives of every race in the East. Several hotels of sorts open, and endless other things which I suppose I mustn't refer to.[24]

I came in on the famous Baghdad railway, sitting on a camp chair in an open truck.

The Turks made desperate efforts to flood half the city, and on one side there is a vast lake only kept out by the railway embankment.[25] Luckily the flood season is now past. The lake too has its advantages, the wind blowing across it is delightfully cool, and absolutely free from dust – such a pleasant change from our own camp.

On the 4th June there was an old Etonian dinner at the chief hotel; who would have thought it three years ago.[26]

---

[24] The development of Mesopotamia had kept pace with the British advance and in Baghdad numerous projects were in hand, overseen by Force 'D"s dedicated political branch under Sir Percy Cox, the Civil Commissioner. These schemes included the recruiting and training of a police force and fire brigade, building new schools, repairing Mosques, monitoring the grain supply, improving sanitation, roads and water supply, not to mention steadying inflation.

[25] F.V.B.W. is referring to the expansion of Lake Aqarquf by the breaching of the Sakhlawiya canal at Falluja by the Turks in March 1917.

[26] Later on in 1917, on November 17th, a 7 course Old Wykehamist dinner was held at Amiens attended by the then headmaster Monty Rendall. Sixty-nine Wykehamists attended. The battle of Passchendaele was in full swing at the time.

73. Landing the English Mails at Basra.

...It is getting hot, but there is a liberal supply of ice to be had here and soda water too, both obtained from shops which existed here before our arrival.

I don't know how long I am to remain here, I came down for 2 days and have already been here 3.

There is no more news.

Very best love,

Your ever loving Son,

Fred. V. B. Witts.

FVB Witts

Capt. R. E.

[Samarrah]

June 18th 1917

Dearest Mother.

Just a line to catch the post. Like you I write every week, except when on the march with no post offices; but it doesn't follow that I catch every mail out from Basra. I now hear that they are only going to run once a fortnight instead of weekly, so that if anything goes wrong there may be no letters for a month: however I shall continue to write each week.

...I have had a very busy week. Two days running I rode thirty miles or more reconnoitring the country.[27] In order to avoid the heat, you have to make such an early start, 4.30. a.m.; it is worse than cub hunting. Two other days I have spent tramping over the country in the neighbourhood of our camp [at Samarrah], with a view to improving roads etc. At present it is so sandy as to be impassable for motors, they all stick and have to be manhandled to the bridge.

[27] F.V.B.W. was reconnoitring the Tigris to the north of Samarrah, beneath Turkish positions at Tekrit.

My clerk is on leave, and with Eastmond away I have to do all the clerical work myself; that is the worst of an Indian unit, you have no one to fall back upon for this work.

It is particularly trying in the awful duststorms, which seem to be on us every day and all day. As I write now I have to blow the dust off the paper each time I get to the end of the line, as by then the beginning of the line is already buried out of sight in the dust.

I am feeling very fit, and every one tells me I look it.

Very best love,
    Your ever loving Son,
        Fred. V. B. Witts.

FVB Witts
    Capt. R.E.

[Samarrah]
June 25th 1917.

Dearest Mother.

Another mail in with your letter of May 1st 1917 also the missing mail with your letter of March 27th. I am glad my name has appeared officially at last, as I believe you were beginning to think me a fraud.

…Although we are pretty uncomfortable out here, I am beginning to think that you are all much worse off at home what with no sugar or poultry and petrol and all the other shortages, coming on the top of such awful weather. Out here the dust has not been so bad this last week, but we have had to pay for it in the shape of hotter weather. However it is an absolute picnic compared with last year. We can buy locally excellent grapes of either colour, real good melons of either variety, tomatoes, cucumbers and green figs! It doesn't sound like the Mesopotamia of last year does it! Grapes and cucumbers are so plentiful just at present, that they are included in the rations issued to all the troops. It should do much to reduce the scurvy which took such a heavy toll last year.[28]

There is no magazine like Blackwood's in my estimation and I am glad you read it and find it interesting.

I am afraid you must find it very lonely, and I am sorry to hear you are so rheumatic. How I long to get home to see you, but we must see the war out first. I am afraid the trouble in Russia will prolong it all considerably. I suppose the Turks will try and recover Baghdad next cold weather. It will be a pleasant change to have them attacking for once. I don't think there is much fear of their being able to turn us out.

---

[28] Candler reports that around 50% of the Indian troops suffered from scurvy in the summer of 1916. (*The Long Road to Baghdad*, vol. I p. 285)

One of my men pulled a 65 lb fish out of the river today, a Mahseer[29] much like a salmon.

No more news

Very best love

Your ever loving Son

Fred. V. B. Witts.

74. Tigris Mahseer.

[Samarrah]
July 2nd 1917.

Dearest Mother.

...I had one very long day this week, shifting our 'flying bridge' to a new site:[30] it meant working in the open from 5 a.m. to 3 p.m. and it is no fun out in the sun after 11 a.m. The 'shimal' blows so hard that the bridge will only 'fly' one way of its own accord, that it does with a vengeance, but it has to be laboriously pulled across again.

Two good fish have been caught this week one of 65 lbs and another of 68 lbs, but they are not such good eating as the smaller ones, though they go round more people.

Very best love,

Your ever loving Son,

Fred. V. B. Witts

[Samarrah]
July 9th 1917.

Dearest Mother.

The first of the fortnightly mails have come in, with a full fortnight's supply of papers and your two letters of May 9th and 15th Blackwoods comes regularly, and is most welcome.

---

[29] A Hindi name applied to any larger species of Barbus, found also in Himalayan rivers and larger rivers around Bombay and Madras.

[30] The 'flying bridge', according to F.V.B.W., was 'a raft of the ordinary four-pontoon type and worked on a 3-in. steel rope, suspended between a tripod on the higher bank and a length of the Baghdad Railway up-ended on the other bank.' (*Light Floating Bridges*, Appendix I, p. 435)

It is hard to believe that Geoffrey [Woodroffe] will be coming up for Sandhurst next year. Which Elm Tree is it that is down at the Dingle?[31] I saw Algy Rushout's death in the paper.

The letter you sent me was from Pearce, your old butler; he wrote to congratulate me on my M.C. He signs himself Corporal, 5th Northamptonshire Regt, Pioneers, B. E. F. He inquired very tenderly after you.

About enclosing paper and envelope each time. There is none to be got out here; but it must be a bother to you to think of it each time. It would do as well to send me a writing pad and envelopes to match occasionally.

I tried to do some shopping in Baghdad, but didn't meet with much success. Nothing to be got but carpets, for which they were asking absurd prices for articles probably made in Birmingham! The Turks and Germans pinched or burnt everything worth having.[32]

Glad to hear Frank is not up at the Front, he has done his share of the trenches; I hope he will get a billet which suits him and which he likes.

No Postcards of Baghdad at present.

We are just entering on the worst bit of the year for climate. I am writing at 10 a.m., the thermometer in the tent is 114°!! What wind we now get, in addition to the dust it brings, is now burning hot. Luckily I am feeling very fit, and have nothing to worry about in the bridging line, as the river is very low, and there is very little road traffic and no river traffic.

The sickness this year is nothing to what it was last year thanks to the better conditions it has been possible to let us live under.[33]

No more news,

Very best love,

Your ever loving Son,

Fred. V. B. Witts.

[Samarrah]

July 16th 1917

Dearest Mother.

No mails in since I last wrote, and it has been a pretty miserable week with the shade temperature up to 120° each day. The tent temperature has been a degree or two higher, and it is hard to realize until experienced. In India you have your comparatively cool bungalow and punkah to fall back upon; out here your tent is a degree or two hotter than the shade outside. My pony which I had in India, and

---

[31] The remaining Dingle elms survived a further sixty years, but died sadly in the 1970s as a result of Dutch Elm disease.

[32] The Turks requisitioned everything they could find before their evacuation, but the city's merchants also managed to hide large stocks of merchandise.

[33] The *Official History* cites the summer sick-list being less than half of what it was in 1916. (Moberly, F. J., *The Mesopotamia Campaign*, vol. IV p. 49)

which went with me to France, had a heatstroke a few days ago, but is, I hope, pulling round. It is very trying for the poor animals standing out in the sun without any shelter at all.

On the 12th there was a Gymkhana race meeting, but it was too hot to thoroughly enjoy it, although it didn't start till 5.15.

I had a great surprise yesterday morning when I saw in Orders that I had been awarded the 'Croix de Guerre'; my name was one of many foreign decorations distributed, including a 'Medaille Militaire' for my havildar, who was with me on Dec 20th, and which pleases me infinitely more. I am particularly glad it is a French one, having served in France, as a decoration from a country which one has never had any connections with, always seems to me a rather silly custom, which should be confined to crowned heads and their relations.

The order reads, 'The following are among the Decorations and Medals awarded by the Allied Powers to the British Forces in Mesopotamia for distinguished services rendered during the course of the campaign:-

Decorations Conferred by the President of the French Republic.

'Croix de Guerre.'

My name appears among the 40 recipients. I have not the slightest notion what it is like. You must find out and let me know.

Would you like to send me a couple of Pears new Shaving Sticks, also one of his Solid Brilliantine; it might get here without melting this time. Also a shaving brush. I know you like doing a little shopping occasionally.

No more news

    With very best love,

        Your ever loving Son

           Fred. V. B. Witts.

                      [Samarrah]

                    July 22nd 1917.

Dearest Mother.

...Another mail has come in with your letter of May 22nd enclosing two silk handkerchiefs, for which many thanks as they are always useful.

There should have been two weeks' mails, but one was sunk en route

Glad to hear about Queenie's Foal. How I long to get home again and see you and everything.

...If you have not already made the purchases I asked for last week, will you get me a medium sized sponge: my present one is old and ragged. I have just been going over my kit to see what I want to keep me going another year or two! It sounds dreadful!

No more news.

    With very best love,

        Your ever loving Son,

           Fred. V. B. Witts.

F.V.B.Witts

    Capt. R. E.

No 2 Bridging Train

[Samarrah]

July 30ᵗʰ 1917.

Dearest Mother.

    Another week has come round again. I think the heat makes the time go faster. It is infernally hot, 127° is an official reading and 132° has been recorded. It is wonderful how anybody keeps going in it. Luckily it is a very dry heat, and there is unlimited water to drink and bathe in. They also give us a certain amount of ice and some soda-water, not bad work considering where we are. It is also very rare to get a day without a breath of wind, and the nights are bearable.

    The parcel has come from Fortnum and Mason containing the Lemonade and Lemon Drops, some of which I am munching now as I write. All most welcome and arrived in perfect condition.

    Another mail has come in this morning; there should have been two but one was sunk. All the usual papers and your letter of June 5ᵗʰ from Harrogate and one from Edith. Tell her I really will write to her next mail. It is too late for this.

    …Eastmond has returned from leave, looking very fit. Nothing else particular happened.

    Just got an invitation to dine with the Divisional General [Maj.-Gen.V. B. Fane of the 7ᵗʰ Division] to meet the Corps Commander [Lt.-Gen. Sir A. S. Cobbe] who is going round inspecting. They are both very genial men.

    Every one is keeping surprisingly fit. From what I hear it is the fellows who go to India on leave who collapse on the return journey probably at the thought of what they have left behind and of what is in front of them.

    The news from Russia is rather discouraging,[34] I suppose it adds a few more years to the war, but after all one year more or less is nothing as things go nowadays.

    Very best love,

Your ever loving Son

Fred.V. B.Witts.

---

[34] The 'Kerensky Offensive' of July 1917, the brainchild of Kerensky, the Provisional Government's Minister for War, was designed to reunite Russia in its defence against German 'imperialism'. After initial success, poor communications and despondent morale slowed the offensive's momentum and it soon succumbed to determined German counter-attacks. Discipline in the Russian forces disintegrated completely and most of the troops simply left their trenches and went home. In Petrograd, an armed protest known as the 'July Days' rose up against the Provisional Government and, as it spread throughout the country, it was joined in readiness by the anti-war Bolsheviks. The Government managed to suppress the uprising and Lenin was exiled to Finland, but the episode consolidated support for Bolshevik radicalism. As far as the war was concerned, Russia was no longer a player.

[Samarrah]
August 6th 1917

Dearest Mother.

…I had a very pleasant dinner on Monday night with the Divisional General, though the Corps Commander failed to turn up.

Bird and the 4th Company are camped just opposite us on the other side of the river, and I was dining with them last night, going and returning in one of our launches.

Farley at present is working in Baghdad. I think I have mentioned we are at Samarrah, which you will see on the map.

The band gave a special performance on Thursday in our camp. A great treat. They have one per division.

No more news
        Very best love
                Your ever loving Son
                        Fred. V. B. Witts.

[Samarrah]
August 12th 1917.

Dearest Mother.

No mail in since I last wrote, and the situation here is unchanged, as the official reports would say. The only item of interest during the week was a Race Meeting, which was a great show of colour and a great social gathering, where one met all one's friends. This is a straggling camp, and these hot dusty days it requires quite undue energy to face say a three mile ride simply to look up someone. There was one race for the local Arabs and the finish was most spectacular as they came in shouting and yelling and waving their arms about. As a return for our hospitality some of the Arabs were handing round their local cigarettes and coffee. This latter is really good though a bit bitter as prepared by them. They serve it up in tiny little china cups with no handle, with a bare mouthful in it. This was perhaps as well, as, having handed you the full cup, they remained with you until you had returned the empty !

The result of the races was my dining out the next two days; with a gunner who was at the Shop [R.M.A. Woolwich] with me, and with an Indian Army fellow who was in the same convalescent home with me up at Murree when I was recovering from enteric.

It is still very hot by day and we have had two of the worst dust storms during the week, but the days are getting noticeably shorter and the nights cooler. It is nearly dark when we start work at 5 a.m.

No more news.
        With very best love
                Your ever loving Son
                        Fred. V. B. Witts.

F.V.B.Witts
    Capt. R.E.

[Samarrah]
August 19th 1917

Dearest Mother.

    …I am glad to hear you have had a bunch of my letters, and hope they have been coming more regularly since. If they haven't it is not because I haven't written!

    I am pleased you have got a Dressing Case for yourself – I want to see it now!

    I have not come across any postcards, and my own photographs have been such a failure that I have given up taking any.

    I have got a long day before me tomorrow, as I am going out on a long reconnaissance. It means a very early start in order to avoid the heat, as although the nights are getting appreciably cooler, it was 114° in our tent this afternoon.

    During the last week, our peace of the last few months has been disturbed by such things as urgent orders received in the middle of the night;[35] and I was out on a long reconnaissance. In fact there are many signs to show, that the slack season, necessitated by the heat, is rapidly coming to an end.

    Last night I was dining with a certain famous Scottish Regiment,[36] who gave a first rate entertainment afterwards. The dinner too was probably bigger and better than you can get at home now, except behind closed doors, and included haggis. Vegetables and fruit are much scarcer now. But water melons are still very plentiful: I am not however very fond of them as they are so tasteless, but being the only antiscorbutic [preventative for scurvy] obtainable one has to eat them for the sake of one's health.

    No more news.

        Very best love,
            Your ever loving Son
              Fred.V. B.Witts.

[Samarrah]
Aug 27th 1917.

Dearest Mother.

    Another mail day has come round, but no mail has come in in the interval for me to reply to or acknowledge. I suppose we are still feeling the effects of the fortnightly mail service, though it was announced that a weekly service has been renewed.

    I had a very long day on the reconnaissance on the 20th. We started off at 3.30 a.m. and got back midday with the temperature in the shade standing at 118° – one of the hottest days we have had this month. and I was not sorry to get back to cover and a

---

[35] It is not clear exactly what these orders were, but General Maude was preparing to renew operations within the Baghdad wilayat to combat reported Turkish movements.

[36] The Black Watch, based in Samarrah.

cool drink. We rode well over thirty miles, and got in touch with the Turkish patrols, who fell back before us and enabled me to see all I wanted, though not without some excitement, as one wily Turk for some reason did not go back with the others, but lay up in a hole, and had some sporting shots at us from an unpleasantly close range as we galloped away.

Nothing else of particular interest during the week until yesterday evening, when I dined out and afterwards attended the opening performance at the Cinema which has just been built here. Fancy a cinema at Samarrah, it must make all the old skeletons turn in their graves and I expect the Turks opposite will be a bit envious when they get to hear. They may think they have got something worth fighting for. However it is the way to win victories, to keep men's spirits up and there are a number of depressing factors – flies, dust, heat, mud etc to be counteracted out here.

We are getting some fresh dates now. They are locally grown but there are very few of them.[37]

No more news.

Your ever loving Son,

Fred. V. B. Witts.

[Samarrah]

Sept 2nd 1917

Dearest Mother.

…I am sorry to hear Pittaway has been called up, but I suppose it is very lucky his being allowed to stay so long. I hope you have succeeded in getting some one to help as you have a large stable on your hands now. It is bad luck too having so few strawberries, though it is good news that you have a good crop of apples.

There are an unlimited number of melons to be got here now, as the Arabs started planting especially for us, and they are just beginning to ripen.

Bird was dining with us last Monday. One of his Officers has just died from enteric in Baghdad – Roche, who took Trevor's place, – a week later and he would have lived to know that he had got the M. C. I see the Gazette is out at home but so far only scraps of it have become known here.

I was very disappointed that the Times only contained a short summary of Maude's despatch. It is only natural of course so as to bring into proper proportion with Haig's. However I should very much like to see it 'in toto'. Could you have it posted out to me – it must be obtainable somewhere, – and also the Mesopotamia Report (in

---

[37] Samarrah is in the northernmost region suitable for growing dates in Mesopotamia; because of the cooler winters, they do not grow in the same abundance as in the south. Further up the Tigris the winters are too cold for effective cultivation.

full).[38] To those of us who were out here then it makes interesting reading to see what was said.

I hope you read in Blackwood's about the Indian Corps in France. It puts very clearly the various points which are presumably overlooked by many who abuse the Indians.[39]

It is not quite so hot but we are having some of the worst duststorms we have ever had so far. I am very well.

Very best love,

Your ever loving Son,

Fred. V. B. Witts.

FVB Witts

Capt. R.E.

[Samarrah]

Sept 10th 1917.

Dearest Mother.

Yesterday was a great day for me: two week's mails arrived including your letters of July 18th and 24th, in which you congratulate me on the Croix de Guerre, and later on came your cable congratulating me on the D.S.O.[40] – my first official intimation that

[38] The Mesopotamian Report was a Commission of Inquiry into the administrative handling of the Mesopotamian Campaign up to the fall of Kut in April 1916. The Commission was made up of 8 members, only one of whom was a soldier and none of whom had visited Mesopotamia or had any extensive experience in the military or civil administration of India. The Commission was appointed by the Government in reaction to public outcry at revelations which had begun to emerge concerning the plight of Force 'D' after the disaster at Ctesiphon. Its aim was to study the evidence and 'apportion blame' where it was warranted. Besides Sir John Nixon, the authorities in India were, unsurprisingly, the most accused; particularly Lord Hardinge, Sir Beauchamp Duff and, to a lesser extent, Sir Percy Lake (when Chief of General Staff at Simla). The report, however, was criticised for inaccuracies, inadequate use of witnesses and, in its efforts to deflect blame away from London, bias against India. Significantly, the *Official History* is damning in its review, reflecting the Government's stance in 1927, its date of publication: 'the Commission in its proceedings did not generally observe the usual rules of evidence…[its] members were lacking in the technical and up-to-date knowledge of military operations and military war organisation required in an enquiry of this nature. It is undoubtedly true that, in a military sense, its report was incomplete and in a few cases inaccurate.' (Moberly, F. J., *The Mesopotamia Campaign*, vol. IV p. 30)

[39] F.V.B.W.'s opinions on this matter have already been expressed in his letter of September 22nd 1916, (p. 106-7) when he related his disgust at the ignorance displayed by four young generals he had met aboard *S.S. Egra*. Slander against the courage and skill of Indian troops was a serious issue within British forces, and one which F.V.B.W., with his extensive experience of living and working with Indians, felt very strongly about.

[40] F.V.B.W. had been awarded the D.S.O. for his success at the Shumran crossing.

I had got it. I must confess that from what was said I anticipated getting something, but I never expected to get the D.S.O. on the top of the Croix de Guerre.

I have had extraordinary luck. For two years nothing, and then for three months work, three medals, a mention in Despatches (I presume from the D.S.O.), and a gold stripe! Not to mention personal congratulations from the Army Commander downwards. All because I had an unique opportunity, absolutely unfailing luck, and was working very much in the limelight, being personally responsible for an essential part of the plan of operations.

I am very glad to say Eastmond, my subaltern, has got the M. C., but I am longing for news of what my men have got. I feel ashamed to have got so much, while they have at present nothing to show for it, when, after all, I owe it all in the end to the splendid way they played up whatever was demanded of them.

I am very glad to read in your letter and also in the Paper that Edward has been mentioned – they must have a pretty rotten [time] of it in the Salonika Force.

…I received a small book from you 'From Dartmouth to the Dardanelles' about a midshipman,[41] which I think I have not hitherto acknowledged or thanked you for. And this mail I mustn't forget the flea-killing soap and grease. It is most useful as there are a number of Sandflies about – one of the worst pests in the insect line. As for the Fly sprayer it was most invaluable in the spring and saved us many hours of horrid torture: but the great heat has one advantage, directly the shade temperature exceeds 110° the flies die off as rapidly as they will reappear again later on when it gets cooler and the Fly sprayer will again be in great demand.

I am sorry to hear about Arthur Heberden; he was at Trinity wasn't he? I hope you have got someone reliable in Pittaway's place: as you say, you have a large nursery to look after. I should so much like to see them.

I am very sorry I have not been able to send you any pictures, but you must remember I am very many miles away from Baghdad – nearly as far as Slaughter from London. And I have given up taking photographs. My efforts met with poor success and then my preoccupations were too great to have any time to worry about it. Stamps I have seen none.

Glad to hear you have had some first hand evidence of Agnes; I expect she does look brown[42] – you would probable mistake <u>me</u> for a nigger!

So glad to hear you are dong so much gardening. I am sure it is very good for you. Frank tells me in a cheery letter, written the night before he crossed, that Aunt Maggie has taken to bicycling.

The past week here has been much like its predecessors. Perhaps a little cooler and more dust. There was another Gymkhana race meeting on Thursday; they are always amusing shows, where you meet everyone. The Arab race this time drew a large entry

---

[41] The memoir of a midshipman in the Dardanelles Campaign, edited by the author's mother (Heinemann, 1916).

[42] Agnes had been in Salonika for about a year, working as an ambulance driver.

and it was a very wild performance: the starters and judges have a very difficult job. In the end the prizes were handed to the Political Officer, to distribute as the Arabs should decide amongst themselves!

No more news,

Very best luck,

Your ever loving Son,

Fred. V. B. Witts.

[Samarrah]
Sept 16th 1917.

Dearest Mother.

No mail in since I last wrote. I have been the recipient of many congratulations from many quarters and it makes me feel I have earned a reputation which I shall not be able to live up to.

The most striking event of the week was the beginning of the end of the hot weather. Two days ago the thermometer in our mess tent failed to reach 100° in the middle of the day for the first time for four months! It was the result of two successive violent dust storms.

On Friday the band was performing in our camp for the third time, and amongst other things played the Merry Widow! Who would have expected to hear it at this desolate corner of the earth.

Did you know my photograph appeared in the Daily Sketch of March 27th, when my M. C. was gazetted. Supplied by Lafayette – did you give them permission? Somebody gave me a copy of it.

If you would like to send me a Christmas present, send me a fly whisk. I have not got one and they are almost a necessity in this country, unless one's horse is to suffer endless torture. When it comes out, I should like to see the part of the Times History of the War, dealing with the operations out here.

For a long time we have had a tame stork attached to us, and it has suddenly disappeared. It was a most fascinating creature and knew no fear. We have also got a wild cat, caught as a kitten and brought up with us. He is not frightened now, and quite friendly but hates being picked up by anyone, and bites and scratches viciously if you try. A cow gives us our daily milk and we have our usual poultry yard. So we are doing pretty well. Dogs abound, but are being killed right out as a case of rabies occurred.

No more news today,

Very best love,

Your ever loving Son,

Fred. V. B. Witts.

I have just been shown another picture of myself in 'War Illustrated' of June 9th!

75. *Daily Sketch*
27ᵗʰ March 1917 page 6:
Captain F. V. B. Witts R.E.,
awarded the M.C.

76. Kazhimain Mosque, Baghdad.

Baghdad, the lodestar that initially had guided Force 'D' to catastrophe, was now a resounding emblem of British success. With the city surrounded by a formative ring of strategic buffers, General Maude had all but satisfied British objectives in Mesopotamia, leaving a question-mark hanging over his plans for the forthcoming winter.

The Turks, meanwhile, had suffered heavily throughout 1917, but intelligence reports indicated that they were not prepared to accept their losses meekly. The Russian collapse had evaporated pressure in Persia and the Caucasus, allowing them to focus more attention and resources on the Mesopotamian and Palestinian fronts. A Turko-German army named the 'Yilderim ('Thunderbolt') Group' was being assembled to recapture Baghdad – an ambition bordering on obsession for the Turkish Commander-in-Chief, Enver Pasha. In September 1917, it appeared likely that, for the coming campaigning season, it would be Force 'D' that was put on the defensive.

Despite the disappointments concerning Russia, morale in Force 'D' was high; Captain Witts' personal attitude to the possibilities of a Turkish advance was positively cavalier. The heat and monotony of the summer, however, had been especially punishing. With the grim prospect of the war continuing for another few years due to Russia's collapse, the troops were eager for any chance to get at the Turks.

CHAPTER VI

TURKEY FALTERS

Letters: Sept 23rd 1917 – April 14th 1918

The *Official History* states that, in autumn 1917, General Maude was 'except for the Russian lapse completely satisfied with his position.'[1] The policy decided on for the winter was to be mainly defensive, but with an element of aggression to tighten the grip on Baghdad and keep troops fresh after their long, lethargic summer.

The closest concentration of Turkish strength lay at Ramadi, on the Euphrates, 20 miles beyond Dhibban, where British engineers wanted to construct a dam on the Sakhlawiya canal to safeguard Baghdad from future floods. Back in July, with uncharacteristic misjudgement, Maude had sent a column on an abortive attempt to seize Ramadi. A determined Turkish resistance and raids from hostile Arabs delivered a heavy toll on British forces, but the greatest enemy had been the incapacitating heat. The arrival of autumn, however, brought with it the opportunity for a second attack on Ramadi.

Whilst preparations were set in motion for an offensive up the Euphrates, the Tigris front had become dormant. G.H.Q. and the War Office had agreed that any further advance in this direction would only lengthen communications without contributing much to the consolidation of Baghdad. Stuck at Samarrah, Captain Witts and his unit were condemned to an indefinite period of further inactivity.

F.V.B. Witts
    Capt. R.E.

[Samarrah]
September 23rd 1917.

Dearest Mother.

No mail in since last I wrote. It is over a fortnight now since we had the last.

The drop in temperature has been maintained, and has had a most noticeable effect on everyone's spirits though it has meant starting to get rid of the large comfortable hot weather tents. In a fortnight I have changed from no sheet or blanket at night up to a sheet and two blankets, and from enjoying a cold bath to enjoying a hot one.

There are no signs of either side doing anything at present out here. We appear to be as suspicious of the Turks, as they are of us.

Yesterday evening I was entertaining one Captain Roosevelt, son of the ex

---

[1] Moberly, F. J., *The Mesopotamia Campaign*, vol. IV p. 46

President, who is now attached to the staff of one of the Generals up here.[2] The last man in the world I should have expected to meet up here!

...I am awfully pleased to say that, in the Gazette of India recently published, containing awards for the Indian troops in Mesopotamia, they have done my sappers extremely well. The Havildar (Indian Sergeant) who was with me when I was wounded has been given the Indian Order of Merit, (I.O.M.), which corresponds to the D.C.M. at home; four of the sappers who were with me then have been given the Indian Distinguished Service Medal, (I.D.S.M.), which takes the place of the Military Medal at home. For the Shumran bridging on Feb 23rd my senior Indian Officer has been given the I.O.M. and two of my N.C.Os the I.D.S.M; this is in addition to the 'Immediate' award, at the time, of the I.D.S.M. to one of my sappers. This is much more than I ever expected to get and in proportion to our size we have received more rewards than any other unit out here. But they have not been done as well as I have! I am particularly pleased that the men who were with me have got eventually what they would have got immediately if I hadn't gone away to Hospital.

Another mail has just come in, bringing your letter of Aug 8th, a letter from Frank, all the usual papers, and the August Blackwood. One complete mail is missing. I wonder if it has gone to the bottom or simply been mislaid somewhere. The August R. E. Journal has also come. I should like the Sapper as well, I still have some men who would take an interest in it.

No other news this week.

> Very best love
> Your ever loving Son
> Fred. V. B. Witts

Sixty-five miles across the desert from Captain Witts' camp at Samarrah, the 15th Division, commanded by Major-General Brooking, began their bombardment of Turkish positions outside Ramadi, alongside the right bank of the Euphrates. Supporting Brooking was a company of Light Armoured Motor Batteries (L.A.M.B.s), first introduced in Mesopotamia in February 1917. Since the July attack, the Turks had strengthened their position, but they were not prepared for the strategic edge afforded by Brooking's L.A.M.B.s. While these vehicles surprised the Turkish right flank, a Cavalry Brigade manoeuvred round their trenches in a wide arc and attacked their rear, cutting off the Turkish supply line up the Euphrates. Realising the hopelessness of their situation, the Turks made desperate attempts during the night to break out of the trap, but the Cavalry Brigade were rigorous in blocking their escape. The following morning, on the 29th September, the Turks surrendered, yielding 3,500 prisoners.

---

[2] Captain Kermit Roosevelt M.C., son of Theodore Roosevelt (US President, 1901-1909) served in the British Motor Machine Gun Corps in Mesopotamia. He chronicled his experiences of the campaign in his book, *War in the Garden of Eden* (New York, 1919).

77. Gufars near the North Bridge, Baghdad.

F.V.B. Witts.
  Capt. R.E.

[Samarrah]
Oct 1st 1917.

Dearest Mother.

The missing mail came in today. It had apparently been round by Colombo, and so took a fortnight longer, coming in a week after the mail that left London a week later. It included your letter of Aug 1st, a letter from Edith for which please thank her, and all the usual papers, also a book, 'The Traitors', sent by you which will be most welcome.[3]

I asked Capt. Farley, who has recently been working in Baghdad to try and get some postcards or stamps: he has failed to get either; I am very sorry as I know how much you would enjoy them, but I cannot do more!

I hope you have managed to get some one in Pittaway's place. You must take care of yourself and not catch cold owing to insufficient coal to warm the house.[4] As you say you will have to go and live in the kitchin, but you must look out for the draughty passages.

The chief event of the week has been our crushing success on the Euphrates,[5] in which of course we played no part being on the other river.

It is one of the best shows we have had out here and is a most auspicious beginning to the cold weather. If we can keep it up there is not much fear of the Turks recapturing

---

[3] *The Traitors*, by E. Phillips Oppenheim, a pioneer of the thriller genre, was published in London in 1902 by Ward Lock. During the war, Oppenheim was appointed to the Ministry of Information and accompanied journalists to France to report on events on the Western Front.

[4] Coal had been rationed in Britain since October 1916 owing to short supplies.

[5] The Battle of Ramadi on 28th-29th September.

Baghdad whatever the Russians do or rather fail to do.[6]

Yesterday I had a game of polo, the first I or my pony have played since December 1914. We are both feeling rather stiff in consequence! The ground is rather dusty, and you occasionally completely lose sight of the ball. But it is very good considering.

I made a ten mile trip down the river in a pontoon the other day. It is most exciting, as it is now at its very lowest and is a succession of pools and small rapids.

We, that is to say all the 1st K. G. O. Sapper and Miners units present here, are giving a Regatta next Saturday. I am running it all, so shall have a fairly busy week, as we are also busy getting ready for the floods which are possible in November.

No letter mails out from home have been sunk recently, but two parcel mails, and I thought I had lost a pair of boots and pair of breeches, but both arrived today having been posted a day later thank goodness!

Very best love

    Your ever loving Son

        Fred. V. B. Witts.

F. V. B. Witts

Capt. R.E.

                    [Samarrah]

                    Oct 7th 1917

Dearest Mother.

No mail come in since I last wrote.

We have been having a sort of Samarrah week. On Tuesday evening one Regiment was at home for a Khattak dance. The Khattaks are Pathans who come from near Kohat, and have a weird dance in which they fling themselves about and brandish swords in a most alarming manner. By bright moonlight, with a roaring fire in the middle, round which they dance, it is a really wonderful sight.

On Thursday there was another race meeting which drew together another large gathering.

Yesterday was our Regatta of which I enclose a Programme. The sketch on the outside represents a view of Samarrah. Appearing above the walls of the town on the left you see the spiral watch tower, further along the smaller of the two domes is

---

[6] Early in October, the new commander of the Russian Caucasus Army, General Prjevalski, made an official communication to Maude regretting that Russian cooperation would not be forthcoming. He did, however, offer Maude the services of a detachment of 15,000 Cossacks, but these were rejected on grounds that they would struggle to reach the British camp in time to be of any practical use, and would be better employed reining in the mutinous elements of Baratoff's force. Later, in December, when the newly installed Communist Government began negotiating peace with Turkey, Maude did accept a detachment of anti-Bolshevik Cossacks, under a certain Colonel Bicharakoff, to come under British command.

78. A Gufar.

covered with blue mosaic and is a very sacred place of Pilgrimage for Mussulmans. The larger dome is covered with gold, and the sun flashes on it and can be seen for miles around. Then come the two slender minarets, a perfect pair covered with very beautiful mosaic work. The tower on the right is the clock tower! It gives you the view I have been gazing upon for five months or more. In the foreground you see the round gufars[7] and an Arab sailing boat. We had a perfect day for it and everything went off most satisfactorily. My men got one of the Prizes in every event which was open to them, and so did very well. There was a very large crowd and every one was very pleased with my arrangements. When I tell you that our refreshments included biscuits, cakes, cigars, cheroots, cigarettes, beer, gingerbeer, lemonade, whiskey, sodawater and vermouth, you will begin to wonder where are the hardships of campaigning in Mespot. Such a week of events too, when we ought to be starting our winter campaign: but this time it is more or less up to the Turks.

Did I tell you another Officer has joined me, one Cargill, many years older than me, who had an engineering job in India before the war. I am prejudiced against bald subalterns!

It is much cooler and if anything dustier. No other news today.

Very best love

Your ever loving Son

Fred. V. B. Witts

Send me out six inches of Croix de Guerre <u>ribbon</u>. I have borrowed a bit from Capt. Farley and a bit of D. S. O. from Major Bird and am feeling very shy!

[7] *Gufars*, also known as coracles or quffars, are amongst the most ancient vessels in the world. They are composed of a circular reed basket in a wooden frame and waterproofed with a sealed layer of bitumen. Herodotus, writing towards the end of the 5th century BC, describes them paddling down the Euphrates to deliver merchandise to Babylon. (Herod. I. 194)

F. V. B. W.itts
   Capt. RE

[Samarrah]
Oct 15th 1917.

Dearest Mother.

Two mails have come in during the week with all the usual papers and your letters of August 14th and August 22nd also a small book by John Buchan[8] — the third or fourth I have received from you recently and all so welcome. I also heard from Aunt Maggie, congratulating me on the Croix de Guerre. By the way I asked you to send me 6 inches of the ribbon last mail: make it 12 inches, as you cannot get it out here, and once put up you have got to keep it going.

Your letters have come with absolute regularity, hitherto only one mail has gone to the bottom — in the Mongolia within site of Bombay![9]

I have just lost Company Sergeant Major Deverell, as he has been promoted Regimental Sergeant Major, so that no further news in any cable will refer to him. I am very sorry to lose him as he has done me very well. I hope he gets some reward.

I am glad to hear Harrogate has been such a success. You must certainly go again: there can be no question of affording it, as your sons can afford to send you there. I have saved £1600 during the war, and far more than made good my previous speculations! I now have £2200 in 5% War Loan, £500 Post Office Saving Certificates in England and £500 Post Office Saving Certificates in India, i.e. £3200 in 5% Gov Security and another £500 about in reasonably sound Industrials. But this is all private please, though I know it will interest you.

I hope you have got your coal all right, and am glad to hear the apples are so good. I think we are better fed out here than you are at home!

I have had to wait nearly three years for my First Mention in Despatches! I think anyone who has been out for 3 years on end with no soft jobs in the time deserves a mention for that alone! I am glad to say my subaltern Eastmond has been mentioned and also some of my men. They all deserve it thoroughly.

It has been an uneventful week. A concert on Wednesday evening — and a very good one too — our only entertainment.

Wednesday morning we had a slight thunderstorm and some rain, — the first rain since May. But it was a month earlier than last year. I hope that does not mean exceptionally high floods. I am more frightened of them, than I am of the Turk.

   Very best love
      Your ever loving Son
         Fred. V. B. Witts.

---

[8] During 1917 John Buchan was made head of the newly formed Ministry of Information (*see* also note 3).

[9] *S.S. Mongolia*, a 9,500 ton steamship, struck a mine, laid by the German commerce raider *Wolf*, and sunk 50 miles west of Bombay on 24th June 1917, claiming 24 lives.

As Captain Witts intimates, the Turkish threat to Baghdad had largely dissipated. The Turko-German Yilderim Group, dubbed as the army to retake the city, had become delayed by the incompletion of the Aleppo-Mosul railway, an essential part of its supply line. Further delays were caused by disagreements between the Yilderim's German commander, General von Falkenhayn, and Enver Pasha. Whilst von Falkenhayn was adamant that German interests could be better served in Palestine than Mesopotamia, Enver Pasha was still intent on recapturing Baghdad for the sake of Ottoman prestige. In December, however, the Turkish commander finally yielded, and the Yilderim Group was transferred to the defence of Jerusalem, arriving there just in time to join the Turkish retreat.

In Mesopotamia, the Turks were trying to avoid confrontation whilst General Maude was trying to force it upon them. Turning his attention back to the east of the country, Maude instructed General Marshall to lead the IIIrd Corps into the Jabal Hamrin hills and engage the wily Ali Ihsan in a conclusive battle. By mid-October, the trap was set; Marshall had split his force into two separate columns which were to converge on the Turkish XIII Corps, driving it up the Diyala River towards Qizil Ribat, where a Cavalry Brigade was waiting in ambush. Marshall's plan, however, had a vital flaw; he had misjudged the water levels on the Diyala. Upon hearing of the two British columns advancing towards him, Ali Ihsan simply forded the river and marched north to Qara Tepe, escaping Marshall's trap.

Back at Samarrah, Captain Witts had almost forgotten there was a war on.

F.V.B. Witts
   Capt. R.E.

[Samarrah]
Oct 22nd 1917.

Dearest Mother.

…It was Lt Gen Lawson R.E., who took me on his staff for manoeuvres one year when I was at Aldershot. I last heard from Sweet Escott when I was wounded. He has retired in the interval. Skipwith is a Major now, and I have not heard of him since early in the war.

I am very glad to see in one of the Times just come that my late Company Sergeant Major Deverell (Apphie called on Mrs Deverell I think) has got the D.C.M. He thoroughly earned it; and I wish we had heard before he left us.

You must find it very hard to keep going, and I am afraid you will feel the winter badly, but I hope Agnes will be at home for a bit and that you will see more of George. The war will be over next year I am certain, and you are very lucky in that all your sons have comparatively safe billets – as safe as any other five brothers in the Army. So we shall be forgathering for a family meeting sometime in 1919, as I see little chance of getting home next year.

It has been an uneventful week, not even a concert to record. I am getting polo regularly twice a week on my old pony. It doesn't sound like war does it?

An antiaircraft gun shell case fell in our kitchin yesterday, but I suppose that is an everyday occurrence in London now.[10] Luckily no damage was done, but our poultry were badly scared.

The climate now is almost perfect: there are only a few flies, very occasional duststorms, and not too hot in the middle of the day. The mornings and evenings are delightful and nights not too cold to be unpleasant.

No more news.

> With very best love
> Your ever loving Son
> Fred. V. B. Witts.

Captain Witts' harmonious lifestyle on the Tigris front was soon to receive a rude awakening. On 22nd October, Shefket Pasha sent a detachment of his XVIII Corps downriver to Huwaislat, 8 miles north of Samarrah. His aim was to divert British forces from chasing Ali Ihsan in the Jabal Hamrin hills. General Cobbe, commanding the Ist Corps in Samarrah, received alarming aerial reports of condensed masses of Turkish infantry assembled on islands in the Tigris (as Captain Witts mentions in his next letter, the inexperienced pilot had mistaken sheep for troops). In response to this information, Cobbe opted for a cautious approach in dealing with the threat. Two days later, having waited for a Cavalry Division and 3rd Division reinforcements to be sent up from Baghdad, the British advance on Huwaislat began. The Turks, meantime, had reverted to their evasive strategy and withdrawn to Daur, 10 miles upriver.

F. V. B. Witts
  Capt. R.E.

[Samarrah]
October 29th 1917.

Dearest Mother.

This is advertised as the Christmas mail, so I must start by wishing you a very happy Christmas, or as happy as it can be under the present circumstances. Let us hope that the war will be over before next Christmas and that we shall all be home again once more to cheer you up. I am sending you our local Christmas card. Please

[10] Zeppelins had bombed London intermittently since 1915, but in June 1917, the frequency of bombing raids increased dramatically with the introduction of the *Gotha* biplane. By May 1918, however, the Germans had lost so many planes (through accident, anti-aircraft fire and British SE-5 fighters) that they were forced to stop bombing.

As you fight for your King and
　　Country
In the thickest of the fray,
Be sure that your King and Country
　　Are thinking of you to-day,
And they send you Christmas Greetings,
　　And messages of love,
On the day when the King of Glory
　　Came down from Heaven above.

To-day from the heart of England
　　Ariseth a mighty prayer,
For the men who fight for England
　　By land, and sea, and air :
" God keep you through all your danger,
　　God help you in all your pain,
God bless you, and bring you safely
　　Back to your homes again ! "

Irlam Briggs.]

JUST because He loved us more than we can tell,
JESUS from His glory came on earth to dwell ;
Hymns of praise we offer, songs of joy we lift
As we thank our Father for His Christmas Gift.

79. Official Christmas card to the troops, 1917.

give my Christmas wishes to all at home. It is too great an effort to write to one and all by the same mail, when I can only repeat the same in each. I have written to Edith, Frank and Aunt Maggie, who wrote to congratulate me on my D. S. O.

The missing mail came in this morning with all the papers, your letter of congratulations of August 28th and a letter from George, for which please thank him. Many thanks for the congratulations: your cable was the first news I got. I have been very lucky. It is time Edward got something.[11] During the week we heard that my Indian Drivers have got five medals between them for gallantry and good work, so I am very pleased.

I am glad to hear that Butler appears to be turning out a success.

…We have had an unsettled week, as the Turk came down to find out what we were doing. He slipped away again before we could close with him, but it upset all our arrangements for polo, sports, races etc. The general commotion caused was rather aggravated by our aeroplanes who kept mistaking sheep for Turks, and brought in quite alarming reports.

I am writing in the middle of a violent duststorm, which probably means rain, and I hear some thunder growling round.

　　　　　Very best love and good wishes,
　　　　　　　Your ever loving Son,
　　　　　　　　　Fred. V. B. Witts.

[11] See Chapter I, p. 44, note 8.

General Cobbe was determined to engage the Turks at Daur, but, after a brief stand-off, they eluded him once again. The next Turkish outpost on the Tigris was at Tekrit, a strong defensive position where Shefket Pasha had concentrated his whole Corps. On November 5th General Cobbe launched his assault on the Turkish trenches, coming up against a dogged resolve which recalled the heroic defences of the Hai Salient and Khudhaira Bend. The outcome, however, was as predicted; on the night of the 5th, Shefket withdrew his force, fighting a valiant rearguard action all the way to Fathah Gorge, 30 miles upstream. The next day, the Ist Corps occupied Tekrit finding few prisoners and no supplies; with their communications already stretched, and with no strategic incentive to push on, General Maude ordered Cobbe to halt his advance.

Captain Witts, meanwhile, had followed the Ist Corps up the Tigris as a spectator. Describing his little expedition as a 'joyride', he was clearly still unconvinced that Force 'D' had anything to fear from the Turks.

FVB Witts
   Capt. R.E.

[Samarrah]
Nov 11th 1917.

Dearest Mother.

I am afraid I missed my New Year's Mail, but you have got to blame the war for it as for many other things. I went out on the evening of Nov 1st for a reconnaissance, expecting to be back in three days at the outside: actually I was out a week, and missed the mail accordingly. I was living in my old 4th Company with Major Bird and Capt. Farley, and made a reconnaissance of the river an excuse to accompany them on a surprise march against the Turk. However the Turk was not to be surprised this time, and fell back before us. I had a great view of the fight at Tekrit from the opposite bank of the river, and only returned when we had occupied it after the Turkish withdrawal.

In a way it was a strenuous time, two long night marches, one of 20 miles on the top of 6 miles earlier in the day, but personally I was practically joyriding and had nothing to worry me, especially as the 4th Coy fed me very well.

There is no fear of the Turks being able to retake Baghdad this winter and I don't think they will trouble to try, but will simply ignore us.

A portion of our train went out and all our Transport has been doing very heavy work.

…I am very sorry to see about Colonel Chester Master.[12]

---

[12] Lieutenant-Colonel Richard Chester-Master D.S.O. of the Abbey Cirencester was killed in action aged 47 on August 30th 1917.

You must be finding the long winter evenings very lonely and trying, but it should be a mild winter this year after last year. 1918 must see the end of the war and some of us home.

I am sending you a Sapper & Miner New Year card, which, like my letter, missed last mail.

Many thanks for sending the soap etc: it is sure to arrive in due course and I will let you know. So far all along only 1 letter mail and 1 parcel for me has been lost, which is remarkably lucky.

…I am also writing to the authorities at the War Office to tell them to send you my Croix de Guerre – they may or may not do so. Anyhow don't be surprised if it comes, but look after it carefully.

Many thanks for sending me a sketch of the Cross and full particulars. I do not know which of the two I have got but imagine it is the bronze one.

When you have got the Croix de Guerre and seen what it actually is: a most acceptable present would be the three miniatures with miniature ribbon as worn in Mess Dress. I must get them sometime and Mess Dress is still worn in India.

You certainly must NOT put C de G on my envelopes, only British Decorations carry such letters after one's name.

I am glad Pittaway's successor is turning out a success and that you have got in some coal; I hope you still have some of it in hand!

I think I am all the better for the hot weather; it has definitely killed those wretched germs which used to cause spots on my face, but from which I have been free now for a year. I consequently feel more presentable and correspondingly more cheerful, as they used to worry me.

Some large fish have been caught opposite our camp during the week. While I was out one of 95 lbs was landed on a rod after 1½ hours playing, and another of 87 lbs on a ground line. The day after I got back one of 131 lbs was caught on a ground line. A magnificent fish and most excellent eating. It was 5 ft 6 inches long and 36 inches largest girth. A Mahseer – a famous fish in India. I think I shall have to get you to send me out a rod and tackle, but I am sure if they started I should move elsewhere before they arrived.[13]

No more news.

With very best love and best wishes for the New Year.

      Your ever loving Son,

          Fred. V. B. Witts.

---

[13] In *Light Floating Bridges*, F.V.B.W. mentions the rather unorthodox fishing methods of the local Arabs: 'The Arabs used to catch them by throwing in a loose bait containing opium: they then swam out and caught the drugged fish which came to the surface with their hands.' (Appendix I, p. 436).

F.V.B. Witts
   Capt. R.E.

[Samarrah]
Nov 19th 1917.

Dearest Mother.

Very little news from this end this week. Major Bird and Capt. Farley dined with us on the 13th previous to their moving elsewhere, and I have had two evenings out with other Roorkee Sappers who are moving. As a result I spent Saturday in bed, having over eaten myself or something! but I believe I am in good company, as I hear General Maude was taken dangerously ill the same day, and that his condition is grave. It looks as if we shall have a new Commander as this is not the country to get well again in quickly. I hope he will be as good a man.

Three mails have arrived during the week – an absolute record – with your letters of Sept 24th from the York Hotel and Oct 3rd & 8th from home. Also your two parcels of Sept 17th & 18th containing Shaving Brush, 2 sticks Pears Shaving Soap; Piece Soap, Beef tea, Lemonade, Flycatchers, Vinolia Brilliantine and Spong. All so civilizing and welcome, particularly the spong, as my old one had faded away some time [ago], but it is a bit big to cart about in a 20 lb kit on Active Service! Every conceivable means of dealing with flies are now issued out here free to every one, so don't trouble to send any more, though it is impossible to have too many.

Thanks awfully for sending the D.S.O. and Croix de Guerre ribbon. It was only last mail that I asked you to send me some, and I was wondering whether my present bit would hold out till the new came three months ahead, and then to my intense surprise and delight I got bits two days later. However send me some more as asked for as it soon gets dirty and untidy. Thanks too for the palm leaf, but I don't know whether I am entitled to it, and if I am, I don't know how to wear it. You might enquire from the Office of the Foreign Decorations, where again I see you have anticipated me and successfully demanded the Cross, which only last mail I wrote to tell them to send to you!

But you must not put C de G after my name in the address – it is not done.

All the usual papers, and Blackwoods and R. E. Journal for October, and an unexpected letter from Geoffrey [Woodroffe], also came. No mail has ever got up here quicker – exactly five weeks for the latest date Times.

I am afraid there has been a long gap in getting any letters from me. It is not for lack of writing regularly.

I am very sorry to see you were caught in a bad air raid. You mustn't stay in London longer than absolutely necessary.

The news from Russia and Italy just at present is about as bad as it possibly can be.[14] Palestine is the only bright spot, and it looks as if the British Flag will be flying over Jerusalem of all places before you get this.[15]

Glad to hear Agnes is back again, and I hope she will be at home a bit to help cheer you up these long winter evenings. There must be ample work for both her and Edith.

Very many thanks for sending a box from F & M. I hope it was not too big! They have recently got very strict out here, and a whole consignment for us from India has been held up as too bulky. Parcel post is all they allow at present.

I should like to see Father Staunton's life.[16]

I am so sorry to hear about Duncan Woodroffe,[17] I was very fond of him.

Always remember if my letters don't roll up, no news is good news. Bad news flies only too fast.

I am glad your War Pension work has been suitably recognised by an allowance of petrol.

You say you don't know where I am. It is Samarrah at present and likely to remain so as far as I can see.

Who is there left I wonder to go out with the Heythrop.[18]

No more news and the orderly is waiting for my letter.

    Very best love,

        Your ever loving Son,

          F. V. B. Witts

On the 19th November, after just two days of illness, General Maude died aged 53. Colonel Willcox, his personal physician, diagnosed 'cardiac failure' as the reason for death, 'consequent on the toxaemia of a very severe cholera

---

[14] The 'October Revolution' from 5th-8th November 1917 (Russia used the Julian calendar) was a Bolshevik coup against the Provisional Government: the dawning of Russia's communist era. At the top of Lenin's manifesto was his pledge to begin immediate negotiations for an armistice with the Central Powers. On 3rd March 1918 the Bolshevik Government signed the treaty of Brest-Litovsk, officially ending Russia's involvement in the war. In Italy, the Caporetto Offensive (24th October-12th November), on the Austro-Italian front, had ended in catastrophe for the Italians with 20,000 casualties and 275,000 taken prisoner.

[15] General Allenby, C-in-C of the Palestinian Campaign, marched into Jerusalem on 9th December 1917, delivering a devastating blow to Ottoman prestige.

[16] The American-born Rev. John Staunton was a pioneering Catholic missionary in the Philippines in the early 20th century.

[17] Duncan Woodroffe was an older brother of George Woodroffe, F.V.B.W.'s brother-in-law. He was Vicar of Banstead in Surrey.

[18] The Heythrop was, and is, the local Upper Slaughter hunt.

injection.'[19] The illness was believed to have been caused accidentally by the consumption of a glass of unpasteurized milk, although rumours persisted in Baghdad and England that Maude had been poisoned; a suggestion strongly repudiated by Colonel Willcox.

The news of Maude's death came as a great shock to the men of Force 'D', the British Army as a whole, and the British and Indian public. The *Official History* asserts that 'his name had so come to be regarded as synonymous with success that his death was looked upon as indeed a national misfortune'[20]. British dignitaries from King George V downwards expressed their grief in public announcements, the following being the closing paragraph of Prime Minister Lloyd George's address to the House of Commons:

> Sir Stanley will always be remembered as one of the great figures of the War, not merely for what he achieved, but for what he was. I know not what destiny may have in store for the famed land which he conquered, but of two things I am certain. The first is, that the whole course of its history will be changed for the better as a result of the victory and the rule of Sir Stanley Maude; and the second is, that his name will always be cherished by the inhabitants of that land as that of the gentlest conqueror who ever entered the gates of Baghdad.

To his army, he was a hero. General Maude had adopted command of Force 'D' after a winter of heavy defeat and a summer of great discomfort; British morale and prestige were at their lowest ebb. Building on the stable foundations of General Lake's administration, he took a measured and assertive approach to the campaign, adroitly working his superiors in London round to his way of thinking. Under his leadership, Force 'D' achieved goals the War Office had dared not think possible. His modesty, compassion and insatiable appetite for work were well known and inspiring to his men. Captain Witts, having become personally acquainted with Maude in the run-up to the Shumran crossing, respected and trusted him as a leader and as a man. Together with the whole of Force 'D', he greeted the news of his death with heart-felt regret.

---

[19] Colonel Willcox's medical report in Callwell, *Life of Sir Stanley Maude*, p. 310.

[20] Moberly, F. J., *The Mesopotamia Campaign*, vol. IV p. 85

80. General Maude's funeral.

F.V.B. Witts
Capt. R.E.

[Samarrah]
Nov 25th 1917.

Dearest Mother.

...General Maude died the day I wrote. Of cholera of all things – the one man in the force whom you would consider immune from the perils and pestilences of war. He is a tremendous loss. The hardest worker out here, he was possessed of wonderful driving power. He had some mad ideas, but got things done.[21]

Now today I hear one of our sapper generals has just died of pneumonia.[22] They seem to be having a run of bad luck.

The weather broke early in the week and we had 18 hours steady but not heavy rain. It has laid the dust splendidly and has been most refreshing as it is the first wash the air has had since April. 48 hours later the inevitable rise in the river came, but so far it has been nothing alarming.

Things are so quiet and settled now – since our recent raid on Tekrit, only one aeroplane even has paid us a visit, – that everyone's thoughts are already turning to the prospects of leave. But the trouble is everyone cannot go: luckily I have the prior claim of any one in the Train, but leave to England is very difficult to get except on the plea of marriage, which I am not contemplating at present. Leave to India in the hot weather is not much relief – it is a long way to go for merely a change of diet. There is a white lady up here now engaged in political work: she was out here before

---

[21] F.V.B.W. previously made mention of General Maude's 'wild schemes' (*see* Feb 11th 1917, p. 141-2). His penchant for deception made it difficult to be certain which schemes he intended to carry through and which he created just to confuse the enemy.

[22] Brigadier-General E. Stokes-Roberts R.E. (Director of Works) died on 22nd November 1917.

the war and speaks Arabic like an Arab, and she knows most of their leading men too. She is the only one to come beyond Baghdad. A Miss Bell by name – she was among the original recipients of the New Order of the British Empire.[23]

No more news today
  Very best love
    Your ever loving Son
      Fred. V. B. Witts.

F. V. B. Witts
  Capt. R.E.

[Samarrah]
Dec 3rd 1917.

Dearest Mother.

Another week has passed, how quickly the time slips by. In December already, and it will be well on in 1918 before you get this. The week brought with it another week's mail including your letter of Oct 16th and all the usual papers, including the Guardian about Duncan Woodroffe. He was such a charming man that he will be greatly missed.

Nothing particular to report from this end. It is getting very cold at nights. Only ½ degree above freezing two nights ago. This indicates hard frosts later on in January; but nothing to what you had in England last winter. They say they are going to give us stoves but I doubt if we shall get them until it is beginning to get warm again. However it is healthier than the heat.

I am sending you a packet of Christmas cards which were issued to each man in the force – the gift of the Women of the Bombay Presidency. Too late I am afraid to fulfil their proper purpose; but I know they will interest you as Picture Postcards.

I had a bit of bad luck on Saturday evening, when my Sergeant Major fell into the river and was drowned. I ought to expect to lose a man occasionally in this way, but it is always the man one can least lose, and under circumstances of the most futile description. The necessary Court of Inquiry into the case quite spoilt my Sunday's rest,

---

[23] Gertrude Bell was an explorer, archaeologist, political officer and author; she had considerable knowledge and experience of the customs, society and language of the Arab people. From November 1915 she had worked in the Arab Bureau at Cairo with the likes of T. E. Lawrence, successfully helping to incite an Arab revolt against the Turks. She was summoned to Basra in March 1916 to start work as a Political Officer, advising Sir Percy Cox, the Civil Commissioner in Mesopotamia. She was later sent to Baghdad to take up office as Oriental Secretary and from then onwards was intricately involved in British relations with Iraq until her death there in 1926.

especially as it will probably lead to a Court Martial.[24]

No more rain, and the river has fallen again nearly to its original level.

Since our visit to Tekrit, we very rarely even get a visit from a hostile aeroplane; and things are very peaceful, and but for the discomfort of always living in tents to which one is getting more or less inured, one would quite forget that there is a war on.

No more news.

With very best love

Your ever loving Son

Fred. V. B. Witts.

81. Lieutenant-General Sir William Marshall.

General Sir William Marshall, former commander of the IIIrd Corps, succeeded General Maude as G.O.C. in Mesopotamia. His task of carrying on where Maude had left off was far from easy; as Captain Witts had discovered first hand in February 1917, Maude was an intensely secretive commander. As a result, there was no record of what Maude's intentions for future operations might have been, and staff officers at G.H.Q. were equally mystified. To clarify the situation, the Chief of Imperial General Staff in London, Sir William Robertson, recapitulated that Marshall's brief was essentially one of aggressive defence; like his predecessor, General Marshall intended to take full advantage of his relatively free rein.

In early December, Marshall despatched a column under Major-General Egerton, the new commander of the IIIrd Corps, into the Jabal Hamrin hills to flush conclusively Ali Ihsan's XIII Corps out of hiding. With Egerton, Marshall sent a party of 1,200 of Baratoff's Cossacks, commanded by the Russian Colonel Bicharakoff who, disgusted by the Bolshevik stance, had placed himself and his men under Marshall's authority.

Despite Russian help, the IIIrd Corps still failed to pin down the Turks; after a short, indecisive battle, Ali Ihsan escaped to the north with the bulk of his force. Although he had failed in his primary mission, General Egerton's capture of the Sakaltutam pass, an important route through the Jabal Hamrin hills, would greatly limit any future movements of the Turkish XIII Corps. At the same time, the large number of Turkish deserters was testament to the poor condition of Ali Ihsan's supply lines and the morale of his troops.

Life at Samarrah, meanwhile, was comfortable but boring.

---

[24] Usually quite sympathetic towards his men, F.V.B.W. displays a surprisingly selfish attitude towards the death of his Sergeant-Major. The need for a Court Martial suggests that someone's incompetence was to blame, perhaps also explaining, to some degree, F.V.B.W.'s frustration in the matter.

F.V.B. Witts
    Capt. R.E.

[Samarrah]
Dec 9th 1917.

Dearest Mother.

No mail since last writing, but your parcels from Fortnum & Mason have arrived. Very many thanks for sending them; they are very welcome, but you mustn't send any more; I ought to be sending you dates and oranges from here instead! They were not packed as well as usual; I was greeted with an awful smell which was found to proceed from a tin of Jugged Hare which had burst in the post!

Nothing of interest to report from this end this week. We had some rain two nights ago, and it is raining again now; but hardly enough to lay the dust, and the river at present shews no signs of rising, but of course the river depends more on the rainfall in the hills.

One of our other columns has been clearing the Turk back a bit, but, as his recent practice has been, he slipped away before things became too unpleasant, and one ton of rice assumed such a large proportion of our total captures, that it was deemed deserving of a special reference in our local communiqués![25]

If he hopes to lure us on to our destruction he is failing dismally.

…Tomorrow morning I have a Court Martial which is rather a trying business and I shall be glad when it is over.

A great programme of events has been arranged for the Baghdad Christmas week. Tennis, Golf and Polo Tournaments, Races, Dinners and Duckshoots – ducks obliging! – everything in fact except dances – and I expect there will be some of those, as there are ample nurses to justify it! However we, up here, are quite out of touch with what goes on in Baghdad, and they are not likely to give us leave there en blocque, unless in the hopes of the Turks hearing of it and venturing to attack us.

It is now six months since I was down there.

> Very best love
> Your ever loving Son
>   Fred. V. B. Witts.

---

[25] F.V.B.W. is referring to the action against Ali Ihsan at Qara Tepe. The ton of rice is not mentioned in any other researched material.

F.V.B. Witts
  Capt. R.E.

No 2 Bridging Train
Mes. Ex: Force
[Samarrah]
Dec 17th 1917.

Dearest Mother.

No mail since I last wrote: it is already the longest time we have been without one and they tell us not to expect it for another ten days, which will mean after Christmas. It must be due to the Italians being driven back [at Caporetto] and dislocation of the mail service through Italy. But we mustn't grouse.

I had two outings during the week, due to some Germans putting some mines in the river 12 miles beyond our outposts. The first day I went out in a car escorted by armoured motor cars to locate the mines. We found them successfully, and the next day I rode out with a cavalry escort with a party to blow them up, which we did most successfully. I had a 36 mile ride, which neither master nor pony have been accustomed to recently but we bore up well! Not a sign either day of any enemy, who I believe are quite 50 miles away.[26] The following day however just to remind us that there is a war still on and that they are within reach, an aeroplane came over and dropped a few bombs; he flew straight over our camp and I thought we were going to get it, but none dropped within half a mile of us.

The river started coming up during the week but changed its mind and went down again.

The outstanding feature of the week has been the cold. The thermometer suddenly dropped nearly 30 degrees and we have been having frost each night, as much as eleven degrees once. They say it will get no colder, I certainly hope it doesn't. I think we feel it more than we should otherwise, after the extreme heat of the summer.

I see in Blackwood's they are advertising a book published by Murray – The Indian Corps in France by Lt Col Merewether & F. E. Smith. Will you get it for me and send it out after reading it? With these intermittent mails, one feels the want of something to read.

Major Bird and Capt. Farley are both leaving the country for some other scene of war; I wish I were going with them as there are strong rumours that they will be nearer home.[27] I am afraid I have got a job and a unit, special to the country, and there

---

[26] Shefket Pasha's XVIII Corps had dug in at Fathah Gorge, on the left bank of the Tigris, 60 miles north of Samarrah.

[27] The relative security of the Mesopotamia Campaign had precipitated a reshuffling of troops. Palestine was now the more decisive theatre in the Middle East and General Allenby needed reinforcements to replace troops he had sent to the Western Front. The 7th (Meerut) Division, including 4th Coy. Bengal Sappers and Miners, left Basra for Palestine (via Egypt) on January 4th 1918 to help in the advance on Damascus.

is little chance of my being shifted.

    With very best love

        Your ever loving Son

            Fred. V. B. Witts.

82. The bridge at Baghdad.

F.V.B. Witts
    Capt. R.E.

                    [Samarrah]
                    Christmas Eve.
                    Dec 24th 1917.

Dearest Mother.

    Still no mail in – it is five weeks now. There were wild rumours of its coming in yesterday, but they did not materialize. It may come in today but not till after the outward mail has gone. It will be most suitable if it comes in tomorrow. I sent you a Christmas cable on the 20th which I hope you got. It was the anniversary of my being wounded and getting the M. C. How the time has past, and yet we seem little nearer the end of the war.[28]

    Eastmond has just gone off to Baghdad for the Christmas week, which includes every form of amusement bar dances. I shall probably go down in the beginning of January for a week or so – floods permitting, the enemy no longer need consideration!

    They tried to bomb our bridge early in the week, but made very bad shots and the bombs fell miles away from anywhere.

    The hard frost has passed off and in its place it has been very foggy and raw like a November day at home – much more unpleasant, but the fogs have kept off moonlight bombing raids which were expected.

    Thursday there was a large Horse Show and we did very well though we didn't get a first. We got three seconds and a third. Second for pack mules and tent pegging, and both second and third for mule carts. Our large mules had to compete against teams of horses, who took the first three prizes, but our team of mules were the last team to be turned out, so were actually winners in their class. We were very pleased with ourselves.

---

[28] Prolonged inactivity seems to have dampened F.V.B.W.'s spirits.

My second subaltern Cargill, who has been with me barely ten weeks has been taken away for another job, so I am rather shorthanded. I don't like changes of officers, you never know what you are going to get these days. And it is most unpleasant in a small mess if you strike one of the wrong sort; as it is we have to put up with an Indian doctor, who is rapidly getting on my nerves!

My two courts martial have been satisfactorily settled, one man being acquitted and the other just escaping getting shot!

We shall be a very small party tomorrow night with Cargill gone and Eastmond away, just myself, Das the doctor, who I could well do without, Finlay my Transport officer, who is a very nice lad whom I am very fond of, and one or possibly two friends from outside. However we have got a plum pudding and shall be drinking your health in Champagne.

May we soon spend a Christmas together again.

    Very best love & good wishes,
     Your ever loving Son,
      Fred.V.B.Witts.

F.V.B.Witts
 Capt. R.E.

                  [Samarrah]
                 Dec 30th 1917.

Dearest Mother.

Mails take so very long and are so uncertain that I am making this my birthday letter, though perhaps I am already behind the time. Very many happy returns of the day, and may you live to enjoy many more in the company once again of all your sons. I am enclosing a little present, which you must spend on yourself as you like. I was only totting up today how much you have been spending on me in the form of newspapers and postage, and I was astonished how much it worked out to; while all the time I have been saving money in a way it is only possible to do in the Army even in wartime, when you are a bachelor fighting in a barren land: in fact if finances were everything, as far as I am concerned I should be praying for the war to go on until it was time for me to retire!

Christmas passed off very quietly. Boxing day brought us two weeks' mails, and two days later a third. All the usual papers – Times, Truth, Bystander & Punch – for the three weeks, besides a copy of Land & Water, and the special Flying edition of the Sphere, a letter from Apphie for Christmas, one from Jack, and your three letters of Oct 22nd, partly written from Brown's Hotel after meeting Frank, Oct 29th & Nov 7th from the York Hotel. All most welcome: so you see nothing ever goes astray and everything gets here eventually. I think I have thanked you for the Fortnum & Mason's box; the Plum Cake from Cheltenham has still to come.

I am glad to hear Frank was so well; the family have been very fortunate in getting slight wounds. The Tetanus inoculation affected me when I was hit a year ago, and I shocked all the hospital nurses by telling them there were fleas in my bed, as I was itching all over!

I am going to ask you to do some shopping for me and send me out a small black comb, 4 to 6 inches long. My own is breaking up. I am hoping to get from you The Times Weekly History of the War – the part dealing with the Fall of Baghdad. I see it is out.

…There is little news from this end: it has been much milder, cloudy, with some rain, as the Daily Graphic would say. In fact we haven't seen the sun for some days, which is rather unique for this country. There have been fogs too, which were rather welcome as we were anticipating moonlight air raids. But we have got the upper hand in the air out here, as in every other department.

On the 28th there was a race meeting in which I entered and rode one of my ponies, but without any success.

On the 2nd I am probably going down to Baghdad for a week, and so my next letter should be from there.

> Very best love,
> Your ever loving Son,
> Fred. V. B. Witts.

F. V. B. Witts
Capt. R.E.

Baghdad
Jan 7th

Dearest Mother.

I came down here for a week's holiday on the 2nd. The train started at daybreak, so I arranged to sleep in it the previous night; when I got down to the station after a late night with my General where I had been dining,[29] it was pouring with rain and there was nothing but open trucks on the train! Luckily I managed to find a tent to sleep in near by, and the rain cleared before starting. But it was a vile night and a vile journey down; it is discomforts like these which makes one want to sit tight in one's own camp.

But here I have been living in the lap of luxury – I am staying with a sapper captain on the G.H.Q. Staff. A motor car met me at the station and brought me to the Mess a very comfortable building. It is now seven months since I slept under a roof, and the last time was when I was down here in June, staying at the same place. It is quite a cheery mess inspite of the presence of two Major Generals – the Gunner and the Sapper, and the Surgeon General; and it is the best possible place to stay in as you

[29]Major-General G. A. Leslie, F.V.B.W.'s former C.R.E. from France, now commander of the 17th Division which had replaced the 7th (Meerut) Division stationed on the Tigris Front.

83. British Residency in Baghdad.

can get a horse to ride, or a motor car or launch or whichever is the most convenient; without these helps it would be a very difficult task to get round all the widely scattered camps, which I wanted to visit.

Four new companies of ours have recently come out of Roorkee and they are camped round about and I have been spending a day with each going out by horse, car, or launch; meeting fellows whom I have not seen for three years or more.

Shopping or rather trying to shop has also kept me busy, but there is very little to buy and it is very hard to find that little. It is no good buying things to take home, as you cannot cart them about with you out here and there is no way of sending them out of the country. I have searched everywhere for postcards of the place but have failed to find a single one.

We had a regular cyclone yesterday evening, blew down our camp and two or three buildings, all accompanied by rain and thunder.

I go back tomorrow sometime.

> Very best love
>> Your ever loving Son
>>> Fred. V. B. Witts.

84. Bazaar scene, Baghdad.

85. Gufars at Baghdad.

F.V.B.Witts
    Capt. R.E.

[Samarrah]
Jan 13th 1918.

Dearest Mother

I came back in the early hours of the 9th, having travelled all night. I was greeted on arrival with the cheerful news that my bridge was broken; however it turned out to be only the Indians' way of saying it had been dismantled for removal to its flood site.

We have been kept very busy ever since to keep the bridge going as the water now is always rising or falling and the bridge has constantly to be adjusted. So far we have suffered no damage which is something to be thankful for. A flood came down the tributaries below us while I was in Baghdad and five bridges were carried away. It is very hard to cope with the conditions.

We have moved down with our bridge to a new camp after more than eight months in the last. It is above flood level which is more than the last was.

No mails in since I went away; it is nearly three weeks since we had any now. It makes it difficult to write letters when you have nothing to answer and it is a crime to talk about what is going on out here.

My journey up was much more comfortable than the journey down. I got into the train at 9 p.m. in one wagon fitted up with baths for wounded, went to bed & slept soundly, and although we got back at 3 a.m. we were not turned out until daylight.

I send you some picture postcards of Basrah which I found in Baghdad. One of them may interest you as it is of my bridge – I have marked it behind. I couldn't find any of Baghdad.

There was a lot of rain up here while I was away, but it has dried up much quicker than I expected.

I bought a number of Polo sticks and balls while in Baghdad and when I get time I hope to get going again.

No more news

Your ever loving Son
Fred.V. B.Witts

In terms of offensive operations, little was currently happening in Mesopotamia, but Captain Witts' tantalising comment 'it is a crime...' may have been a reference to the venturesome *Dunsterforce* mission in Persia and the Caucasus. Peace negotiations between Russia and the Central Powers, initiated on 22nd December 1917, had filled the British Imperial Staff with worry that Russia's collapse would not only open Force 'D"s Persian flank, but could also open India to the possibility of a Turko-German invasion. Considering the state of the Turkish army in Mesopotamia, these concerns may seem groundless, but they were founded on the knowledge that 40,000 Austro-German prisoners, held by the Russians in Trans-Caucasia and Russian Turkestan, were bound to be released with the signing of a peace treaty.

The War Office's solution to the problem was to create *Dunsterforce*: a detachment of 1,000 picked men under the Russian speaking Major-General L. C. Dunsterville. Their ambitious mission was to travel across Persia into Trans-Caucasia, and raise Georgian and Armenian militias to fill the void left by the Russian Caucasus Army. In late January 1918 *Dunsterforce* left Hamadan, in western Persia, with an escort of armoured cars and a fleet of 750 lorries carrying supplies from Baghdad. Two weeks later, the expedition reached the Caspian port of Enzeli, having travelled 200 miles across land ravaged by famine. At the port, *Dunsterforce* was confronted by a hostile mass of Bolshevik troops, numbering around 3,000, which stubbornly refused to let them pass. The situation was extremely delicate; the British were completely isolated with no hope of support from Baghdad should violence break out. Fortunately, through General Dunsterville's exceptional powers of diplomacy, a battle was narrowly avoided and the Bolsheviks allowed the British to retire back to Hamadan unscathed. Having been repulsed at the first serious hurdle, *Dunsterforce* had been an expensive failure; however, another opportunity for adventure would soon arise. In the meantime, General Dunsterville employed his men industriously in famine relief work in the hard-hit region around Hamadan.

F.V.B. Witts
  Capt. R.E.

[Samarrah]
Jan 21st 1918.

Dearest Mother.

Two mails have come in together since last writing, bringing all the usual papers and also Blackwoods Land & Water and the Despatches which were just what I wanted. Your two letters of Nov 13th & 14th with your Christmas Card, and the cake from Cheltenham in excellent condition but being devoured only too rapidly. The fly whisk has come too: it is tophole and just what I wanted, thanks awfully for sending it, and my pony will be equally grateful in the spring when the flies get bad again.

The week has been uneventful, no rain to speak of and river has been falling steadily. I have been having quite a gay time & dined out three times, lunch twice & tea once.

One of my dinners was with the Corps Commander, a very charming man.[30] Another with the Navy who have at last managed to get up here.

There is a lot of talk about leave, but very little mention of leave home, and I am afraid it is too much to hope for under present conditions.

86. Lieutenant-General Sir Alexander Cobbe.

The floods a fortnight ago caused a colossal smash at one of the bridges lower down, reminiscent of my experiences of April 1916. I am afraid we are in for a thin time of it too during the next three months, but there is nothing more to do but hope for the best. They have supplied us with lifebelts all round, so there is not much chance of getting drowned!

We have had no bombing raids lately, I think I told you how they greeted us on New Year's Day by dropping bombs at 12.1 a.m. just as every one was singing 'Auld Lang Syne'. But they have not been since.

There is no more news today. I am keeping extraordinarily well though my poor old teeth are gradually falling to bits!

Very best love,

Your ever loving Son,

Fred. V. B. Witts

87. Bridge of boats over the Tigris, broken up by storm.

---

[30] Lieutenant-General Sir A. S. Cobbe V.C. K.B.C. D.S.O. Cobbe won his V.C. at Erigo in Somaliland in 1902 for saving a wounded orderly in a stream of enemy fire.

F. V. B. Witts
Capt. R.E.

[Samarrah]
Jan 28th 1918.

Dearest Mother.

…Not much news from this end. Compared with the previous week it has been very quiet and I have only dined out once – a farewell dinner! I was to have gone out to some races and dinner afterwards, but most unexpectedly I had to cancel it.

A beautifully fine week culminated in a hurricane last night, which nearly blew our bridge out of the water though without damaging it. It was accompanied by rain and several tents were levelled. It has been very stormy all day wind & rain and now thunder and lightning, and the river will rise again, but it won't worry me.

I find it very hard to write as I have got a bit of news which took me very much by surprise and which I don't know yet what it means, but such as it is I must not mention it. You must be content with guessing and reading between the lines.[31]

I am afraid I never realized when I wrote you my birthday letter that you would be 70 on Feb 18th. How the time does fly. I shall be thirty next year and have to think seriously about marrying! May you live to enjoy a good old age and see us all back at home again soon.

Well I must stop now as I am very busy, being off to Baghdad in the morning.
Very best love
    Your ever loving Son
        Fred. V. B. Witts

F. V. B. Witts
Capt. R.E.

[Baghdad]
Feb 6th 1918.

Dearest Mother.

I came down to Baghdad on Jan 29th and have had a very busy time since, as two of my three subalterns have been seedy.

…Yes I got the life saving waistcoat you sent me, and since then I have managed to get lifebelts issued to all my men, so there is not much chance of our getting drowned!

---

[31] This intriguing 'bit of news' was orders for No. 2 Mobile Bridging Train to prepare for transfer from the Tigris to the Euphrates front, via Baghdad. Having been stagnating in Samarrah for 9 months, the change of scenery and the promise of some activity was very welcome to F.V.B.W. and his men.

88. View over Baghdad.

Yes I have met General Maude's successor; last year round Kut, when we were in his corps.[32]

Certainly return the earlier copies of the Sapper which you have so far kept for me.

Very pleased to see Jack's name mentioned in Despatches.

It is quite the longest letter I have had from you for ages! I hope your poor old fingers were none the worse for the effort. But if you realize that I look forward to your letters, as much as I know you do to mine, you may be tempted to repeat the performance! You have the advantage of being able to talk about what is going on, whereas I have to keep quiet and find the process rather difficult.

This time my journey down was done in comparative comfort, sitting on a camp chair in a closed cattle truck or its equivalent.

I have met three or four friends whom I have not seen for a year or more, as this place is of course the local metropolis, where everyone drifts to off and on.

We had a violent gale the other night accompanied by some rain, and I was glad to be away from my responsibilities: one less storm to be faced!

No more news.

> Very best love,
> Your ever loving Son.
> Fred. V. B. Witts.

---

[32] F.V.B.W. had received a personal telegram from General Marshall on 23rd February 1917, congratulating him and his unit on their success at the Shumran crossing, but he does not specifically mention when he met him in person.

Hit, 40 miles upriver of Ramadi, was the next Turkish outpost on the
Euphrates and the target of the next British advance. The town was a good
source of liquid bitumen (necessary for tarring boats and roads) and was of
some strategic importance; but the greatest reason for renewing the advance
up the Euphrates was to keep the troops active and morale high.

   No. 2 Mobile Bridging Train set off from Samarrah at very short notice,
leaving their pontoon bridge behind and picking up an entirely new set of
equipment and materials in Baghdad.

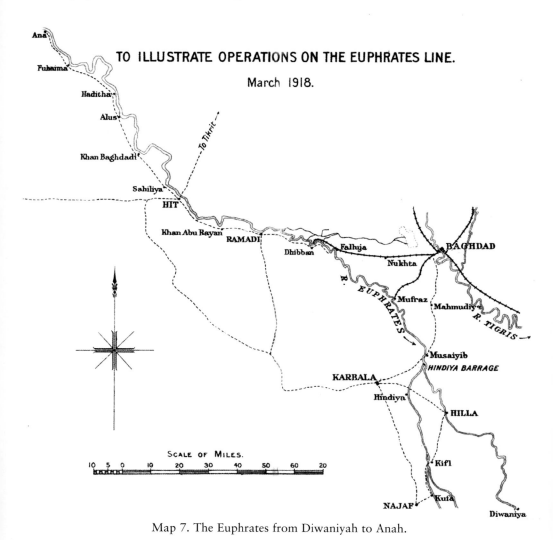

Map 7. The Euphrates from Diwaniyah to Anah.

F. V. B. Witts

[Falluja]
Feb 13th 1918.

Dearest Mother.

It is time for another letter, though it is hard to know what to talk about, when one has no letter to answer and one mustn't talk about ones own doings.

But you will probably have gathered that we have changed our quarters: where we are I shall be only able to let you know later.[33]

Both my subalterns have recovered again, and, instead, for a couple of days I thought I was going sick as a nasty swelling developed under my tongue. However judicious treatment with hot water brought it to a head and a small stone, the size of a cherry stone, popped out. It was a stone in the gland or something. It has left no ill effects.

I tried to see a dentist while in Baghdad as my poor old teeth are tumbling to bits, but he was booked up for ten days ahead, so there was nothing doing.

They are talking about leave again but I am afraid my chances of getting to England are very small and I am not particularly keen on going to India.

After two days of very cold wind, there is a decided feel of hot weather in the air today. But so far we have had only half our normal allowance of rain, so we can expect some more wet days.

Believed to be some shooting in our new quarters. I have got my gun and cartridges but the close season will soon be on us.

Absolutely no more news.

Very best love
Your ever loving Son
Fred. V. B. Witts

I shall be thinking of you on your 70th birthday on the 18th. Very many happy returns of the day and may you live to see us home again.

F. V. B. Witts
Capt.

[Ramadi]
February 18th 1918.

Dearest Mother.

I must begin by wishing you many happy returns of your birthday. Three score years and ten is a good old age but may you live to four score. I sent you a cable of congratulations on the 13th, and hope you got it in time but I have since heard that

---

[33] At this stage, No. 2 Mobile Bridging Train was stationed at Falluja, on the Euphrates, 40 miles west of Baghdad.

cable communication is interrupted: so it may arrive late. I wonder if you are at Slaughter, at any rate you won't be alone.

Leave regulations have come round, but there is not a mention of leave to England. It is of course impossible for every one, who wants to, to go; and there must be many with really urgent private reasons. It hits you hardest, mother, as I know how you are longing to see me. But if it is not this year it is bound to be next. I only hope Edward, who can put up real good urgent private reasons, will get home.[34] The younger son is always destined to be the exile.

…Yes I went up with the force to Tekrit, but we didn't stay there long as the Turks retreated quite fifty miles further north, and there was no advantage to be gained but much inconvenience.

It must be very dreary and lonely not being able to get about. I am glad you find the Foot Muff so useful… What bad luck you have in striking air raids each time you go to town. You must hear more guns and bombs than I do out here.[35]

We have done a bit more marching since last writing, but I don't think we have finished yet.[36] So far we have been extraordinarily lucky in our weather, as lucky as we were unlucky last year, when we made a practice of getting bogged. The marching conditions have been perfect in every way for once – Not too hot, no dust, no rain, good roads & everything – it is hard to believe in Mesopotamia.

Well there is no more I can say without giving things away.

Very best love,

    Your ever loving Son,

        Fred. V. B. Witts.

                                [Ramadi]

                            Feb 24th 1918

Dearest Mother.

As we are moving further away it is time to write again on the chance of catching the next mail, but it is rather problematical as there is no Post Office with us and letters sent may get left in some one's pocket. Needless to say no mail has reached me in the interval. We are down on the lowest scale of kit and rations: it is a tremendous change after our months' sedentary life.

---

[34] Edward was the eldest son and had inherited the family estate in Upper Slaughter. His consequent responsibilities might have helped him in an application for leave.

[35] Compared with WWII figures, bombing raids on London in WWI caused few casualties (835 in total) and little material damage. The psychological effect, however, was great: air raids shattered the age-old illusion that Britain, as an island, was almost invulnerable to invasion. Another significant effect was on industry; with frequent daytime raids, factory production was disrupted as workers hurried to find shelter.

[36] F.V.B.W. and his unit had advanced up to Ramadi.

We have just had three very strenuous days[37] – the most strenuous since last April – and we have actually heard a bullet again, but so far off that you needn't get alarmed! In any case it will be all over by the time you get this.

The weather has continued to be extraordinarily favourable for marching etc; though the roads have not been quite so good in one or two places, but so far we have not actually stuck anywhere.

Nothing has happened yet likely to appear in a communiqué, except perhaps the capture of 30 prisoners the other day.[38] Anyhow you will know that if anything happens in the immediate future from <u>now</u> (time of writing) we shall be involved, though not seriously.

I have chased a few duck but have not got anything more and they are few and far between and not easy to get near.

There is not much prospect of any further developments in the leave question until we settle down again.

With nothing to write about and no letters to answer, I have no more news today. With very best love

      Your ever loving Son
        Fred. V. B. Witts

Yesterday was the Anniversary of the crossing of the Tigris at Shumran. It will always be a red letter day in my Calendar. Owing to circumstances we were unable to celebrate it in any way at all. We shall have to keep it later!

F. V. B. Witts
      Capt.

                      [Khan Abu Rayan]
                      March 4th 1918.

My dearest Mother.

Two mails have just come in with the alarming news of your operation. Thank God it was a success and I have been spared the anxiety of those with you, by getting your letter and George's of Jan 9th, saying how you were, at the same time as the first intimation. It is sweet of you to write to me and address the envelope and also address January Blackwood's at a time when you should have been doing absolutely nothing. George tells me how brave you were over it all, and how you longed for us. I only wish I could have been there. I have applied for leave to England, but I am afraid I

---

[37] Up to this point, No. 2 Mobile Bridging Train had been employed in road maintenance.

[38] General Brooking's 15th Division had advanced to Khan Abu Rayan, 20 miles south-east of Hit, where they had paused to wait for supplies to be dumped and communications to be established properly. The 30 prisoners mentioned by F.V.B.W. might have been taken on Brooking's arrival at Khan Abu Rayan, or by one of his reconnoitring parties.

have not the remotest chance of getting it. But this year must see peace. I do so hope Edward gets leave; I think he must have as much right as most fellows.

…You say you think I must be looking thin. Not a bit of it! A friend whom I met the other day, who hadn't seen me for over three years, said he had never seen me looking better. And he's right!

I was very pleased to see Frank's name in Despatches. It is up to George now!

Very many thanks for the silk handkerchief – a most acceptable present at any time as my own are worn to rags; also for the 8 inches of the 3 ribbons; I am now well set up, and shall have no excuse for appearing improperly dressed.

…Yes, I got the plum cake from Cheltenham and think I have acknowledged it before. It was jolly good.

…We are still in the same place as when I last wrote. Weather has been unsettled, but it has been very good taking it all the way round with a tendency to get warmer.

You will have probably gathered that we left our old abode and are now on the other of the two big rivers out here, having marched 164 miles in the shift. We are all glad to see another bit of the country – rotten though it is, and though it means leaving comfortable almost semi-permanent quarters. Our chief grouse out here is that the Turk won't put up a fight, because he can't, and we can't chase after him because of supply difficulties.

I do so hope that the operation didn't hurt you much and that you have quite recovered from the effects of it. You must write and tell me truthfully exactly how you feel. It is the only way to stop me worrying.

With very best love,

Your ever loving Son,

Fred. V. B. Witts.

As Captain Witts had guessed would happen, the Turks withdrew from Hit before Brooking could engage them in battle. Interestingly, according to his essay, *Light Floating Bridges*, the Turkish retreat was precipitated by an aerial reconnaissance report which mistook Captain Witts' bridging column, measuring two miles in length, for a substantial reinforcement of British artillery.[39] By Captain Witts' own admission, this was virtually the extent of No. 2 Bridging Train's impact on operations on the Euphrates. Time was otherwise spent 'building bridges that were never used.'[40]

On the 9th March, General Brooking occupied Hit, and the next day he advanced a further 5 miles to Sahiliya, also without meeting any opposition. The apparently pusillanimous character of Turkish tactics had begun to tickle the pride of the headstrong Khalil Pasha; he dismissed the Euphrates commander,

[39] Witts, F. V. B., *Light Floating Bridges*, (Appendix I, p. 437). How F.V.B.W. came by this information is a mystery.

[40] Ibid.

Subri Bey, replacing him with Nazmi Bey, under the clear understanding that he was expected to stand and fight. At Khan Baghdadi, 20 miles north-west of Sahiliya, the Turks prepared themselves hurriedly for battle.

[Hit]
March 23rd 1918.

Dearest Mother.

I am afraid I have missed two mails. This is partly due to unexpected moves on mail day and partly to my putting it off in the hope of getting another mail with later news of you and how you are. But none have come so far and if I wait any longer I shall only miss another mail.

Not that I have got much news to talk about. The Turk does not want to fight out here, and slips away at the last minute each time he is threatened. Leave opens on April 1st, but only to India I am afraid; I asked for leave to England but have got the expected refusal. I feel I want a change, I can't exactly say a rest, as things are very quiet out here, and I suppose I shall be going to India but I am wondering where. Roorkee I suppose and then the hills. But the journey is so long and trying that it is hardly worth while, and then it means getting back out here just at the hottest time.

How I wonder how you are, but no news is good news, so I must be satisfied.

Since last writing we have been across a strip of petroleum bearing country.[41] I have never seen such a desolate waste. Black outcrops of bitumen rock, and black springs of liquid bitumen bubbling up. The worst going I have struck out here, and after the heavy rain we've had, it became a regular bog.

Now I am sitting on the bank of the river facing an island about half a mile long and a hundred yards broad, which is the most fertile spot I have so far met in this blighted country. Dates of course, barley, oranges, apricots, vine, all growing in profusion, though not unfortunately bearing fruit just at present. What a country of contrasts it is. It is irrigated by the most wonderful water wheels ever made by man to go round thirty foot diameter made of any old bits of stick tied together by withies or the equivalent, with a tree trunk as axle, they have earthen pots tied on by withies all

89. Waterwheels at Hit.

41 The region around Hit.

round the rim, to make them revolve 'floats' of dried palm leaves are also fixed to the rim; the water pressure against these floats turns the wheels, the water is lifted in the pots, and runs out into a channel when the pot turns over at the top. They are carried on large masonry structures which look like the beginnings of a railway viaduct. In one case I have seen, there are eight of these wheels in a row. To ensure sufficient force of water at low water, dams are built right out into the middle of the rim, much to the troubles of navigation.

During the last ten days we have had the heaviest rain of the winter, and camps became marshes: now there is a regular hot weather feeling in the air.

Very best love
        Your ever loving Son
                Fred. V. B. Witts.

On 26th March, a little further upriver from the tranquil scene described by Captain Witts, General Brooking launched his attack on Khan Baghdadi. The Turkish lines were rapidly overpowered and a determined chase up the Euphrates rounded up their disorderly retreat: it was a consummate victory. A total of 5,000 prisoners were taken, including the special prize of Niazim Bey, the luckless Turkish commander. After Kut, it was the greatest haul of prisoners in the campaign.

Surprisingly, Captain Witts makes no mention of the victory, but upon closer inspection, it seems likely that at least one, possibly two, of his letters have been lost as there is a three week break in his correspondence, with no customary apology for his failure to write.

F. V. B. Witts
    Capt.

[Hit]
April 14th 1918.

Dearest Mother.

...Since last writing we have been living a life of peace and leisure. Absolutely nothing doing and nothing to do – a welcome change from our previous strenuous days. But we are still on 'operation scale' of rations and have been now for seven weeks: it is one of the few hardships we have to put up with as compared with France, but it is ruinous for my poor teeth. I am writing now with a swollen face, though it has passed its worst and is going down again. If my leave ever materializes – none has hitherto – I fancy I shall spend most of it with the dentist.

The news from France is still rather alarming; we have just read of the latest Hun attack apparently with considerable success on the bit of line I know so well, and which has not altered for three years.[42]

I am sending you a Turkish postcard which I picked up, it has two strange stamps on it with the Jerusalem postmark. I don't know what they are but I am sure they will interest you.

I wonder how you are. It will be well on in the summer before you get this. You must take care of yourself for our sakes, as you are always reminding me to do for yours!

It has come on to blow and rain again, when we all thought it was over and that we had settled down for the hot weather. It means shutting up my small tent, so that I can hardly see to write. How I yearn for a civilized existence again! As I imagine every one else does.

My pony, which I have had with me over four years, got rather badly cut about the other night after breaking loose, but I hope will get all right again. He was with me in France & came on here with me.

This river has come down in a small flood since last writing but it is never anything like as bad as the other. It is extraordinary how both of them get much wider when they leave the alluvial and strike the rocky ground.

    Very best love

        Your ever loving Son

           Fred. V. B. Witts.

By the start of the hot season in 1918, Enver Pasha's cherished hopes of reclaiming the 'City of Caliphs' were manifestly dead. With successive defeats, a poor supply line and no hope of reinforcements, Turkish morale had plummeted, and with it, so had her quantitative military strength.[43] With this in mind, the Allied Supreme War Council ruled out Mesopotamia as a decisive theatre in the war, deciding that it would be Allenby's campaign in Palestine which would determine the fate of the Turks.

Although hardly surprising, this news was not the slightest bit welcome to the men of Force 'D'. Compulsory inertia, especially when the Allies were being stretched to breaking point on other fronts, was comparable to a prison term. Stuck at Hit and surrounded by bitumen springs belching out fetid fumes, the summer of 1918 promised to be especially unpleasant for Captain Witts and his men.

---

[42] On the 21st March, the first of three German assaults, known collectively as the 'Spring Offensives', was launched on the Western Front in the hope that the war in France could be won before U.S. troops arrived in numbers. The first phase, named the Kaiserschlacht Offensive, using extra divisions freed from the Eastern Front, was directed against the Allied line near Arras. Having achieved startling success initially, the speed of the offensive, led by light, rapid groups of elite 'stormtroopers', overran supply vehicles by such a margin that sheer exhaustion set in, stalling the advance short of Amiens, the principal target.

[43] The Turkish Army in Mesopotamia at this time amounted to just 9,000 rifles and 60 guns.

CHAPTER VII

VICTORY

Letters: April 19ᵗʰ 1918 – Jan 4ᵗʰ 1919

From its very inception, Force 'D' had struggled with the notion of fighting in a sideshow with little tangible effect on the war. In the summer of 1918, this sense of ineffectiveness and isolation became more apparent than ever. While Force 'D' sat idle in Mesopotamia, on the Western Front the Allies were fighting for sheer survival against the momentous German Spring Offensive, and in Palestine General Allenby was making headway in an elaborate diversion into Transjordan, supported by Arabs risen in revolt against Ottoman rule.[1] Despite the pressing need for reinforcements in both these theatres, and the comparative tranquillity of the campaign in Mesopotamia, the Imperial General Staff was adamant that a large-scale transfer of troops from Mesopotamia would invite disaster. The Turks were down, but not out, and further threats from the east necessitated a strong British force to remain active in the region.[2]

Captain Witts, meanwhile, had managed to negotiate his escape for the short-term; but in his heart, he would rather have been heading west to war in France, than east to leave in India.

---

[1] The Arab Revolt erupted in June 1916 under the banner of the Hashemite Sharif Hussein Ibn Ali of the Hejaz, the coastal region along the western edge of the Arabian Peninsula including the holy cities of Mecca and Medina. Sharif Hussein was known by the British to have nationalistic aspirations; through the work of the Arab Bureau, a British diplomatic organisation made up of Arabists such as Gertrude Bell and T. E. Lawrence, a deal was brokered in October 1915 between the British High Commissioner in Cairo, Sir Henry McMahon, and Sharif Hussein. In return for British guarantees of an independent Hashemite Empire in the Middle East, the Sharif promised to drum up a rebellion against Ottoman sovereignty. The Revolt was confined initially to the Hejaz, but, with the celebrated help of Colonel Lawrence, British liaison officer to Hussein's charismatic son, Feisal, it spread to Syria, Palestine and Transjordan, providing indispensable assistance to Allenby's campaign.

[2] The land east of Mesopotamia was teeming with anti-British intrigue: in northern Persia, Turko-German agents had convinced the *Jangalis*, a powerful revolutionary movement led by Mirza Kuchik Khan, to oppose all British action by force; in Afghanistan, German spies were endeavouring to bribe the Afghan Amir, Habibullah, to break his neutrality and allow Central Powers forces to pass through his country to invade India; meanwhile, in Turkistan, 40,000 Austro-German prisoners of war, formerly under Russian guard, still remained unaccounted for.

F.V.B.Witts
 Capt.

[Ramadi]
April 19th 1918.

Dearest Mother.

Just a line to let you know I have started on leave. I cabled you, as soon as I knew, to continue sending my letters here, but that a cable to Cox, Bombay would find me. But it is no use my reiterating all this, as I shall probably be back here again by the time you get this. The last letter to arrive from you was dated Jan 19th just three months ago!

I don't know yet where I am going. I shall go to Roorkee first to pick up some kit and fix up one or two jobs at the depot; I shall then probably go on to Mussourie which is the nearest hill station to Roorkee or to Simla. In either case my chief occupation will be with the dentist. I am glad to say my face is all right again, but it must be seen to properly.

I have just completed the first stage of the journey – 50 miles in a Ford van and I have had my full share of discomfort already. We got caught in the heaviest rain of the year, and, as there are no metalled roads out here, naturally got bogged, and had a nine mile tramp in the dark & rain to the nearest post, where I found little comfort. I got it pulled out by horses this morning and completed the first stage; but for 24 hours my sole food consisted of two army biscuits and two mugs of tea. I anticipate further troubles as both rivers are now coming down in highest flood. Is leave to <u>India</u> worth it?

The news from France makes one more anxious each day. The latest we have heard as I write is the capture of Bailleul and evacuation of the Ypres salient – after holding it through thick & thin all this time.[3] It is the worst part of this show – the feeling that we are not helping and cannot help in any way to win the war: it is like being interned. If there are any further developments out here, I expect them to be in the direction of Persia, to keep the peace and prevent German penetration and intrigue.

The latest rumour says Major Bird, who is now Brevet Lt Colonel, and Capt. Farley are in Italy: but probably you have more definite news, if so let me know.[4]

Very best love

 Your ever loving Son,
  Fred.V. B.Witts.

---

[3] The second of the German Spring Offensives, known as the 'Lys Offensive', was launched against the Ypres Salient in Flanders on 9th April, aiming to drive the Allied forces all the way to Dunkirk and cut British supply lines. After overwhelming success on day 1, German momentum faded; the onslaught lasted a further 19 days but was brought to a standstill about 20 miles short of Dunkirk. As had been the case in the Kaiserschlacht Offensive, sheer exhaustion had been the main burden on the German attackers. Casualties had been heavy on both sides, but with the looming arrival of U.S. forces, the issue was far more pressing for the Central Powers.

[4] They were actually in Palestine, as F.V.B.W. later discovered.

At sea
H. T. Chakdara.
May 5th 1918.

Dearest Mother.

It is over a fortnight since I last wrote, but I have been rapidly getting nearer home – postally speaking – and this letter, which will be posted the day after tomorrow at Bombay, may get home before the last.

I last wrote from Ramadi on completion of the first stage of my journey. The roads were quagmires so it was useless to think of going on by car, and I walked the next twenty miles to railhead, whence the train took us to Baghdad. Here we found the railway below had been broken by the rain and floods. This meant we should have to go by river and consequently we had to wait three days for a boat. We eventually got the best boat on the river and had a very comfortable and very quick journey to Basra of only three days, steaming only by day. What a change since I last came on leave, when I was living on an iron barge with no domestic arrangements of any kind, and having to make our own arrangements for food. This time I had a comfortable properly fitted up cabin, and there was a proper saloon where meals were served which would do credit to an ocean liner. The growth and expansion at Basrah was even more striking. It is a very sickening reflexion that, now that everything is on a proper footing out here and well run, there is no enemy anywhere near to strafe. There seems to be a lot of energy wasted without in any way helping to win the war.[5] However possibly there may be something doing in Persia, if they try and work down that way towards India and Afghanistan.

…All the usual papers and a Land & Water, & Church Family about the new Warden of Radley [have arrived].[6] I am sorry to see the price of the Times has gone up to 3d this means 2/3d a week with postage – which is tremendous, I must think about stopping it…I am so sorry and distressed to hear you have been laid up again, and do so hope you are all right again now and have recovered some of your old strength, and that the gout has all passed off. Many thanks for the comb, which also arrived. Yes I got the Official Dispatches you sent me, some time ago. Farley & Bird are in Palestine. I left that division when I left the 4th Coy over two years ago to take

---

[5] Under British occupation, Basra had risen from its squalid beginnings into a burgeoning international port and trade centre. Metalled roads, railway connections, electricity, piped water, sanitary facilities, hospitals, ice factories, schools and accommodation were just some of the improvements made. The port, which, upon F.V.B.W.'s arrival, had been the epitome of inefficiency, was now fully modernised and equipped, complete with an impressive 3,300 foot wharf. The expense, however, had been extreme; F.V.B.W.'s frustration at the apparent waste of it all, considering the evaporation of an active enemy, was echoed throughout Force 'D', and later, by the general public in Britain. But having said that, it was largely thanks to Basra's development and the improvements made to communications that Force 'D' found itself in such a dominant position.

[6] Rev. Adam Fox, Warden from 1918-1924.

my present job, and as long as I hold it there is not the slightest chance of my going elsewhere.

Many thanks for the *Times Engineering* Supplement, which was most interesting.

I hope Edward managed to get his special leave and is with you by this time. I am sorry to hear you are losing Mrs Wilcox and that the horses must be sold, it is bad luck having to break up the establishment, and I know how much you must feel it.[7]

I also asked for special leave to England, but it was 'regretted it couldn't be sanctioned' – which is really only to be expected.

This is the same ship which brought me on leave two years ago; small but very comfortable.[8] So far it has been very pleasant – cool and calm. Coming back we shall have first to face the monsoon and then the midsummer heat of the gulf! I have not yet decided where to go. A day or two's shopping in Bombay, then to Roorkee and then to Simla or Mussourie for the dentist.

No more news.

      Very best love

          Your ever loving Son.

            Fred. V. B. Witts

90. 'The Leave Train' (The *Bystanders* 'Fragments from France').

[7] After Canon Witts' death in 1913, the family had been burdened financially by Death Duties.

[8] See F.V.B.W.'s letter of 13th August 1916, chapter II, p. 101-2.

[Roorkee]
May 13th 1918

Dearest Mother.

Just a line to keep you informed of my wanderings.

I got into Bombay on the 8th and stayed there one night, doing a certain amount of shopping and going to the theatre. There are no lighting restrictions there and the only sign of the war is the petrol restrictions, however three of us managed to hire a very comfortable car for the two days. What a difference sailing along in a silent car on a perfect surface, and being jolted to death in a Ford van in Mespot!

I had to come up to Delhi in charge of a troop train and incidentally carry despatches for the Viceroy. The train in front of us collided with another and we arrived at Delhi ten hours late at 2 a.m. – the pleasures of travel!

I spent that day in Delhi, getting rid of the despatches and sightseeing, this time devoting my attention to the fort; it is a wonderful sight now, but nothing to what it must have been in the days of the Moghul Emperors.[9] But it is too hot for this sort of thing or I should like to spend my leave going round such places as Agra. I have got a room at Simla and am going up there tomorrow to place myself in the hands of the dentist.

No letters from you, but they have not had time to catch me up.

With very best love,

Your ever loving Son,

Fred. V. B. Witts.

UNITED SERVICE CLUB,
SIMLA.

May 21st 1918.

Dearest Mother.

Here I am back at my old haunt.

…I came up on the 16th and was lucky enough to get a very good suite of rooms; it sounds swagger doesn't it; I have a sitting room with a private verandah, a bedroom and a bathroom: but as I only use the whole combination for sleeping and dressing etc it is rather wasted. However one appreciates a little space to dress in after a poky little tent.

I found it hotter up here than I expected, but not unpleasant and in fact it is much nicer than when I was up here two years ago in the rains, when one lived in clouds and mist. At present it is beautifully fine with an occasional storm to make things fresher.

I am leading a life of absolute loaf up here, with the exception of visits to the dentist. There is quite a good American one here – whom I went to two years ago.

---

[9] The Red Fort in Delhi was constructed in 1639 by Emperor Shah Jahan. He also built the Taj Mahal at Agra.

He started work [on] my first visit by pulling out all my broken stumps. He did it very well without hurting me a bit, but my mouth has naturally been a bit sore since. However I am very pleased to see the last of them. I have come to the conclusion that Packe rather messed me up when he took them out originally. I shall have to have a new plate, and have several teeth to stop and mend, so that I shall be kept pretty busy. It will be a great relief if I can return with my mouth completely set in order.

I have met several friends up here, so that it is not as lonely as I expected.

    With very best love,

        Your ever loving Son,

            Fred. V. B. Witts.

                                    [Simla]

                             May 28th 1918.

Dearest Mother.

…Many thanks for all the ribbons. I am well set up now, and have ample. I am so glad you have got the Croix de Guerre. As you tell me it has the palm across it, I have now put up the palm you have sent me; I am now going to ask you to send out some more say half a dozen. You will be surprised, but the little pins behind break off very easily and make them useless. This happened to the first one you sent me some time ago, and is liable to happen each time you put on a fresh piece of ribbon. I don't know about the D. S. O. and M. C. medals. How did Frank get his? I think I have to wait until I go to an investiture by the King, or Viceroy out here. Many thanks also for the arm badges: but I think Mrs Farley has made a mistake. They are given for service 'overseas', not for France or any other theatre in particular. I have been 'overseas' for the <u>whole</u> of the war and am therefore, I believe, entitled to the lot. However nobody is wearing them out here at present, and so many are entitled to wear the lot!

…The air-raids in London must be awful, and to think that you should be more worried by the guns when ill in hospital than your soldier son on so-called active service! It makes me furious and brings home how out in the blue we are.

You often ask me in several letters if I have received something such as the Mesopotamia Dispatches. I try and acknowledge everything as they come, and you may be quite certain if anything does <u>not</u> come, which you say in your letters you have sent, I should scream out and let you know at once. The only thing I can think of, the whole time I have been in Mespot, which failed to arrive, was the first lot of solidified brilliantine which you sent, and which I have always imagined melted on the way and was thrown away by the postal people! Everything you send fetches up sooner or later and is most welcome.

…As I have told you, I did my best to get home on urgent private affairs as soon as I heard of your illness. It went up to G.H.Q., but there are only a few allowed

91. Postcard looking down to the ford in Upper Slaughter.

home, and there are so many fellows, who have stronger claims – very often the only surviving son of a widow, the others having been killed in the war. My subaltern, Eastmond, has been out in the east six years without getting home; he is the eldest son of a widowed invalid mother. His only brother is at Aden and there are financial matters to clear up. He too is trying to get home, but with no success so far. It is one of the greatest trials of the war, and it is most unfair that it should fall on the old. However we must live on and hope for the best.

So many thanks for ordering the miniature medals. Messkit is still worn in India by those who have it, as being far cooler, and pleasanter, and messkit is not complete without one's miniature medals.

I am so glad Frank got leave in February: he seems to have got a fortnight – better than they did us in 1915; but I expect a longer change is necessary now.[10]

It was indeed bad luck getting flue on the way down to St Leonards, but I hope you are quite strong again now, and enjoying the summer at Slaughter as far as it is possible.

Since last writing my main occupation has been with the dentist whom I have been to four times. My gums are healing wonderfully well and he is making me a new plate as the old one no longer fits. I am also having three teeth built up again and one ordinary filling. With any luck he will finish with me tomorrow.

I have been to the local theatre twice, where quite a good company perform different plays every other night. Otherwise I have been loafing purely and simply, and thoroughly appreciating the good food and comforts of a good club. It is surprisingly warm up here, but of course heaven compared with the hell down in the plains. The monsoon is not expected for a fortnight yet.

Hoping you are quite well again,

With very best love,

Your ever loving Son.

Fred. V. B. Witts.

[10] F.V.B.W. was only given a week's leave in June 1915 when his company was stationed in the trenches of the Béthune region of northern France. This was the last time he had seen his mother.

[Simla]
June 3rd 1918.

Dearest Mother.

...I am very glad to say I have finished with the dentist – except for the bill! He has given me a new plate which at any rate fits better than the last, and has I hope removed all likely sources of trouble. It is worth coming here simply for this, as I was having a good deal of trouble and pain in Mespot.

I have been to the theatre three times this week. There is a very good company performing there, and I have had some real good laughs. They start at the fashionable hour of 9.30 – just when everything is closing down in London – however there are not the same reasons for early closing, as there are no coal fires or gas lamps: the place is lighted by electricity run by waterpower in the hills. Moreover the late hour gives you a good excuse for a late breakfast next morning. The sapper general who was with the Indian Corps in France has been up on a visit and I dined with him one night, but other wise I have steered clear of brass hats.

My only appearance in Society was at a moonlight picnic the previous night. Amongst the pine trees and deodars – perfectly still with a full moon – it would have been most soothing, if one could only have gazed and dreamed, instead of having to make oneself agreeable!

The monsoon has given notice of its imminent arrival. Two days ago, a violent thunderstorm, and yesterday a succession of them and deluges of rain, which has laid the dust and made it cooler and fresher, though when the sun reappears it will be very steamy. The first thunderstorms on the approach of the monsoon are always a wonderful sight. The sky aflame with lightening with a majestic background of clouds tumbling over each other.

The news from France is again very bad – it almost looks as if they may get to Paris.[11] And here I am doing nothing to help and the same will be the case in Mespot.

Hoping you are really well again

    With very best love,

        Your ever loving Son,

          Fred. V. B. Witts.

---

[11] On 27th May, the third and final phase of the Spring Offensive was launched. Known as the Third Battle of the Aisne, it was directed towards Paris with the Chemin des Dames Ridge as the principal strategic target. On the first day of battle, shock German stormtroopers advanced a record 13 miles whilst German artillery inflicted severe casualties on the tightly packed French lines of defence. As a result of such rapid progress, the town of Soissons fell on the 29th and the River Marne, just 37 miles from Paris, was reached on June 3rd. But General Ludendorff, the German C-in-C, had still not learnt the lessons of Kaiserschlacht and Lys; the speed of the German assault once again completely outstretched supplies. Mounting casualties and total exhaustion eventually ground the offensive to a halt.

ROORKEE, U. P.
INDIA.

June 9th 1918

Dearest Mother.

...I left Simla on the 7th in the midst of a tremendous thunderstorm. I had had a quiet time but plenty of sleep and good food, but not altogether sorry to move. Roorkee is quite a different place since I was here three weeks ago, owing to the arrival of the monsoon. It poured in torrents all last night. Everything is green and fresh, and it is 15 degrees cooler, but of course very damp, which will make it very trying when it warms up again.

...I have had to change my servant, as my present one has had enough of Mesopotamia and made a small fortune, and wants to remain behind – I don't altogether blame him, but it is very hard to get any one in his place.[12] Their wages have gone up so enormously in India that there is no inducement for them to go out to Mespot. I have only just got one in his place, and he is a Christian, which I am sorry to say makes one rather shy of him.[13]

No more news, hoping you are quite fit.

With very best love,
Your ever loving Son,
Fred. V. B. Witts.

F.V.B. W.itts
Capt.

Ex – Hospital Ship 'Varela.'[14]
June 17th 1918.

Dearest Mother.

I ought to have written from Bombay, but was very busy and met a number of friends. I spent two days there shopping hard – the Army & Navy Stores should pay an increased dividend this year! I found some papers waiting for me at Cox's, but no

---

[12] Even on the front line, British officers kept servants for domestic chores such as cooking, ironing and cleaning. On the Western Front these men would have doubled up as soldiers, but in Mesopotamia, Force 'D' had a mass of followers completely disconnected from military duties, being employed and paid privately by officers to carry out mainly household tasks.

[13] F.V.B.W. was probably concerned that, as the rest of men in his unit were either Muslim (mainly), Sikh or Hindu, a Christian servant would be something of an unknown quantity and struggle to fit in.

[14] Built in Newcastle-upon-Tyne in 1914 by Swan, Hunter and Wigham Richardson Ltd., the *Varela* served as a hospital ship in Basra from 1915-17, before becoming an ambulance transport. From 1920 she returned to commercial duties in the Persian Gulf Service until the outbreak of WWII, when she was employed as a troop carrier. Having survived the war she was sold for scrap in 1951.

luck with any letters.

The journey down to Bombay was hot and the train crowded chiefly [with] fellows returning to Mespot. The monsoon hadn't reached Central India.

As you have noticed we are on a late Hospital Ship, now known as an Ambulance Transport: in other words it is a hospital ship with the white paint and red cross washed out, and used for taking passengers when not required for sick and wounded. You would imagine it would be most comfortable, but there are 87 officers on board and only accommodation for 11: the remainder of us are all in one of the men's wards packed like sardines, and I have quite changed my views of the luxury of the modern hospital ship, if this may be taken as a fair sample.

It is hard to imagine what it would have been like if we had had the weather we had every reason to expect – bad monsoon weather in the Arabian Sea followed by fierce heat in the gulf. We have been extraordinarily lucky however – only a heavy swell in the open, so that port holes could be left open and we could sleep on deck, and now in the Gulf we have a strong head wind and I have caught a cold in my head instead of dying of heatstroke which would have been more seasonable.

I had my photograph taken at Bombay for <u>your</u> benefit, but shall not send a copy unless they are a success. As you know I hate having it done.

We get in to Basra tomorrow evening, and I expect my next letter will be written on the steamer on the way up but it may be too hot. I gather I am not going back to the same place, but don't know yet where the train has moved to. If they don't make it a major's job, I may be going elsewhere, as one can't afford to sacrifice even acting promotion in order to keep one's job.

With very best love,

Your ever loving Son

Fred. V. B. Witts.

As Captain Witts predicted when he departed on leave, the direction of Force 'D"s offensive objectives had veered dramatically towards the east: to Persia and Trans-Caucasia. The Azerbaijani port of Baku, on the Caspian Sea, was under threat of attack from a Turkish army; if successful, the oil reserves of Trans-Caucasia would fall into the hands of the Central Powers, boosting their fighting capacity on all fronts.

The Imperial General Staff in London related these concerns to General Marshall, and ordered him to send *Dunsterforce* to Baku. General Dunsterville, based in Hamadan with his force of 1,000 elite troops, began preparations for an advance through Persia to the Caspian port of Enzeli, where, back in February, Bolshevik forces had compelled him to abort his first mission into Trans-Caucasia. From there, Dunsterville's plan was to sail to Baku and join the fight against the Turks, adding professional backbone to the civilian resistance.

Map 8. Operations of *Dunsterforce*, 1918.

General Marshall considered the mission impractical from the start; the difficulties of maintaining a 1000 mile supply line into the Caucasus across hostile Persian territory, were, in his view, intolerable.[15] The War Office, however, had determined that *Dunsterforce* should become a part of Force 'D' (on its first, abortive mission in February 1918, *Dunsterforce* was independent of Force 'D'), and thus under Marshall's direct responsibility. Reluctantly, Marshall sent a small number of men to Hamadan to join *Dunsterforce*, but he was unwilling to increase the demand for supplies by too great a margin. He also put Colonel Bicharakoff's Cossack detachment, based in the Persian city of Qazvin, at General Dunsterville's disposal. Concurrently, in Mesopotamia, to protect Dunsterville's tenuous supply line, Marshall sent the IIIrd Corps into Southern Kurdistan to disperse any lurking

---

[15] The revolutionary *Jangalis*, officered by Germans, were active in northern Persia.

remnants of the Turkish XIII Corps.

General Egerton, commander of the IIIrd Corps, began his advance into Kurdistan on 24th April, but he was unable to commit the Turks to a conclusive fight. The towns of Kifri and Kirkuk, the latter a principal trading centre in Southern Kurdistan, were occupied without opposition, although Egerton did manage to capture the Turkish garrison at Tuz Khurmalti, 10 miles south of Kirkuk. Turkish morale was evidently rock-bottom and, after General Egerton's sortie, there seemed little chance of any hostile interference with the *Dunsterforce* mission from the direction of Southern Kurdistan.

The occupation of Kirkuk heralded the start of the slack season in Mesopotamia; into this sultry atmosphere, Captain Witts returned to his unit at the Euphrates town of Sahiliya, to sit out the heat in slothful inactivity.

F.V.B. Witts
    Capt. R.E.

               [Dhibban]
           June 28th 1918

Dearest Mother.

Here I am back to the land! I spent two days in Basra, including a very cheery evening with a friend who is now a colonel, and then on by train to Amara – a day there and then a palatial steamer took us to Kut where once again we entrained for Baghdad, arriving on the morning of the 26th. Here I interviewed the powers that be about myself and my unit and spent one night, dining at the Hotel Maude, followed by a moonlight trip in a hospital launch with a number of nurses, including one who nursed me while I was in hospital at Amara wounded. Last night I came on to the Euphrates railhead [Dhibban, 10 miles beyond Falluja] where I find my transport spending the hot weather. I have been away two months and ten days.

I find many changes of which the most personal is that I am losing my senior subaltern Eastmond who is going back to India to command a new unit after two years with me. We are split up for the time being, my sapper and bridge being near where I left them sixty miles further on [at Sahiliya, 10 miles beyond Hit]. As one subaltern is on leave, until Eastmond is replaced we shall be only two, that means one at each camp by himself – rather a lonely prospect.

About myself my promotion to acting Major by virtue of my job has been recommended to India: if it is approved as I have every reason to hope, well and good, if not, I have been promised the command of a Field Company carrying with it acting Major's rank. But it means turning out another fellow, so I hope things will pan out nicely. The only trouble now is that India sometimes takes six months to consider such a question, while I shall continue in a state of uncertainty of what is going to happen.

But for the numerous and constant changes – with no porters hanging about to

92. Hotel Maude, Baghdad.

shift one's kit, as is the case at home I suppose, but one's kit returning from leave is very expanded – the journey up is very well done:- meals and fans on the steamers, and resthouses with fans and food and iced drinks at the various places you have to change. How different from 1916, when one had to fend for oneself.

...Thanks awfully for getting the miniature medals for me. I am afraid the D.S.O. was very expensive. Keep them for me for the present: they are no use to me out here, and I should not have worn them in India if I had had them. I am sure you like having them to shew to people! At any rate in the absence of the proper thing.

I am so glad Frank has been confirmed as Brigade Major.

The 7th Hussars are three miles from here; so I may meet Frank Rickards – Aunt Sybil's cook's young man,[16] whom you mention as being in Carrie's Class once.

I enclose a few Persian stamps I picked up in Baghdad on my way through.

I am so glad you are stronger again – the splendid length of your letters is an excellent indication most welcome to me in two ways. How can you think I should get tired of reading 'your long yarns' as you call them?

I do so hope Edward has managed to get leave and get home by this time. I suppose George has gone across to France: it is very bad luck being left with none of your five sons in England, but you must be proud to have so many to serve for the country, and we have been extraordinarily lucky so far. Fancy German prisoners at Northleach![17] The fighting on the North West Frontier was quite a picnic.[18]

Yes, when we came over to the Euphrates in February we marched across from Baghdad to Feluja some forty miles of desert.

Many thanks for the picture postcard of the Dingle & bridge.[19]

[16] F.V.B.W.'s Aunt Sybil was the widow of his paternal uncle George Witts. She lived at Leckhampton in Cheltenham.

[17] The Northleach prison had been built in 1791 under the supervision of the distinguished prison reformer Sir George Onesiphorus Paul.

[18] The North West Frontier is the region encompassing the volatile Afghan/Indian border. F.V.B.W. was posted there at Kohat and Fort Lockhart in 1912-13.

[19] Although the Dingle had been built by Canon Witts in 1904 as a Dower House for Mrs Witts, it is surprising that no mention is ever made of it when Mrs Witts, and others, were talking of the possibility of her having to leave the Manor in the last year or two of her life.

I am pouring with sweat as I write. It is 113° in the tent and only 11 a.m.:- it will be nearer 120° by 2 p.m! The worst of taking first leave. No more news.

Very best love

     Your ever loving Son

         Fred. V. B. Witts

F. V. B. Witts

    Capt.

                                [Sahiliya]

                             July 7th 1918.

Dearest Mother.

I got back on the 2nd stopping at Divn H.Q. for a night on the way up, and making one night's involuntary stop at Hit through the wheel of my Ford Van breaking. I have no luck travelling in a car in this country; as you will remember I stuck in the mud on the way down! Luckily this time I was able to get another car to the rescue.

Eastmond left on the morning of the 5th a great loss to me – and for the moment I am alone, but an Indian Regt are camped alongside and I dine with them. Our luck was out while I was away, our bridge being broken up by a violent hurricane, which swept down the river, lasting a bare hour. It must have been like the early days in 1916.

One of my Indian Officers died in my absence on his way on leave and one third of my N.C.O.s have gone back to India for the new armies they are raising; so you can imagine I have plenty to do.[20]

Whether the sixty miles up the river makes the difference, or whether it is simply a cool snap, I don't know but it is nothing like so hot up here as when I wrote a week ago. The 'Shimal' or North West wind is blowing with gratifying persistence, though it occasionally gives me qualms for the safety of the bridge, and stirs up the dust in an annoying way, but luckily I am right on the river's edge and very free from dust.

The Turks have sent a few troops down to face us, but they keep a long way off except for an occasional patrol, which as often as not we manage to capture.[21]

A parcel of vegetable seeds has just arrived – cucumbers, water melons, ordinary melons, tomatoes, beans, brinjal, gourd & pumpkin – and I am going to start a garden, though it is a bit late in the year and we may move before it ripens.

---

[20] Many new combatants were being recruited and trained in India to create 67 new infantry battalions, primarily for action in Salonika. To assist in their training and organisation, and to inject a degree of experience into their ranks, a large proportion of Indian officers and men were sent from Mesopotamia to serve in these new battalions.

[21] After the victory at Khan Baghdadi, the Turks had been chased a further 60 miles up the Euphrates to their supply base at Anah, losing many men as casualties and prisoners en route. The Turkish threat on the Euphrates had now almost completely evaporated and desertion amongst there remaining ranks was becoming more common.

…I am very well and quite glad to be done with travelling for a bit. Someone has been talking in Parliament, and they are going to be a bit freeer with English leave; I must ask again, though they are sure to say it is too soon after my Indian leave.

Very best love,

Your ever loving Son,

Fred. V. B. Witts.

[Sahiliya]
July 14th 1918.

Dearest Mother.

…Your accounts of the food situation are not encouraging[22] – you must be nearly starving, and undergoing much worse hardships than we out here, I do so hope you will be able to keep the old home open inspite of all, but your own health is far more important, and you must shut the house up during the winter, if you can't get enough coal to be dry and comfortable. What would home be without you?

I may meet Major Gibbs: his regiment is at present camped about three miles from my downstream camp. Fancy Fred Collett in an aeroplane, I can imagine some excitement in the village.[23]

I wonder what sort of a job Jack Cheetham will get if called up.

Yes, you must get a second 'Jerry' and fourwheel pony cart, as it is very bad for you not to be able to get about.

The R. E. is not a sufficiently dangerous job for rapid promotion in Field Units; you can only get it by going to technical jobs such as railways etc, which are not in my line. However I hope you will see me as Acting Major before the year is out.

You ask me if I want anything: it seems to me that it is us out here who ought to ask you at home if we can send you anything!

Your letter of May 13th gives me the first details of the nature of your operation in January. You must have had a very bad time; I am so glad to hear you had no pain and liked the Doctors: it was very bad luck getting flue and gout on the top of it.

Fancy Joan [Woodroffe] old enough to be left alone at Wimbledon.[24] How time does fly. I shall be thirty next year, though I find it hard to believe it; I must think

---

[22] Britain was largely reliant on imports from Canada and the U.S.A. for food. Stocks had depleted severely since February 1917 when the German Navy implemented a policy of unrestricted submarine warfare, targeting merchant shipping on the Atlantic. As a result, on top of a coal ration, a sugar ration was introduced at the start of 1918, and by April, meat, butter, cheese and margarine were also on the ration list. The Government also requisitioned around 3 million acres of land for cultivation, to be farmed by the newly established Women's Land Army. By and large, the measures taken were a success and there were no reported cases of starvation in Britain during the war.

[23] Fred Collett was brother of George Collett whom F.V.B.W. noticed on the casualty list at Rawal Pindi Hospital, Amara in 1917 (see letter of Jan 3rd 1917, Chapter III, p. 128). Fred served in the Royal Flying Corps.

about getting married, but penniless nurses are the only things in the line of brides out here, and India is not much better!

I am so sorry to hear Edward has not succeeded in getting leave yet.

Fancy 40 or 50 chickens on the lawn,[25] our poultry farm had to be reduced when we moved in the winter, and we have never been able to make it up again.

No news this end. It has been another cool week, but is stoking up again.

Very best love,

Your ever loving Son,

Fred. V. B. Witts.

F.V.B. Witts

[Sahiliya]

July 21st 1918.

Dearest Mother.

...I think I told you I am messing with the regiment alongside – the 6th Jats[26] – while I am alone. I find one of them – Young by name – a Captain (acting I think) is a nephew of the Cunards and has often stayed at Notgrove in recent years. Rather strange! He was also at Cheltenham College, so knows all the country round. They are a very young and cheery crowd, and I am the Father of them in both seniority and age.

On Tuesday July 23rd I shall have completed eleven years service, and should, but for the war, have just been getting my captaincy! As it is I am already getting anxious about my majority!

We are in a very peaceful spot, the two lots of us alone in a secluded spot as usual on the banks of the river which is about a quarter of a mile wide here – deep in places and very shallow in others and rapidly getting shallower. There are date gardens all along the bank with these wonderful 'naurs' or water wheels drowning out their whining chant day and night. They are quite the most wonderful and most artistic thing to be seen in Mespot.[27]

...Amongst the date palms, all sorts of vegetables and fruit are grown. We are at present getting from this source onions, tomatoes, pumpkins, ladies fingers and brinjal [aubergine] the two latter being common in the East, but possibly strange to you; we are also getting delicious figs, which poor old Father would have appreciated immensely. There are also peaches, grapes and pomegranates rapidly ripening. It sounds too good for Mespot! We have also started our own little vegetable garden, – tomatoes, cucumbers, water melons, sweet melons, beans, pumpkins, gourds and brinjal – on a sandbank in the middle of the river!

[25] Household chicken coops and vegetable allotments were amongst measures used to boost food production in Britain.

[26] The Jats were a Sikh regiment hailing from Punjab.

[27] See F.V.B.W.'s letter of March 23rd 1918, chapter VI, p. 221-2, for a detailed description.

I was inoculated again against cholera just to please the doctors. It is just as well to be on the safe side.

No more news

        With very best love

                Your ever loving Son

                        Fred. V. B. Witts.

F. V. B. Witts

    Capt.

                                      [Sahiliya]

                                  July 28th 1918.

Dearest Mother.

...Yes, your 'very hot between 70 & 80 in the shade' represents our minimum night temperature just at present. The maximum day reading hovers between 110 and 120, but hasn't touched that mark yet in my tent.

It is a great Trial not being able to get a carriage for a drive. In my little unit I have nearly three hundred vehicles and over nine hundred animals!

I am sorry to hear you came in for another raid. It seems to be your luck. We never see an enemy plane here now: an occasional bomb would break the monotony of our existence.

How I should like to spend June at Slaughter again. I have been fishing here this week; I think I told you I brought back a salmon rod with me. But the water is not clear enough yet, and I haven't caught anything.

I should like to give you an R.E. brooch: I have seen all sorts of varieties advertised by different firms. Pick out one you like and let me know the damage.

An indication of a probable move would justly rouse the wrath of the censor, but sitting still doing nothing doesn't help in anyway to win the war.

As I have mentioned, I am hoping to be an Acting Major ere long; our casualties are not heavy enough to give rise to the extraordinary rapid promotion of the Infantry; one cannot have it both ways. Bird has gone as C.R.E. to a Divn, and if I had stuck to the 4th Company I should be commanding and Acting Major. Now Farley has it. I had a long letter from Bird from Palestine yesterday. I must say I wish I were over there. But I can't complain at my present job, which brought me the opportunity of a lifetime, followed by a mention and three decorations all of which were <u>earned</u> in a space of three months. One doesn't like throwing it over from personal ambition. I become a permanent major in July 1922!

I am glad Agnes has been making use of my old clothes!

Fancy Gerald Tuck Lt Col! it makes one think one is getting left.[28]

---

[28] Lieutenant-Colonel Gerald Tuck was a Woodroffe cousin. He was commanding officer in the Cambridgeshire Battalion in the Suffolk Regiment and was awarded the D.S.O. for bravery in January 1918. He also won the Croix de Guerre and was mentioned in Despatches in both WWI and WWII.

93. The Manor, Upper Slaughter (from the Vineyards).

I had my photograph taken in India, but they're not come yet. I must write about them.

All sorts of books I should like to see, but one can't cart a library about with one, so that it is impossible to have a lot of expensive books sent out.

Send the Pears Soap along, 'I shan't be happy till I get it.'![29] You did very well out of the old Graphics and waste paper, but your doctor's bills were very high: you must let your children know if you are having difficulty in making both ends meet. As a bachelor at present, I am rolling in wealth, and if I became acting Major it will be worse still!

The present news from France is the best since March 21st, I only hope General Smuts is right when he says he thinks the tables have <u>finally</u> turned.[30]

---

[29] 'He won't be happy 'till he gets it!' was a famous advertising slogan for Pears Soap Co. featuring a picture of a baby reaching out of his bath for a bar of soap.

[30] The tripartite 'Spring Offensive', launched on March 21st, had cost Germany roughly a million casualties, crippling her strength beyond regeneration without gaining the decisive breakthrough she needed to win the war. With deficiencies in men and supplies, plummeting morale, economic collapse on the horizon and the imminent arrival of massive American reinforcements, the German C-in-C, General Ludendorff, had little choice but to try to maintain a relentless offensive in the desperate hope that victory could be snatched from the jaws of defeat. For the Second Battle of the Marne, launched on 15th July, Ludendorff had summoned 42 German divisions, mostly ragged and exhausted, for a two pronged attack against Allied positions on the River Marne and the Reims district. After some initial German gains, the Allied forces, with the first traces of U.S. support, recovered themselves to launch a massive counter-attack, inducing a full-scale German retreat back behind the Rivers Aisne and Vesle. Casualties were heavy on both sides but the Germans suffered worse; Allied success on the Marne inspired other counter-offensives up the whole of the Western Front, generating a momentum which would prove unstoppable, finally precipitating the end of the war.

I left one little point out of my description of this place last week: the date gardens, and cultivation only occupy a narrow level strip of land from 0 to 200 yards wide along each bank: beyond this you get an abrupt rise of 30 feet and then the desert extending to the Tigris on one side and to Palestine on the other! I think my earlier description would give the idea of cultivation and date gardens as far as the eye could see.

Have spent another very uneventful week, and Eastmond's relief has not joined yet.

You must cheer up and hold on, Mother, we've all got to see it through.

With very best love,

      Your ever loving Son

         Fred. V. B. Witts.

Seven hundred miles to the north-east of Captain Witts' base at Sahiliya, a small vanguard of British troops under Colonel Stokes arrived in Baku to assess the situation for General Dunsterville. The Russian Colonel Bicharakoff, meanwhile, had realised that his only chance of gaining a foothold in the Caucasus was to join the Bolsheviks as regional commander of the Red Army. With troops of a variable quality, he was operating against the Turks north of Baku around Derbend, with equally variable success.

The defenders of Baku, as Colonel Stokes discovered them, were about 8,000 in number, with little military training and of five different political orientations, making them ill-disciplined and uncoordinated as a unit. He determined, however, that Baku could be saved with British support, as long as that support was delivered urgently and followed by the immediate despatch of reinforcements by General Marshall.

Marshall, however, was struggling to keep *Dunsterforce* supplied over such a distance as it was. Waiting at Enzeli with the rest of his men, General Dunsterville was now faced with a difficult dilemma: whether to throw his small band of adventurers into a hornet's nest with no guarantee of success or reinforcements, or to abort the mission there and then, leaving Baku to the mercies of the pitiless Turk.[31] The Baku population, meanwhile, which included many Armenians, clamoured for British help.

Although Captain Witts was part of the same Expeditionary Force, his monotonous routine on the Euphrates could hardly have been more distinct from the activities of *Dunsterforce* on the Caspian Sea. Consistently good news from Europe, however, improved his morale.

---

[31] The Armenian atrocities, amongst other examples of brutality, had given the Turks a reputation for cruelty.

F.V.B. Witts

[Sahiliya]
Aug 4th 1918.

Dearest Mother.

...Today we start the fifth year of the War, and with it I qualify for my fifth chevron − red and 4 blue. They simply denote service overseas and I have been overseas every day of the war, as India counts as overseas for a British service Officer like myself although employed with the Indian Army. You must send them along to me some time.

It is no use speculating how much longer the war is going on. The latest news we have had from France is the brightest for many a day. It is equally useless speculating what the army will be like after the war: there should be little further use for it in our lifetime except in India, and India will be no white man's country when all these reforms which have been introduced develope.[32] So one is in rather a dilemma. But one doesn't like to throw up a definite monthly wage and a certain pension too lightheartedly.

I have had no luck with my fishing, partly due to an unexpected avalanche of work, and partly to the insects which thrive on the river bank and drive me away.

One of my subalterns has rejoined me from my other camp, and I shall probably be going down there this week.

It has been hot all the week but nothing desperate.

I have just moved into a little hut which I have had built. It is about 8 to 10 degrees cooler than a tent in the heat of the day.

Very best love,
Your ever loving Son,
Fred. V. B. Witts.

F.V.B. Witts

[Dhibban]
Aug 11th 1918.

Dearest Mother.

...As I mentioned in my last letter, I have come down to my other camp [at Dhibban], and unfortunately didn't bring my mail with me, as I have arrived to find my subaltern in hospital; consequently I may have to stay longer than I intended.

What a narrow escape Frank had; I am glad I didn't realize he was in the 50th

---

[32] The Montague-Chelmsford Report of 1918 detailed a series of reforms to allow the gradual introduction of self-governing institutions to India. The reforms were realised in the Government of India Act of 1919.

Divn or I should have been very anxious.[33] I hope his wound will heal up all right – the face is a nasty place.

I am awfully pleased to see Edward's D.S.O. In many ways he has got the worst of all of us. He must have been mentioned again in Despatches though I didn't notice it. But he would prefer leave to the D.S.O! I wish he could get it.[34]

I chose one of the hottest days to come down here in a car, but stopped a night en route at Divn H.Q. to talk business. It is all together hotter down here and the flies are much worse. We nearly got stuck in the deep dust this time, instead of the mud as when I went on leave.

I wonder what job Jack Cheetham will get, I always understood he was unfit in some way. He must be pretty fed up at being roped in as a private, when he could easily have got a commission earlier on. But if he kept a bailiff to do all the dirty work, it was only natural that he should be called up.[35]

I had another try fishing, but without success and have come to the conclusion that the fish of Euphrates are not sportsmen!

Tomorrow Grouse shooting opens, and there are some round the camp, but not expecting to be here long I came as light as possible and didn't bring a gun.

      With very best love
        Your ever loving Son
          Fred. V. B. Witts

You will notice I am using a borrowed envelope with the Supply & Transport Corps crest.

In the Caucasus, the die had finally been cast; *Dunsterforce* had joined the defenders of Baku. But as British troops hurried to bolster the defensive lines, the civilian militias began falling back into the city, apparently expecting the small band of British troops to take over the entire defence of the town. Already, General Dunsterville had resolved sombrely that evacuation, not liberation, would be the eventual outcome of his expedition. Evacuation, however, was not going to be straight-forward; the harbour was controlled by Bolshevik sailors determined to obstruct forcibly his escape.

Captain Witts, meanwhile, vegetating on the Euphrates, had less taxing things to focus his mind on.

---

[33] The 50th (Northumberland) Division took a severe blow in the Third Battle of the Aisne (27th May – 3rd June 1918) – the battle F.V.B.W. was referring to when he wrote 'the news from France is again very bad …' (3rd June 1918). Ironically, the 50th Division had been placed on the Aisne specifically to avoid serious action, having already suffered heavy losses on the Somme and Lys battlefields. According to Kipling's *The Irish Guards in the Great War* (p. 293), Frank Witts was wounded on the 25th May, two days before the start of the main German attack, but no further details are given.

[34] See Chapter I, p. 44, note 8.

[35] The Universal Service Bill finally got the better of F.V.B.W.'s cousin, Jack Cheetham.

F.V.B. Witts
        Capt.

[Dhibban]
Aug 18ᵗʰ 1918.

Dearest Mother.

...I have only men, mules and vehicles to think about here though plenty of each. Half the men have hardly one year's service, but they are supposed to perform efficiently work performed by British Drivers in France. It is a misnomer to call them men, they are all boys, some of them 17 or less, not 10 per cent can write, and they have no idea of the meaning of property, cleanliness or time. His mind is a blank, and he speaks no known language. So you can imagine the results are rather disheartening, and yet people at home seem to think it is as easy to raise an Army in India as in England; they forget that the recruit has to be educated <u>from the very beginning</u> besides being taught soldiering.

The Mules are getting old and warworn, like all of us, and consequently very difficult to keep in condition, and the vehicles have a predilection for falling to pieces owing to a lack of roads, and to the effect of the fierce sun on the unseasoned wood of which they are made. So you will see, there is plenty to do.

My tent was visited by an Arab the other night. I was lucky to lose nothing but a box belonging to the unfortunate fellow sick was lifted. I have now six Arabs under my guard and some one will be punished, but I am afraid there is little chance of recovering the lost stuff, which is all one really cares about.

They are making open references to Officers visiting Teheran in Persia, which shows how the ramifications of Mes: Ex: Force are growing.[36]

The weather varies tremendously, we have had some very cool days for the time of year, but yesterday felt like the hottest day we have had, and there was not a breath of wind. Today a violent duststorm is blowing. However the worst must not be over.

Hoping all's well at home,

        With very best love

                Your ever loving Son,

                        Fred. V. B. Witts.

It is splendid news we are getting from France the last ten days. I only hope it holds![37]

---

[36] In Teheran, anti-British insurgents were growing bolder, encouraged by the Persian Government's refusal to adopt a positive attitude towards the British military presence in the land. Meantime, further north, a strong Turkish column had been noted advancing eastwards from Tabriz. As F.V.B.W. had predicted, Force 'D''s sphere of responsibility had expanded significantly eastwards.

[37] The Battle of Amiens on August 8ᵗʰ was the first major Allied counter-offensive of 1918. The Australian and Canadian Corps achieved an advance of 7 miles, prompting Ludendorff to describe it as 'the blackest day of the German Army in the history of the war.'

F.V.B. Witts
  Capt.

            [Dhibban]
            August 26th 1918

Dearest Mother.

 …I have just seen in the paper Edward's mention – which I knew the D.S.O. implied – and Jack's M.B.E. It is splendid and I am awfully pleased, how bucked he will be. I must write to him and Edward to as soon as I get back to my paper and envelopes.

 It is very curious how often our name appears in the Times for the week June 10th – 16th. First of all there's Edward's D.S.O., a day or two later his name again appears amongst mentions & Frank's as wounded, a day later Jack's appears, and two days later the name of a Capt. Witts M.C., R.A.M.C. as wounded but you must of course have noticed it.

 The news from France is good, as is the only news I've got, namely that the last week it has been decidedly cooler! It looks as if the Germans intended to turn their attention to Russia again.[38] You will have seen in the paper that Mes: Ex: Force now extends right up to the Caspian Sea: it must be very interesting up that side and I am sorry that there is very little chance of my getting up there.

 My sick subaltern has returned from Baghdad, so I am no longer alone, which is a great thing.

 My photographs have come from Bombay, but they are so disgusting that I can't make up my mind to send them on.

 I am absolutely hard up for news, with no mail in and absolutely nothing doing here. Not intending to stay long, I brought neither my gun or rod when I came down or might have amused myself with them.

 Very best love
   Your ever loving Son
     Fred. V. B. Witts.

F.V.B. Witts

            [Dhibban]
            Sept 1st 1918.

Dearest Mother.

 No mail for nearly a month now and there are sinister rumours of their being torpedoed or mined in the Mediterranean, though one more optimistic rumour asserts that the damaged mail boat was got into Malta – so we may see them yet.

---

[38] Despite intermittent fighting between the Bolsheviks and Turks in the Caucasus, on 25th August 1918, German diplomats managed to persuade the Bolshevik Government to sign a second treaty with Germany. In return for German help in Finland to stop the anti-communist White Guard from attacking Russia, the Bolsheviks promised to fight Allied forces recently landed in Murmansk, in northern Russia. The agreement also conceded to Germany the use of the Bolshevik fleet in the Black Sea and a third of Baku's oil production should the port end up under Bolshevik control.

I have sent off my photographs in a separate packet, registered. I hope they will fetch up all right and that you will appreciate them. I consulted my friends who said they were worth sending on – in fact thought them rather good. They are for private family circulation only, and I should like Aunt Maggie to have one.

I came back to my headquarters on the 29th, but it is not for long, as we are again going through what came as such a surprise in January but in exactly reverse way. So now you know![39]

I think things were brought to a climax by the sudden drop in the temperature ten days ago – but now unfortunately it has stoked up again which will not be pleasant.

Nine of us went out shooting today (Sept 1st) but didn't meet with much success, there were a few partridge about and a number of pigeon, but we didn't work it very well: I also saw a solitary snipe and four duck.[40]

The river appears to have nearly dried up while I've been away, and you can now wade across three hundred out of the four hundred yards of width.

Rumour says that my acting majority is sanctioned, but I have not heard officially yet.

No more news

   With very best love

     Your ever loving Son

       Fred. V. B. Witts.

F. V. B. Witts
  Capt.

             [Dhibban]
            Sept 10th 1918.

Dearest Mother

 …I much enjoy getting Land & Water as it has such interesting articles, though Hilaire Belloc gets on my nerves! But it is a great pleasure inspite of Hilaire Belloc.[41]

Your long yarn of June 25th in reply to 4 letters of mine is most delightful, but I am afraid a tremendous strain on your poor old fingers. Many thanks for the Times map with Frank's wanderings marked on it. He was very lucky to get away.

---

[39] F.V.B.W. is referring to the intriguing comment he made in his letter of January 28th 1918 (p. 214). That 'bit of news' was orders for the movement of his unit from the Tigris to the Euphrates. No. 2 Mobile Bridging Train had now been ordered back to the Tigris front.

[40] F.V.B.W. and his colleagues seemed to be keeping to the English shooting season.

[41] Hilaire Belloc, editor of *Land & Water* from 1914-1920, was a fervent Catholic with determined views. Although widely recognised as a brilliant journalist, his obstinate character, often reflected in his writing and public debates, strongly divided people's opinion of him.

I am sorry to hear George may be out in France again now. Only two days ago I met a man – Vine by name – who knew him at Sidbury Training Camp and told me it would be a shame if he were sent out again. As a matter of fact no mention has ever been made in any letter of what was wrong with him, but I imagine shell shock or something analogous.[42]

I hope Frank has got a job in England too for a bit. He has seen his share of fighting. He ought to come out here for a change!

I am sorry to hear you won't be able to keep the kitchin fire going; I don't think you ought to spend the winter at Slaughter. You should go somewhere warmer and drier.

…I shall be interested to hear how Jack Cheetham gets on in his new career!

We have said goodbye to our summer quarters and have accomplished the first portion of the journey in great comfort by river. We are now waiting for room on a train. It has been a week of packing up and handing over.

We are having a series of windless days which are as a consequence very warm.

This extraordinary influenza epidemic which has been going round the world threatened to pay us a visit but it seems to be passing off again without any particular ravages. It seems to be a thing to get and to get over it.[43]

No more news,

       With very best love,

           Your ever loving Son,

              Fred. V. B. Witts.

Up on the Caspian things were reaching fever pitch. On the 12th September, having already decided that Baku was doomed and evacuation the only sensible option, General Dunsterville was warned by an Arab deserter that the Turks were planning a determined attack at dawn on the 14th. Unable to convince the Provisional Government in Baku to organise an immediate evacuation, or to allow his force to leave the city without obstruction, Dunsterville had little choice but to prepare for the coming onslaught. The defenders, spread out across the 14 mile front line on the outskirts of the city, consisted of a mixture of British, Russians, Armenians and sparsely trained

---

[42] George Witts had suffered from gas inhalation and shell shock but the details are unknown.

[43] The primary symptoms of influenza (Spanish flu) took the form of a common cold, hence F.V.B.W.'s relatively casual attitude, but infection could often end in death. The pandemic swiftly covered the globe killing an estimated 50-100 million people in 1918-19 – a staggering total far outreaching the numbers killed in over four years of war. Curiously, the disease was of a strain which targeted the able-bodied over infants or the elderly, but in Mesopotamia, as F.V.B.W. asserts, the men were lucky to be in a region only sparsely penetrated by the disease. Nonetheless its effects were still extremely serious for Force 'D', as F.V.B.W. relates in later letters.

Baku militias which made up the bulk of the force.

The Turkish attack, when it started, immediately overwhelmed the Baku men, demanding a brave intervention by British troops to plug the gap and stall the Turkish advance. However, with an effective force of only 1500 men (Bicharakoff had sent 500 of his Cossacks from Derbend), Dunsterville knew that the battle was hopeless. Towards the evening, with a lull in the fighting, he seized the chance to extricate his British troops. Under cover of darkness, *Dunsterforce* secretly boarded their transport, certain that, if detected, they would be attacked by their former comrades in arms. In the event, their plot to escape was discovered in Baku harbour; the alarm was raised, but it was too late to stop them. With characteristic pluck, *Dunsterforce* made its escape out into the Caspian, leaving Baku doomed to its fate.

The operations around Baku provoked considerable criticism when they came to light in Britain. The mission had achieved very little and, by all appearances, had been destined to fail on account of its lack of manpower, a derivative of its problems with communications. However, whatever the mission's reception at home, in Mesopotamia, the likes of Captain Witts were only too jealous that they themselves had not taken part in such a sterling adventure.

[Tekrit]

Sept 16th 1918.

Dearest Mother.

…We are now trying to settle down at our new home which begins and ends with the same letter as the name of the river begins with.

I got here yesterday morning after stopping two days in Baghdad, where I saw two or three friends.

We are having another heat spell, and the thermometer stands at 118 in my tent as I write – we could not bring our huts along with us! Thank goodness, we did not have to walk but were able to do the latter part of the journey by train.

We paid this place a flying visit last November, and I probably described it then.[44] We are camped just upstream of the town on a cliff some 100 feet immediately above the river, which is here very deep and hard to get at. The other bank for nearly three miles is low-lying and dead flat and consequently completely overlooked from our tents. Beyond the three miles there is the ruin of an old canal and the desert plateau, which is not a third as high as our side.

I am disappointed to say that India has refused to allow my present job to carry the acting rank of Major with it. I am therefore putting in for a transfer to a Field Company. I don't know when it will come off, as apparently they wish me to stay

[44] F.V.B.W. watched the Battle of Tekrit on 5th November 1917 as an observer (11th Nov 1917, p. 197-8).

with this unit, but they must give me my due if they want me to stay. I shall be very sorry to move but one has to look to one's own future occasionally.

No more news,

> With very best love,
>> Your ever loving Son,
>>> Fred. V. B. Witts.

F. V. B. Witts

[Tekrit]
Sept 23rd 1918.

Dearest Mother.

...I see in the Times that one is given a Royal Warrant of appointment to the D.S.O., I am writing to ask them to send it to you. You must take care of it when you get it.

News is very good: Austria talking about peace and successful pushes reported from Salonika and Palestine, not to mention the Western Front;[45] only here is there nothing doing except a withdrawal from Baku. It looks as if we were in for another peaceful cold weather with the floods our worst enemy, though they are enough to turn our hair grey. Perhaps Turkey will throw up the sponge if we get a real move on in Palestine and Salonika. I hope Edward's all right.[46]

Do what you think best with the Stag's head and black bear. It is a pity to send them to Rowland Ward as long as any one is at Slaughter, as then no one derives any pleasure from them.[47]

Longley appears to have recovered, what happens to him this autumn as his five years are up?[48]

The hope of an early peace next year will bear you up through the coming winter,

---

[45] Austria appealed to President Wilson on September 15th to arrange a preliminary peace conference to stop hostilities; in Salonika the Allies had launched a successful attack from Albania on the Bulgarian forces in the Vardar Valley, precipitating their surrender; the Battle of Megiddo on September 19th had broken Turko-German lines in Palestine and opened the road to Damascus; on the Western Front the battles of Havrincourt (12th Sept) and Epehy (18th Sept) kept up the momentum of Allied success with a devastating effect on German morale.

[46] F.V.B.W.'s brother, Edward, was posted in Salonika and presumably took part in the Vardar Offensive from the 15th-29th September. Although ending in Bulgaria's capitulation, the fighting was by no means one-sided; the battle of Lake Dorian in the Vadar Valley, fought on the 18th-19th September by predominantly British and Greek troops, ended in 20,000 Allied casualties to a mere 2-5,000 Bulgarian.

[47] Rowland Ward Ltd. was a notable taxidermist in Piccadilly. The black bear in question was shot by F.V.B.W. on a walking and shooting expedition to Kashmir in 1913.

[48] F.V.B.W. is talking about Longley's 5 years of service as rector of Upper Slaughter.

as things look brighter now than they ever have: I am really beginning to think another year may see it over.

We have settled down in our new camp but are being split up so I shall be on the move off and on.

Spanish influenza is running through our men, and at the moment we have 33% down with it. Luckily it is not bad and doesn't last long.

No more news,

    With very best love,

        Your ever loving Son

          Fred. V. B. Witts.

                            [Samarrah]

                    September 30th 1918.

Dearest Mother.

No mail to answer, but this is probably due to my being away from headquarters for a week inspecting at the spot we spent eight months in last year. Things are much the same as they were and we still get luscious melons.

We are all wondering how the sweeping victory in Palestine is going to affect the situation out here.[49] I suppose the few remaining Turks will vanish, and we shall be left with even less *raison d'étre* than before. I wish I was out there with the 4th Coy, especially now that I am leaving my present job, but one cannot have everything, and I have done extraordinarily well out of my present job, which I should not have done with the 4th Coy.

The hot weather is rapidly coming to an end. The nights and early mornings are quite cold and one wants two blankets, but to ensure that life does not become too much of a bed of roses for us, the flies are now appearing again in swarms.

I have just sent two of my men on leave to England, so I may get away next year and it looks as if peace is within the bounds of possibility by then.

I don't know yet when I shall leave the unit or what unit I shall go to: but my application has been accepted – as it was bound to be. I shall be very sorry in many ways; but one can't see all one's juniors being made Major without a protest!

No more news. Hoping you are all keeping fit.

    With very best love,

        Your ever loving Son,

          Fred. V. B. Witts.

---

[49] The Battle of Megiddo on the 19th September culminated in the unopposed occupation of Damascus on 30th September and the total collapse of Turkish dominion in Palestine.

[Tekrit]

Oct 9th 1918.

Dearest Mother.

…Frank's letter was dated August 30th – more than three weeks later, it is wonderful what difference posting in France makes, as my latest Times from London is August 13th. He tells me I've been mentioned in Despatches. I am very fortunate as I had little to do during the period in question.

…They are still arguing about my fate; apparently the powers that be do not want to lose me from my present job and have again asked that I may be given acting rank so as not to forfeit promotion by staying on. But it looks as if the war would be over before they make up their minds! Today's news – Germany accepting Wilson's 14 points as a basis for negotiation and asking him to arrange an immediate armistice is the most stupendous since 1914, if only as an indication of the conditions in Germany. I imagine it will lead to nothing unless they climb down completely.[50]

…Very sorry to hear the strawberries were so bad – and we out here almost living on melons. Also about the coal; I don't think you will be able to carry on at Slaughter with that small amount and hope you will go to the South Coast or somewhere at any rate for a month or two.

…I am so pleased to hear Edward's been home: what a pleasant surprise it must have been to you! You must have enjoyed his getting some petrol and taking you to Guiting and Cheltenham.

…I am not altogether surprised to hear Longley has given notice to Edward and wants to sell: but it is a great worry to you and Edward, and means the breaking up of the estate. He evidently intends to stay on! But his extra allowances come to an end this year, don't they?

Fancy a Slaughter man in a kilt. It is the absolute limit.

India is certainly going to be no place after the war – except for possible further scraps – but one wonders if England will be either! I am entitled to go home as soon as they can spare me after the war.

I am so very glad to read Edward is so well and fit, as I had gathered otherwise from earlier letters. It is splendid his getting an opportunity to settle everything up. It is Stow Fair[51] in three days time – I hope he gets a good price for the mare and youngster.

---

[50] Germany and Austria were desperate to end the war but afraid that an outright surrender would remove all their leverage in negotiation, leaving them vulnerable to harsh terms. Consequently, on 4th October, the German High Command drafted a 'Peace Note' for the attention of the American President (Austria's earlier appeal for an armistice on Sept 15 had been rejected by Wilson). The Note was a request for Wilson to agree to an armistice, but by no means an offer of surrender. On the basis of Wilson's 14 points, published in January 1918, the German High Command thought that he would be more sympathetic to their terms than either Britain or France.

[51] Stow Fair had been taking place twice a year, spring and autumn, since time immemorial.

I should like to take you to Waterville again – do you remember your excursion on your own in the bay? I hope you won't follow Edward's suggestion of trying to learn to drive the Ford!

Many thanks for the two large Palm leaves, but they are for full dress only; what I wanted was the miniature palm leave, about half an inch long, the same as you sent me before, to wear on the ribbon in ordinary every day kit: I shall be delighted if you can send me out say 4 or 6. Don't send the other two big ones.

What an awful idea, your keeping rabbits in the stables.

I hope by now you will have got the photos I sent.

No more news.

> With my best love,
> > Your ever loving Son,
> > > Fred. V. B. Witts.

F. V. B. Witts
> Capt.

> > [Tekrit]
> > Oct 20ᵗʰ 1918.

Dearest Mother.

I am afraid I have missed a mail, but have been very busy and moving about.

…You have splendid news of Edward and all the rest of the family. Fancy East having a Ford reaping machine, and Edith driving it too. What changes the War has brought about.

I am so glad to hear you could walk to Bourton, but you must take care and not overdo things.[52]

The news everywhere is extraordinarily good. Last night we heard of the dramatic entry of a single aeroplane into Ostend, and that the Bosche had not damaged Lille before evacuating.

Wilson in his replies to Germany seems to hit the right nail on the head each time.[53] We are daily expecting to hear of an armistice with Turkey and are wondering whether we shall get in another blow out here before it is all over.[54]

---

[52] There are still those who walk between Upper Slaughter and Bourton-on-the-Water on a regular basis.

[53] On the 8ᵗʰ October, Wilson formally rejected Germany's 'Peace Note', declaring that he would make no attempt to negotiate an armistice while German forces still remained in occupied territories.

[54] On that same day, General Townshend, acting as an emissary for the Turkish Government, arrived at Mitylene with a proposal for peace. Whilst incarcerated in Prinkipo, Townshend had made many influential friends among Enver Pasha's enemies. Once Enver and the whole Ministry had resigned in response to popular unrest, one of Townshend's acquaintances, Izzet Pasha, was appointed Grand Vizier and War Minister. Townshend immediately wrote to Izzet offering to negotiate peace terms with the British Government on Turkey's behalf in return for his personal liberty.

I was out on a reconnaissance a week ago and saw a Turk for the first time since the spring operations on the Euphrates. We played hide and seek for a bit but he was anxious to keep out of our way.

During the last week we have had to pack up all our Summer outfit, and are down to bare necessities again. One misses a big tent in the middle of the day, as it has been quite unpleasantly hot the last week but the nights are quite cold. It is hard to know what to put on in the early morning, when you shiver if you only wear what you will be able to wear in the middle of the day.

No more news which the censor won't object to!

> Hoping you are keeping fit.
>> With very best love,
>>> Your ever loving Son,
>>> Fred. V. B. Witts

By October 1918, the Central Powers were collapsing internally and on all fronts; there was a unanimous wish to end the war. In Mesopotamia, Ali Ihsan Pasha, former commander of the Turkish XIII Corps, had assumed overall command from Khalil, but the army he inherited had lost all substance and vitality. Meanwhile, the Turkish surrender of Aleppo, Ali Ihsan's main supply base, left him trapped and isolated – easy prey for a final *coup de grace* by Marshall.

General Marshall, however, was less enamoured with the prospect of chasing the Turks 250 miles up the Tigris to Mosul. Lengthy communications into Persia and the Caucasus had left him short of supply transport, and the road ahead offered strong defensive positions which had been prepared over many months. The battles of the Hai Salient and Khudhaira bend had demonstrated that the Turks could not be underestimated when the stakes were down. Marshall's own force, meantime, had been weakened by a sudden outbreak of influenza and by a high proportion of inexperienced new recruits.

Nevertheless, an advance was to be made, much to the delight of Captain Witts. In preparation, No. 2 Mobile Bridging Train was augmented with the addition of half of No. 3 Bridging Train, recently also converted into a 'mobile' unit, giving Captain Witts a total bridging capacity of 750yds.

Writing to his mother after the Armistice with Turkey, signed on October 30th, Captain Witts was able to talk freely about his part in the final push of the campaign.

F.V.B. Witts
    Capt.

[Fathah Gorge]
Nov 8th 1918.

Dearest Mother.

It is a disgraceful long time since I wrote – it must be nearly three weeks. I can only plead that we have been busy putting finishing touches to master Turk, and as a consequence have been out of touch of all postal facilities. Now I am getting in closer touch again and the news as I write is that Austria has been downed and concluded an armistice and that Germany has sent delegates to interview Foch.[55] It really looks as if the war is coming to an end, and is of course already for us out here, though it is very hard to believe and there may be some rounding up of disturbers of the peace to be done in the wilds of Persia or Central Asia.[56] For the same reason as I've been able to send no mails, no mails have reached us. It is particularly unfortunate as I am afraid I've missed the Christmas mail, but if it has been in the cause of an accomplished peace, I am sure you will forgive me. Anyhow all best wishes for Christmas and the New Year and if the war is not over before you get this, may the New Year bring an early peace and us all home to Slaughter once more. In any case the prospects will be much brighter than they have been the last four Christmases! Let's hope the coal shortage will not be too trying for you.

And now for our doings out here, which appear rather paltry and puny beside what is happening elsewhere, but which have been quite a success. With an armistice fixed, I don't think the censor can object to an account of our doings.

We marched out from Tekrit on the 21st two days march up [to Baiji], where we bridged the Tigris on the night of the 23rd, next day the Turks retired from their first position [Fathah Gorge] and we marched on another 15 miles and bridged the river again that night – we thought of advertising a nightly performance, place of performance uncertain! Next day I pushed on with what was left [of the bridging material] to the Lesser Zab another 15 mile march over the vilest going, right across the front of the fight which was in full swing, but we luckily escaped attention from the Turk Guns. Next day after dodging a few shells we put a bridge over the Lesser Zab while the fight still went on on the other side of the Tigris. This was the 26th, that night the Turk again retired [to Sharqat, on the right bank of the Tigris], our

---

[55] The Allied crossing of the River Piave on October 27th, capturing 7,000 Austrians, brought about the crumbling of the Austrian defence on the Italian Front. The next day, Austria made a formal request to the Allies for an armistice, which came into effect on November 4th. Three days later, on the morning of 7th November, General Foch, C-in-C of Allied armies on the Western Front, received a wireless message informing him that German armistice delegates would cross the front line onto French-occupied soil to discuss terms for an armistice.

[56] The Armistice stopped all hostilities with Turkey, but, in Persia and Central Asia, hostile Bolshevik influence and anti-British insurgents would be harder to subdue.

94. Armistice proclamation in
Baghdad 31/10/18.

Cavalry having forded the Tigris 30 miles up behind them & cutting off [their] retreat.[57] On the 27th I had to send on a detachment with an infantry column racing to help the cavalry, as it appeared touch and go whether we should capture the Turks or the Turks our cavalry. I had to stay myself with my main portion. It was perhaps rather lucky as that day I developed Spanish Flue – of all times, and for the next three days had a temperature of 103°; for the first two days I had to keep out and about, but then I was able to take two days complete rest and soon threw it off.

The Turks, some 11,000 & 51 guns, surrendered on the 30th and the armistice was fixed on the 31st. On Nov 1st I had to march through 30 miles to join my advance detachment, and next day built yet another bridge over the Tigris [at Hadraniya, 15 miles north of Sharqat] to help people sort themselves out. We also rescued one of our own guns which had been given up for lost in the river after trying to ford it. Our only trouble was rations, which were often two days behind hand and we had to draw in our belts a bit. However on the 5th, we started back towards railhead so as to ease the ration situation: on the 6th I got back to the Lesser Zab and on the 7th to Fathah to our bridge put up on Oct 24th where I am writing from.

We are all wondering now what will happen to us all. I should like to get up to Mosul but there is not much chance unless the Turks have destroyed their bridge, which is unlikely in view of the Armistice. After that the sooner I can get home to you and Slaughter the better I shall be pleased: but I am afraid the breaking up of the force out here will be a slow job whenever it may start, and we shall have to wait our turn.

We had our first heavy rain yesterday and last night, but I am glad to say I have completely recovered from the flue.

Hoping you are quite fit.

With very best Christmas wishes to you & all

      Your ever loving Son.

          Fred. V. B. Witts.

---

[57] In *Light Floating Bridges*, F.V.B.W. gives the following description of the cavalry's fording of the Tigris: 'the 18-pdrs., with which the horse artillery were specially armed, completely disappeared from view in the middle of the ford, which was almost a rapid. A number of men and horses were drowned, and one gun washed away but recovered by a subaltern of mine some days later. However, the Turks thought the river absolutely unfordable and were completely surprised. It was a great 'finale' to the campaign.' (Appendix I, p. 427).

The principal terms of the Armistice, signed on board the *Agamemnon* off the island of Mudros on 30th October, were as follows: the immediate demobilisation of the Turkish military; unhindered passage through the Bosphorus for Allied ships; the evacuation of all Arab territories formerly part of the Ottoman Empire; the release of all prisoners of war; the dismemberment of all ties with the Central Powers; and the acceptance of a continued Allied military occupation of both the Dardanelles and Bosphorus forts. The agreement would later be criticised for its lack of provision for the Armenians, whose abominable sufferings were to continue in the post-war years. For the moment, however, it was greeted with elation by Force 'D'; finally, a victorious homecoming was truly on the horizon.

F.V.B. Witts
    Capt.

[Fathah Gorge]
Nov 15th 1918.

Dearest Mother.

...As last week's was a belated Christmas letter this must be a New Year letter, so let me wish you and all the happiest and brightest of New Years, which, now that the war is over, is a real possibility instead of the mere phrase it has been for the last four years. Let us hope 1919 will see me home.

The good news of the German Armistice reached me at 10 p.m. on the 11th at Qalât al Shargât (the ruins of Asshur – the capital of ancient Assyria) which has been the Turkish Headquarters some forty miles above our present Camp at Fathah gorge, where the Tigris breaks through the Jebel Hamrin Hills. I went up by car to

95. Fathah Gorge.

inspect a possible bridge site, and captured bridging material: the road crosses the hills and heavy rain had made it almost impassable, in fact without the help of men working on the road and in one case of a team of Artillery horses we should never have got back. As it was it took five hours each way. I stayed at certain Divn H. Q. up there and also twice saw our Corps Commander [General Cobbe], who of course was very pleased with his achievements and very amiable; it was he who refused to allow me to go to a Field Company to enable me to get my acting majority, as he said that I could not be replaced in my present job owing to my special experience especially in view of the operations then in view, and that I must be made a major in my present job. That is not however in his power; it is however in his power to recommend me for a Brevet, which would be worth years of acting rank – apart from pay; and in view of the fact that he made me sacrifice acting rank and pay, and that we did all that was required of us in the recent show, which was such a complete success, I am living in hopes, but it wouldn't materialize for nearly a year, and I may be disappointed. This is strictly private, but I know it will interest you.

Now that the war is over, and my unit will probably be amongst the first to demobilize at any rate partially; it is quite possible that they will send me to a Field Company, on the other hand the end of the war may put a stop to the expansion of Field Companies at present intended. However things are too uncertain to make speculation profitable, and demobilization especially out here will be a very slow business and complicated in many ways.

What scenes there must have been in London on Nov 11th, and how thankful every one must have been. The thought of it all makes one feel terribly far away out here. The future, which one didn't worry about much, until the war was definitely won, now looms up seriously. I think the next four years will be as perilous for the British Empire & England, and as full of momentous changes as the last four; let's hope we manage to pull through without falling out among ourselves. As for myself, I don't know what to make of it, but I have a sort of feeling that no one at home, who have been right through France will have any use for men from the Indian Army who have simply dabbled in war in Mespot: they will say we know nothing about anything and treat us accordingly.[58] On the other hand I have no wish to spend my life in India, and the recent innovation of King's Commissions for Indians is not likely to make it more attractive.[59] Further it is hard to say what job one would get in India. I should like to get on the Staff now, but a fellow with no staff experience

---

[58] At a time of national triumph this was a gloomy premonition of things to come. It is an accurate reflection, however, of the frustration and tinge of shame felt by some British troops at their comparatively cushy time in Mesopotamia in 1918.

[59] The King's Commission for Indians (K.C.I.) allowed Indian personnel to rise through the ranks of the Indian Army and join the officer class. Like the Government of India Act of 1919, previously mentioned by F.V.B.W., the introduction of the K.C.I. was another example of political pressure in India forcing the hand of the British.

is hardly likely to stand an earthly chance; with so many knocking about who have and who will be released by the inevitable reduction of the army.

I was very pleased to get a mention – which incidentally and privately increases my chance of a brevet – very many thanks for your congratulations.

I am very sorry to hear the Glebe is being sold, and I do so hope Edward was able to buy it.[60]

Edith seems to be doing her bit pretty thoroughly at Slaughter. I am so glad to hear the harvest is so good, except the apples. For the last month we have been living on nothing but bully beef, biscuit and some socalled tinned vegetable – and we didn't always get any of them, and the thought of something fresh makes one's mouth water. A month's course of biscuits was too much for my new plate, which cracked but luckily did not break under the strain! We have not got back to bread yet! I have been trying to shoot a sandgrouse or a partridge but the few there are about are very illusive, and my eye appears to be somewhat deranged shall I say.

…You must look upon my photographs, if they have ever reached you, as a Christmas present. Your letter is full of interesting items of Slaughter news; thanks so much for them, as I greatly enjoy hearing about every one and everything. I hope the cheeses will turn out a success and not poison every one!

I am afraid my letters have been arriving very spasmodically; but it is not entirely my fault. I write as regularly as circumstances permit, but the departure of posts and the chances of their catching connections at Basra and Bombay complicate matters.

So glad to hear you have had massage for your right arm and that it has done you good. I hope you will get a good price for your Devonshire farm:[61] it seems wise to sell with the uncertain future.

You say every one travels about with their rations; it sounds more like Mespot than England.

No more news,

With very best love & good wishes,

Your ever loving Son,

Fred. V. B. Witts.

F.V.B. Witts
    Capt.

[Fathah Gorge]
Nov 23rd 1918.

Dearest Mother.

…Fancy melons at 8/- each and we can get them out here for a few pennies! I hope the massage has done your arm good: I wonder if you met Gen Willoughby, I

---

[60] The Glebe was Church land.

[61] Mrs Witts would have inherited Devonshire property from her mother, Mrs Bourne (née Jane Hole).

96. Craw (or Cray) fishing at Aston Brook August 1915.

have come across him on two or three occasions out here.[62]

Your chief item of news is Jack's engagement. I am very pleased indeed, it is quite time one of us got married. It is disappointing the wedding not coming off in England, but these are unusual times.

It is very sad to think that the Glebe is gone, and that all our old memories of shooting parties and cray fishing cannot repeat themselves.

But these are days of vast changes and I should not be surprised to see revolutionary alterations in land ownership. I hope you will get a good price for your Devonshire property. I hope you have managed to sell the car too.

I met Major Wingfield, who was at Slaughter the other day: he is on the staff of the − − Divn out here, where I was staying a night.[63] We neither recognised each other until we heard our names! He asked to be remembered to you and every one, and seemed very fit.

I hope the cheese making has turned out a success.

Have you got my photographs?

Everything points to our staying in our present camp for the time being, and we are therefore settling down to make ourselves as comfortable as possible: we are right in the mouth of the gorge where the river breaks through the Jebel Hamrin hills and are expecting some excitement when it comes down in flood. There are several small oil springs at the spot running into the river,[64] which makes our water supply a difficult matter, as the surface of the river is covered with it. It also spoils all our

[62] Brigadier-General Willoughby, Deputy Adjutant and Quartermaster General, IIIrd Corps.

[63] The Wingfield family have lived at Great Barrington for many years.

[64] The Mosul wilayat (the region through which the Lesser Zab flows) was the most oil-rich of the three Mesopotamian wilayats (the oilfields of Arabistan being in Persia). This factor came into prominence in 1919-20 when Britain and France squabbled over the distribution of mandates.

clothes, which are covered with black oily stains. Unfortunately there is not quite enough to be of value in stilling the troubled waters in a storm. The hills are very rugged and barren, rising to some 1000 feet at their highest point, and form a very sharply defined ridge. The road through the gorge is very difficult, and the main road makes a 40 mile deviation through the desert.

There are two coveys of partridges – one on each bank – they give me a certain amount of sport and exercise but little food, and are now getting rather wary!

Very best love,

Your ever loving Son,

Fred. V. B. Witts.

F. V. B. Witts

Capt.

[Fathah Gorge]

Dec 1st 1918.

Dearest Mother.

...It has been colder and the rain has held off but it looks threatening again. The rain three weeks ago beats all Mesopotamian records for the 24 hour fall, – we always seem to be beating some Mespot record, so it is getting monotonous! However now we are off the absolute dead level plain, one does not notice it so much, as the water runs off instead of converting the country first into a lake and then into a quagmire.

We have utilized a slack week to make ourselves more comfortable, and have got up all our heavy kit and two large tents also a stove, which is most comfortable at nights. We have already built a decent cookhouse and chicken run (!) and land gravel (really shingle) paths between our tents, and utilized old Turkish wire entanglements to make a handsome and effective fence round the camp, as we are all alone – 3 miles from the nearest camp –, and Arabs are expert thieves. I am afraid you will think all this sounds horribly permanent, but I believe in making oneself as comfortable as possible: it helps to keep us fit.

Not a word yet about leave, or breaking up the force; all they have done so far in this line is to ask for the names of any one willing to stay on here. You will be thankful to hear they have not got mine. In another month's time it will be three years since I landed at Basrah.

We have been shooting and eating coots, I have always thought they were rather objectional, but we find them a very pleasant change. They come and sit on the water above the bridge.

No more news, hoping you are all fit.

With very best love,

Your ever loving Son,

Fred. V. B. Witts.

I enclose my voting proxy paper for you, I am afraid it will be much too late for the election but there may be a second 'ere long.[65] I don't know whether I am entitled to a vote – the laws change so quickly! Fill in name of constituency!

F.V. B. Witts
    Capt.

Dec 8th 1918.

Dearest Mother.

Another fortnight's mail in since last writing, with all the usual papers, including the October Blackwood, a Land & Water, and a Tatler as an extra, and your two letters of Oct 1st & 8th; these contain further details of Jack's engagement [to Gulielma Richardson], including his duplicate letter. He seems to have fallen on his feet – I am so delighted; I can imagine your disappointment at missing the wedding. These additions to the family make it even more necessary that I should get home!

But there is not a word of leave or of breaking up the force yet.

No I have not been to Kubela,[66] it is one of the most holy of Mahommedan cities, and visits are not allowed: I have not managed to get down to that part of the world at all, and I am wondering if I shall ever get a chance of seeing the ruins of Babylon,[67] though I imagine the ruins of Asshur,[68] which I saw the other day, are just as interesting if not as well known. All these ruins seem much of a muchness to me. Which book of Mespot have you now got, you must let me know.

I think you were very wise to sell your car when you did, I should think second-hand cars will be a drag on the market now. You won't find it as simple to get rid of the Brougham and Victoria.[69] You mustn't allow yourself to be depressed at parting

---

[65] Polling for the 1918 General Election began on 14th December and the count began on the 28th. It was the first British Election in which women could vote. David Lloyd George was re-appointed Prime Minister, leading a coalition of Liberals and Conservatives (under Andrew Bonar Law).

[66] The city of Karbala, founded in AD 680, grew up around the site of Hussein ibn Ali's martyrdom. Hussein was the grandson of the Prophet Muhammad and, according to members of the Shi'ite sect, the rightful heir to the Caliphate. The city holds his tomb and is a great place of pilgrimage for Shi'ites.

[67] Babylon was the ancient capital of the south Semitic kingdom of Babylonia. It was most prosperous under the Chaldean kings when it was described in admiration by Herodotus (I.178-187). The city continued to prosper under the Persians (who conquered it in 538 B.C.) and Selucids but declined rapidly under the Parthians and was in ruins by the time the Emperor Trajan visited it in A.D. 115.

[68] Asshur (or Assur) was the first capital of Assyria. It grew up around a great temple of the god Assur c. 3000 BC and was the Assyrian Kingdom's religious centre, continuing to prosper through to the Parthian age.

[69] Brougham and Victoria were models of luxury Cadillacs. The 2 and 4-passenger Victorias were first introduced in 1906 as the *Model K Light Runabout* and *Model M Light Tourer*. The later 3-passenger design, introduced in 1915, had a formal leather top and carriage bows, followed up in 1917 by a convertible version, 'Vicky'. The 5-passenger Brougham, or Standard Sedan, was first introduced in 1916.

with all these things, they are of little account as long as your large family is spared to you.

Fancy no fire before Michaelmas, and even then no coal. But I suppose it means just a little more to burn later on. I suppose the coal situation has not been so acute as expected before the Armistice, what with the release (I suppose) of miners and the recovery of French coalfields.

We have got an oilstove, and it is very welcome now, as we are in the middle of a spell of wet and windy weather. This is the fourth day in succession, not that the total fall of rain has been heavy. There's been a good deal in the hills and the river rose during last night to half as wide again as it had been before, pulling us all out of bed at 2 a.m. to make the necessary arrangements. Luckily with the whole country in our occupation we now get ample warning from upstream a point which saves much anxiety, and was of course impossible before the armistice.

We had the Mesopotamia Geological expert in to dinner last night, and he was most interesting: he recommends investing in Mesopotamia oil if a company is started![70] There is no doubt about it being here.

No more news.

> Very best love & good wishes,
> Your ever loving Son,
> Fred. V. B. Witts.

POST OFFICE TELEGRAPHS.   14 DE

This Form must accompany any inquiry respecting this Telegram.   18

Office of Origin and Service Instructions.

PHMS: *Baghdad Lilb*   *Handed in at}* 12.5pm *Received here at}* 9.45pm

    TO{ *Lco Witts. Upper Slaughter,*

    Best Christmas wishes coming home months leave
> *Fred Witts*

---

[70] Visits from competing international oil prospectors in 1919-20, representing companies such as the US Standard Oil Co., spread distrust amongst the Allies (see note 62) and promoted an unfavourable image of colonialism to the local Arabs.

F.V.B. Witts

    Capt. R.E.

[Red Sea]

H. T. Egra.[71]

Jan 4th 1919.

Dearest Mother.

I have not written since most unexpectedly and at very short notice I got a month's leave home, as I imagined I should get home before any letter. They now say that this ship will not take us beyond Egypt, and that we may be delayed there some days.

I am therefore writing to give you more warning than was possible in my original cable or will be possible in the cable I shall send from Egypt, in which I shall try and tell you our date of departure and probable date of arrival. But we have not the slightest notice whether we shall go round by sea, or be sent via Marseilles or Taranto.

In any case I shall make for Brown's Hotel[72] and hope to find you there with my clothes! I will wire you there time and station of arrival if I get the chance.

I left behind a suitcase and leather portmanteau containing various articles of kit and hope you will be able to look them up, and bring them along inspite of the absence of porters etc! We have come straight round from Basra so that I have nothing with me except uniform, luckily both hot and cold. I also left behind a British Warm greatcoat which I should also like and which may not be in the suit case or portmanteau.

I shall have a lot to do in London, shopping, business and dentist and shall probably have to spend most of the 28 days there.

…The voyage has been like any other. There are 92 Officers and 1400 other ranks on board – all leave details or demobilizers.

We embarked on Christmas Day in pouring rain, & so, but for the fact that we were bound for Blighty, it would have been the most dismal Christmas I've ever spent.

I'll keep other news till we meet.

Au revoir and very best love,

    Your ever loving Son,

        Fred. V. B. Witts.

---

[71] F.V.B.W. had sailed on the *Egra* in 1916 from Bombay to Basra (September 22nd 1916, p. 106-7).

[72] Brown's Hotel is in Albemarle street, Mayfair.

The war had been over for two months but little had changed in Mesopotamia; any immediate trace of a Turkish threat had vanished long before the signing of the Armistice. In the intervening period, the irrepressible question of whether, in the context of the whole war, the sacrifices made in Mesopotamia had been worthwhile, was bound to surface.

Force 'D' had fulfilled their primary mission of protecting the oil fields Arabistan; they had captured Baghdad to the great benefit of British prestige; and they had held down and defeated a large Turkish army. But the cost had been great; 35,000 men had died in battle and through sickness,[73] and untold quantities of funds and resources had been spent. Meanwhile, the ignominious title of 'SIDESHOW' would forever besmirch the campaign's achievements.

The real answer to the question of the campaign's worth, must also be based on the forthcoming years in Mesopotamia. The war was over, but Britain's challenge to build a workable, independent state out of a politically barren corner of the old Ottoman Empire had only just begun.

For Captain Witts, the campaign had offered brief moments of brilliance in a sea of inactivity. Those moments, however, had been extraordinary. For the time being, Captain Witts' future belonged in Mesopotamia, and he would continue to benefit from it.

---

[73] This may seem like a negligible total when compared to casualty statistics from the Western Front, but, proportionally, casualty rates in Mesopotamian battles from 1915-17 were roughly equal to, and sometimes higher, than those on the Western Front.

CHAPTER VIII

PEACE

Letters: March 15ᵗʰ –July 13ᵗʰ 1919

The collapse of the Ottoman Empire left a power vacuum in Mesopotamia which had to be filled, but conflicting loyalties led to an uncertain stance for the British Civil Administration, the political arm of Force 'D'.[1] The Empire's division, come the end of the war, had been under fervent diplomatic discussion since 1915. The result was a confused mass of public and private agreements. Collectively, these agreements failed to establish any cohesive political direction regarding the British role and her objectives in Mesopotamia. Early on in the campaign against the Turks, the Indian Government had pronounced designs for an outright annexation of the Basra wilayat as well as veiled control of Baghdad behind the façade of an Arab figurehead. The Sykes-Picot Agreement between Britain, France and Russia was signed in May 1916. It carved Syria (plus the Mosul wilayat) and Mesopotamia into respective French and British dominions, leaving Palestine under international control. The Agreement was essentially a manifestation of imperialist greed, but most unsavoury was its total invalidation of an earlier diplomatic contract laid out in correspondence between Sir Henry McMahon, British High Commissioner in Egypt, and Hussein ibn Ali, Sharif of Mecca, in October 1915. In return for Hussein leading a widespread Arab Revolt against the Turks, McMahon had pledged to give him and his family kingship over an independent Arab Federation comprising Arabia, Syria (except Lebanon which was reserved for France), Mesopotamia and, although later denied, Palestine.[2]

With these two contradictory positions, the line to be taken by the Civil Administration after the war was unclear. Pressure from the hugely influential U.S. President, Woodrow Wilson, to promote self-determination in the Middle East, led to an apparently encouraging but actually grudging policy for the sponsorship of Arab independence, encapsulated in the Anglo-French Declaration of 8ᵗʰ November 1918. Based on the doctrine of Wilson's 14 Points, it stated that, 'France and Great Britain are agreed to encourage

---

[1] The Civil Administration, headed by Lieutenant-Colonel A. T. Wilson, the Acting Civil Commissioner after the war, was the provisional Government in Mesopotamia. It was made up of a group of young British administrators, known as Political Officers, who were installed as regional governors or 'advisers' to native leaders throughout the country, imposing the rule of the Civil Administration. Their duties were wide-ranging and included the collection of revenue, overseeing municipal projects, presiding over judicial matters when required, providing subsidies, promoting trade and commerce and keeping the peace. Essentially, they were the senior authority in their sphere of influence with the power, if necessary, to call upon military assistance from British forces.

and assist in the establishment of indigenous Governments and Administrations in Syria and Mesopotamia.'³ Annexation along the lines of the Sykes-Picot Agreement had been ruled out, and the promises to Sharif Hussein of a Hashemite Kingdom had been sidestepped; what remained was a vague and impractical policy lacking any appreciable understanding of the political, racial, religious and economic vagaries of the country.

Militarily, it was necessary to retain some measure of strength to avoid the country collapsing into anarchy, although partial demobilisation was

97. Sharif Hussein.

already in full swing and military costs were being cut wherever possible. On his return from leave, Captain Witts was perfectly aware that, one way or the other, British involvement in Mesopotamia was to be for the long-term. The proportion of military involvement, however, would be determined by forthcoming events. Nonetheless, for the present, minds were still focused on the past 4 years of war; nothing could extinguish the joyous facts that the fighting had finally ended and the war was won.

---

² The question of Palestine was never actually mentioned in the correspondence between McMahon and Hussein but both parties later claimed that there had been an unspoken understanding that the region would fall under their jurisdiction. The issue provided a massive and lasting source of controversy, compounded by the Balfour Declaration of 1917 under which the British Government favoured the creation of a Jewish homeland in Palestine.

³ The Anglo-French Declaration was essentially an official confirmation of the panegyric 'Maude Proclamation' (*see* Chapter V, p. 160, note 2), which intended to portray the British as liberators rather than conquerors.

Palace Hotel Telephono: No. 83
Grand Hotel de Turin
Turin
March 15th 1919

Dearest Mother.

Our train leisurely pulled up at a siding about three miles out of the town this morning and announced its probable intention of not going on for another five or six days. So we got out and walked into the R.T.O's office at the Central Station. He hopes to push us on at 8 o'clock tonight but it is not yet certain. So we came in here for a meal and a bath the first of each that we have had since leaving London.

The U.S.S. Nopatin[4] was a comfortable boat, but we had a rough crossing. She didn't move about as much as I expected but quivered from bow to stern as if she was going to drop to pieces when we met a wave. We left at six and got into Havre at 3 – not Cherbourg as anticipated. They just gave us time to have an omelette or rather two to be precise and then pushed us out to a way-side station and into a train which did not start till midnight. They might have given us time for a proper dinner.

It was an empty trooptrain returning to Taranto – empty cattle trucks except for two Italian second class coaches into which our party of about thirty had to squash. They wouldn't let us use the comfortable hospital coach absolutely empty and likely to remain so unless we can conjure up a temperature! We came past Versailles and woke at Dijon yesterday morning, passed Aix-les-bains in the evening and through the Mont Cenis during the night. Rather disappointing, as it is very pretty just now with snow very low, and masses of primroses about.

Best love,

Your ever loving Son,

    Fred.V. B.Witts.

F.V.B.Witts
    Capt.

Taranto
Italy.
March 20th 1919.

Dearest Mother.

Got in here this morning after eight nights in all in the train, and found your very welcome letter of March 12th.

---

[4] *U.S.S. Nopatin* was a transport ship built in 1913 by Harlan & Hollingsworth, Wiimington, Delaware. She was used for ferrying American troops over the English Channel to France in 1918. After the war, the *Nopatin* was rechristened the *De Witt Clinton* and employed as a passenger steamer on the Hudson river in New York state, before once again operating as a troop carrier in the English Channel on America's entry into WWII. After the Allied victory, she was finally re-named *Galilah* and served as a passenger liner for ZIM Israeli lines.

Don't worry about my face, it is practically all right again now thanks to a week in the train without a shave and starving![5]

The ink in the restcamp mess, where I am writing, has run out, so I must carry on in pencil.

We go on board tonight or tomorrow morning on the Canberra, the same boat as brought us to Marseilles in January – an Australian boat and very comfortable which is nice.

I hope you got my letter from Turin where we spent the best part of a day. From there onwards our train could only move in fits and starts. We struggled to Bologna and had to stop there as it were to recover breath, for six hours or more, and so on all down the coast. The trouble was it was always impossible to find out how long we were going to stop anywhere but we usually managed to stretch our legs and get a hot meal each day. The Italians know how to charge all right, and didn't seem to be out to make things pleasant for the English. I am not a bit sorry to have the journey behind us.

At our long halt yesterday just outside Brindisi we saw an Italian aeroplane crash from a great height. He was apparently doing stunts and overdid it.

The trees and fields are all beautifully green but it is surprisingly cold for the South of Italy this time of year. I was very glad of my Gilgit boots.

Very best love,

     Your ever loving Son,

        Fred. V. B. Witts.

                    H. M. T. Canberra

                      Mediterranean.

                      March 24th 1919.

Dearest Mother.

We are due in at Port Said late tonight or early tomorrow and I shall then post this as what happens next – whether we go straight through, or hang about Egypt – is of course quite uncertain. If we have to hang about, I shall do my best to get up to Cairo, but I think it is extremely doubtful if they will let us in view of the recent trouble in Egypt.[6]

We got away from Taranto on the afternoon of the 21st after one night there. There was almost a gale blowing and it was very unpleasant the first 24 hours but since then

---

[5] F.V.B.W. may have suffered another outbreak of the 'Baghdad Boil', although a beard and stringent diet make a questionable cure.

[6] In early March 1919, British authorities exiled Saad Zaghlul, the leader of the nationalist Waqf party, to subdue demands for an independent Egypt. The banishment, however, had an adverse effect; on 9th March public demonstrations, predominantly non-violent, broke out in Cairo and rapidly spread throughout the country.

it couldn't have been pleasanter. There are a mixed crowd on board including some extraordinary specimens of the Royal Air Force, who are luckily only going to Egypt, as are most of those on board. Some are for India, and a small cheery party for Mespot, including a Flying man of a more ordinary species. There are also a crowd of ladies and civilians wearing armbands with S. P. R. F. on them, which led to great speculation as to what it stood for – the Society for the Propagation of something being the nearest we could get to it. Eventually it turned out to be Syria and Palestine Relief Fund under the leadership of Lord Lamington.[7] There are no troops on board which makes it very nice and all berths only 2/3rds full. By an extraordinary coincidence I was allotted exactly the same berth as I had coming over, but this time only two instead of three in a very large cabin.

I find that most of the fellows who came on leave with me returned by this boat <u>three weeks ago</u>, immediately on the expiration of their one month's leave. I was very lucky.

Very best love,
      Your ever loving Son,
            Fred. V. B. Witts

[Suez]
March 28th 1919.

Dearest Mother.

As anticipated we got into Port Said late on the evening of the 25th, landed on the morning of the 26th, spent that day and night there and came on here by train yesterday. Here we are under canvas, but have a comfortable mess. There is no news when we are going on, but it will probably be in three or four days time, and I shall try and write again when I know. There are apparently few or no boats running direct to Basra, and we shall have to go to Bombay first: so goodness knows when if ever I shall get back to my unit.

There was little in Port Said to make one suspect that the country was in revolt. Two large Dutch liners were in, and the place was full of tourists of all nationalities busy shopping. The British guard on the Post and Telegraph offices seemed an ordinary war precaution. It was only on reaching the thoroughfare dividing the Arab from the European quarters that there was anything to show that on the 21st the Arabs and

---

[7] S.P.R.F. was launched in 1916 by Rennie MacInnes, Anglican Bishop in Jerusalem, to supply aid and medical assistance to civilians displaced or suffering from the effects of the war in Syria and Palestine. Charles Lord Lamington (1860-1940), leader of the expedition encountered by F.V.B.W., was a British politician and administrator who served as Governor of Queensland (1896-1901) and Bombay (1903-1907) before serving as a commissioner to S.P.R.F. after the war. His most famous accolade, however, was as founding father of Australia's national cake, the 'lamington', a square sponge-cake dipped in chocolate sauce and sprinkled with shredded coconut. Although extremely popular in Queensland, Lord Lamington himself is reported to have described his edible namesake as 'that bloody poofy woolly biscuit!' (*The New Zealand Herald*, 6th Oct 2007).

Egyptians had tried to rush the European quarter (and failed miserably). We found every cross road held by a strong British guard with a machine gun pointing down each street into the Arab quarter: but no one seemed to take any notice of it and business seemed to be going on as usual, though no Europeans were allowed into the Arab quarter.

During the day a warning came in that there was a scheme afoot to poison all British Troops and we were ordered not to buy anything in the shape of fruit, drink or food outside.

Coming along yesterday we found the railway guarded all the way, and being repaired in one place where they had tried to pull it up.

There has been no trouble here at Suez so far and the many British troops that there are in readiness do not show themselves at all, and life appears quite normal, and one wanders about freely, though, personally, with a revolver in my pocket.

Things have been very serious along the Nile. A number of British Officers, variously reported up to 30 in all, have been murdered, and enormous damage done to the railways and telegraph lines, which have been destroyed far and wide.[8] Communication was only kept up by aeroplane, though the main lines Alexandria, Cairo and the Canal are again running irregularly.

The whole thing seems extraordinarily futile, as the Egyptians and the Bedouins have hardly an arm between them – the Egyptian Army and Police are not affected – whereas the country is flooded with British and Indian troops trying to get back to England and India respectively. Many unfortunate demobilized men from Mespot have been roped in and re armed and detained much to their disgust.

I thought of wiring to Milne Cheetham[9] to get me a job, but I don't think there is any shortage, or that there would be anything particularly interesting to do.

The whole situation is rather like a number of midges worrying one in summer.[10]

No more news.

> Very best love,
> Your ever loving Son,
> Fred. V. B. Witts.

[8] British efforts to quash the uprising had resulted in roughly 30 British, 30 other European and 800 Egyptian deaths.

[9] Sir Milne Cheetham, F.V.B.W.'s cousin through Jack Cheetham, had temporarily replaced Lord Wingate as British High Commissioner in Egypt in January 1919, while Wingate was recalled to London to attend conferences.

[10] F.V.B.W. misjudged dramatically the potency of the revolution. The country was so united in its demand for a constitutional government that strikes effectively brought it to a nation-wide standstill, resisting all British efforts to restore her authority. By the time that three different High Commissioners, Lord Wingate, Sir Milne Cheetham and General Sir Edmund Allenby, had agreed that the nationalist fervour running through Egypt was irrepressible by force or other means, Whitehall finally decreed that a deputation of the Waqf party should be permitted to travel to Paris to present their case at the Peace Conference. Less than three years later, on 18th February 1922, Egypt was declared an independent state.

98. The Hospital Ship
Erinpura.

[Suez]
March 31st 1919.

Dearest Mother.

We are expecting to embark today on the 'Erinpura'[11] a B. I. [Battle Injury] Ambulance Transport for Bombay, so goodness only knows when we shall reach Baghdad. Some of our party went on yesterday in an awful tramp, and I was thankful not to be with them. Our boat though not luxurious will be passably comfortable or should be.

I am afraid my chief pal will miss the boat as he had to go to Cairo on duty two days ago and it is doubtful if he can get back in time. I should like to wait for him, but I must push on as, as it is, I shall not reach Baghdad till May!

There have been no developements here and everything is quiet and normal. This is an awful spot to wait in, none could be worse, and I shall be glad to be out of it. Absolutely nothing to do. We have been here five nights now. Our only two diversions were a fracas with the Egyptian Police over the gentleman driving our cab; we at first took the side of law and order, as we thought, and were much surprised when a strong patrol of British Military Police arrived and scattered the Gipy Police to the four winds, leaving our conveyance and driver free to proceed. No wonder there is unrest in Egypt!

The other show was a concert given by the party of Russian Officers, escaped or released from somewhere and passing through to Vladivostock. About fifty of them.

---

[11] The merchant schooner, *H.M.A.T.* [His Majesty's Auxiliary Transport] *Erinpura*, had a long and varied life in the service of the British Navy. Built in 1911 by W. Denny & Bros. in Dumbarton, she acted as a trooper, hospital ship and ambulance transport during the war until she ran aground on the Mushejera Reef in the Red Sea on 6th June 1919, shortly after F.V.B.W.'s own voyage to Bombay. She was salvaged and her damaged bow was replaced. She then returned to merchant duties until, on the outbreak of war in 1939, she was re-employed for trooping. She made numerous voyages until, in May 1943, her service ended tragically when she was hit by German bombers off Benghazi, and sunk with the loss of roughly 650 men.

They sang extraordinarily well. The evening finished with speeches and toasts in Russian, French and English, followed by the two national anthems. They sang theirs – the old hymn tunes – very well indeed.

We have been spending our days wandering about aimlessly, usually ending up at the Hotel Bel Air, the only respectable pub in the place, for a drink or a meal. It has been quite hot – unusually so for the place.

No more news.

> With very best love,
> Your ever loving Son.
> Fred. V. B. Witts.

> H.M.A.T. Erinpura.
> Arabian Sea. April 8th 1919.

Dearest Mother.

We are due in to Bombay late this evening. It is very unlikely that we shall go on to Basra by this ship; possibly we shall be transhipped immediately on to a Basra boat, but more likely we shall land tomorrow morning for two or three days, and I shall not be sorry to stretch my legs, though I don't want to stop long.

Our departure from Suez was enlivened by the desperate efforts made by my particular friend [Norrie Fuller], who had gone to Cairo on duty, to catch the ship. He is a 60th Rifle man now in the R.A.F. He got my wire, warning him we were going, at 9.30 a.m. At 9.45 a.m. he wired me he was starting immediately by aeroplane: I got this at 11.15 just as we were going on board, and promptly approached the authorities with a view of holding the ship up a few minutes, but met with little sympathy: at 12.15 he arrived at the aerodrome and on ringing up the authorities he was told he was too late and couldn't come. Luckily I rang him up on another telephone a minute later on the chance, not knowing he had arrived, and told him to ignore the authorities and come on board. He collected his kit and was down at the ship by 1 p.m. within 3½ hours of getting my wire at Cairo. The authorities were very annoyed, and I got severely choked off, but as there was ample room on the ship they could not say anything. So he came along with us and we have been a very cheery crowd. He said he found Cairo apparently absolutely normal, but he was only there a day and a half.

The voyage has been quite the pleasantest I have ever had. Besides excellent company, we have been extraordinarily fortunate in our weather, and I have never known it so cool either in the Red Sea or Arabian Sea; there has always been plenty of wind without its being rough. The ship too is the most comfortable and best run B. I. boat I have been on. In everything except name it is a regular hospital ship, full of Indian sick. We occupy the empty British Officers quarters. It is extraordinarily clean for ships these days, and the food is good. I have been playing less bridge than I usually do at sea, but it has been of an highly entertaining nature, and I have been winning more or less consistently.

We passed close in to Perim on the morning of the 4th, but passed Aden some way out as it was getting dusk the same evening.

I will write again from Bombay.

Very best love,

   Your ever loving Son,

     Fred. V. B. Witts

P.S. You will be glad to know my face has completely healed again.

TAJ MAHAL HOTEL, BOMBAY

April 15th 1919.

Dearest Mother.

We landed on the 10th, and I posted my letter written on board. Three of us were very lucky in getting rooms here as the place is absolutely full up. Hundreds of people pouring in from Mespot and all parts of India, and staying here waiting for passages home. I have met a large number of friends here including one of the R. E. Generals from Mespot. My unit was, when he left, where I left it [Fathah Gorge], and I shall certainly go straight back to the same job. I discussed my future with him, and as a result decided to try and get a nomination into the Staff College preferably the home one at Camberley or failing that the Indian at Quetta. He introduced me to the Director of Staff Duties out here who told me all about it. I am taking back with me a personal letter for the Commander in Chief at Baghdad [General Cobbe] – who knows me well, asking him to nominate me. I have certainly more chance of getting something out of Mespot where I am known, than anywhere else; so I shall stay out there until this is decided one way or the other. If there is nothing doing I shall ask for home. It was great luck meeting the General. My other R. E. General friend from Mespot is now head of the R. E. in India which may be useful.

On the 11th the day after landing, I got roped in to do best man at the wedding of a fellow who came out with us and whose best man failed him at the last moment. I suppose being best man is the first step towards getting married? At any rate one gets to know what one has to do at one's own wedding.

We ought to have gone on to Mespot on the 12th, but meeting so many friends we decided to miss a boat and are sailing tomorrow morning on the *Varela* a hospital transport.[12] It has been one mad succession of luncheons teas and dinners here or at the Yacht Club alongside, and I have thoroughly enjoyed meeting so many friends.

The *New Zealand* is in the harbour with Jellicoe on board.[13] The cousin of the

---

12 F.V.B.W. had sailed in the *Varela* from Bombay once before (see June 17th 1918, Chapter VII, p. 232-3).

13 Admiral John Jellicoe, 1st Earl Jellicoe, commanded the Grand Fleet at the famous Battle of Jutland (31st May–1st June 1916), the largest naval battle of WWI. He was promoted to First Sea Lord in November 1916 but his pessimistic outlook upon Allied chances of overall victory prompted Prime Minister Lloyd George to replace him with Admiral Wemyss in December 1917. After the war, Jellicoe served as Governor-General of New Zealand from September 1920 – November 1924.

third of our trio is also there, and yesterday we went on board and saw all over the ship, which was most interesting. Tonight we are dining some of them at the Club.

As in Egypt we have come in for riots and rows; there were riots here on the 11th and troops were called out. There has been serious trouble at Ahmedebad near here and upcountry at Lahore and Amritsar. They have now started pulling up the lines and telegraphs. Goodness knows how it will develope or straighten out.[14] In Mespot we appear to be going back to the quietest spot on the earth at the moment.

I think I've told you all the news. I sent you a cable yesterday telling you of my progress.

Very best love,

Your ever loving Son,

Fred. V. B. Witts.

F. V. B. Witts

H. T. Varela No. 2 Bridging Train
Mes: Ex: Force.
10 a.m. April 22nd 1919.

Dearest Mother.

We are due in in Basra in an hour's time after a pleasant but uneventful voyage. We left Bombay on the afternoon of the 16th and touched at Bushire yesterday remaining there some six hours dropping mails, passengers and some 250 tons of fresh water, which is unobtainable there in any quantity. You only get a bird's eye view of the place as owing to shallow water, ships anchor about four miles out: but a bird's eye view was quite enough.

Some fellows amused themselves fishing while we were at anchor, but only caught an indifferent type of mud fish. One small shark was hooked, but managed to get off.

We were very lucky to catch the tide in the early hours of the morning and get over the bar or we should have been waiting about twenty four hours.

We have had extraordinarily good weather throughout: a strong head wind without being rough, with the result that it has been positively cold. It will be all the more trying launching out into the Mespot heat.

I expect to stay a day or so in Basra and then on up to Baghdad.

---

[14] Public resentment at the passing of the 'Rowlatt Bill', which gave the Indian Government the right to imprison suspected terrorists without trial, had overflowed throughout the Punjab. In retaliation to the Bill, a *hartal* (a comprehensive strike in all shops, factories, offices and institutions) was organised in Lahore and Amritsar on 30th March and 6th April, spreading riots and destruction across the Punjab and beyond. Angry mobs attacked post offices and Government buildings and tore down telegraph wires, killing five Englishmen in the violence. In Amritsar, on the 13th April, General Dyer of the 29th Punjabis decided upon shock tactics to restore order. Having blockaded the exits, he ordered his soldiers to fire upon a peaceful gathering at the public square of Jallianwala Bagh, killing 379 citizens.

We had a great dinner at the Yacht Club the night before we left Bombay entertaining our friends from the *New Zealand*. It is out and out the best club outside England.

This is the ship I came back from leave in India in last June. 90 of us sleeping between decks. This time however we've been very comfortable.

Very best love,

Your ever loving Son,

Fred. V. B. Witts

By the time that Captain Witts returned to Mesopotamia, the war had been over for nearly 6 months. However, from a political perspective, there were very few signs of progress. The League of Nations had outlined a system of provisional government whereby a powerful nation would be given a mandate to nurture a weaker country's political, social and economic growth, until it was able to flourish on its own as a fully independent state. Britain was the only reasonable candidate for the Mesopotamian mandate, but its finalisation was pending on peace being signed with Turkey.[15] Until the mandate had been confirmed, the British Government forbade the Civil Administration from making any formal declaration of policy to the Mesopotamian people or giving any substantial indication of their long-term political commitment to the country. Meantime, the all-British administration, with the use of Indian clerks, contradicted any literal interpretation of the Anglo-French Declaration's pledge to 'encourage and assist in the establishment of [an] indigenous government in Mesopotamia.' Despite this, the population was, at this stage, far more concerned with rebuilding livelihoods after the ravages of 4 years of war, than with political wrangling.

Initially, the Civil Administration was relatively popular. In the latter years of the war, the areas of Mesopotamia under British control had undergone substantial schemes of development. After the Armistice, cuts were made to the funding of the Civil Administration, but improvements were still made to agriculture, irrigation and infrastructure, although generally on a smaller scale. Political officers integrated themselves into town communities and often developed friendships with prominent inhabitants; their efficient administration, bringing law and commercial prosperity to many regions, was usually welcomed. In Baghdad and Basra, development programmes that had been initiated during the war were continued. On the surface, Mesopotamia was progressing peacefully, despite political inconsistencies with the promises made in the Anglo-French Declaration. Captain Witts, meanwhile, arrived in the country with his mind focused on his career; in his ambition to get to Staff College, he would start by getting advice from the very top.

---

[15] The British Government was nervous of precipitating the signing of a peace treaty with Turkey until America had made a decision on whether it was to accept the mandate for Armenia.

99. View of Baghdad downstream of the British Residency.

F.V. B. Witts
    Capt.

Baghdad (No 2 Bridging Train)
Mes. Ex. Force.
April 29th 1919.

Dearest Mother

I am writing from Baghdad where I arrived yesterday morning. I stayed one night in Basra and came on the next evening by train to Amara and then by river to Kut: owing to the strong current this stage took the unusually long time of three days. I spent the few hours we had in Kut on going to look at the old Kut of the siege fame, which is some four miles from the new Kut and which I have never previously seen except from a distance. It is three years today since they surrendered.

I went to G.H.Q. yesterday morning, presented the letter I collected in Bombay and had an interview with General Cobbe, the present C-in-C out here. He is a most charming gentleman, and told me he thought I was looking extraordinarily well, which by the way is the opinion of all my friends out here whom I have met so far. He told me the War Office refuse to entertain any nominations for the Staff College in the case of fellows like myself with no staff experience, so he suggested I had better collect some staff experience with a view of getting into the Staff College later – my present youth is also against me, much to my surprise. With this in view he arranged for me to be attached to the R.E. Branch of G.H.Q. as an understudy to see how I take to staff work – I think he suspects that three years independence running my own show will have spoilt me for it, as probably it has. I am to be given some minor staff job when one becomes vacant, provided I give satisfaction in my present probation! It is like starting all over again, but one must have some sort of goal

100. View of Baghdad upstream of the British Residency.

in life, and the Staff College seems a suitable one for me at the moment, so I must lump it! It will do me good not being my own master for a change! The General was very nice about it all and appeared to be all out to help me; I already owe him a lot as I learnt that, thanks to his putting up such a strong case for me, the War Office reversed the decision of India and sanctioned my getting the acting rank of Major. It is very satisfactory winning one's case, but it is a bit late in the day as of course I have to relinquish it if I get a Staff job, but it has been arranged that as long as I am only attached to G.H.Q. I am to retain my present appointment as O.C. of the Bridging Train and with it the rank and what chiefly matters the extra £20 a month which it brings.

The only fly in the ointment which may still upset everything is the difficulty of finding some one to carry on the Bridging Train work for me, as the fellow – Wotherspoon – who has been doing it while I was away, will naturally want to go on leave.

I am going up by tonight's train and shall be with them tomorrow, I shall stay about a week and then, if everything is fixed up, shall return here to G.H.Q.

Continue addressing everything as usual as it is only a temporary appointment and I can get the letters diverted from Basra equally quickly and easily.

It is much cooler here than I anticipated and this morning I was actually shivering.

No more news.

      With very best love,
          Your ever loving Son,
            Fred. V. B. Witts.

F.V.B. Witts
Major.

Fathah Gorge. No. 2 Bridging Train
Mes: Ex: Force.
May 4th 1919.

Dearest Mother.

Edward's birthday: please wish him many happy returns if at home.

I got up to railhead at Baiji [across the Tigris from Fathah, on the right bank] on Wednesday morning April 30th, and, finding a large detachment of my unit there, spent the day and night with them. I came on here to my headquarters on May 1st, and found my old tent just as I had left it.

Everything is just the same as when I left, except in my 4½ months absence things have been made very comfortable – huts built, garden sown with both vegetables and flowers, a lawn laid out and a tennis court. No bridge to worry about, as it was dismantled in February owing to high floods and is still sitting high and dry on the bank. Wotherspoon, whom I left behind in charge, did extraordinarily well dismantling just in the nick of time and saved everything. The two other bridges between us and Baghdad were swept clean away with enormous loss of material.

The floods should now be over, but it is doubtful if we rebuild the bridge before June.

My orders to go down to G. H. Q. have come through and I am probably going on Wednesday, as there are races in Baghdad the next day. One of my subalterns has gone sick and Wotherspoon wants to be demobilized or get leave so I may have to return in a month's time.

I found all your October, November and December mails including your Christmas present and numerous Christmas cards. Many thanks for them all. I have also got your two letters of March 18th and 24th I missed the second letter at Taranto, and so am delighted to hear Jack has got an Acting Majority. He managed to beat me alright!

I shall be interested to hear who is elected guardian.[16]

Everyone remarks how awfully well I am looking and how much the holiday has done me good. I am already beginning to wonder how things will plan out, and if I shall be able to get back next year. My ambitions to get a staff job as a stepping stone to the Staff College may however cause difficulties.

Your envelopes fit very well and have consequently arrived intact.

Fancy more snow after my departure!

I am very glad to hear Aunt Sybil's horse is getting better. I nearly told the Vet to kill it!

Many thanks for all the usual papers including the Deanery Magazine.

Very best love,

Your ever loving Son,

Fred. V. B. Witts.

---

[16] The Guardian was a village position equating to a governor of the poor.

101. Baghdad Racecourse.   102. The Grand Stand at the Baghdad Races.

OFFICERS' CLUB,
BAGHDAD.

No 2 Bridging Train
Mes: Ex: Force
Sunday May 11th 1919.

Dearest Mother.

I came down here on Wednesday night arriving for breakfast on Thursday, as the train takes twelve hours to do the 134 miles from Baiji – the railhead nine miles below Fathah.

My Colonel is at present out on tour but comes back on Tuesday, and as Thursday and Saturday were occupied with the Baghdad May Races, I have so far had nothing to do: and I am very much afraid that ordinarily there will be little for me to do. If so I shall try and get a change, but I must go steady or I shall make myself unpopular. I could never survive a hot weather in Baghdad with no work. Anyhow I somehow don't think I shall stay long in my present job.

I was very glad to get in to the Races as, apart from the racing, which was quite entertaining and provided good sport, one meets every one one knows, as they come in from outstations. But a very large number have been demobilized or at any rate left the country, as of course the number of troops out here has been very largely reduced while I was away. The youngest de Wend Fenton was riding and had rather a nasty fall but escaped with a strained shoulder.

I am living in quite a comfortable mess, but its members are rather old and dull – perhaps they will improve with closer acquaintance – so I am feeling a bit lonely. Fuller, my friend of the journey out, is now in Baghdad, but he is too busy for me to see much of him which is rather disappointing: he is now Private Secretary to the Civil Commissioner [Lt.-Col. A. T. Wilson] – a very nice billet. I have been offered two good civil jobs out here, but apart from my own wish to get home as soon as circumstances admit, I doubt very much if I could get away from the Army, and it would mean burning one's boats behind one in that line, at a time too when the future prospects and conditions of service out here are very indefinite.

There are all sorts of rumours flying about of trouble with Afghanistan,[17] and it might affect us out here: so perhaps there may yet be some more work for the Army to do. The more I think of it the more I dislike the idea of the Army in peace again. Anyhow I must stick it for another three years when I am due for the lordly pension of £120 a year!

You will gather I am feeling rather restless as to the future.

No more news,

>   Very best love,
>>   Your ever loving Son,
>>>   Fred. V. B. Witts.

Aerial Mail

F. V. B. Witts
>   Major R.E.

>>>>   No 2 Bridging Train
>>>>   Mes: Ex: Force
>>>>   [Baghdad]
>>>>   May 12th 1919.

Dearest Mother.

I had only just posted my weekly letter this morning when it was announced that an 'aerial mail' direct across to Egypt would leave tomorrow morning. It should get there quicker, but it is impossible to say how quick or how many earlier letters it may forestall: on the other hand I am told that on the last occasion an aerial mail was sent it took longer than the ordinary mail as it got hung up in Egypt: if this should happen again, there is no need to read any further.

My name has appeared in Orders as an acting Major and I am consequently now masquerading as such; but it won't be for long, as if I get a Staff job I shall have to revert to substantive rank again.

I came down to the Engineer-in-Chief's at G. H. Q. in Baghdad on the 8th, but have found very little to do so far, and somehow don't expect to stay long. I was really never intended to come here at all, but General Cobbe has now gone on leave, and I must go warily or I shall be very unpopular. In the meantime I am keeping my present appointment with the Bridging Train, so that I retain my acting

---

[17] Good relations had existed between the British and Afghan Amir Habibullah during the war, but in February 1919, Habibullah was assassinated and the title of Amir was claimed by his volatile son, Amanhullah. To deflect suspicion that he had committed patricide, Amanhullah seized upon the growing surge of nationalism in Afghanistan, declaring a *jihad* against the British. His pretext was religious outrage against General Dyer's massacre of Punjabis in Amritsar, despite the majority of casualties being Hindus and Sikhs. By early May 1919, an Afghan force had crossed the frontier into India and taken the village of Bagh, thus provoking the Third Afghan War.

rank and can always go back there.

Remember to continue to send letters and papers to the old address, as my present billet is decidedly temporary.

I spent a week with the Train before coming back here.

It is keeping extraordinarily cool for the time of year, and we have just had a shower of rain, which will keep it cool still longer.

I don't think I mentioned the completely changed aspect of the river between Amara and Kut. Instead of waste land, it is now a belt of crops along each bank, irrigated by rain and flood water only: it is simply the result of peace again, and the high price we pay for grain etc. It has nothing to do with our irrigation schemes,[18] but it makes the country look much more hospitable and on the other hand has caused a vast increase in the mosquitoes, sandflies and other insects, confirming my opinion that irrigation will render this country as unpleasant as India.

Very best love,

  Your ever loving Son,

   Fred. V. B. Witts

F.V.B. Witts

 Major R. E.

             No 2 Bridging Train.

                [Baghdad]

              May 18th 1919.

Dearest Mother.

Your letter of April 1st from Settle arrived during the week, as you see they are coming through much faster than during the war. I expect all the papers arrived safely, but I have told them to keep them with the Train, as down here I can see all I want to, whereas they would be sadly missed up there: any special paper or magazine you send will however be sent on.

I was very interested to read your description of Stainford Hall and the Ribble. I wish I had been with you, as I should have liked to have seen it. I shall be interested to hear what Edward decides to do with it. Many thanks for the enclosure from Cox. I wonder who has been elected Guardian: these village squabbles are rather humerous...I hope you went for a massage and that it's done you a lot of good. Glad to hear the car is running well, and that the problem of getting it up to the front door has been solved.

I have had an uneventful week, but am feeling a bit more at home and have had a

---

[18] Ambitious schemes to restore Mesopotamia to its former glory as the 'granary of the world' had been undertaken by the British with some success. However, in 1919 the Irrigation Directorate was suffering from a drop in funding following its transfer from military to civil responsibility. But as F.V.B.W. relates, peace brought a healthy return to local agriculture along the Tigris, helped by the high demand for grain.

little more work to do. Another three weeks or a month will see me away I expect, and then I shall probably go up the line again, as the 18th Divn H.Q. [located at Mosul] want me, which is rather pleasing. But I may still have to go back to my Train, as with the Afghan trouble on the top of trouble in India, it is impossible to get reliefs sent out to this country, and my subalterns the senior of whom has just been made an acting captain, are all temporary fellows clamouring to get away more or less.

You will be glad to hear that the more I think of it the less I like the idea of permanent employment in this country.

We had a violent hurricane on the 15th, lasting about half an hour, followed by terrific hail and thunder. The wind lashed the river into a raging sea in about ten minutes, and any pontoon bridge would have been destroyed straight away. As a consequence it is extraordinarily cool.

I have played Tennis twice this week and am improving!

Very best love,

> Your ever loving Son,
> Fred. V. B. Witts.

F. V. B. Witts
  Major R.E.

> [Baghdad]
> No. 2 Bridging Train
> Mes: Ex: Force.
> May 25th 1919.

Dearest Mother.

I got your letter of April 8th from Fallowfield yesterday. I am very glad to hear you have been having your arm massaged and hope it is all the better for it. So pleased the car is running well, and that you are using it and that Agnes likes driving it.

You say you are thinking of going away for ten days to save coal; it makes me think of the enormous extra amount burnt while I was at home, and makes me feel guilty of driving you out. I am glad Edwin [Brassey] is the new Guardian.[19]

All the papers have, as I explained last week, been intercepted by my unit, but I have no doubt they all arrived as usual.

I don't expect to remain here much longer. The 17th Divn have now written in asking for me to be attached to their G branch: their home is at present just outside Baghdad. It will probably have to be decided tomorrow whether I am to go there or to the 18th at Mosul.

In neither case is any definite job involved, but I haven't got anything like enough to do in my present office.

---

[19] Lieutenant-Colonel Edwin Brassey D.S.O. M.C. lived at Copse Hill; the house had been built in the 1870s for his father as a hunting box.

I have had a very dull and uninteresting week including two days in bed. I went to the doctor for a dose, and he peremptorily ordered me to bed, though there was absolutely nothing wrong. A ride and a game of tennis my only recreation.

But there is usually something on in the evenings, either dining out or someone dining with me, and failing that there are two cinemas quite close, though the cinema usually sends me to sleep.

I am living in luxury – comfortable room, mess and office with electric light and fans complete. It's the first I've indulged in since the war started! so I feel I am entitled to it, and it is to be very short lived.

With very best love,
   Your ever loving Son,
     Fred. V. B. Witts.

Peace reigned on the Mesopotamian plain. Although the British mandate had still not been confirmed, and Arabs remained very poorly represented in the central government, there had been little sign of rising agitation. Kurdistan, however, was a different matter.

The Kurds, living in the mountainous region to the north-east of the Mosul wilayat, were distinct from their Arab neighbours in creed, culture and ethnicity. Neither party shared much affection for the other. Consequently, uniting these two races as a single nation with Baghdad as the seat of the civil power was not going to be an easy task. In early 1919 the idea of an independent state of Southern Kurdistan[20] was explored for the first time in the region's history. However, after initial excitement, the scheme was rejected as impracticable, with most prominent Kurdish tribal chieftains and townsmen agreeing on the matter. The intense rivalries between Kurdish tribes, their economic reliance on Lower Mesopotamia, and the lack of a suitable candidate to lead the country as Amir, were, amongst other problems, insurmountable obstacles. No foundation existed on which to build a new state. Direct British administration, meanwhile, was also problematic.

The Kurds generally distrusted the British, and not without reason. In May 1918, General Egerton's sortie into Southern Kurdistan ended in tragedy for many of the inhabitants of Kirkuk. Having reached Kirkuk and put the Turk to flight, Egerton withdrew his force to shorten his supply lines; in so doing, he sacrificed those inhabitants who had befriended the British to a brutal revenge at the hands of the Turks. In 1919 convincing reports of large-scale demobilisation of British forces meant that many Kurds were unwilling to risk cooperating with the British for fear of Turkish retribution. Meanwhile,

---

[20] The northern and eastern extremities of Kurdistan stretch beyond the boundaries of the Mosul wilayat into Turkey and Persia respectively. The region of Kurdistan within the Mosul wilayat is called Southern Kurdistan.

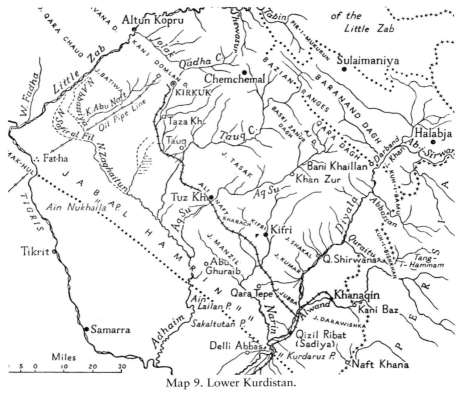

Map 9. Lower Kurdistan.

Turkish intrigue, active throughout Kurdistan, nurtured traditional fears of Arab domination or religious persecution under British suzerainty. Nevertheless, Kurdish territories were still administered through a network of British political officers, some achieving greater success than others in imposing the law of the Civil Administration.

In the south-eastern Kurdish district of Sulaimaniya, the Civil Administration tried a different approach, more directly in line with the Anglo-French Declaration. They appointed the influential Sheikh Mahmud as Governor of Sulaimaniya, but a clash of values determined that the partnership would not be harmonious. Sheikh Mahmud was a tempestuous, juvenile character whose administration was founded solely on a system of patronage designed to enrich him at the expense of others. On the appointment of the formidable Major Soane as political officer in Sulaimaniya, Mahmud's influence began to wane and he became more vocal in his objections towards British supremacy in Southern Kurdistan. On 23rd May 1919, in a desperate attempt to reassert his authority, Sheikh Mahmud launched a

103. Sheikh Mahmud.

revolt with 300 warriors, mustered over the border in Persian Kurdistan. Having imprisoned the British administrative staff in Sulaimaniya town, he proclaimed himself Amir of all Kurdistan and appealed to surrounding tribes to join him in his nationalist revolt.

The eruption of unrest in Sulaimaniya was directly relevant to Captain Witts' own fate as he had been on the point of joining the 18th Division, based in Mosul.

F.V. B. Witts
  Major R. E.

Baghdad
Sunday June 1st 1919.

Dearest Mother.

...I am very pleased to hear the garden is beginning to look up and recover its former glory.

My immediate fate is not yet decided. There is trouble in Southern Kurdistan on the Persian border of Mespot, and, possibly owing to more important preoccupations on this score, 18th Divn have not yet replied about myself. In the meantime – on Wednesday evening – a wire comes in from India asking if I can be spared to return there.[21] From my position at G.H.Q., I have been able to have a good say in the matter, but I don't know definitely yet whether I am to go or not. You may be surprised to hear that personally I have been using all my influence to get out of going, because I am certain I am only wanted for duty at the Depot at Roorkee – to release someone else for the Frontier and I have, at the moment, every prospect of getting a good start on the Staff out here. But I wish they would make up their minds. I don't like all this waiting about not knowing what's going to happen. But something will be decided any day now, and I am almost certain to move one day this week.

Things looked rather bad in April in India, but quietened down in a remarkable way thanks to firm handling.[22] The Amir should have made his attack three weeks

---

[21] In light of the current unrest in India, Simla was anxious to recover its military and civil officers, often irrespective of Mesopotamia's needs which had been multiplied by the strains of large-scale demobilisation.

[22] F.V.B.W. is possibly referring to the massacre at Jallianwala Bagh in Amritsar – an incident on which public opinion was divided in England. Like most Englishmen of his time, F.V.B.W. was opposed to the Independence Movement in India, and as an officer and advocate of military discipline, he is unlikely to have been disposed tolerantly to the disregard shown to British military authority. An approval, however, of the extreme brutality of Dyer's methods contradicts the personal affection that F.V.B.W. clearly had for his Indian troops, often displayed by his praise for their bravery and commitment to duty. Another possibility, considering the large number of Indian, especially Punjabi, troops in Mesopotamia, is that they may have only been exposed to a diluted version of events. In any case, despite F.V.B.W.'s assertion that the situation had been initially 'quietened down', Dyer's 'firm handling' only solidified resentment against the British Raj in the long run.

earlier; as it is, it is of course only a matter of time and trouble.[23] You will have noticed Thal mentioned as being shelled by the Afghans. It was in my district when I was on the Frontier.[24] It is much too hot for scrapping to be amusing up there now!!

    With very best love,

        Your ever loving Son,

           Fred. V. B. Witts.

(Did you ever get my letters from Turin & Taranto?)

The letter below is from Mrs Witts to her son, the first of her post-war letters to have survived.

                    Adelphi Hotel

                    [Harrogate]

                    June 4th 1919.

Dearest Fred,

    I have just sent you a cable and I hope worded it rightly? I am so pleased – Frank has the D.S.O.! it was in yesterday's paper & again today. I sent you a yarn yesterday at Hawkes hill & let me know if you got it all right. I am so delighted & no one to speak of it to!

    …dearest love tell me if I address you properly & warmest congratulations[25] god bless and preserve you

    Your loving mother

        MH Broome Witts

I send you a sheet from here as I have not one handy! I wonder if mine is the first letter you get

[23] On paper, the Afghan army was far inferior to the Indian, but the tumultuous efforts of the war and large-scale demobilisation had left the Indian Army under strength, with a wasted appetite for prolonged conflict. If, as F.V.B.W. suggests, the Afghans had struck in sequence with the Punjabi uprisings, the Indian Army would have been in difficulty, although Amanhullah would not have had his pretext for going to war in the first place (see note 19). After a series of skirmishes lasting just a month, both sides were eager to negotiate a peace, the outcome of which fell largely in favour of the Afghans.

[24] From March 1912 to May 1913 F.V.B.W. was posted as Assistant Garrison Engineer at Kohat and Fort Lockhart in the Thal district of the North-West Frontier, bordering Afghanistan.

[25] Mrs Witts is referring to F.V.B.W.'s promotion to Acting Major.

F.V. B. Witts
    Major R. E.

G. H. Q.
June 8th 1919.

Dearest Mother.

...It was the tin box and <u>both</u> suitcases (packed in a wooden box) that I wanted sent if I wired for them. Things are far too unsettled and uncertain to say anything definite at present.

...Fancy heavy snow at the end of April! It was very nice for you having Frank back on leave: I am glad to hear he looks so well.

I should very much like to get home next year if it could be managed, but I can't afford to miss a good opportunity, which staying on here another year might give me. But let's hope it won't be necessary. You will notice that I am still writing from G.H.Q. and have not moved as expected. I got definite orders during the week posting me as G.S.O. II [General Services Officer] 17th Divn, followed three hours later by orders to stand fast for the present, the reason apparently being developments in Southern Kurdistan and a demand for Staff Officers there. So I may have to go up there instead, but it is the wrong time of year for scrapping out here. At any rate I am apparently to get a definite job fairly soon.

I can't think what they wanted 12 cottages at Slaughter for, or 6 for that matter? I only hope they will build something decent.

104. *Cheltenham Chronicle* 13th August 1910: The wedding of Jack Kennard and Frances Witts (F.V.B.W.'s first cousin) 9th August 1910 at Lower Guiting (Guiting Power).

I am interested to hear Jack has gone to Constantinople, much more entertaining than Salonika I should think. I am rather surprised to hear Jack Kennard[26] is chucking the navy, as he must be very young for a Captain, but perhaps he thinks he has not got much else out of the war: I should think Francie would be pleased, as I never envy a sailor's wife. I think I would chuck the army if I had a comfortable billet to walk into.

The latest news from India rather points to the Afghan show fizzling out, but one never knows how sincere they are in their requests for an armistice. Out here the situation is much the same – it certainly hasn't improved. I think you will find Sulaimaniya on your map, more or less due east of Fathah – my proper home; that is the centre of the trouble, the Kurds have rebelled and imprisoned our Political Officers etc: the difficulty is the inaccessibility of the place. The conditions are in many ways like the North West Frontier of India.[27]

It is beginning to get warm and has been up to 111, but living in luxury with fans and electric light, one hardly notices it.

No more news, though I may be able to add definite news about myself before actually posting this.

Very best love,

Your ever loving Son,

Fred. V. B. Witts.

Sweeping cuts made to Mesopotamia's military budget had left Force 'D' in a weak condition. In Sulaimaniya, this was made patently apparent by the meagreness of the detachment sent from Kirkuk to put down the revolt. It was an ill-planned and under-prepared relief attempt and was easily repulsed by Mahmud's band of rebels. As well as conceding heavy casualties, the failed attempt damaged British prestige in the region, encouraging support for Sheikh Mahmud amongst outlying tribes. Major-General Fraser, meanwhile, commanding the 18th Division, was assembling a stronger 'South Kurdistan Force' at Kirkuk to deal decisively with Mahmud. For a short time Major Witts believed he was to join the expedition.

---

[26] Jack Kennard's wife, Francie, was F.V.B.W.'s first cousin on his father's side.

[27] This was familiar topography for experienced soldiers of the Indian Army, but the majority of troops stationed in Kurdistan in 1919 were new recruits, untrained in mountainous warfare. Most of the veterans of the North West Frontier had either been demobilised or been killed upon the flat plains of the Basra and Baghdad wilayats during the war.

F. V. B. Witts
  Major R. E.

G. H. Q.
June 15th 1919.

Dearest Mother.

No mail in since last writing. One is due in Baghdad today and another during the week, but as my letters go up to Fathah and back, it means I don't get them until three or four days later.

On the other hand I was delighted to get your cable announcing Frank's forthcoming marriage to Ruth Brocklebank.[28] It wasn't such a surprise as it might have been as only a few days before I had got your letter hinting at the possibility. I cabled my congratulations and have written by this mail. I have told him to let you know what he would like as a wedding present from me and I now enclose a cheque for £20 to meet the cost. Will you fix it all up for me? I know you will like choosing something. I am doing it like this so that he may get it before the wedding if possible. I do so wish I could be at home to attend. It makes me realize it is time I started looking about for a wife; but there's nothing doing out here and the only thing is to get home as soon as possible. It is rather sad contemplating the break up of the family, but I haven't seen Frank for nearly four years and not since 1913 for any length of time.

You will be surprised to notice that I am still at G.H.Q., and in fact my situation is absolutely unchanged since I last wrote. I can't afford to make myself unpopular by trying to force the pace, and must wait on events. But I was told unofficially yesterday, that it was now unlikely that I should go to the 18th Divn or Kurdistan force and that it was going to be decided today, whether I was to be allowed to go to the 17th Divn forthwith. I hope it will be yes, if not I must try and find out something definite, as I can't pretend to be doing much or learning much in my present job. I may be able to add something definite before posting.

It has been a very quiet uneventful week, and extraordinarily cool. One day the thermometer didn't touch 90°, when by all the rules it should be somewhere about 110° or 115°. So what with fans and my present comfortable surroundings I am experiencing quite a different Mesopotamia to what I have been used to, and, needless to say, far more comfortable and pleasant generally.

My present daily programme is called 6.30, breakfast 7.30, office 8 − 1 and 2 − 4, and tennis or a ride in the evening, followed by a dinner party somewhere two or three times a week. What I have been used to, and what I should be doing now if I were with the Bridging Train would be, called 4.30, parade and work 5 − 10 with breakfast thrown in, and parade again in the evening 5 − 7, entailing that awful seven hours in the middle of the day with nothing to do, and no means of keeping cool.

[28] The Brocklebanks of Liverpool were a wealthy shipping family, associated with the Cunard line for many years.

Two very different pictures.

No more news at the moment.

Very best love,

Your ever loving Son,

Fred.V.B.Witts

By the 17th June the 'South Kurdistan Force' was poised to crush Sheikh Mahmud's revolt. The rocky terrain and sweltering conditions were favourable to the Kurdish insurgents. On top of the narrow Darband-i-Baziyan pass, 30 miles west of Sulaimaniya town, they waited in ambush for the British column. General Fraser, however, was prepared; his men skilfully outmanoeuvred Mahmud's force by scaling the precipitous heights of the pass and surprising them with an attack from the rear. The rebels scattered immediately and the battle was over in minutes. Sheikh Mahmud was captured and a cavalry squadron was sent post-haste to free the British prisoners incarcerated in Sulaimaniya town. The rebellion had been subdued successfully but, with the innate volatility of the Kurdish tribes, there was no guarantee that peace would be lasting. As for Sheikh Mahmud, he was eventually reprieved.

Major Witts, meanwhile, had finally joined a division: the 17th, stationed just outside Baghdad.

F.V.B.Witts

Major

17th Divn H.Q.

[Nr Baghdad]

Sunday June 22nd 1919.

Dearest Mother.

…Very many thanks indeed for your cable and congratulations sent from Harrogate which reached me on Wednesday.[29] I am of course very pleased: I have been extraordinarily lucky to get so much out of the war.

You will see I have at last moved out to 17th Divn, and what with this and your cable, I am in particularly good spirits. I am only here for 'temporary attachment to the General Staff' to learn the work, and I don't know what it will lead to. They have gone back on the order posting me here as G.S.O II. when the vacancy occurs; another officer had previously been posted, I am not surprised, as I was astounded at their apparent intention to push me straight into the job. The present man is off on leave at the end of the month, and I shall then act until his successor arrives. He is at present on leave in India and was last heard of with a job at Simla, so he may not return. In the meantime I

---

[29] F.V.B.W. is referring to congratulations given for his promotion to Acting Major.

retain my appointment as O.C. No 2 B.T. and can always fall back on it, if nothing else turns up. Please continue addressing letters to the Bridging Train as before; it will only lead to confusion and loss of letters altering it before I settle down.

Last night a Colonel Dent of the Intelligence Staff out here was dining here: he is just back from England via Constantinople, where he apparently saw quite a lot of Jack, who, he tells me, was very well and apparently thoroughly enjoying life. Col Milward, who is G.S.O. I of this division, then asked me if I had a brother in the Bantam battalion of the Glosters! He was Brigade Major of George's brigade in France in 1916 and knew him. It was rather curious hearing of two brothers at the same moment.

…Many thanks for forwarding Rowland Ward's bill and for writing to him. Please send on all and any bills as they arrive, and don't tear them up. I had quite forgotten I owed him anything!

You don't seem to be having much in the way of weather, and now, according to Reuters, you have a regular drought and are praying for rain. Out here it still continues to keep extraordinarily cool for the time of year.

Many thanks for the Outlooks.

I am glad to hear Edith has her passport. I wonder when they will sail.[30] It is great to hear that the car is such a success and the chauffeur too apparently

I see from your cable you have been up to Harrogate; I hope it has done you a world of good and that your arm is better.

And now I must describe my new surroundings. They are not quite as luxurious as I have been used to the last six weeks, but still comfortable enough – fans and electric light, but the house is not quite so well built: in two important respects it is far superior. The mess itself is much more comfortable and better run, and would do credit to a mess in India in peace-time. The building is beautifully situated on one of the prettiest reaches of the Tigris I have seen – palm groves and gardens on both banks as far as the eye can see, a wonderful contrast to the tumbledown buildings of Baghdad which I have been gazing on for the past six weeks. The sunset effects are beautiful. We are about 2½ miles above Baghdad city – 4 miles from G.H.Q.

General Leslie, who commands the Division, is on leave. He was my C.R.E. all the time I was in France, so knows me well: and I have met all the staff at various times and places, so feel quite at home.

I played polo on Friday and hope to play regularly if I can raise another pony. Today I am lunching with the Doctor [Capt. C.A. Wood], who was with the Train when I was wounded, and whom I have to thank for the complete recovery of my thumb. I haven't seen him for two years.

> Very best love
> > Your ever loving Son,
> > Fred. V. B. Witts.

---

[30] Edith and Edward were planning a trip to Rhodesia. *See* also Chapter I, p. 44, note 8.

105. Hillah from the south-east.

F.V.B. Witts
  Major

[Hillah]
Sunday June 29th 1919.

Dearest Mother.

...Our Divisional Area covers half of Mesopotamia and this place Hillah – on the Euphrates some 60 miles South of Baghdad – is the headquarters of one of our brigades: I've been sent down to get to know the troops and the lie of the land. I came down by train Thursday night with Martin whom I am relieving and who came to say goodbye, and am staying at Bde H.Q. We spent Friday visiting the various regiments here: Martin returned Friday night, and yesterday I paid a flying visit to Diwaniyeh, 54 miles by road further down the river.

I left at 5 a.m. in a Ford van and got down for breakfast at 7.45: it is a very good road for this country. I came back again in the evening. There are some cavalry down there.

I have been wanting to see this part of the country, but it is too hot to enjoy joyriding this time of year – it is at last beginning to get really hot. Hillah itself is quite pretty: the branch of the Euphrates it is on is only some fifty yards wide, and has beautiful gardens on each bank looking refreshingly green: it is not spoilt by the enormous bunds which the Tigris has to keep the floods in – But I was sadly disappointed with my journey yesterday through one of the 'granaries of the world'. The first ten miles the conditions are as here, but after that the road runs through absolutely flat fields, intersected with irrigation canals – really deep ditches lined by large ugly banks of excavated earth: not a tree to relieve the monotony, and looking absolutely dry & burnt up, not a green thing in sight. I've no further use for 'granaries of the world' and have quite made up my mind that Mespot will never be a white man's country. It may be wonderfully fertile but that's not enough by itself.

This afternoon I am going out to see the ruins of Babylon: they too are very disappointing, but I shall not be disappointed as I don't expect much, whereas I did regards the country in general.

Tomorrow I was to go to Kufa and Nejf [principle towns of the Shi'ite sect], but a wire came in this morning that peace has at last been signed,[31] so tomorrow's a holiday and I am not to go till Tuesday unless I am recalled to Baghdad in the interval, as I was due back that day. Tomorrow I may now go to see the Hindiyah Barrage[32] or the ruins of the Tower of Babel or both, but as I said earlier, it is too hot for joyriding except in the early morning and for an hour in the evening.

I do not suppose that signing peace with Germany will make much difference to us out here. I have my doubts as to whether you will be any better off at home.

I had two afternoon's polo the first half of last week . And this inspite of the fact that my pony was lame though not bad. I had the use of four other ponies of sorts; only one of them any particular good but all of them easy rides.

No more news.
      Very best love,
          Your ever loving Son,
            Fred. V. B. Witts.

F. V. B. Witts
Major

                        H. Q. 17th Division.
                              [Nr Baghdad]
                        Sunday July 6th 1919.

Dearest Mother.

I wrote last Sunday from Hillah. That afternoon I went out to see the ruins of Babylon. I wasn't disappointed, because, as I told you, I didn't expect to see much. Except for the absolute enthusiast there is little to see – a large collection of brick walls which have been dug out. The lion of Babylon, and the carving on the walls is about the only things of interest to the layman, though bricks with cuneiform writing on them can still be picked up, and the bitumen mortar in which the bricks are laid

---

[31] Peace with Germany was finally signed on 28th June 1919 at Versailles.

[32] Built between 1911 and 1914, the Hindiyah Barrage was designed to regulate inundations in the Mid-Euphrates basin, supplying water to irrigation channels all year round for the benefit of cultivation. It was a magnificent feat of engineering, coincidentally designed by a Briton, Sir William Willcocks, but by 1919, it was in need of urgent repairs which were not forthcoming due to cuts in the funding of the Irrigation Directorate.

106. Ruins of Ancient Babylon.

is rather curious. I really enjoyed the six mile trip up the river in a launch more than anything else, as it is a very pretty stretch – uniquely so for this country.

That evening we celebrated the signing of the peace treaty by letting off every light, flare and rocket any one could lay hands on. It had an extraordinarily good effect on the river, amongst the palm trees, one of which caught fire and added to the general effect. The actual banks were lined with thousands of tiny earthernware oil lamps.

Monday I went up to the barrage across the Euphrates at Hindiyah – the one bit of enterprise the Turks showed. It is worth seeing from an engineering point of view. It meant a run of some 20 miles by car, but as the road was very rough it meant 1½ hours each way.

108. Hindiyah Barrage.

108. Najaf.

Tuesday was a very long day. We, that is the local Brigadier, his Brigade Major, and myself, left at 6 a.m. by motor trolley on the narrow guage railway. It passes quite close to the reputed remains of the Tower of Babel – an enormous mound with the remains of a large tower on it, which appears to have been struck by lightning. An hour and a half's run brought us to Kifl, a small and uninteresting village where a launch was waiting for us and took us down to Kufa in another 1½ hours. Except for the last reach near Kufa, the river was not particularly beautiful, though it lacked the utter repulsiveness one associates with the Tigris.

From Kufa half an hour's run in a car across the desert brought us to our goal Nejf. This is one of <u>the</u> four sacred cities of the Mahommedan world. In appearance it is an inferior edition of Samarrah, though much larger. On the highest ground in the centre stands the golden mosque, which is a remarkable sight when viewed from a long distance with the sun on it through a mirage. The whole city is surrounded by a large wall, and stands in the most absolute desert imaginable. Clustering close up to the walls are millions of graves, as it is the dearest ambition of certain sects of Mahommedans to be buried within the sight of the Mosque. It is a common sight on all roads leading there to see funeral parties from all over the Mahommedan world. There was trouble there last year, when they murdered our Political Officer, and we blockaded the place until they complied with our terms.[33] We went down to

---

[33] Captain William Marshall was murdered on 19th March 1918 amid rumours that the Turks were about to throw the British out of Mesopotamia. In retaliation, General Marshall, commanding Force 'D', demanded the unconditional surrender of the perpetrators plus another 100 men for deportation to India as POWs. A fine of 1,000 rifles and Rs.50,000 was also exacted on the people and, as F.V.B.W. relates, a blockade was brought down on the city until these demands were met. A nervous period followed due to Najaf's religious significance, but peace was maintained, and by the 4th May Marshall's demands had been met and the blockade was duly lifted.

inspect our present defensive arrangements. We afterwards motored back to Kufa and lunched with the Dorset battalion stationed there. I couldn't help pitying them! At 2.30 we started back the way we came, getting back to Hillah at 7, as the launch trip took 3 hours against the stream. At 9 p.m. I entrained for Baghdad, getting back here at daylight after a most interesting week.

I was delighted to find on return your two letters of May 15th and 20th – the latter from Elma's and enclosing the Taranto letter which missed me. And today I have got yours of May 29th and one from Frank personally announcing his engagement, lucky fellow!!

I am glad to hear Canon Bazeley has been up. Did he have time to look at the books in the study! Fancy Miss Cambray getting married![34]

I am so glad you went to see Elma and found everything so pleasant.[35] I have promised Jack two armchairs as a wedding present when they are ready for them.

With two new sisters-in-law I shall feel quite a stranger in the family!

I am glad you found the keys and instructions re my boxes, though I am beginning to wonder if I shall ever want them sent out. I hope not.

I am getting polo regularly on any odd pony I can raise. It gives one some exercise at any rate. But I've not had a game of tennis since the day I came out here from Baghdad.

No more news.

> Very best love,
>> Your ever loving Son,
>>> Fred. V. B. Witts.

F. V. B. Witts
Major.

> H Q. 17th Division
> [Nr Baghdad]
> Thursday July 13th 1919.

Dearest Mother.

No letters since last writing, as the mail boat caught fire between Bombay and Basra and had to put back to Bombay. However a fortnight's mails are due at the end of this week.

I met a friend in Baghdad on Thursday just out from England direct – quicker than the mails – who had seen the Gazette containing my brevet, and confirmed your cable, which unfortunately arrived in rather a mutilated condition and although I was morally certain of what it implied, I couldn't be absolutely positive. It is very pleasant to know that having once put up my crown, I shall not have to take it down again!

---

[34] The Cambrays were an old Slaughter family. Properties in the village retain their name to this day.

[35] Gulielma Richardson was recently engaged to F.V.B.W.'s brother, Jack.

India wired for me again on Friday saying they were sending a sapper relief. G.H.Q replied I couldn't be spared until the G.S.O. II demanded from India for this Division arrived. They wired again later suggesting the name of another sapper of similar standing go instead. I don't know how it will plan out, and may have to go.

My G.S.O. I. is off on leave tomorrow and nobody else is coming for the moment, so I shall have to do his work too. It makes me responsible for the peace ceremonial parade being held at Baghdad next Saturday the 19th. It is going to be a busy week for me; as has the last both in work and play. I dined in Baghdad three times and have had more than enough work to keep me fully occupied.

It has been decidedly hotter this week but it is very different for me to the previous summer spent under canvas.

No more news.

      Very best love,

          Your ever loving Son,

            Fred. V. B. Witts.

Major Witts' lifestyle of office work mixed with a healthy dose of sightseeing, dinners and recreation reflects an outward appearance of stability in Mesopotamia. Peace celebrations, not war, were his greatest occupation in the summer of 1919. The unrest in Kurdistan, the only substantial fly in the ointment since the end of the war, had been subdued and British administration in the region had been reinstated successfully. Beneath the placid veneer, however, was an atmosphere of distrust.

British policy in Mesopotamia was still racked by ambiguity. The delay in signing the mandate and the Civil Administration's refusal, in the interim, to confirm its permanent objectives, had left the population uncertain about their future. Britain's various pledges, namely the Anglo-French Declaration, promising an indigenous Government in Mesopotamia, and the Sharif Hussein–Sir Henry McMahon Agreement, promising the establishment of a Hashemite kingdom, had not been forgotten. However, there was little evidence that Britain intended to fulfil her obligations.

The Civil Administration's continual reluctance to share political power with the Arabs frustrated the ambitious Baghdad intelligentsia. It also roused suspicion that Britain was seeking to impose colonial rule in Mesopotamia. On the other hand, extensive demobilisation, necessitated by the end of the war and Britain's growing economic crisis, heightened fears that Britain was on the verge of abandoning the country. Civil anarchy would undoubtedly follow such an event, succeeded, possibly, by the return of the Turks.

Despite the concerns of the population, and cuts in funding for civil projects, political dissension in Arab Mesopotamia was not yet a major worry for the Civil Administration. Through the success of irrigation and agricultural schemes, and the growth of trade, the country was enjoying greater prosperity than it had done for many years. For the time being the general population on the Mesopotamian plain was distracted from raising hostile political objections. In Southern Kurdistan, however, the economic benefits of British administration were less forthcoming. In addition, as had already been demonstrated by the rising of Sheikh Mahmud, the population was less disposed to submit to the authority of the Civil Administration. Turkish intrigue, meanwhile, especially in the borderlands near Ottoman Kurdistan, was a driving force in stirring up trouble for the British. One rebellion had been suppressed, but the innately volatile character of Kurdish society dictated that further unrest would soon follow. As a promising young officer eager for staff experience, Major Witts was hoping to be involved when it did.

CHAPTER IX

KURDISH BELLIGERENCE

Letters: July 20th – Dec. 10th 1919

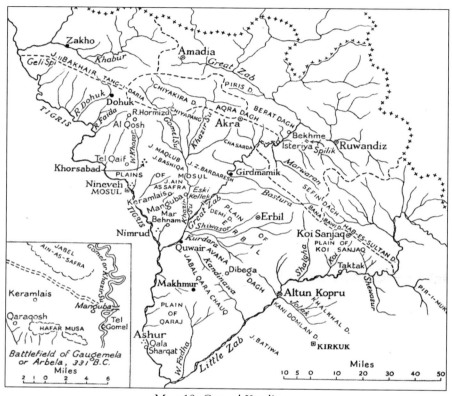

Map 10. Central Kurdistan

'That we could have avoided rousing the hostility of the Aghawat[1] was from the first impossible.'[2] In 1919, the driving principles of the British Administration, namely: order, justice and humanity, axioms of Anglican Christian idealism, were incompatible with the ancient rule of the Aghawat, threatening its very existence. Traditional Kurdish society was savage and shackled, ruled for centuries on a basis of tyranny and repression. The British had already experienced Kurdish caprice once with the rebellion of Sheikh Mahmud, but, as A. T. Wilson, the Civil Commissioner, rightly asserted, the gulf between Kurdish and British ideals would make further conflict inevitable.

---

[1] The Kurdish tribal leadership.

[2] Wilson, A. T., *A Clash of Loyalties*, p. 154

On the night of the 14ᵗʰ July, in the town of Amadiya, just south of the provisional Turkish border, a band of insurgents broke into the British compound and killed the political officer, his deputy and a British sapper. The temerity of this action was chiefly attributed to two factors: first, religious animosity, drummed up by the ubiquitous presence of Turkish intrigue so close to the border of Ottoman Kurdistan, and secondly, the complete lack of a substantial British military force in the area to deter acts of violence. On the first factor, the existence of Turkish agents, mainly Kurds who had served in the Turkish army, was an impossible problem for the British to confront head-on in a province so recently delivered from nearly four centuries of Ottoman rule. The second factor, however, could be remedied, but, as Mahmud's rebellion had demonstrated, without any speed and only by straining the depleted military resources in Mesopotamia. Nevertheless, it was essential that British supremacy should be established in the Amadiya district, and that reprisals should be carried out with resolution so that any further acts of insurgency would be discouraged throughout Southern Kurdistan.

Meanwhile, in Lower Mesopotamia, the British were celebrating 'Peace Month' – a medley of dinners, dances and celebrations. On the surface all remained quiet, although, in view of the murders in Amadiya, the peace celebrations had taken on a tinge of irony. Overall, however, it was an unusually joyous time to be in Mesopotamia, and Major Witts, with his pleasant weekly routine combining desk work, sport and an extensive social calendar, was out to enjoy it while it lasted.

F. V. B. Witts
Major

H.Q. 17ᵗʰ Division
[Nr Baghdad]
July 20ᵗʰ 1919.

Dearest Mother.

No letters yet though they should arrive any day, as the mail came in six days ago with all the papers containing the Birthday Awards and Mesopotamia mentions. I am naturally very pleased.

We've had a very strenuous week celebrating the German Peace Treaty – out here another little war has started during the week! It has been made more strenuous for me by the departure during the week – on Tuesday – of my G.S.O. I on six months leave home. For the moment no one has come to act for him, and I am consequently acting G.S.O. I. as well as G.S.O. II. – very nice for me as it ought to give me all the more chance of getting a permanent job after my liking.

This made me responsible for the big ceremonial parade of all troops in and around Baghdad. It went off very successfully but I am glad to have it behind me. My General

[Maj.-Gen. G. Leslie] was in command of the Parade, and I marched past with him at the head of the troops. This was yesterday morning the 19th. It was followed in the evening by a tremendous display of fireworks and illuminations on the river in Baghdad: altogether quite a good show though we nearly got sunk cruising about in a launch in the dark. Two separate fires were started in the city which added to the illuminations as well as to the general excitement. The Arabs think we are madder than ever now. After the fireworks we toured round visiting all the leading lights starting with the Commander-in-Chief[3] and finishing up with the Military Governor who had a dance on. It was a long enough day for us who did it in luxury – some 20 hours, for the troops it was 24 hours on end! A quaint sort of 'holiday' for the troops!

109. Pony. F.V.B.W. has written: 'This pony was mine later on'.

Last Monday there was a dance at the Club and we had most of the nurses from the big hospital to dinner first of all. A most awful show! One couldn't escape doing one's duty.

Wednesday we ourselves gave a dance (after a dinner in quiet) and it was a great show. But all these things mean late hours and I now feel I could sleep for a week on end. There have been various other minor excitements too.

I am playing polo regularly three days a week, and have now a second pony, or rather horse, permanently lent to me to use. He is not an easy pony to play, but one gets plenty of exercise which is the main thing.

Monday morning.

The expected mail came in yesterday evening. Your letters of June 3rd and 4th and 11th from Harrogate and one from Agnes and one from Edward. Very many thanks for your congratulations and theirs, though possibly Edward has moved by this time. I am so pleased about Frank; he is the only one of us who has really been through the thick of it.

I am very glad to hear the Doctor gives such a good report. I should like to give something to Summerfields[4] – whatever Frank gives. Fix it up with him and let me know.

Yes it is a pity the little bridge by the sheep pond has had to go, but these days most sentiment has to go to the wind.

[3] General Sir George MacMunn, former Inspector General of Communications, was the new C-in-C.

[4] F.V.B.W.'s Oxford prep school.

I will answer the rest of your letters next week, as I must stop now if I am to catch the mail.

Very best love,

Your ever loving Son,

Fred. V. B. Witts

F.V.B. Witts

Major.

H.Q. 17th Division.

[Nr Baghdad]

July 27th 1919.

Dearest Mother.

…I am glad to hear they are reviving the village cricket: it is so long since I played that I almost forget how to use a bat!

I am surprised to hear Fred Bateman has had to go back to Palestine.

I have been getting regular polo and have improved a little, but I have only one mount deserving the name of polo pony.

Your letter of congratulations was the first to reach me. One of the greatest pleasures to me in getting a brevet is the knowledge of how pleased you will be.

I was equally pleased at getting another mention though I suppose I couldn't have got the brevet without it.

…I am surprised to hear you did not take advantage of the aeroplanes at Harrogate to go for a trip! A large Handley Page[5] arrived here from Cairo two days ago, and we went down to see it yesterday evening.

You certainly have had a serious drought, but remember we get no rain for five months on end, but of course it is the normal thing and irrigation take its place. It

110. A Handley-Page aeroplane.

[5] Originally built as heavy bombers, Handley Page aircraft were redesigned to become some of the first passenger planes after the war.

reads rather quaintly to us to see in the Times headings 'Intense Heat' and to read 'the blazing power of the sun seemed overpowering' and to discover finally that the maximum shade temperature was 82° – a point below which the thermometer out here never falls for weeks on end.

…We have changed our General during the week: the Brigadier, who was in command, having been ordered to the North West Frontier: he was a very nice man and I am sorry to lose him, but his successor is equally nice – he went home on leave with me and we played bridge together in a tournament.[6]

We have had a comparatively quiet week though I celebrated July 23rd – the date of my first commission with a little dinner party. I attach importance to the date now rather as being the completion of another year towards the number necessary for a pension – I have now done 12 out of 15. It also marks an increase of pay when I have to give up my acting majority: the brevet majority carries no extra pay on the Indian Establishment.

What with my job, polo and an occasional game of tennis, I am keeping extraordinarily fit and in very high spirits. But I don't intend to stay out here one minute longer than necessary to give me a chance of the Staff College. I have heard nothing more about having to go back to India, though I am afraid it remains a very real possibility.

No more news,

Very best love,

Your ever loving Son,

Fred. V. B. Witts.

F. V. B. Witts
Major.

> H.Q. 17th Division.
> Mes: Ex: Force.
> [Nr Baghdad]
> August 3rd 1919.

Dearest Mother.

No more letters since I last wrote. India are still making efforts to get me back but G.H.Q. continue to fight for me. India wired last Saturday to know if I had embarked! G.H.Q in their reply pointed out that there was no grounds for imagining I should have and that I could not be spared until a G.S.O.II actually arrived for this Division. India also announced they were sending a G.S.O. II., so G.H.Q. added I was wanted for another staff job and that they could send another sapper – Chater, of my own term, – immediately. I don't know how it will all turn out, but unless there

---

[6] It is uncertain whom F.V.B.W. is referring to. General MacMunn had taken the job of C-in-C in May, and General Leslie remained in command of the 17th Division well into 1920.

is some special bridging job, which has not been mentioned hitherto, India can hardly refuse to accept Chater in my place and could hardly raise the question again. Chater has just got married and is very keen to get back to his wife in India. So it would suit us both.

I am much too well off and am having much too good a time to want to move. In fact I am being absolutely spoilt, though I feel I have earned it after three solid years of supreme discomfort. Very pleasant and interesting work with the right proportion out of doors, and not too much of it, polo three days a week, tennis any other day one cares, dining out three or four times each week! Dances once or twice a week! But I must explain we are having a sort of 'Peace Month', during which all restrictions on the nursing sisters dancing

111. Lieutenant-Colonel Sir A. T. Wilson.

have been removed. There is only another week to go, but it is being made the most of. Tomorrow, Monday, there is a jumping show. Wednesday we are giving another dance. Thursday and Saturday are the Summer races; and there are other dances as well. Not that the dancing interests me, but it doesn't matter as there are always ten times as many men as girls: however one sees everyone and has a very cheery evening of it.

I have improved quite a lot too in my polo and tennis and consequently get much more fun out of it. I have been hitting the ball with some precision at both. For the moment I have got the use of three animals of sorts and so get as much as I want.

It has been much hotter this last week, but living in a house under a fan I have not felt it at all. Not that it has anywhere near approached anything to talk about. It has been a wonderfully cool summer so far and we have started into August which means we have broken the back of it.

I am dining out tonight with my General at the Civil Commissioners – the Head of the Administration of the Occupied Territories [A. T. Wilson] –: I have more or less got the run of his house as his Personal Assistant is my friend Fuller who came out from England with me. It will be the fourth night I'm dining out in succession. It is lucky the General is too, as I think he's getting rather fed up at being deserted night after night!

Very best love,

Your ever loving Son,

Fred. V. B. Witts.

In contrast to Captain Witts' carefree lifestyle in Baghdad, in the Amadiya district of Kurdistan, the 'South Kurdistan Force' was ready to avenge the murders of British political staff. Under the new command of Brigadier-General Cassels, a thorough scouring of the landscape began on August 1st, aiming to make a lasting impression on the Kurds. Hostile ambushes were beaten off, ringleaders were weeded out, and tribesmen were disarmed. However, the difficulties of the mountainous landscape and the aggression of the tribes were effectively turning a single operation into a prolonged war. But, if the Civil Administration was to make any progress in Kurdistan, it was agreed that thorough action had to be taken, which meant drawing more troops from the south to join the operations.

F.V. B. Witts
    Major.

H.Q. 17th Division
[Nr Baghdad]
August 10th 1919.

Dearest Mother.

No mail to answer. There has been some delay in the shipping line owing to plague or something.

The 'Peace Month' has I am glad to say come to an end. Monday's jumping show was a washout as far as I was concerned as a sudden little war tied me down here at H.Q.[7]

Our dance on Wednesday was a great success in every way: every one here from the Commander-in-Chief down. I also heard that India were getting reconciled to the fact that they were not going to get me back. I got one of my subalterns down from the Bridging Train that morning and he returns this evening – a very pleasant change for him from the dust and dirt of Fathah. Thursday's racing was an absolute failure. It turned out to be the hottest day in the year – not that it was really hot – only 115° – but there was not a breath of wind and it was rather damp. It was physically impossible to take any interest in anything but the cold drinks. That night I had an amusing dinner party in Baghdad.

Yesterday's racing was a great success. It was just as hot, but it was dry and there was a good breeze, so everyone did not look like drowned rats as on Thursday. Two of the hospitals gave dances on Friday and yesterday but I did not patronise them.

Friday I got news that my happy existence here was to come to an abrupt end. The G.S.O. II asked for from India for this Division is due at the end of this week, and at

---

[7] The latest episode of the action in Kurdistan was an attack on Suwaira, a British camp just west of Amadiya, by a hostile gathering of the Guli tribe. Having initially been caught unawares, British forces were soon able to drive the Gulis off. Interestingly, the rebels were discovered to be laden with Turkish arms and equipment, suggesting that the attack had been incited by Turkish authorities over the border, not far to the north.

the same time I am wanted to act as G.S.O. II with the 'South Kurdistan Force' with headquarters at Kirkuk which you will find on the map – about 40 miles N.W. of Fathah. So I expect to be moving to Kirkuk at the end of this week.

It is I am told not at all a bad place and has excellent billets. But I shall miss the electric fans and lights we have here. However we shall be half way through August when I leave, so I oughtn't to grouse, as at the worst there can be only six weeks of heat.

I shall also miss the polo, tennis and all round gaity of life in Baghdad, where I have a crowd of friends. I had hoped to see the hot weather out here, but pickers can't be choosers. It is really not at all a bad job, as it is an independent little show, as it doesn't run to a G.S.O. I. South Kurdistan has, nominally, been completely subdued: actually however there is a certain amount of raiding going on from over the Persian border.[8] So we may have a certain amount of excitement and something to do. It is only an acting job, and I continue to draw pay and hold rank as O. C. No 2 Bridging Train: but it may lead to something definite.

No mail in and nothing more to add this morning (Monday) so I must stop or I shall miss the mail.

Very best love,

> Your ever loving Son,
>> Fred.V. B.Witts.

Back in England, Major Witts' brother, Frank, had just been married to his fiancée, Ruth Brocklebank, at Satterthwaite in Cumberland. In one of the earliest surviving post-war letters to her son, Mrs Witts gives a detailed account of the wedding.

> THE MANOR,
> UPPER SLAUGHTER,GLOS.
> August 12. 1919.

Dearest Fred

…The heat has been very great & we have not had rain for months, it will soon be serious here & everywhere water is getting scarce. I believe Edward is going to make over the Reading Room & stables to a Com: at a nominal rent for a 'Slaughter Hall' for village use. To return to him if ever dropped –…our old friend Millett who worked with uncle George is going to send us some ideas…Elma is here & alas we don't know yet when Jack will get away some say not till there is peace with Turkey I don't believe in the peace doings!

---

[8] F.V.B.W.'s use of the word 'nominally' shows an understanding of the Kurdish problem. Tribes were liable to rise up at any point and the mountainous landscape made it exceptionally difficult for the British to keep hold of disturbances. Raids over the Persian border, meanwhile, did not become a serious concern for the British, although unrest in the town of Rowanduz, in close proximity to Persia, had reached such a pitch that the resident British political staff had been forced to evacuate.

...Next day on to Ullverston very pretty route, lunched there & at 2.30 to Brocklebanks 2 cars met us one a Rolls Royce the 13 miles was soon done- over the hills to a lovely place with a huge modern house with every comfort & luxury but still rather like an Hotel – Tennis court roses in abundance & shrubs- mixed shooting, a few grouse pheasants woodcock and snipe...

August 7th wedding at 2.15. Church wee no organ – very little music beautifully decorated Capt. Agnew was best man & he & Frank in uniform- Bride had her sister & one friend as Bridesmaids & cut the cake with Frank's sword – some kind friend took a photo but I doubt if we see it – They went to church in the Rolls Royce beautifully decorated with flowers & white ribbons. A large local garden party afterwards Frank & Ruth left about 4.15 & did the 70 miles by 7.30 in the Rolls Royce – all went well – no speeches – all very quiet...

Frank gave the bride diamond & sapphire rings & earrings, she gave him a beautiful fitted Dressing case – not too large but handy. Mr.Brocklebank gave Ruth a cheque & a fitted Dressing case & Mrs B a canteen of knives & silver spoons & forks besides the silver – several books & pictures there is one here from Sophie, she was in Dorset & so declined but Jack [Cheetham] & Mabel ought to have gone especially as Jack went North on the 5th too lazy of them! Annie gave a silver butter knife Mr & Mrs Ketteringham carving knife & fork!...

It seems as if the dear old family of 5 generations here was to pass out of knowledge and an upstart like Willes to rule the roost with a cad of a parson [Mr Longley].[9] Forgive my outbursts it does me good – all the old places are being sold even Mrs. Stevens wants to let & go. Edward thinks the Gov. will soon <u>take all</u> as we are nearly bankrupt.[10] I shall have to come to you and George for a home – when you have both permanent jobs somewhere – George looks very old & is not strong he will stick on as long as he can I think. Elma is tall & fair – I think you will like both your new sisters – our manservant wishes to leave on Sat: for an Hotel...- God bless you.

Jack Cheetham & I want to put an old Gloucestershire Cross in the village as a thanks offering[11] which would be nice dearest love – come home soon. Shall I leave here & get a home for you and George somewhere I fear Ed won't marry with Edith at hand!

Your loving mother

MHB Witts

[9] Relations between the Witts family in the Manor and the Willes family in the Manor House seem not to have been harmonious.

[10] The Witts family had been heavily burdened by death duties since the death of F.V.B.W.'s father in 1913. Britain's post-war economic recession heightened the financial strain.

[11] Upper Slaughter is one of 32 villages in England and Wales known as 'Thankful Villages', having lost no men or women in the war. Upper Slaughter's remarkable luck continued in WWII, although that is not to say that those serving in either war, as well as their families, did not suffer from their experiences. In the event the Village Hall became Upper Slaughter's thanksgiving memorial, and no cross was erected.

F.V.B.Witts.

Major

H.Q. 17ᵗʰ Division
[Nr Baghdad]
Saturday August 16ᵗʰ 1919.

Dearest Mother.

...It should not be very long before I move from there [Kirkuk] to Mosul. I shall spend one night with the bridging train at Fathah on my way through. I've had a very cheery week to finish up with. Some excellent polo and a dinner party every night – dining out one night and a party of our own the next. I feel rather sad at going back to Mesopotamia as I knew it before

...I am sorry to hear there's East Coast Fever on Edward's farm. I hope it won't touch his herd.

...I am sorry to hear you have been so long without servants, and hope you are better off now.

...Splendid beating Lower Slaughter: George made a good score. I shall be interested to hear the truth about Eyford.

No more news and I'm busy packing.

Very best love,

Your ever loving Son,

Fred.V. B.Witts

H.Q. 18ᵗʰ Division
[Mosul]
Friday August 22ⁿᵈ 1919.

Dearest Mother

When I last wrote I was expecting to go to Kirkuk next day. At the last moment I was ordered up here most urgently in the same capacity, i.e. to act as G.S.O. II.

I came up to Baiji on Sunday night and was supposed to come straight on here, but it was impossible to fix up, so I had time to go up to Fathah for half an hour and see my Bridging Train. They all seemed very well and cheerful. Monday night I came on to absolute railhead as railway is in process of being carried on to Sherqat. Three Ford vans met me at dawn and took me into Sherqat, where I was on Armistice night. After a hurried meal, I could only get two vans on, so dumped some of my kit.[12] I got into Mosul at 1.30, having left railhead at 5.30 – i.e. eight hours going less half an hour for breakfast. This may be nothing in a comfortable car on a good metalled road, but in a rickety Ford van on Mesopotamia roads in the middle of the day in the middle of the

---

[12] Three Ford vans may seem excessive to carry one's kit, but the vans were far more compact than modern vehicles. An officer's usual kit would have included a large tent, a mosquito net, a camp bed, camp furniture, a stove and cooking utensils besides other personal items.

112. Mosul.

hot weather it is a bit of a strain. My abandoned kit arrived yesterday.

I was immediately plunged into work, without any respite, in connection with the little war we are waging with Central Kurdistan,[13] and found I was in for a very different life to what I've been leading recently.

All work, for the moment entirely office, and absolutely no time for play or exercise other than that obtained by walking to and from the office, some 300 yds from the mess, three or four times a day.

The mess is very comfortable, and I have got a better room and better office than I had at 17 Div H.Q. but the electric fans and lights are a bit weak, though it is everything to have them at all. No more news or time. No mail in

Very best love,

Your ever loving Son,

Fred. V. B. Witts

113. Kurds of the Rowanduz District.

[13] Although the term 'Southern' Kurdistan refers to all of Kurdistan lying within the provisional boundaries of the Mosul wilayat, the northern region bordering Turkish Kurdistan (i.e. the Zakho, Amadiya and Rowanduz districts) is sometimes referred to as 'Central' Kurdistan.

114. Flying over Southern Kurdistan.

F.V.B. Witts
Major

18th Divn H.Q.
Mosul.
Thursday August 28th 1919.

Dearest Mother.

I have not yet got used to my change of locality, and have only just been reminded that the mail leaves tonight.

…I am glad to hear you and Edith have been helping Frank set up his house. What exactly is the job he has got and what is his address? It is hard to realize he is a married man by this time. He is very lucky to get a shooting box for his honeymoon. I shall be quite satisfied with whatever you settle to do about my present. I am very interested to hear what everyone is giving him.

…Where is the new reading room or Slaughter Hall. Is it the old one brought into regular use again?

Until yesterday things had continued the same as I described last week. Plenty of work all day with no time for exercise or recreation.

Yesterday however was a day to be remembered as I went up in an aeroplane for the first time. No mere joyride either. If you look on your map I think you will find Rowanduz marked about 120 miles East of Mosul, not far from the Persian Border. For the last six months it has been occupied by our Politicial Officers, but was evacuated three weeks ago owing to the disturbed state of the country.[14] There have recently been rumours of intertribal fighting in the place, and two planes were ordered to go and see what was happening there and report the result to our nearest post some 20 miles away. I was told to go with them.

The first five minutes were rather alarming but after that I thoroughly enjoyed it. Rowanduz is in mountainous country and we had to cross hills 7000 feet high,

---

[14] *See* W. R. Hay's *Two Years in Kurdistan* (Sidgwick & Jackson, 1921) for a detailed account of his experiences as Chief Political Officer in the Erbil district from 1919-1920.

and then come down to about 2000 feet in a more or less narrow valley. There was a prospect of being fired on but everything was absolutely peaceful and we finally came down to within 200 feet of the town, and the inhabitants shewed great interest in us as they had never seen a plane anywhere near before. We climbed up out of the valley again, and flew off to look for our post in an uncertain place [probably Aqrah]: I was immensely pleased with myself as I spotted it straight away and had some difficulty in convincing my very experienced pilot, who afterwards congratulated me on my effort.

We went down within 10 feet of the ground much to the delight of the garrison, who are more or less cut off from the outer world, and dropt a message. And then home. It took us three hours and we covered some three hundred miles in all.

115. Rowanduz Gorge.

I have been wanting to go up for some time, and was very pleased to get the opportunity. It was an ideal flying day as far as it ever can be in a Mespot Summer. We left at 5.30 and it was quite hot enough when we got back at 8.30. One can't wear a topi, so it is liable to catch one's head.

Yesterday I also managed to get out for a ride, and rode through the Town and over the bridge to the ruins of Nineveh which are even more uninteresting than those of Babylon if that is possible. The town of Mosul is much more solid than that of Baghdad, as stone is available for building. It is a sort of alabaster which cuts very nicely into slabs, but is so soft that you can hammer a nail into it.

The little war we are directing goes on merrily just North of Zakho and Amadia which you may find marked on your map. They are some 80 miles North of Mosul.

No more news.

Very best love,

Your ever loving Son,

Fred. V. B. Witts.

F. V. B. Witts

Major

H.Q. 18th Division

Mosul

September 4th 1919.

Dearest Mother.

...I shall be interested to hear if Edward accepts the offer for the Yorkshire property. I am sorry to hear the strawberries have been so few owing to the rain. I shall be interested to hear if you go to town or Cheltenham: you certainly must move somewhere. I should like Lord French's book 1914 very much indeed.[15] Many thanks for all the extra papers – Round Table, Fortnightly, National and Spectator, though just at the moment I have not got time to read any of them.

I am sorry to hear the victory fête was such a dud show. It seems to have been the same all over the place. The real outburst of spontaneous rejoicing was at the Armistice and it was hard to work it all up again. I think they might have given a little more thought to the soldiers. All peace celebrations fall rather flat out here, where we are up to our necks in a war, which nobody seems to know or care about at home.

I am very sorry to hear Geoffrey has not got into Sandhurst.[16] I am glad to hear Edward has good news again from the farm. Many thanks for calling my attention to my name being in the Gazette as acting Major, as I should not have noticed it otherwise.

...Will you send me 12 inches of the new war ribbon – orange with white black & blue edging. One can't get it out here. Also of the victory ribbon – the double rainbow. And any others which I may be entitled to which they may issue. I should also like 12 inches of the 1914–15 star ribbon, of which I could only get a very little when I was at home.

You will be relieved to hear I've done no more flying. My work continues at the same pitch, but will shortly probably ease off a bit as I shall have wiped off all the accumulated arrears. I have been out for one more ride and this evening I hope to get out for a short walk with a gun, though there is not much to shoot close by. My ponies have not got up yet.

The Central Kurdistan war still continues: we failed to bring off the coup the other day which might have ended it, as the Kurds scattered and avoided a fight.[17]

---

[15] Published by Constable & Co. in 1919. *See* footnote (p. 339-40) for F.V.B.W.'s letter of Jan. 4th 1920.

[16] It is not known why Geoffrey Woodroffe failed to get into Sandhurst in 1919. Having lost a first cousin, Neville Woodroffe (2nd Lieutenant in the Irish Guards), at Ypres in November 1914, he was especially keen to fight but was too young to enlist. On the outbreak of WWII he signed up immediately with the Territorials. As a Lieutenant-Colonel he landed at D-Day on Juno beach commanding a Canadian anti-tank battalion. He was one of the oldest serving officers to land on the beaches on D-Day. He campaigned all the way into Germany, where he was involved in post-war reconstruction.

[17] F.V.B.W. is referring to General Wooldridge's clash with the Guli at Birnuna, a village just south of the provisional Turkish border. The impossible terrain prevented Wooldridge's brigade from achieving a victory.

We are now getting involved in complications with Turkey, as the other day one of our planes bombed a village on their side of the armistice line! However we've sent our apologies!

As soon as it is over the present General here [Brig-Gen. Cassels] leaves to command a Cavalry Division in Palestine. He is only officiating here for the real man [Maj.-Gen. Sir T. Fraser], who is on leave. I am sorry as he has known me well for three years: I seem to be losing all my influential friends. Cobbe whom I interviewed as C in C out here on my return has retired, seeing nothing better to be got: I had great hopes from him! It is rather disappointing.

It is decidedly cooler, and one can definitely say the hot weather is over. We get most excellent grapes and sweet melons and peaches here which are all a great luxury.

No more news.

> Very best of love,
>> Your ever loving Son,
>>> Fred. V. B. Witts.

F.V. B. Witts
Major

> H.Q. 18th Division.
> Mosul
> September 14th 1919.

Dearest Mother.

No mail in since I last wrote and I have consequently nothing to answer. Here things have carried on much the same except there has been a bit of a lull in our little war. I've had the same long office hours with the same lack of opportunity for exercise, though I've twice been out with a gun; but there's nothing within walking distance except pigeon and yesterday I saw a solitary quail.

However I've had two days in the country one premeditated and the other not so. Taking the last first as it came first. Two planes were going off bombing Rowanduz way in continuation of the show that took me out there the previous week.[18] One had to land at Erbil, which you will find marked on the map some 50 miles South East of here, to pick up an officer to point out the particular village to bomb. As Erbil is quite the most interesting place to visit in Mespot, I got permission to go in the plane as far as Erbil. We had an uneventful flight though we had some difficulty in finding the aerodrome. The machine was to pick me up again 1½ hours or so later, but it never

---

[18] Aerial bombardment was an innovative and, primarily, a cost-effective way of dealing out immediate reprisals on recalcitrant tribes. Mr. Winston Churchill, Secretary of State for War and Air, was a chief advocate for plans to increase dramatically the R.A.F.'s role in Mesopotamia as a means of reducing the costs sustained in garrisoning the country.

116. Erbil.

117. Erbil from the south.

returned, and the escorting plane landed instead and told me they didn't know what had happened. They went to look for it, but couldn't see a sign and I had an anxious morning until I heard they had landed safely and had been seen by tribesmen making their way towards one of our posts, which they reached 24 hours later. I had to return here by car, and I was very lucky in getting one that day, but it took 3½ hours to do the 75 miles round by road, including being ferried across the Greater Zab, as against the 45 minutes by air. I got back here just in time for tea instead of breakfast and the General swore he would never let me go out again as it had been a busy day: however we shall see. Instead of getting only an hour or so in Erbil, I spent the whole morning there. Its an old Assyrian city built on a large circular mound some 200 feet high with a high wall all round the top, and only one gateway and that a very imposing concern. I arrived in the middle of some political show and was introduced to the local Mayor – a Turk who is now serving us!

Two days later I had to escort the Times Correspondent up to Zakho just behind our 'front' and the furthest he was allowed to go. 75 miles by car over a very bad road taking 5½ hours; at the end a pass has to be crossed some 1500 feet rise: some of the bends are so sharp that even a Ford cannot get round without reversing. We stayed there a couple of hours and then started back another 5½ hours uninteresting drive as there is nothing to see on the way except the Pass. Eleven hours in a car over Mespot roads is a long day. Zakho town is curiously situated on an island, our camp lies on the

118. Zakho camp.

top of a high hill forming a sort of natural fortress, from the top you get an excellent view of the surrounding country and of the mountains in which our columns are operating. The hills are covered with vineyards producing excellent grapes. The Times Correspondent was not a particularly interesting man; he is on his way to Teheran and has asked me to come and stay with him there. The day I was stranded at Erbil he was a passenger in the other machine, so he may write and describe his visit to Mosul.[19]

 No more news,

   Very best love,

    Your ever loving Son,

     Fred. V. B. Witts.

By mid-September, G.H.Q. in Baghdad had agreed that punitive operations in the Amadiya district had achieved satisfactory results, and the region was suitably calmed. However, on their return to base at Mosul, a British column was ambushed by Goyan tribesmen hailing from the Zakho district, where Major Witts had recently escorted the correspondent for *The Times*. Back in April, Goyan tribesmen had lured Zakho's deputy political officer, Captain A. Pearson, from the town and murdered him. This crime had gone largely unpunished due to the impracticalities of sending troops into the difficult terrain of the Zakho district. In the light of this second ambush, however, it was decided that these difficulties had to be overcome. A determined sortie was thus sent into the very heart of Goyan territory. Major Witts, with his recently acquired knowledge of the region, was enlisted to help with aerial reconnaissance.

F. V. B. Witts

 Major

            H.Q. 18th Division

                Mosul

           September 18th 1919.

Dearest Mother.

 Two mails in since I last wrote, with your letters of Aug 4th and 12th, the latter containing a full report of Frank's wedding. Very many thanks indeed for it: you can't imagine how I have enjoyed hearing all the details. I am so pleased everything went so well. They seem to have had a very nice lot of presents. I expect you were very tired by the time you got home, but I am glad you had plenty of the family to take care of you. How I wish I had been there instead of sweltering at the Baghdad races on the hottest day of the year. There is no doubt about it that the 'old order changes'

---

[19] See Appendix XII for *The Times* article entitled 'A Little War in Kurdistan'.

but I can't quote: it is very noticeable in the army, and I am rapidly coming to the conclusion that England will be no place to live in. I seriously think, you ought to settle down in a smaller house: with all these servant and coal difficulties,[20] Slaughter is too much of a good thing, much as I hate the idea of your not staying there till Edward marries. Wherever you are will be my home till I marry, much as I hate the idea of no longer being able to look on Slaughter as such.

I am sorry to hear George looks so old and is not strong.

I have had quite an interesting week including two flights into Central Kurdistan on bombing raids: I've not been doing it for joyriding, though I enjoy the change and experience, but to try and pick up the best track for our columns to follow: it's made me feel I'm taking a more active part in our little war, instead of only sitting in an office writing and thinking

The first day things didn't go as well as they might owing to various little contretemps owing to machines failing to start etc. We had to hang about for three quarters of an hour over the aerodrome, and landed twice to find out what was up. But it gave me a good opportunity of studying Mosul from the air. Finally our machine had to be left and only four of us went instead of five. We worked in two pairs, our pair did their job, but the others went off and, as they confessed two days later on going a second time, bombed the wrong place! Not that it mattered much, as it was also hostile. In this mountainous country with totally inaccurate maps it is wonderful they can find their way about at all.

Two days later things were very much better, we all five got off in a bunch and dropped 28 bombs into a village [Karoar] about the size of Slaughter. Several of them straight through the huts.[21] We were going again this morning, but it was stopped. It is far worse country than that round Rowanduz. You may find Zakho and Amadia marked on the map, some 80 miles North of Mosul: it is the mountainous country north of that line. We had to cross hills of 9000 feet. I would much sooner fly over it than walk through it!

The General is away for a couple of days and I'm having quite a holiday; I dined out last night for the first time and am dining out again tonight; this morning I went out for a shoot, but it wasn't very successful, the sand grouse were very high and the cartridges very old – over three years – apart from crooked shooting, and I only got

---

[20] Strike action in Britain had created a coal shortage, pushing up prices of available stocks. Non-essentials such as household servants had to be cut back in light of the family's financial difficulties.

[21] The use of aerial bombardment in Mesopotamia was devastatingly effective. In 1919, as has been the case with the Iraq war of the early 21st century, it attracted criticism for its indiscriminate killing of civilians and its propensity for human error (*see also* F.V.B.W.'s letter of September 4th 1919, p. 313-4). In 1924, Squadron Leader Arthur ('Bomber') Harris wrote 'they [the Arabs and Kurds] now know what real bombing means, in casualties and damage; they know that within forty-five minutes a full-sized village can be practically wiped out with a third of its inhabitants injured or killed…' (McDowall, D., *A Modern History of the Kurds*, p. 180).

four with about 20 cartridges. However it was a pleasant morning in the country.

Very best love,

Your ever loving Son,

Fred. V. B. Witts.

F. V. B. Witts

Major

H. Q. 18th Division.

Mosul

Thursday September 25th.

Dearest Mother.

Since last writing, your letter of August 19th has arrived – very much quicker than has lately been the case. It is certainly very handy having the Post Office at Mrs Guy's.

Yes it's very sad parting with the glebe: how has East finally fixed up his farm arrangements? I hope the butler has been a success. I hope Agnes has written to tell me all about St Andrews, but I am afraid I already owe her a letter. Sorry to hear the chauffeur is likely to go. I heard from Apphie by the same mail: it is very sad Geoffrey failing. Yes you see very little in the papers about Constantinople and Mesopotamia; we certainly feel that we are entirely forgotten, and with a little war on, it's rather trying.

… I've been getting a little shooting: the day our flight didn't come off, we shot pigeon on the aerodrome instead and I got a dozen. Today, the General being out in the country, I took the opportunity to go out too after sandgrouse. We had a very pleasant morning and got 24.

I am sending some surcharged Mosul stamps.

Very best love

Your ever loving Son

Fred. V. B. Witts.

F. V. B. Witts

Major.

H.Q. 18th Divn. Mosul.

Oct 2nd 1919.

Dearest Mother.

… The railway strike news from England looks pretty black, I wonder what it will all lead to and where it will end.[22]

---

[22] The 'Model Strike' of October 1919, so-called because of the generally peaceful behaviour of strikers, was the result of a disputed agreement between Railway Unions and the Government on the standardisation of pay. Known as 'war-wages', the agreement was designed to bring about pay cuts to some grades of workers, but the strikers were demanding increased pay and the abolition of the war-wages agreement.

Our war still goes on and there's been a certain amount of scrapping this week. It is very hard to catch the Kurd in his mountains. But it must stop soon, and then I'm told I shall be sent off somewhere else, though I don't know where. It's rather trying all this shifting about, but if one wants something one has to put up with these little worries. Anyhow the hot weather is over and I've worked through it under perfect conditions.

They've appointed me officiating G.S.O. 2 here, which means I have had to give up my job as O.C. No 2 B.T. and with it the acting rank of Major and the pay it carries. I retain my Brevet of course, and get extra staff pay, but go down considerably on the transaction. However I was <u>very</u> well paid before and can't pretend to be underpaid now.

I had a very amusing evening the other day, when I managed to get out to dinner with the chief Political Officer in these parts, whom I have known well out here.[23] Our own mess is rather quiet and subdued, as one can't get away from the little war we're waging.

No more news,

Very best love,

Your ever loving Son,

Fred. V. B. Witts.

119. Brevet Lieutenant-
Colonel G. Leachman.

[23] Brevet Lieutenant-Colonel G. Leachman, Political Officer to Mosul, was a renowned character in the Civil Administration. An explorer and long-term British agent in Arabia, he was dark skinned, fluent in Arabic and so in tune with Arab culture that he was able to disguise himself as a Bedouin and infiltrate Arab circles effortlessly. By the time of F.V.B.W.'s acquaintance, he was a household name amongst the Arabs of numerous tribes, most of whom revered him, with many even naming their children after him. On Leachman's entertaining, a fellow political officer serving in Mosul, Wallace Lyon, wrote in his Memoirs: 'He would lead a carousal in the mess till all but he had flown to bed…[and] give orders for champagne by the case' (Fieldhouse, D. K., *Kurds, Arabs and Britons*, p. 64). He was murdered by Khamis, son of Sheikh Dhari, at Falluja on 12th August 1920 over what is believed to have been a personal dispute.

F.V. B. Witts

Major

H.Q. 18th Divn.

Mosul.

Oct 9th 1919.

Dearest Mother.

Still no mail to answer. Its ages now since one came in.

News has just come in that the railway strike is over. What an anxious and trying time you must have had. The trouble is I am afraid it won't be the last of them. We have had a strike down the line out here though I know no details: the Postal Services were recently made into a Civil Department and they have celebrated the change by going on strike: though this doesn't account for the delay in the mails.

I've had a strenuous and quite exciting time since last writing. That evening owing to heavy storms all communication with the columns broke down, and the General decided to send me through next day with orders, and to bring back a report the following day. I left by aeroplane in rain and wind at 6. a.m. the next morning and was safely deposited about 7 a.m. on Zakho aerodrome where I found a horse and escort of six awaiting me. Then followed a 35 mile ride through the mountains involving crossing three passes with ascents and descents of 1000', 2500', and 3000' respectively. The horses had to be led at least half the way, and one slipped over the edge and was only saved by a tree below. The path was a mere goattrack, going up and down literal stone staircases or crossing sloping slabs of rock. It was raining steadily all the time – snow at the top of the highest pass – 8000' – and I was very relieved, and rather surprised when I found the columns just before dark after 10½ hours going. They were amazed to see me, how had I got them, why hadn't I been scuppered en route. I stayed the night and returned next day – fine this time – but, instead of a plane, a car had to bring me home. It unfortunately broke down and I spent the night out in the blue. Coming back was a beautiful day and I thoroughly enjoyed it, magnificent mountain scenery and beautiful fresh cool air, and the country alive with chikor – the Himalayan Partridge. It was particularly interesting seeing it after reading so much about it in reports, and flying over it twice. The column reached and burnt the village [Karoar] we had previously bombed and then started home, and we all hope our little war is over.

Next day I had to represent the General at a Garden party in the Mosul Civil Hospital. I found myself surrounded by all sorts of ecclesiastical celebrities – an R. C. Archbishop, a Chaldean Bishop, a Papal Nuntio and crowds of others.[24] It was

---

[24] In *A Clash of Loyalties*, Wilson makes mention of the Papal Nuncio, Monsignor Martin, who arrived in Mesopotamia determined to safeguard the special interests and privileges of the country's small Roman Catholic community, who had enjoyed singular immunities as French protégés under the Turks. Under Monsignor Martin's banner flocked Christian delegates of the Chaldean, Armenian and Assyrian churches, all making special requests and greatly embarrassing the Civil Administration's earnest endeavours to promote an image of religious impartiality (p. 214-215).

however quite entertaining studying every one around one, the most mixed and motley crowd imaginable.

Since then I've been leading a more normal existence and have had neither a ride nor a shoot. There will be a certain amount of work winding things up; but in another ten days things should be much quieter, unless I am moved to another centre of activity.

The last two days we've had the most violent thunderstorms accompanied by thunder and rain. It is much cooler consequently. In fact one can have no legitimate grouse against the weather now.

> Very best love,
>> Your ever loving Son,
>>> Fred.V. B. Witts.

As Major Witts had hoped, the razing of Karoar, the principal village of the Goyan tribe, was the symbolic end to the 'little war' in Central Kurdistan. However, although the region had once again been subdued outwardly, the series of expeditions, which had cost considerable casualties and expense, could in no way guarantee against a resurgence of hostilities. In Britain, pressure was building on the Government to give reasonable explanations for the ongoing fighting in Kurdistan. The myth of Arab and Kurdish gratitude for British patronage was beginning to wear thin, helped by the growing attention of the media. *The Times* Middle East correspondent, whom Major Witts had escorted to Zakho and with whom he had undoubtedly conversed at some length, wrote the following piece on 23rd September:

> I imagine that the view held by many English people about Mesopotamia is that the local inhabitants will welcome us because we have saved them from the Turks, and that the country only needs developing to repay a large expenditure of English lives and English money. Neither of these ideals will bear much examination... from the political point of view we are asking the Arab [and Kurd] to exchange his pride and independence for a little Western civilisation, the profits of which must be largely absorbed by the expenses of the administration.

The bitter taste of war was still on the lips of the British public, and the struggling economy cried out for a reduction in all foreign expenditure. In response to national feeling, the Foreign Office in London pressed for an evacuation of British forces from Kurdistan. Their suggestion, however, was rebuked vehemently by the Civil Commissioner, A. T. Wilson. Conscious of the obligations that the Civil Administration now held towards their allies in Kurdistan, Wilson asserted that the region was being governed 'not by force but by consent.'[25] He believed that pockets of insurgency had only flared up in response to Turkish propaganda which, in course of time, would lose its potency. According to Wilson, the essential desires of the Kurds, lodged behind a fearful screen of tribal loyalty, were civilisation and stability under a British regime. If, however, the Kurds were to be left to their own devices, as was being suggested by the Foreign Office, tribal anarchy would take over and intrigue would spread unchecked. Eventually the Turks would bring Southern Kurdistan back under their suzerainty, creating greater long-term problems for the British.[26]

For the moment, the British Government was convinced; the Civil Administration was allowed to retain its responsibilities in Southern Kurdistan. It seemed that Major Witts, however, would play little part in any further operations in the region; having seen his first bit of action since the end of the war, albeit in a reconnoitring role, the powers-that-be had decided to move him on once again.

F.V.B. Witts

   Major

H.Q. 18th Division

Mosul.

Oct 16th 1919.

Dearest Mother.

...I hope the Butler has been a success and that you've got a decent cook. I am sorry to hear the Chauffeur has probably left by this time. I am so glad Elma has been making such a good stay. Very many thanks for all the papers particularly for the North Country one with an account of Frank's wedding. Your description of things in England does not surprise me after what I've seen in Reuters and the papers: it makes one look about for somewhere else to make a home, but it won't be in your time, so don't worry on that score.

I had a very busy two days working with the General [Cassels] on his Despatch and Recommendations. I put in a solid 36 hours actual work in the 48. I may tell you straight you needn't expect to see my name, though he was kind enough to thank me properly and give me a pat on the back for that ride the other day. He left this morning for India en route for his new Cavalry Division in Palestine. He's a great loss, as he's an outstanding man. We gave him a farewell dinner last night. However I'm not going to have a chance of missing him, as he had hardly left before a wire came ordering me to Basrah to relieve the G.S.O. II Lines of Communications, who is off on leave to India. There is no place in Mespot I want to go to less, but I suppose I

[25] Wilson, A. T., *A Clash of Loyalties*, p. 143

[26] Ibid. p.143-146

must take what comes: anyhow it is a purely temporary job, and the present occupant can hardly be away more than ten weeks. It is quite a good climate in the winter, though of course nothing like as nice as this, and will give me an opportunity of seeing a different part of the country, but I do dislike being moved about, just as I have settled down and got to know people. I shall not move sooner than I need as every day it gets cooler down there. But I am afraid another week or ten days will see me on the move again.

With our campaign over and no anxieties I started polo again on Monday, and distinguished myself by falling off without damage to anyone however. I am playing again this afternoon, but then I think my ponies will have to start down country.

I went for a joyride with the aeroplanes this morning both to speed General Cassels on his way, and to welcome back the first lot of troops from the war. It was rather exciting as the pilot was playing all sorts of tricks, but both General and troops were very pleased.

I had a morning out on Tuesday, trying to shoot something. We however struck a bad spot and I only fired three cartridges and got one partridge – However it was a delightful morning in the country and we had a very pleasant picnic.

No other news this time.

Very best love,

> Your ever loving Son,
> Fred.V. B. Witts.

F.V.B. Witts

Major

> Mosul.
> Oct 23rd 1919.

Dearest Mother.

…It is very sad losing one's old friends but I gather Canon Nisbet's death must have been a happy release.

As you will observe, I've not moved yet but am off on the 29th to Baghdad where I am taking a week's leave to look up all my friends; I shall be staying with Fuller, who came out with me, at the Civil Commissioner's. I then go on to Basrah to the Headquarters of the Inspector General of Communications [Brig.-Gen. H. Nepean] where I shall be my own master as the sole representative of the General Staff. It is only acting of course, but I hope I may get a permanent appointment later. They won't make me G.S.O. 3. apparently – too senior or something. I had a very nice wire from General Cassels – our late Divisional Commander – from Baghdad on his way down, advising me to go and adding he was speaking to the Commander in Chief for me.

We've had a real Bishop and his wife staying for us for three nights – the Bishop of Nagpur (India) on a visit to the troops. A genial and pleasant man. We were rather frightened at the thought of Mrs Bishop – never having had a lady in the mess, but she was used to roughing it, and we had no difficulty in entertaining and looking after her. She asked to go up in an aeroplane and was duly sent, it falling to me to chaperone her to the aerodrome. She enjoyed it. She rather reminded me of Aunt Maggie except that she was far from handsome…

I went out shooting on Sunday after attending early service, at which the Bishop officiated, but it was too late for the sandgrouse however we got a few black partridges nine to be precise. I hope to get a day in the country tomorrow. I've been doing great execution with the pigeons from the roof of our mess, which they fly over in large numbers each morning. Two days ago I got 18, and this morning I got 20, I was in great form getting two right and lefts running and only using 29 cartridges.

No more news today,

Very best love,

Your ever loving Son,

Fred. V. B. Witts.

F. V. B. Witts

Major

Baghdad.

Nov 2nd 1919.

Dearest Mother.

I left Mosul on the 30th; I was to have come on the 29th, but the aeroplane which was to bring me down wasn't quite ready. I sent my kit off by 3 cars to railhead that morning. As a result of staying an extra day I got another mail with all the papers and your letter of the 23rd Sept. We got away all right on the 30th, and were in Baghdad in 2½ hours – as against 2 days by road and rail. We had an odd machine with a patched up engine making it even odds that we might have to land en route, so we didn't come in a bee line but followed the road and railway making it about 250 miles. Otherwise we should have been down in 2 hours or so. It is certainly the way to get about in this country. It was a beautiful day and I thoroughly enjoyed seeing the country from the air and picking up all my old bridge and camp sites. I had two days shooting before leaving Mosul, but we didn't get much – 15 sandgrouse, 10 black partridges and a snipe.

I may not be going to Basrah after all. I interviewed the G.C.S. [General Commander Staff] at G.H.Q. yesterday and as luck would have it a Brigade Majorship in the 17th Divn became vacant yesterday. On paper it is not as good a job as G.S.O. II at Basrah, which I was told I should probably get permanently. But it is better in every other way. If I go to the L of C [Lines of Communications] I go on British Rates of pay, whereas in an Indian Division I remain on Indian Rates, so that I get better pay as B.M. than as G.S.O. 2 at Basrah, where moreover there is no General Staff work worth speaking of. The Brigade Commander (51st) [Brig.-Gen. F. E. Coningham] and

Divn Gen [Maj.-Gen. G. A. Leslie] have both asked for me and I have been told to stand fast here, while they look for some one else to go to Basrah. It would suit me much better as I have a lot of friends in and around Baghdad, though we should be someway outside.

No more news

Very best love.

Your ever loving Son

Fred. V. B. Witts

While the next stage of Major Witts' career was being disputed between Basra and Baghdad, events in Southern Kurdistan intervened to decide the matter. In the north-eastern Aqrah district, familiar to Major Witts from the air, a lifelong feud between the Barzani and Zibari tribes had been reconciled in favour of a united hatred for the Civil Administration. On November 2nd, the new chief political officer of the Mosul wilayat, Mr J. H. Bill (who had recently succeeded Lieut.-Col. Leachman) and a British army officer were murdered in a combined Zibari and Barzani ambush. Bill had exacted a fine on two Zibari chiefs in punishment for their retainers shooting at a gendarme. He had thus incensed the dangerous pride of the Aghawat, whose fears of subjugation and curtailment had been carefully nurtured by Turkish propaganda. Having committed the murders, the band of insurgents turned their ire upon the nearby town of Aqrah, which they plundered without resistance over the next few days.

The inhabitants of Aqrah, meanwhile, appealed earnestly to the British to come and rid them of the malefactors. In response, General MacMunn

120. Kurdish tribesmen at Rania, 1919.

arranged for the immediate dispatch of a punitive column, precipitating the decision for Major Witts' fate.

F.V.B. Witts
Major

> Future Address: 51st Inf Brigade
> Mes: Ex: Force
> Nov 9th 1919.

Dearest Mother.

Events have moved quickly since I last wrote. First and foremost I've got the job I wanted and am now Brigade Major, 51st Inf Brigade. Please address my letters accordingly in future.

In the meantime however on Nov 4th, news came of a rising at Akra, E.N.E. of Mosul about 60 miles out, and the murder of two British Officers. Having just come from that part of the world, and having flown over Akra my last trip from Mosul – incidently with one of the murdered officers in the other aeroplane – I was in great request and was immediately summoned to G.H.Q. to give my views on the murder and the country. I heard nothing more till the 7th, when, within two hours of receiving definite orders to take up my appointment in the 51st Bde, I was ordered to stand fast and learnt I was to be Brigade Major to the Column being organised for punitive purposes. Much as I was pleased, I was not altogether surprised, in view of my special knowledge of local conditions, gathered in the last 2½ months. I moved across to my old home, 17th Div H.Q., yesterday as the column is being partly organised here, but I return to Mosul this week. Six weeks at the very outside should see it all over and me back with 51st Inf Bde before Christmas. But one never knows how things will turn out.

I forgot to mention in my last letter that Fuller, whom I was to have stayed with, went to hospital and was operated on for appendicitis 4 days before I came down. He passed me on to the aerodrome where I have been staying till yesterday, and have had a very cheery time. I have seen a lot of Fuller, and am glad to say he comes out of hospital tomorrow

The first theatrical company to visit Baghdad has been performing this last week and I have been to two quite good shows. Not to mention a dinner party somewhere each night.

…I am afraid the chances of the Staff College in 1920 are nil, and very very poor in the following year. However one must live and hope.

I must stop now as I've got a lot of work to do.

> Very best love and Christmas wishes to all,
> Your ever loving Son
> Fred.V. B. Witts.

F.V.B. Witts
  Major

Mosul.
Nov 14th 1919.

Dearest Mother.

…once again very best wishes for Christmas and the New Year. I wonder where you will be spending it and who with. Let's hope it will be a warmer and cheerier one than the last: though I'm afraid you will get no cable from me announcing my early arrival on leave, I don't know where I shall spend it I hope Baghdad, but we may still be up in these parts. I enclose a snapshot of myself taken on the aerodrome at Baghdad: they say it is rather a good one of me. I'm afraid I've nothing to send in the way of a present or Christmas Card, but I know there's nothing you will like better than a photo.

I came up here on Tuesday – the 11th – by air, having the luck to get a lift in a machine coming up to fetch a pilot back: it took 3¼ hours this time as we had a strong wind against us part of the way. I am not staying at my old home, but at the Cav Bde H.Q. where we are organising our Column Headquarters. The Column Commander is due today and we move out in 4 or 5 days.

Yesterday I motored out some 40 miles to our advanced troops, and then rode on another 16 to within 2 miles of Akra, which was seized and looted by the revolting tribesmen. I had a strong escort, but we saw not a soul and had a most uneventful day, though I saw all I wanted to and much more than I expected to. It was a long ride – some 35 miles the round trip – and we didn't get back to the advanced post till an hour after dark and found them on the point of turning out troops to look for us. The road back was too bad to think of coming on in the dark, so we stayed the night there and came in this morning, doing a little shooting on the way. Not much to shoot but we saw a few black partridges and also a flock of geese feeding in the open which we fired on with rifles without success.

It is much colder up here than at Baghdad and there's been frost already. We shall have a very cold time of it in the hills. Luckily they are allowing us plenty of kit. It will probably be wet too though so far the weather has held wonderfully. I am very lucky to get the job and am very pleased and only hope we may have a chance of doing something; but the blighters usually run at the sight of any number of troops and refuse to fight, in which case we shall have nothing to do but burn their villages as it is impossible to follow them right up into the far hills. It can't be a long show as the whole country is snowed up later on. We shall be cut off from the post, so letters may be a bit intermittent.

I am feeling extraordinarily well, and every one remarks on how fit I look.

I will write again before going out.

Very best wishes for Christmas and the New Year,
      and very best love,
            Your ever loving Son,
                  Fred. V. B. Witts.

122. The result of a stunt.

121. Kurdish scenery near Rayat.

F.V.B. Witts
Major

[Mosul]
Nov 19ᵗʰ 1919.

Dearest Mother.

…What a terrible time you must have had during the railway strike. The papers make terrible reading and I can quite understand you being upset about it all.[27] It is bad luck Frank having to move so soon after settling in.

My trouble about getting to the Staff College is that I'm too young and junior and have not had enough Staff experience.

…Our little force is nearly concentrated and we ourselves go out by car to join them near Akra the day after tomorrow. During the week we've been busy organising and getting things together. I went out with the planes one morning on a reconnaissance to have a look at the country we have got to operate in. It is pretty fierce. We have to cross two mountain ranges, each over 5000 feet to reach our objective, each involving an ascent and descent of 3000 feet; the paths are mere tracks and we shall have difficulty with our pack transport. Luckily the distance is not much – some 15 miles. It is a hopeless place for an aeroplane to land and I was relieved when we were over the plains again as the engine was going very rough. I was out with the 'stunt' pilot of Mespot, and he put me through it when we were safely over Mosul again. Luckily it is not safe to do much with the type of machine they have out here, but it was enough to make my head swim and to be quite relieved when we had made the most perfect landing I have yet experienced. You will probably be relieved

---

[27] The strike, demanding increased pay and the abolition of the war-wages agreement, ended in complete success for the Railway Unions, demonstrating their power to sway the Government – a worrying notion for Britain's middle and upper classes as it encouraged strike action across the board.

that with my present job I shall not get another chance of flying as far as the present operations are concerned: but it is not really so very dangerous as is proved by the fact that, though we've been scrapping for the last six months, the R.A.F. have not had a single casualty.

I have been out to dinner every night since I came up!

Very best New Year wishes,

Your ever loving Son

Fred.V. B.Witts

YORK HOTEL,
ALBEMARLE STREET, W.
Telephone No. 612 REGENT
Telegraphic Address: 'HOTELIER, PICCY, LONDON.'
Nov: 20.1919

Dearest Fred,

I can catch the mail in London so send you a line tho my regular letter has gone. You will see in the Times of Saturday about your doings I enclose the wee map can you put a line across your flight? & return it – all interests me. I feel all the better for London, but it is no longer the <u>comfortable</u> place it used to be. Edward writes he has a berth on the Edinburgh Castle for Dec 12. We must try & get Edith on board too if possible as they will be afloat for Xmas.

Jack & Elma have been with us for lunches and teas, but I think it will be best for them to get abroad as Elma is rightly anxious to save until Jack has a job- he wants a bit of rest. Frank has not got his orders yet & so is at Southsea- but I shall go home with George after our visit to Canterbury. Jack admired my Squirrels (yours) very

Map 11. Area north of Mosul.

much they are so very warm & the muff warmer than any other. I wanted my mole skin done up but the price asked is £66 rather too much as I should think I could buy a new one for that.

Best Xmas wishes & may you soon be home. George & I have dentist & other disagreeable jobs-

dearest love

    Yr loving Mother

        MH Broome Witts

    F.V.B. Witts

    Major

                                In the Mountains

                                Nov 29th 1919.

Dearest Mother.

Just a line to catch a convoy going down tomorrow. We have reached the principal objective of our expedition – the scene of the murder [Bira Kapra village, just outside Aqra] – without any opposition worthy of the name. But the road was very bad – a mere goat track – and the weather awful the first two days. Now it is beautifully fine but freezes hard at night. We stay here at the most a week and then start back.

It is a very pleasant change from the plains and I am enjoying myself and my job hugely.

I am extraordinarily fit.

Very best love,

    Your ever loving Son,

        Fred.V. B. Witts.

    F.V.B. Witts

    Major

                                      [Mosul]

                                  Dec 10th 1919.

Dearest Mother.

Very many thanks for your three letters of Oct 21st, 22nd & 28th, which all reached me on return from our little war yesterday. Also all the usual papers and the medal ribbons – very many thanks for them. They are impossible to get out here, and I shall now be able to dress myself up.

…If it is not too cold and damp for you and difficult to keep up, I am very glad to hear you are staying on at Slaughter, but you must put your health first. I am very pleased to hear the Tennis Court and other improvements are getting on so fast.

There was a cable from the Times Correspondent I took round in the Times of

Sept 13th I think or thereabouts with a very short description of his visit.[28] I hope Frank may have got to the Staff College. I am afraid I have a very remote chance at present. They expect you to go to the Quetta Staff College from here. This last time they only sent one to Camberley – a Lieut Colonel commanding his Regiment! I think I must stay on sufficiently long to establish a claim to Staff work. So far my jobs have been acting or officiating, though I am now a full blown permanent Brigade Major, which is not so bad in view of the many reductions. This last little war might have helped me – if there had been any war but the Kurds all fled on our approach – a compliment to the earlier punitive columns, when I was on the directing staff here.

We had a splendid fortnight, bar the first two days, and it has done me a world of good. All the hard exercise and open air life was a delightful change, and I am feeling and looking extraordinarily well. We had one magnificent morning's shooting 61 chikor – or mountain partridge rather like the frenchman at home but twice the size – and one mush deer; and we lived on venison & game the whole time. Not to mention fish, which were successfully bombed in the Greater Zab, some 100 fish representing 350 lbs dead weight being collected after exploding only 4 lbs of guncotton. It was very cold at nights but we had unlimited wood and sat round blazing log fires in the evenings. The weather looked as if it was going to break on our way back, and we did have a little rain and crossed the passes in the clouds but nothing to make the road difficult as on the way out. Bira Kapra was our centre for a week from which we worked in various directions, I think you will find it marked on your map.

I am staying up here a few days partly to finish up our little show, and partly on what I call war leave for our little war. Then I move down to my permanent home at Daurah just below Baghdad where the 51st Bde H.Q. are.

I am rather fond of Mosul; it has a very good climate for Mespot, I know everybody here and it is a self contained place not too scattered which is the fault of Baghdad.

We were extraordinarily fortunate in our weather: every one prophesied rain would stop the whole show if it did not actually cause a small disaster: it has held off in a marvellous way. I suppose it will make up for it later.

No more news,

    Very best love,

        Your ever loving Son,

            Fred. V. B. Witts

---

[28] See Appendix XII for *The Times* article, 'A Little War in Kurdistan.'

Once again, the tribes of Central Kurdistan had been subdued, but this time the lesson had hit home – not for the Kurds, but for the British. The Aghawat in Central Kurdistan was never willingly going to give up its power, and the British lacked the strength to take it forcibly. Harmful Turkish intrigue, meanwhile, could not be curtailed with the resources available to the Civil Administration. A determined re-settlement of political officers to these areas would only lead to more murders and raids, followed by an evaporation of the culprits into the mountains at the first sight of a punitive column. As a result, British outposts fell back on a line running from Aqrah to Dohuk, leaving trouble spots such as Amadiya and Zakho outside British administration.

Meanwhile, on the Mesopotamian plain, the past thirteen months since the signing of the Armistice had been comparatively calm. In his excursions around Kurdistan, Major Witts had missed little more than dinners and races in Baghdad. The political situation, however, was starting to cause problems.

The promise of independence made in the Anglo-French Declaration had encouraged the growth of nationalism in Mesopotamia. However, Arabs were still remarkably under-represented in the Civil Administration, and completely absent from high offices containing any substantial degree of responsibility or power. As a result, the disenchanted Baghdad intelligentsia were growing hostile, and the city was fast becoming a hotbed of political intrigue. Meanwhile, on the Upper Euphrates, Britain's failure to fulfil her pledge to Sharif Hussein of the Hejaz, for the establishment of a Hashemite Kingdom in Mesopotamia, was surfacing with dangerous alacrity. An energetic stream of seditious propaganda had begun to flow over the border from Syria.

As a counter-measure to growing unrest, the Civil Administration desperately needed to confirm its intentions to create an independent state in Mesopotamia. However, with the British mandate and peace with Turkey still unsigned, the Civil Commissioner and his staff were still forbidden to make any official statements on British policy in the country. Major Witts was soon to find himself embroiled in another war.

CHAPTER X

THE RISE OF NATIONALISM
Letters: Dec 20th 1919 – June 15th 1920

Throughout 1919, the Arab Government of Syria, established in Damascus under Amir Feisal after the war, was engaged in an aggressive pursuit of absolute independence. The Anglo-French Declaration and the Hussein-McMahon Agreement applied equally to Syria as to Mesopotamia; these pledges had given impetus to nationalist ambition. French aspirations, meanwhile, to secure the mandate for Syria, were a dreaded prospect. France's poor reputation as a colonial ruler in North Africa and for her open favouritism to Christian minorities strengthened Syrian resolve to secure their independence; for this, the Damascus Government looked to Britian for support.

Having been promised autonomy under a Hashemite ruler by the British, the Sharifian party held them responsible for guaranteeing the fulfilment of this pledge. Therefore, when Britain renounced these responsibilities effectively by withdrawing from Syria in October 1919,[1] opening the door for French intervention, a deep resentment was fomented within the Damascus Government, particularly within the extremist wing of the Sharifian party, Ahd-al-Iraqi.[2]

The Civil Administration's failure to begin establishing an Arab Government in Mesopotamia had not passed unnoticed by this group. Since April, they had been busy promoting nationalist propaganda on the Upper Euphrates, encouraging grievances among local tribes about taxation, political representation, and religious differences. When Britain withdrew from Syria, ending all hopes for independence, Ahd-al-Iraqi intensified their efforts to create a nationalist movement in Mesopotamia. They hoped to assume control of the country in the wake of Syria's inevitable submission to the French with the signing of the mandate.

On 11th December 1919, the first violent demonstration of anti-British feeling occurred on the Upper Euphrates. The Syrian town of Dair-ez-Zor, close to the provisional Mesopotamian border, was administrated by a British political officer, posted there at the special request of the inhabitants

---

[1] Up to this point, the remnants of the Palestinian Expeditionary Force had remained in Syria since the end of the war.

[2] Ahd-al-Iraqi was a secret nationalist society. Its members were Mesopotamian nationals, former officers in the Ottoman army who had betrayed the Turks to join Sharif Hussein's Revolt against Ottoman rule. Many had fought alongside Amir Feisal and now occupied prominent positions in the Damascus Government.

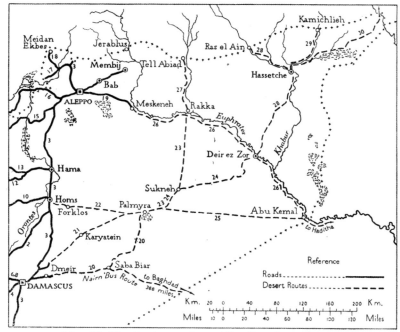

Map 12. The Euphrates from Albu Kemal to Aleppo

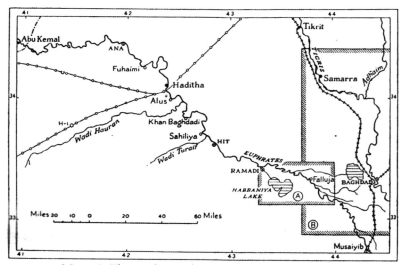

Map 13. The Euphrates from Baghdad to Albu Kemal

to preserve law and order. A raid by local tribesmen, incited by Ahd-al-Iraqi, was made on the town and the political officer was imprisoned.

The Civil Administration felt powerless to respond effectively to this act of hostility. Dair-ez-Zor was over three hundred miles from Baghdad and British military resources were already overstretched. From a diplomatic perspective, sending an armed column into Syria could be highly damaging to international relations. The Damascus Government denied all responsibility and was impervious to diplomatic pressure. Even appeals to Amir Feisal, a British ally, to restore British administration in Dair-ez-Zor were to no avail, highlighting the limitations of his power and the relative strength of Ahd-al-Iraqi. Eventually, without the courage to act assertively, the Civil Administration agreed to withdraw from the town. The lives of the political staff had been saved, but at the expense of a damaging loss of prestige which would add considerable weight to anti-British propaganda in the region. Lieutenant-General Sir Aylmer Haldane, G.O.C. in Mesopotamia from March 1920 to 1922, declared that the 'acceptance of this insult' was so significant that 'from that time [forward] the subsequent rising in Iraq was…a matter of absolute certainty.'[3]Haldane was speaking with the advantage of hindsight, but the fact was that British weakness had been exposed and a window of opportunity had been opened for her enemies to exploit.

Whilst these events were unfolding in the Syrian borderlands, in the vicinity of Baghdad Major Witts was settling back into the daily discomforts of camp life as Brigade Major of the 51st Bde. On the bright side, the holiday season was upon Force 'D', and various dinners and celebrations were soon to follow. For the time being, little concern was attached to rumours of tribal unrest on the distant Upper Euphrates.

No mails since last writing,   H.Q. 51st Brigade.
    but a mail is expected any day.   [Daurah]
                                                              Mes: Ex: Force.
                                                      Saturday Dec 20th 1919.

Dearest Mother.

I have at last got down to a permanent job. I came down from Mosul last Saturday and was lucky in again getting a lift down by aeroplane: it saves so much time and trouble.

We are under canvas about eight miles below Baghdad by road. So that in these days of economy and consequent lack of means of transport,[4] it is not easy to get in unless one makes a business of it, which I did on Wednesday when I spent the night with my friend Fuller at the Civil Commissioners.

It is rather a come down being under canvas once more after living in the lap of luxury for six months. The rain is going to be very unpleasant though we have got good

---

[3] Haldane, A., *The Insurrection in Mesopotamia*, 1922, p. 33.

[4] Amid the economic turmoil of the post-war period, Britain had retained ongoing military commitments in Egypt, Persia, Turkey, India, Palestine, Russia, and Mesopotamia, not to mention Ireland, loading intolerable burdens upon the resources of the Empire. Mr. Churchill, Colonial Secretary, was charged with finding a releasing valve to ease the pressure on the economy and identified Mesopotamia as the most suitable theatre in which to enforce cuts. He thus imposed even greater strains on Force 'D''s shrinking resources.

large tents which we never had in the days of the war, and good stoves but no roads or anything approaching it. And I have seen quite enough of Mesopotamian mud.

The General [Leslie] has been to Bombay to meet his wife and returns in a day or two with her. They are going to live in our camp, though by themselves. He is a charming man, and was temporarily commanding 17th Divn while I was with them.

For two or three days everything looked as if we should be moving out again, up the Euphrates this time, in view of developments at Dier-ez-Zor, but the present indications are that it will all blow over. In any case I hope they will wait till after the New Year.

I tried to send you a Christmas cable but the cables are so overcrowded they asked us not to send them.

A telephone message has just come in that leave and demobilization which have been stopped for a week are open again. So I suppose its peace, not war.

Very best love.

> Your ever loving Son
> Fred. V. B. Witts.

> H.Q. 51st Inf Bde.
> [Daurah]
> Mes: Ex: Force.
> Christmas Eve 1919.

Dearest Mother.

I am off by tonight's train to the 17th Divn H.Q. Christmas shooting camp at Beled Ruz, 20 miles odd beyond Baquba, and may not be back in time to catch the next mail out.

…The Times is full of Mesopotamia and Kurdistan for once in a way, and it is quite cheering to think someone is taking some interest in us. Those on Kurdistan were written at Mosul by the Correspondent who was then under my charge. It was to avenge the two officers who were killed that I went back to Mosul and out on a punitive expedition. It is not a bad country to soldier in as we always have something to do. I am returning the little map you sent and have marked in red the line of some of my trips in the air: in blue I have marked the line of my ride after flying to Zakho.[5]

I am so glad to hear Jack is home again, also that Edward has at last got his passage to South Africa. I hope Edward was able to take Edith with him. I also had a Christmas letter from Frank; they seem to keep him hanging about a long time.

£66 seems a lot for having your mole skin done up.

Christmas is going to be a gay time for those actually in Baghdad. Dances most nights; but we are too far out without making an absolute complete night of it. I am going in [for] the New Year's Eve Ball, but that will be all.

Very best love,

> Your ever loving Son,
> Fred. V. B. Witts.

---

[5] See Map 11. p. 329, for F.V.B.W.'s map.

123. *Cheltenham Chronicle* 16th July 1910: The wedding of Jack Cheetham and Mabel Witts (F.V.B.W.'s first cousin) on July 7th 1910 at Lower Guiting (Guiting Power).

THE MANOR,
UPPER SLAUGHTER,
GLOS.
Dec.30.1919.

Dearest Fred

Yours of Nov. 19th came on the 27 and Nov. 14th today – both most welcome I am charmed with the photo & like it better than anything. This must be your birthday letter & I send you a wee present may you have many happy years– I thought people went to the Staff College to <u>learn</u> & not <u>after</u> having experience. However I am pleased because you like your job– I have found the place on the map but it is not spelt quite as you did – yours is on the coast near Beirut – whereas the other is just North of Bagdad as you say– & towards a lake.[6] I hope you will have a chance of doing your bit tho <u>I</u> don't want fighting, My Neuritis is better & I hope soon to get back the use of my legs!! Sophie's marriage will take place I believe about the middle of Jan[y] as there is nothing to wait for; Mr. Richardson is nearer my age than Sophie's – a J.P. for Sheffield & county a good churchman & I should think a good sort all round from his photo, he does not hunt or shoot: he has a nice house & garden in Sheffield

---

[6] Mrs Witts must have been quite confused on Mesopotamian geography. F.V.B.W.'s letters of November 14th and 19th were both written from Mosul and talk about operations in Akrah, just 60 miles away to the north-east. Neither are near any substantial lakes and, more confusingly, Beirut, lying about 500 miles to the south-west, is never mentioned by F.V.B.W. and has no immediate connection with Mesopotamia.

124. Eyford Park (side). Eyford was the home of Jack and Mabel Cheetham.

& Sophie says more money than she has so he is not marrying her for that; it may take place in London: Mabel says nothing! but she is getting more like her mother but alas without her mother's good qualities.

– I have only been to Eyford once during the War & then I asked myself – the Heythrop are round here now every week as rabies broke out Banbury way & they cant take the hounds there. It is mild & damp, rain most days which is everything for the new Turf putting down & the trees & shrubs we are planting – I am doing it up at the Dingle along the wall in the field so as to shut out the road- I wish we had given Emily notice in Sept to move out in march as if Edward decides to do the warming & electric light I gather we shall have to be out of the house 2 or 3 months & I don't know where to go, Agnes wants to take up oil painting as a business,[7] Com: Wright R.N does it at the Bridges & taught her – he had lessons in Paris.

I expect Ed & Edith will be landing now. Old Bee is dead at L.Slaughter… Jack [Kennard] & Francie are settled at Falkirk- he in business on half pay-

I believe we shall be fighting again before long everything seems so unsettled even in England – Best of wishes for 1920 and your birthday.

Yr loving Mother

MH Broome Witts

[7] The two paintings in the Colour Section of the Manor at Upper Slaughter are by Agnes Witts (Illustrations 6 & 7). Also a painting of Wyck Hill (Illustration 8).

125. *Cheltenham Chronicle* 13th August 1910: The wedding of Jack Kennard and Frances Witts (F.V.B.W.'s first cousin) 9th August 1910 at Lower Guiting (Guiting Power).

F. V. B. Witts.
Major

H.Q. 51st Inf: Bde.
[Daurah]
Mesopotamia.
Jan 4th 1920.

Dearest Mother.

...I am sorry to hear Edith considers my Godson Peter [Apphie's son] a thoroughly naughty boy. It is nearly time he went to school. Frank is very lucky to get a small furnished house. Many thanks for sending 'A Private in the Guards'[8] which I am reading and find very interesting. Don't send me Lord French's book if it is so bad.[9] One I should like would be 'Rudyard Kipling's Verse: Inclusive Edition 1885 – 1918' in three volumes published by Messrs Hodder & Stoughton; I have not seen the price mentioned.

I had a great Christmas shoot at the 17th Divn H.Q. Christmas camp at Beled Ruz which you will probably see on your map. The first day we got with seven guns 106 head, including 69 partridges, 16 snipe and 8 geese: the second day with seven guns 103 head made up in much the same way. The third day three of us got 80 head, chiefly partridges, the fourth day we explored Mendali which you should find N

---

[8] An autobiographical account of life on the Western Front by Pte. Stephen Graham, published by Cassell & Co. Ltd, London.

[9] Lord French's *1914* (Constable & Co., 1919) has been widely criticised for its inaccuracies. In an article entitled *French and 1914: His Defence of His Memoirs Examined*, the historian Bullitt Lowry goes so far to describe *1914* as 'one of the most unfortunate books ever written' (*Military Affairs*, Vol. 45, No. 2 (Apr., 1981) p. 79).

E of Baghdad close to the Persian frontier, some 30 miles from Beled Ruz, but did not strike any good shooting and only got a few sandgrouse on the way. Altogether I got 82 head to my own gun made up of 56 partridges, 11 snipe, 6 duck, 3 geese 5 sandgrouse and 1 quail. I was very pleased with my shooting. We had perfect weather, and the Divn made excellent arrangements and altogether ran a perfect show. The gun you gave me has turned out a great success and fits me perfectly.

I got back on the morning of the 29th.

On New Year's eve I went to the R.A.F. fancy dress 'bal masque'. I wore a brand new Turkish Officer's uniform, picked up in the Mosul Bazaar. It was a great show for Baghdad wonderfully well done. It was too far out to get in from our camp, so they very kindly put me up at the Aerodrome, where I found all my flying friends from Mosul down on leave, and didn't drag myself away until the following evening. One of them astonished people here by flying over for a glass of beer the following morning, landing on a football ground just by my tent.

The weather is behaving wonderfully for the country and the time of year. We've had one heavy fall so far, about 24 hours of it, and it dried up marvellously quickly. I am afraid it is too good to last.

Today I have been out with the Baghdad Bobbery pack who met down our way. They are persian grey hounds, hunting jack at night. We had two good runs. But it was absolutely open level plain with nothing to jump or scramble through.

Very best love

Your ever loving Son

Fred. V. B. Witts.

F. V. B. Witts

Major

H.Q. 51st Inf Bde.

[Daurah]

Mesopotamia.

January 11th 1920.

Dearest Mother.

…This should arrive about your birthday. Very many happy returns of the day and may you live to enjoy many more. I wish I was to be at home to celebrate it with you as last year. I hope I may be next, but things are so very indefinite and one has to think of one's career and make the most of what opportunities one may get. I am enclosing a birthday present, which I want you to spend on yourself as you like. The present rate of rupee makes one feel sick, though on the other hand it makes one appear to spend fabulous sums out here, as of course the expenditure in rupees remains the same.

Very many thanks for your good wishes for the New Year. I am glad you were to have a Christmas party, even though it had to be a bit early.

No news this week. We've started polo in our new home, and hope to play three days a week. I went in to Baghdad for one night for the last week of the theatrical company which have been performing here the last 2½ months and are now returning to India. I stayed at the Serai — a sort of boarding house with suites of rooms, where many married officers live with their wives. They are fairly comfortable there, but otherwise Mesopotamia is no place for ladies. I think it is very premature their coming out at this time, and many may live to regret it. There are no suitable arrangements for any large numbers, and the country is very unsettled.[10] Nearly every week alarms and excitements appear from some quarter of the country with great regularity. The British troops are now all new, and the Indians old and warworn and pining to get back to India.

No more news.

Your ever loving Son,

Fred.V. B. Witts

As Major Witts intimated in his letter home, Mesopotamia was far from settled. Instead of easing the tension on the Upper Euphrates, the Civil Administration's submission to Ahd-al-Iraqi demands at Dair-ez-Zor had inflamed it. The chief protagonist, a Mesopotamian adventurer named Ramadhan-al-Shallash, had taken courage from the demonstration of British weakness. Styling himself as the 'Governor of the Euphrates', he was becoming increasingly audacious in inciting local tribes to commit acts of violence. On 11th January 1920, he demanded that the British withdraw all their forces as far as the Wadi Hawran, roughly 170 miles downriver from the River Khabur, the provisional border between Syria and Mesopotamia. When the Civil Administration refused to comply, Ramadhan attacked Albu Kemal, the northernmost British outpost on the Euphrates, with a band of indoctrinated local tribesmen. He specifically targeted notable friends of the Civil Administration, destroying their property and violating their women. The British response to this affront was ineffectual once again. Logistical difficulties and the absence of a mandate were the Civil Administration's excuses for its forbearance; but, to the Arabs, it simply expressed either serious weakness or apathy. Nationalist sentiment and disillusionment with the British administration spread rapidly down the Euphrates.

---

[10] By January 1920 there were nearly a thousand British women and children staying in Mesopotamia (Wilson, A. T., *A Clash of Loyalties*, p. 272). The influx promoted an undesirable image of colonialism and, as F.V.B.W. asserted intuitively, signified a gross misjudgement of the country's stability.

Upper Slaughter.

The Great War, 1914=1919.

To *Major E.F.B.Witts. D.S.O. Glouc. Regt.*

THE women of Upper Slaughter wish to express to you their grateful recognition of your services in the Great War, and tender this small token of their appreciation and thanks for your help towards the attainment of victory.

126. 'The women of Upper Slaughter thank Major E.F.B. Witts (F.V.B.W.'s eldest brother) ...' F.V.B.W. received one similar.

F.V. B. Witts
   Major

H.Q. 51ˢᵗ Bde.
[Daurah]
Mesopotamia.
January 18ᵗʰ 1920.

Dearest Mother.

Many thanks for your letter of Dec 9ᵗʰ and the papers. How you must have enjoyed Jack's and Frank's visit with their wives; it still seems so curious to me. I am glad to hear Edith managed to get a passage in the same ship as Edward. You will certainly miss him. He has been home nearly a year now. So sorry to hear your rheumatics are worrying you again.

I shall much value the framed card of thanks from the Women of Slaughter, though I don't know whether professional soldiers should get it. I got one of my mention in dispatch certificates the other day.

The week produced its usual tale of unrest and movement of troops.[11] At one time it looked as if Brigade Headquarters might have to move up the Euphrates, but things have quietened down for the moment. Otherwise there has been little doing in the week. The rain has kept off in a marvellous way after threatening to deluge us on two or three days. We are getting our polo regularly but it is very inferior as there are too many beginners.

I went in to Baghdad one evening, and dined and slept with my friend Fuller at

---

[11] Although, up to this point, British forces had done very little to punish or curtail acts of insurgency on the Upper Euphrates, more troops were finally being moved to the region.

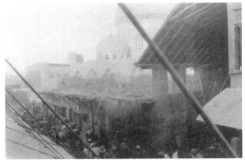

127. The bazaar, Baghdad.

the Civil Commissioners. I had hoped to do some shopping next morning, but had
to dash back here for a job of work. One might as well be 100 miles away for all the
benefit we get out of Baghdad.

The Commander in Chief out here has just gone off to India to take up the job of
Quarter Master General. His successor is a total stranger to most people out here.[12]

No more news.

> Very best love,
>> Your ever loving Son,
>>> Fred.V. B. Witts.

F.V. B. Witts
Major.

[Baghdad]
Mesopotamia.
January 25th 1920.

Dearest Mother.

I came in to Baghdad yesterday evening preparatory
to an early start this morning for a shoot down Kut
way: but a violent storm sprang up during the night
and not only did we have to abandon the shoot, but I
have been unable to get back to Daurah – our camp
– and have to stay another night here. The heavy
gale coinciding with a bit of a flood on the river has
rendered all the bridges unsafe and they have been
closed to traffic, and there is too big a sea running for a
launch. Unless I write now, I shall miss the mail, but I
have not got your letter which arrived yesterday with

128. Floods on Maude Bridge.

[12] Lieutenant-General Sir Aylmer Haldane, General MacMunn's successor, was a veteran of the Western
Front and entirely unfamiliar with Mesopotamia. He did not actually arrive in the country until March, two
months after General MacMunn's departure. In the interim General Leslie officiated as Acting C-in-C.

me to answer in detail. A day like this I am very thankful I am not at my old job – the bridging train – : my same old bridge is over the river near our camp, and I shall not be a bit surprised to hear it has been destroyed.

It is very disappointing as it should have been a first rate shoot – the Civil Commissioner's – and I haven't been out since our Christmas camp... I have been lucky to escape from my camp on a day like this and to spend it in the luxury of very comfortable quarters.

It has been an uneventful week. We have been getting our polo regularly and only a very little rain. It is a pity it didn't rain more today as it is badly wanted.

Yesterday morning we had a small ceremonial parade, when our C-in-C presented decorations to certain officers. There appeared to be more Generals and other redtab gentlemen on parade than others.

No more news.

> Very best love,
>> Your ever loving Son,
>>> Fred. V. B. Witts.

F. V. B. Witts.
Major

> H.Q. 51ˢᵗ Inf Bde.
> [Daurah]
> Mesopotamia.
> Feb 8ᵗʰ 1920.

Dearest Mother.

...Saturday there was a day's racing in Baghdad, followed in the evening by a ball given by the bachelors, of which I am one, under the name of the 'Black Diamonds'. Both were most successful. I was surprised to see how many ladies there are now in Baghdad: – nearly all officers' wives. Every one was there from the G.O. C-in-C downwards. The present temporary C-in-C [Leslie] was my Colonel in France. I am dining and sleeping with them on Thursday – it may help my getting to the Staff College! I stayed the night in Baghdad at the Aerodrome where the dance was held in one of the hangars where a special floor was put down.

Just before the races we had a fire in our camp – the tent next but one to mine. There was a strong wind blowing and I thought it was all up with my kit. However we managed to cut down

129. Major-General G. Leslie.

the tent between and save both, but it was almost a miracle. Two officers lost every stitch of stuff they possess out here. One it doesn't affect much as he was just being demobilized, but the other had only just arrived from England and had some of his wife's kit.

No more news,

With very best love,

Your ever loving Son,

Fred. V. B. Witts

F. V. B. Witts

Major

H.Q. 51ˢᵗ Inf Bde.

[Daurah]

Mesopotamia.

Feb 16ᵗʰ 1920.

Dearest Mother.

Many thanks for your letter of Jan 6ᵗʰ and all the papers. Letters are coming much quicker nowadays, getting to Baghdad in just the month. I suppose shipping is more regular and possibly they come across France. The through line Basra to Baghdad is now in working order which saves time this end.

I am sorry to hear your leg has been so bad, it must be very painful; but I hope the treatment has done it good. Aunt Sybil must be very pleased to have you staying there.

What a lot of planting you have done at Slaughter; I shan't recognise the place when I get home. I know the author of 'With the Turks in Captivity'.[13] He was at Roorkee with me, and was the Bridging expert before me.

We are all wondering what they are going to do with this country. I wish they would hurry up and decide for everyone's sake.

An uneventful week. The rain still manages to keep off and we get our polo regularly. I have bought you a silk Persian rug: I hope you will like it when I manage to get it home to you.[14] It has been bitterly cold. A hard frost each morning – my sponge frozen stiff in my tent: it is hard to realize how soon we shall be grousing at the heat!

Large numbers of soldier's families are arriving. I think it is very premature. The country is too unsettled to start with and then there is no proper accommodation.

[13] Francis Yeats-Brown, the author of *With the Turks in Captivity* (1919) and, most famously, *Lives of a Bengal Lancer* (1930), a memoir of his army life in India from 1905-1914. In WWI he was a member of the Royal Flying Corps in France and Mesopotamia. In 1915 his plane was shot down behind Turkish lines and he was taken prisoner; *With the Turks in Captivity* is an account of his experiences.

[14] See Illustration 18 in the Colour Section.

They all have to go into tents and it will be very hard on the children.[15]

Fuller's Mother is arriving this week on a visit; her husband died last summer. He takes her home again in or about April. I shall miss him, as we've become fast friends. But she is comparatively young and he is in a position to make the best of arrangements. I am certain it would never do for me to ask you out.

No more news,

> Very best love
>> Your ever loving Son
>>> Fred. V. B. Witts

> THE MANOR,
> UPPER SLAUGHTER,
> GLOS.
> Feb 18. 1920.

My darling Boy-

You are too good to your old mother sending me such a large cheque. I shall get something one day & hand it on to your wife! God bless you. Yours of Jan 11th reached me a few days ago. I am getting better, having lost my pains I feel so weak so I am seeing one of our new Drs!!

Of course you must put your career first & take whatever turns up to your advantage. I hope my small cheque arrived safely. I wish it had been more I can hardly think your place a good abode for women yet! And the unrest seems going on as the Turks are killing people off still![16] We have lovely spring weather everything too forward. We went down to see Aunt Sybil on the 16th her birthday she must be 78 or 79 – & is wonderful. Frank hopes they have secured a house in Chester Square but it is not finally settled he was on duty for the Opening of Parliament mounted as second in command & keeps his birthday on the 22nd on duty at Buckingham Palace: but he seems to like his work which makes it nice. Jack & Elma are enjoying Nice & I don't suppose will be back before May as Jack is improving in health and losing his

---

[15] In *The Insurrection in Mesopotamia* Haldane agrees with F.V.B.W. on 'the fundamental unsuitability of Mesopotamia as a place of residence for white women and children' (p. 61). However, accommodation was being built at Karind, in Persia (with the permission of the Shah), 60 miles east of Khaniqin, where the climate was cooler. Curiously, Haldane chose to transpose G.H.Q. from Baghdad to Karind in the summer months for health reasons, despite the obvious political and logistical disadvantages of running a military occupation from a foreign country.

[16] Mustafa Kemal's nationalist movement in Turkey had risen to strength in the wake of Allied vacillation in finalising a peace treaty. In January 1920, Kemalist forces attacked and drove out French troops occupying Armenian Cilicia. On the promise of Allied protection, the region had been largely repatriated by Armenian refugees throughout 1919; upon France's departure, nearly 50,000 Armenians in the Marash district were massacred at the hands of Kemalist troops.

lumbago. No news of Ed & Edith since I last wrote the mail should be in today.

I am posting you Rudyard Kipling's works next week complete in small volumes, they are only published like that or else 3 large ones which are clumpy so I hope you will like them. Ash Wed: a bad day to keep a feast however we had Commander Wright to dinner last night his wife was away, he is a great artist in oils & Agnes takes lessons from 11 to 1 most days! Edwin Brassey has started building cottages at L.Slaughter: I expect he would have done it here if the silly Parish Council had not applied & now they will have to be done by rates. Edward & Jack Cheetham don't want any! Jim is going strong and Ben Day over 80. I am changing my chauffeur & hope for the best. I expect soon to see 'Sophie and Sam' as they are due home – Edward wants to get her shooting if he can: as 'Sam' doesn't shoot or hunt– too old I expect. They are going to put a cross up at Weston Subedge[17] as a war memorial it will be nice– I want one here someday in the middle of a village– just a plain one.

The snowdrops are lovely & the new Tennis Lawn with yews round one end look nice– also a Victory oak in the pleasure ground, rockery end, and an acacia the other end – hope you will see them some day– Best of love

 take care of yourself

  Yr loving old Mother

   MH Broome Witts

As British families arrived by the boat-load in Basra, six hundred miles up the Euphrates, the Damascus Government was beginning to show its true colours in the absence of the pro-British Amir Feisal, who was attending the peace talks in Paris. While Ramadhan-al-Shallash had been branded a maverick, beyond the Government's control, the official appointment of the zealous Mesopotamian, Maulud al Khalaf, as Governor of the Dair-ez-Zor district, indisputably confirmed Ahd-al-Iraqi as the political spearhead of the Damascus Government.

Under Maulud's supervision, the well-subsidised propaganda campaign against the British accelerated with a vengeance. Letters were sent throughout Mesopotamia to notable Sheikhs urging them to take up the nationalist banner, while agents, sent to the sacred Shi'ite cities of Karbala and Najaf, persuaded clerics to support their call for a *jihad* against foreign despotism. In response, the Civil Administration finally agreed that a show of force was necessary to stifle the spread of sedition. In order to remind local tribes that the land south of the Khabur River was still under British jurisdiction, a small British force was sent up the Euphrates to Salihiyah, 25 miles north of Albu

---

[17] Mrs Witts had been brought up in Western Subedge. Her father, Canon George Drinkwater Bourne, had been rector there from 1846 until 1901. Their house, the Old Rectory, is now called Canonbourne.

Kemal, to establish a military outpost in closer proximity to the provisional national boundary. The gesture, however, was hopelessly inadequate. It only served to ignite the passions of local tribes who were already stirred to the point of revolt by incessant intrigue. Under the leadership of Syrian army officers, the local tribes rose in another vigorous assault on Albu Kemal. Once more, the Damascus Government was warned either to restrain its officials or to face military reprisals and cuts in British subsidies (which, ironically, were funding the propaganda campaign). When British demands were once again ignored, Major Witts' 51st Brigade was ordered to report to Albu Kemal to restore order and to punish surrounding tribes within the Khabur border.

F.V. B. Witts
    Major

H.Q. 51st Inf. Bde.
[Daurah]
Mesopotamia.
February 22nd 1920.

Dearest Mother.

...I dined and slept the night on Thursday with the acting Commander-in-Chief – Gen Leslie who was my Colonel in France, I think you met him and his wife at the Station seeing off the leave train. He has a marriageable daughter-in-law,[18] but not dangerously attractive, though there is not much to choose from out here!!

Thursday our long threatened order to move came along. The situation on the Euphrates far from improving seems to be growing worse – Turkish and Arab Intrigue.[19] More troops are moving and we have got to go and take over command. We move on Wednesday to Albu Kemal, which I expect you will find marked on the map, by car some 300 miles up the Euphrates. It will take us at least 3 days to do it. We are praying for decent weather!

There is no regular postal service, so communications will be at very irregular intervals, and you mustn't be surprised at long gaps without news or even letters getting lost.

I don't know how long we shall be up there, but there is a remote chance of my getting five or six months leave from about April 15th. But it is not much more than remote. If I got a nomination for Quetta I should then go straight back to India in September.

---

[18] It is unclear what F.V.B.W. means by 'marriageable daughter-in-law'.

[19] A Turkish force had gathered at Ras-al-Ain on the Armistice line separating Turkey and Syria. Agents had been sent into Mesopotamia to stir up unrest in the hope that an opportunity would arise out of British weakness to re-establish Turkish authority on the Upper Euphrates.

It has been very cold again – a hard frost this morning.

With very best love,

>Your ever loving Son
>>Fred.V. B.Witts.

F.V. B.Witts

>Major

>>>>[Albu Kemal]
>>>>March 2nd 1920.

Dearest Mother.

Just a line to let you know we got here safely. We had a bit of luck, as a convoy was attacked two hours after we had passed and another the next day – that is yesterday.[20] The telegraph line is down and for the moment we are cut off from the outer world: this letter is going by aeroplane taking news to Baghdad.

I am very fit and enjoying the change of work – back to war again.

I must stop to catch the plane.

Very best love,

>Your ever loving Son,
>>Fred.V. B.Witts.

F.V. B.Witts.

>Major

>>>>[Albu Kemal]
>>>>March 11th 1920.

Dearest Mother.

No letters since leaving Baghdad and we are practically cut off from the world by distance. This is going by aeroplane as far as Anah, and I hope by car on.

After two days torrential rain which flooded the country we have had a spell of decent weather.

There has been a certain amount of scrapping, but the Arabs took a bad knock on the last show which may improve the situation.

I am extraordinarily fit.

Best love

>Your ever loving Son
>>Fred.V. B.Witts

---

[20] Raiding had become endemic on the road towards Albu Kemal and beyond. It not only endangered travellers, but it also had a disastrous effect on trade along the prosperous Aleppo-Baghdad route.

130. Fortified town of Salihiya.

[Albu Kemal]
March 15th 1920.

Dearest Mother.

No mails have reached us since we left Baghdad, but one is on the way up now and should reach us in two days time. But there is a convoy going down today, so I mustn't miss the opportunity of sending a line.

After a scare that we were all going to starve owing to the non arrival of a food convoy, we have put in three days good work punishing the tribes and getting some of our own back. On the 12th we marched 25 miles up to Salihiyah, which you may find on the map, and which at the moment is our furthest outpost. On the 13th, we overran a large bend in the river some four miles across and three miles deep, and destroyed every village on it, bringing in their livestock.[21] Yesterday we returned here, dealing with another two mile stretch on the way down.

In view of developments elsewhere the situation is interesting to say the least of it,[22] and my leave looks rather doubtful. However professionally I suppose I am very lucky to be where I am though I don't look forward to a hot weather here.

Salihiyah is a most interesting old Roman ruin, and I wish I hadn't been so

[21] The punitive tactics employed by the British in Mesopotamia were hardly sophisticated and had a variable success rate in deterring further rebellion. By burning crops and villages and taking livestock, the aim was to inconvenience tribesmen to a maximum degree, whilst rounding up active insurgents to face trial. However, for some impoverished villagers, the repercussions of these measures would have been far greater than an inconvenience.

[22] On 11th March 1920 Amir Abdullah, Feisal's brother, was unofficially crowned King of Mesopotamia by the Syrian Congress in Damascus. In light of the Congress' invented authority, the coronation was clearly absurd. However, the event created a rallying point for nationalist zeal. Abdullah was eventually selected by the British to be Amir of Trans-Jordan in 1921, and became King in 1946.

preoccupied and could have spent some time messing round. It is quite the most interesting ruin I have seen in Mesopotamia. A large solidly built stone fort some 400 yds square, no stones less than 3 ft by 18'. Some excellent arches etc remain. Some coins have been found and it would be a most interesting place to open up as it has not been touched at present.[23]

The weather is treating us very kindly inspite of two most violent duststorms yesterday afternoon.

No more news,

> Very best love,
>
> Your ever loving Son,
>
> Fred.V. B. Witts.

Please pass on my news to everyone, as I really am very busy.

> H.Q. 51st Inf: Bde.
> [Albu Kemal]
> March 21st 1920.

Dearest Mother.

It was very nice to get a week's mails by car three days ago, and another week's by aeroplane yesterday.

I am sorry to hear you cannot get rid of the pains in your right leg: it must be very worrying. It is splendid to hear you have been having such good weather.

…I am afraid the prospects of my getting home this summer are not very bright. I put in for six months leave just before coming up here, but they have now turned it down for the moment owing to the present state of affairs. I have not come across the book you name 'History and Antiquities of Mesopotamia'; and there is no chance of finding it in this out of the way spot.

We have had one more scrap since I last wrote, when we went out to destroy more villages, but the Arabs kept away and only fired at long range. We have been bombing them heavily: I went out one day as I wanted to correct a map. It was a beautiful morning and I thoroughly enjoyed it: it is child's play after flying over the Kurdistan

---

[23] Salihiyah, also known as Dura-Europus ('Dura' locally meaning 'fortress'), was a Seleucid city founded around 300BC, shortly after Alexander of Macedon's conquest of Asia. Thriving as a cosmopolitan trade centre and garrison town, Salihiyah passed between Seleucid, Parthian and Roman hands until, in AD 230, it was destroyed in a Sassanid siege which plunged it into seventeen centuries of obscurity. In the absence of Gertrude Bell, the celebrated archaeologist, who was occupied with administrative work in Baghdad, the American Egyptologist, Henry James Breasted, was summoned to inspect the site. He visited Salihiyah in April 1920 under a strong British escort and immediately discovered a wealth of beautiful frescoes, wonderfully preserved by their burial under makeshift Roman ramparts constructed during the Sassanid siege. Since the 1920s there have been a number of further excavations uncovering a great quantity and variety of artefacts, making Salihiyah an important archaeological site.

Mountains. Moreover it is such a short distance from the aerodrome which itself is at our door. I put in some good work with the Lewis Gun too. At the moment everything points to the tribes having had enough and wanting to throw their hand in. Some of the shaikhs have already come in and the rest should be in by tomorrow evening. This should improve the immediate local situation, but there is no knowing what further developments may come from the [Syrian] Arab Govt.

There is nothing to do here, and it is not safe to wander far from the town: so it would be very dull if one wasn't kept very busy.

We have a very comfortable billet, but it won't be very nice if we have to spend the hot weather here.

This morning I have been attending a sort of miniature Peace Conference.

I don't know when I shall get a chance of sending this away. But I have it ready to go by aeroplane or car, should the opportunity occur.

Very best love,

    Your ever loving Son,

        Fred. V. B. Witts.

                       H.Q. 51st Inf: Bde.

                          [Albu Kemal]

                       March 25th 1920.

Dearest Mother.

I wrote a letter four or five days ago, but it is still on my table as there has been no chance of sending it away. A motor convoy is going down tomorrow, so I am writing another line. It brought in a belated week's mail with your letter of Jan 28th: it was given to an officer to bring up, and he took just four weeks getting here, which gives you an idea of the conditions.

…Since last writing, we have had a mixed existence; our advanced post and also our first L of C post behind have both been attacked, but on each case the Arabs took it in the neck without casualties to us. Then a message arrives from a party seventy miles out in the desert, doing a reconnaissance towards Palestine, that they have been raided and lost everything they possess except their shirts, and one of their number wounded. They ask for a doctor urgently. Our only doctor is sent off on a pony with two black slaves as guides for his 70 mile ride into the desert: I am thankful I am not a doctor! He doesn't speak a word of the language or know anything about the East.

I've also been attending a local peace Conference, which has been successful as far as it goes, as half our enemy Arabs have come in and agreed to our terms. We are now concentrating on the other half.

No more news.

    Very best love.

        Your ever loving Son,

           Fred. V. B. Witts.

1. F.V.B.W. in his mid-twenties.

2. Oil painting of Mrs Margaret Witts (F.V.B.W.'s mother).

The Armorial Bearings of
FREDERICK VAVASOUR BROOME WITTS
late of Chesterton, Cirencester, co: Gloucester, C.B., C.B.E., D.S.O., M.C., D.L.,
Major General in the Army and Lieutenant-Governor, Royal Hospital, Chelsea.

College of Arms
London

I. J. Matthew

Rouge Dragon Pursuivant of Arms.

3. F.V.B.W.'s Coat of Arms, incorporating the Witts Coat of Arms with his medals, many awarded in Mesopotamia. It can be seen on the memorial tablet at the Royal Hospital, Chelsea (*see* colour illustration 22).

4. Canon Broome Witts (F.V.B.W.'s father); he was sometimes referred to by F.V.B.W., in his letters, as 'Dear old father'.

5. Mrs Margaret Witts (F.V.B.W.'s mother).

6. Oil painting by Agnes Witts (F.V.B.W.'s youngest sister) of the front of the Manor, Upper Slaughter.

7. Oil painting by Agnes Witts of the back of the Manor, Upper Slaughter.

8. Oil painting by Agnes Witts (F.V.B.W.'s youngest sister) of Wyck Hill House (*see* p. 118, note 6).

9. Oil painting of Guiting Grange by Susan Boone. Guiting Grange was the home of F.V.B.W.'s Aunt Maggie (Mrs Waddingham Witts). It was inherited from her, first by her daughter Sophie, and then by her daughter Francie.

10. (*Above left*) F.V.B.W. as a Cadet, stepping into the back garden at the Manor.
11. (*Above right and below*) Hand-painted Christmas cards from Mrs Witts to F.V.B.W., 1918.

12. Envelopes sent to F.V.B.W. in Mesopotamia, 1920.

13. Coloured print of the crossing of the Tigris at the Shumran bend February 23rd 1917.

14. The Maude Proclamation in Arabic (*see* p. 160, note 2).

PROCLAMATION.

To the people of the Wilayat of Baghdad.

IN the name of my King and in the name of the peoples over whom he rules I address you as follows:

OUR Military operations have as their object the defeat of the enemy and the driving of him from these territories. In order to complete this task I am charged with absolute and supreme control of all regions in which British troops operate; but our armies do not come into your cities and lands as conquerors or enemies, but as liberators.

SINCE the days of Hulagu your citizens have been subject to the tyranny of strangers, your palaces have fallen into ruins, your gardens have sunken in desolation and your forefathers and yourselves have groaned in bondage. Your sons have been carried off to wars not of your seeking, your wealth has been stripped from you by unjust men and squandered in distant places.

SINCE the days of Midhat, the Turks have talked of reforms; yet do not the ruins and wastes of to-day testify to the vanity of those promises?

IT is the wish not only of my King and his peoples, but it is also the wish of the great Nations with whom he is in alliance, that you should prosper even as in the past when your lands were fertile, when your ancestors gave to the world Literature and Science and Art, and when Baghdad City was one of the wonders of the world.

BETWEEN your people and the dominions of my King there has been a close bond of interest. For 200 years have the merchants of Baghdad and Great Britain traded together in mutual profit and friendship. On the other hand, the Germans and Turks who have despoiled you and yours, have, for 20 years, made Baghdad a centre of power from which to assail the power of the British and the Allies of the British in Persia and Arabia, therefore the British Government cannot remain indifferent as to what takes place in your country, now, or in the future, for in duty to the interests of the British people and their Allies, the British Government cannot risk that being done in Baghdad again which has been done by Turks and Germans during the war.

BUT you, people of Baghdad, whose commercial prosperity and whose safety from oppression and invasion must ever be a matter of the closest concern to the British Government, are not to understand, that it is the wish of the British Government to impose upon you alien institutions. It is the hope of the British Government that the aspirations of your philosophers and writers shall be realised once again, that the people of Baghdad shall flourish, and shall enjoy their wealth and substance under institutions which are in consonance with their sacred laws and with their racial ideals.

IN the Hijaz, the Arabs have expelled the Turks and Germans who oppressed them and proclaimed Sharif Husain as their King, and his Lordship rules in independence and freedom and is the Ally of the Nations who are fighting against the power of Turkey and Germany: so indeed are the noble Arabs, the Lords of Kuwait, Najd and 'Asir.

MANY noble Arabs have perished in the cause of freedom at the hands of those alien rulers the Turks who oppressed them. It is the determination of the Government of Great Britain and the Great Powers allied to Great Britain that these noble Arabs shall not have suffered in vain. It is the hope and desire of the British people and of the Nations in alliance with them that the Arab race may rise once more to greatness and renown amongst the peoples of the Earth and that it shall bind itself to this end in unity and concord.

O people of Baghdad, remember that for 26 generations you have suffered under strange tyrants who have ever endeavoured to set one Arab house against another in order that they might profit by your dissensions. This policy is abhorrent to Great Britain and her Allies for there can be neither peace nor prosperity where there is enmity and misgovernment. Therefore I am commanded to invite you, through your Nobles and Elders and Representatives, to participate in the management of your civil affairs in collaboration with the Political Representatives of Great Britain, who accompany the British Army, so that you may unite with your kinsman in the North, East, South and West, in realizing the aspirations of your Race.

(Sd) F. S. MAUDE, LIEUTENANT-GENERAL,
Commanding the British Forces in 'Iraq.

S.G.P.B.—2095—3255—1,500—7 3-18.

15. The Maude Proclamation in English (*see* p. 160, note 2).

16. Eastern Bank, Baghdad cheque book *c*. 1920. It is interesting that the bank's name was recorded not only in English and Arabic, but also in Hebrew.

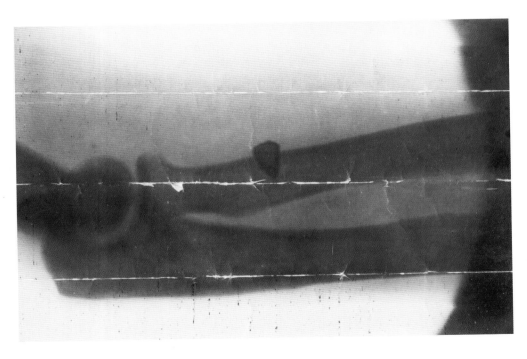

17. X-Ray: 'bullet in my arm 20th December 1916'.

18. The silk Kashan rug which F.V.B.W. sent home to his mother in 1920 with his friend
Norrie Fuller. It arrived shortly before she died.

19. Statue of the 'Winged Figure of Victory' commemorating the deeds of the Bengal Sappers and Miners. Please see Appendix XVIII. The plaque on the base depicts the crossing of the Tigris at Shumran, with the minarets of Baghdad and the Spiral Mosque of Samarrah on the horizon (photos by Lieutenant-Colonel Charles Holman, R.E. Museum, Chatham).

20. Postcard of the Thomas Denny
stained glass window at the east end of
the chapel in Upper Slaughter church.
Please see Appendix XVII (photo by
Clive Barda).

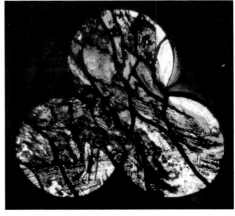

21. Photo of the Trefoil stained glass
window on the north side of the
chapel in Upper Slaughter Church.
Please see Appendix XVII (photo by
Clive Barda).

IN MEMORY OF
MAJOR-GENERAL
SIR
ALEXANDER DOUGLAS CAMPBELL
KBE CB DADJMC COMMANDER LEGION OF MERIT U.S.A
1899 - 1980

LIEUTENANT - GOVERNOR & SECRETARY
OF THIS ROYAL HOSPITAL
1957 - 1962

IN MEMORY OF
MAJOR-GENERAL
FREDERICK VAVASOUR BROOME WITTS
CB, CBE, DSO, MC, KStJ, DL, CROIX de GUERRE
1889 - 1969

SAPPER STAFF OFFICER & COMMANDER

LIEUTENANT-GOVERNOR & SECRETARY
OF THIS ROYAL HOSPITAL 1944-1948
COMMISSIONER 1948-1957

IN MEMORY OF CAPTAIN
CHARLES GRAHAM
TROUGHTON DEAN M.B.E.
ROYAL ARTILLERY 1914-1921
CAPTAIN OF INVALIDS 1929-1963
AND ADJUTANT 1939-1952
ROYAL HOSPITAL CHELSEA
AUTHOR OF A HISTORY OF
THIS ROYAL HOSPITAL
DIED 30TH OCTOBER 1963
IN HIS 70TH YEAR
This tablet is erected by his widow son & daughter

22. F.V.B.W.'s memorial tablet at the Royal Hospital, Chelsea. He served there as Lieutenant-Governor from 1944 until 1948 and as a Commissioner from 1948 until 1957.

F.V. B.Witts
   Major

[Albu Kemal]
March 30th 1920.

Dearest Mother.

Many thanks for your letter of Feb 18th – your birthday, which came up by air from Baghdad and was delivered with one from Frank in a message bag dropped by the aeroplane on the field of battle! as we moved out for three days thirty miles upstream of this place to strafe a section of the tribes which still remain hostile. We came back yesterday after a very successful show and found the rest of the mail – papers etc – on arrival. The only unfortunate incident was that my staff Captain doing observer in an aeroplane stopped a bullet in the leg. He is not bad, but it leaves me single handed for some time as we are very short of officers up here thanks to casualties and sickness.

We are hoping for an early settlement as a result of our strafe, which would mean our returning nearer Baghdad. Though this is not a bad spot in its way: the climate is wonderful for Mesopotamia. We are still wearing our thick clothes, while they must be sweltering in the heat down below.

Do you notice how Swan and Edgar's shares have gone up lately. They have doubled in price since I put £200 into them: I wish I had put more into them. I have been in financial luck lately. Two and a half years ago I put about £400 of savings into the Indian War Loan: I sold out the other day and transfered it home by cable getting just £900 thanks to the rise in the Rupee: I wish I had put all my savings into India and kept them till now!

I am glad to hear the pains have gone but am sorry you are so weak. You must take care of yourself for my sake – as you are always telling me! You must be glad the winter is over.

Very many thanks for posting Rudyard Kipling's Works. I look forward to their arrival.

I must stop as this is going down by air to Baghdad, and the machine is just leaving.

With very best love,
      Your ever loving Son,
         Fred.V. B.Witts.

F.V. B. Witts
  Major

[Albu Kemal]
April 4th 1920.
Easter Sunday.

Dearest Mother.

No mails in since I last wrote but there's a motor convoy going tomorrow so I must send a line as one never knows when one will get another opportunity.

I've spent an unusual Easter Day out in armoured cars strafing the hostile tribes: with good results too as this evening they want to come in. I hope they may and let us get back to peace and quiet.

It is beginning to get hot and the days have come when one must wear a topi. However if the tribes pay up we ought to get a move on in the right direction within a fortnight – not before I'm afraid.

> No more news today,
> Your ever loving Son,
> Fred.V. B. Witts.

THE MANOR,
UPPER SLAUGHTER,
GLOS.
April 7. 1920

Dearest Fred –

Yours of March 2nd came last week so the aeroplane did me a good turn! & I was glad to hear you were fit & well – things seem very unrestful your way & in Ireland [24] – I am much distressed I cant take Frank & Ruth in for want of servants; Frank has had flue & wants a change- & does not like an Hotel. No news of anyone else the S African mails are still very uncertain. Agnes has gone to Apphie for a few days. I have seen no one – one of East's daughters was married here Saturday. The Reading rooms are to be opened in about a month & I believe I am to be asked to do it & present War Medals to the school children – Capt. Willes is making a swimming Bath in his field beyond our pond, & it wont hold!!! he seems to have plenty of money to throw away & is a most extraordinary man – Hunting ends this week.

We are busy with poultry – George looks after them & we have a lot of young chickens. Mabel keeps no end, she has no housemaid! no servants now will stay in

---

[24] Towards the end of March 1920, the British Government introduced the notorious 'Black and Tans' Reserve Force into the ranks of the Royal Irish Constabulary to deal with the growing momentum of the Irish revolution. So-called because of their initially varied uniforms, the 'Black and Tans' were, for the most part, war veterans with little training in policing. They soon became loathed in Ireland for their thuggish behaviour and indiscriminate attacks on civilians, consolidating hatred for the British and support for nationalist values.

the Country – too dull – Wyck Hill[25] is for sale & Sapperton Park. Emily comes back this week – Michael motors over from Aldershot where he is in Barracks. I wish you were there with a job & could do the same. This is a dull letter but there is no news. We have Gen: Townshend book on Mesopotamia.[26] George says it is very interesting but I don't think you were there then, it is his defence about Kut – Best of love- take care of yourself.

Yr loving old Mother

MHB Witts

F.V. B. Witts

  Major

[Albu Kemal]

April 11th 1920.

Dearest Mother.

No mail for a week, and I don't know when this will go down.

We had hoped to have finally settled things by this time, but the last people to settle have been too long paying up their fine so we have started strafing them again: I only hope it will bring them to heel soon: though it will mean our returning to the heat of Baghdad and a tent. Although it warmed up a lot, it is still delightfully cool for the time of year up here.

There is not much to do, when work gets a bit slack: I have started learning to drive a Ford van in my spare time, and I find taking the air occasionally in an aeroplane a very good tonic.

The aerodrome is literally at our door, within 50 yards of our billet, and at night the aeroplanes are wheeled right up to the billet for safety.

I had hoped to have got down to Baghdad this week, but I am afraid there is not a chance for another fortnight. My friend Fuller is off home at the beginning of May, and I want to see him before he goes.

My own leave has been definitely stopped which is rather disappointing though perhaps not very surprising. However one cannot get everything in this world, and I am very lucky to be getting all this experience. My general tells me he is recommending me for a Brevet Lieut Colonelcy, but there is not a hope of my getting it; anyhow it is pleasing to hear it said.

I ought to hear soon about the Quetta Staff College, though I wish it were Camberley.

No more news.

Very best love,

Your ever loving Son,

Fred. V. B. Witts.

---

[25] See Illustration 8 in the Colour Section for an oil-painting of Wyck Hill by Agnes Witts.

[26] Townshend, C. V., *My Campaign in Mesopotamia* (Thornton Butterworth Ltd, 1920).

F.V. B. Witts
Major

H.Q. 51ˢᵗ Inf Bde.
[Albu Kemal]
April 23ʳᵈ 1920.

Dearest Mother.

A fortnight's mail came in yesterday with your letters of March 3ʳᵈ and 9ᵗʰ, and all the usual papers. Particularly welcome as there is not so much doing at the moment and literature is very scarce. So glad to hear my squirrel furs are so warm, and that your new chauffeur seems a success. I should certainly much prefer Camberley to Quetta, but it is better to try and make certain of one than miss both: I don't think I can complain of my luck and not getting on fast enough!!

I am very keen to see the new Tennis Lawn and shrubs, but I am afraid it won't be this year.

India have just asked me to spend my leave there later on to give advice on bridging! A fine way of spending one's leave!

There seems no immediate prospect of getting away from here, though we are gradually squeezing our fines out of the tribes; but there are bigger questions arising from the Peace Conference.[27] At the moment everything is very peaceful and the roads are quite safe which is a refreshing change.

I have had a very quiet week. One morning I took the air to point out the boundary of the hostile tribe; another day I spent in the country looking at defensive positions: it was the first real exercise I had had for some time, and it did me a lot of good.

I am threatened with trouble with my teeth and shall have to go to India for that if for no other reason: the dentists out here are not much good, and their stuff is spoilt by the climate.

It is beginning to warm up but is still delightfully cool compared with Baghdad where fans and ice are the order of the day. They have promised us a billet if we go back to Baghdad, which is something.[28]

My General has just had his leave to England stopped and is very fed up!

With very best love,
    Your ever loving Son,
        Fred. V. B. Witts.

---

[27] Heads of Government from Britain, France and Italy had finally met in San Remo, northern Italy, to discuss the fate of the Ottoman Empire and conclude the distribution of mandates. With the Armenian question still unresolved in the U.S.A., the American delegate took no active part in the discussions, sitting only as an observer throughout the Conference.

[28] The commandeering of private homes was a great source of resentment for merchants and other property owners. Wallace Lyon, a political officer stationed in the Mosul wilayat at the time, affirmed that 'the British, military and civil, had possession of nearly all the best houses in the capital, and the attitude of the British to the inhabitants was in general the same as what had made them so unpopular in India' (Fieldhouse, D. K., *Kurds, Arabs and Britons*, p. 72).

H.Q. 51st Inf: Bde
Mes: Ex: Force.
[Albu Kemal]
April 30th 1920.

Dearest Mother.

…I am so sorry to hear you are such a cripple and George bad too.

Fuller should be leaving Baghdad about now for England with his Mother and the silk carpet: I had hoped to have been back before he left and am very sorry to miss him: I hope the silk carpet will get home.[29]

I looked up the Daily Graphic of March 18th; it is certainly an excellent likeness of Frank.

We have had an uneventful week but expect to be moving back soon, and shall be quite sorry to leave our present good billets. It is still reasonably cool though we have had a succession of unpleasant sandstorms.

It is two months today since we got up here after running the gauntlet – as we now know – of a large raiding party who were out to do us in. We never expected to be here so long, but it is always the case.

Apart from one's work there is little to do up here: I have been continuing my efforts to learn to drive a Ford, and could get home alright now if I was stranded in the desert with my driver ill, but I don't know how I should get on in a crowded thoroughfare.

Some enthusiasts have been trying to fish but have not caught anything yet. My only exercise consists of a walk before breakfast and another after tea!

No more news,

Very best love,

Your ever loving Son,

Fred. V. B. Witts

THE MANOR,
UPPER SLAUGHTER,
GLOS.
May 3. 1920.

Dearest Fred –

I am beginning my letter early as it is decided I must go to a Nursing home for a Rest Cure to regain my strength so I go to Chelt tomorrow under a Dr. My pains are much better but I am so weak something must be done. I shall add a line later.

On April 30th I got 4 letters from you March 11th, 15th, 21st and 22nd all most welcome & I let everyone know the news. I am so glad you keep fit.

I cant find the name on the map – Tennis is beginning at Stow & the Rooks will soon be ready to shoot!

---

[29] See Illustration 18 in the Colour Section.

May 4th Edward's birthday 41 today. A Major Daniel[30] has been in this village calling on Captain Swayes & he asked if there was a relation here of Witts in India!! So he must have met you – I wish I had seen him. Good bye dear old boy best love

Yr loving old Mother

MHB Witts

THE MANOR,
UPPER SLAUGHTER,
GLOS.
May 12.1920
Stow Fair![31]

Dearest Fred

Yours of March 30 came 3 days ago. Glad you got letters & papers- No I had not noticed Swan and Edgar but <u>Harrods</u> have taken it over and that Firm is I believe paying enormously – glad of your good luck. No news of Jack and Elma Edward writes they hope to be home about Xmas- Mealie's doing very well and all looking well. I am in Chelt in a Nursing home for 10 days but hope to be home soon long before you get this. The Dr wanted me to have a 'rest cure' and my legs put under the X-rays which has been done and nothing found wrong. It is only weakness and I already feel a lot better and can walk across the room much stronger. I daresay it may be months before I get strong if ever quite as before but one can't expect it at 72. & I shall be able to enjoy the garden & sit about & get a motor ride so one may be thankful. Frank is at Pirbright in Camp for 3 weeks. Ruth with her sister near Newbury pulling up after an operation in her throat but she has got over it well – they have their house 7, Chester Square London SW – and hope to get in, in June – George & Agnes were here yesterday & George addressed some of your papers. Edwin Brassey has left the Army as Lt Col: Frank has been to court and got his DSO. And I have a capital picture of him and Ruth leaving the Palace! which I hope to show you some day. One of the Nurses here has been at Bagdad & all over that country. Tennis has begun. I am doing my best to get strong or I should not be here!!

dearest love

Your loving mother

MHB Witts

131. Buckingham Palace Investiture 1920: Frank and Ruth Witts.

[30] Major Daniel had just returned from Staff work in Mesopotamia (June 26th 1920, Chapter XI).

[31] See note 51 Chapter VII, p. 252.

In Mesopotamia, meanwhile, the verdict of the San Remo Conference, finally deciding the fate of the Ottoman Empire, was causing a stir. As predicted, the mandates for Lebanon and Syria had fallen to France, while Great Britain had been awarded those for Palestine, Mesopotamia and Trans-Jordan. In the fifteen months since the signing of the Armistice, the Civil Administration had been hampered severely by its inability to confirm any long-term policy in Mesopotamia. Now, with the acceptance of the mandate, it could finally shed its provisional character and begin working towards a model of independence which took both Mesopotamian and British interests into account. However, by spring 1920, the political and social climate in Mesopotamia had turned against the Civil Administration and the mandate.

Grievances were widespread, even without the catalytic effect of Syrian propaganda. In rural areas, tribes unfamiliar with assertive government resented the efficient collection of revenue; in Baghdad, political dissidence had continued to rise in the absence of any reasonable attempt to begin integrating Arabs into government; throughout the country the dominance of a Christian power over a mainly Muslim population presented an unshakable moral dilemma. That is not to say, however, that the Civil Administration was without a strong support base. Political stability and the subsequent expansion of agriculture, infrastructure and trade, were reasons enough for the majority of the population to turn a blind eye to the Administration's flaws. But, as had been demonstrated repeatedly in the war against the Turks, tribal allegiance would depend on Britain's ability to maintain its role as the superior military force in Mesopotamia.

F. V. B. Witts
   Major

H.Q. 51st Inf Bde.
[Anah]
May 13th 1920.

Dearest Mother.

Just a line to let you know I am quite fit. The last week has been very full of incident, and I have had a very busy time, starting with an international (!) conference on May 5th, when I motored up fifty miles with the Political Officer to meet the representatives of the Arab Government and fix a new boundary.[32] This was fixed up, but the local Arabs naturally thought our withdrawal a sign of weakness and started worrying us at every conceivable opportunity and we have been scrapping with them nearly every day.

---

[32] The boundary with Syria was established on a line just below Albu Kemal, making a retirement of British forces necessary.

We got down here on the 11th after quite an exciting journey and now they are worrying the line down below us. I think they want to turn us out of the country! – I for one should not be sorry to go!

We have got a very nice billet, but being over three miles away from camp not half so convenient. It is built right out into the river which is quite pretty here, and we get a very nice breeze.

I must stop to catch the down convoy.

Very best love,

> Your ever loving Son,
>> Fred. V. B. Witts

THE MANOR,
UPPER SLAUGHTER,
GLOS.
Royal Nursing Home Chelt:
May 19 1920.

Dearest Fred

Yours of Easter Sunday came on the 17th & I hope by now you have done with the tribes. Forgive this bad writing but I am mostly in bed & my fountain pen is coming to an end! George brought my car down yesterday and we went to Birdlip and back by the Seven Springs – the country looked lovely. I go home Sat the 22 & hope to have much benefited by the rest & massage. It is only my back is so weak – 'worn out' I expect so I must just take life easy. Geoffrey is coming to us for Whitsuntide. Tennis at Stow begins this week. George & Mabel are playing in the tournament Agnes & Com: Wright. I have no news of Jack & Elma but I see letters are all held up out there [in France] with strikes – the outlook in England is very bad – they say 'lean years' are coming as of old. Stow Fair was a success & horses sold well. I have some lovely lilies of the valley from home they are just out. Old Jim & Ben Day are going strong. Your Godson Peter, otherwise John Edward goes to a preparatory school at Eastbourne in Sept. I believe is rather a sharp little chap – Joan is grown up! & Geoffrey learning office work so as to go abroad when he is 21. I believe they have got him with some firm.

Best of love I am doing my best to get strong

> Yr loving old Mother
>> M H B Witts

[Anah]
May 20th 1920.

Dearest Mother.

…Rudyard Kipling's books also arrived: I have been looking forward to them for ages and they are doubly appreciated up here where there is nothing to read.

I was very relieved to see them arrive. It is the first convoy that has not been fired on for a fortnight. It also had a complete new outfit of summer suitings and boots and shoes for me. So I am completely set up again now.

I have been having a rather harassed time what with incessant raids on our convoys and a violent hurricane which blew all our aeroplanes away. The raids are I suppose the natural result of our withdrawal from Albu Kemal and may stop when it is seen we don't intend to go further at any rate for present.

As if scrapping with the Arabs was not sufficient, there has been a certain amount of bickering amongst our own people which has taken all my tact and a lot of my time to smooth over. The net result is that I am very behindhand with my office work, not that that really matters.

My friend Fuller left for England on May 3rd. I am very sorry he has gone, and not to see him before he left. I hope he has taken a carpet back for you.

All my friends seem to be leaving the country – the only thing is to clear out oneself. No news of Quetta yet, I am afraid I can have no chance.

My teeth want attention badly, otherwise I am keeping extraordinarily fit.

No more news tonight,

> Very best love,
>> Your ever loving Son,
>>> Fred. V. B. Witts.

> THE MANOR,
> UPPER SLAUGHTER,
> GLOS.
> May 26, 1920.

Dearest Fred

Best congratulations your name was in yesterday's paper in the Despatches. I am so glad to hear what the general says in your letter of April 11th it is nice & cheering. I saw in the paper of May 22nd that on the 5th May Albu Kemal was handed over & our troops moved down – so I expect you have changed your quarters?

I got home Sat 22nd & am better tho frightfully weak & the great heat wave we have now on is not helping me. Apphie is here looking after me. Geoffrey only had 3 days he is 6ft, quite tall enough. Jack & Elma are in London. Jack looking for a job, may get one in Constantinople! but does not know. I wish they had a home to go to. Everything is very forward – gooseberries lilies in perfection. It is a bit disappointing about your leave but it cant be helped & I do wish for Camberley but there seems such a block everywhere. England is almost too full! George & Agnes have gone to the Stow Tennis Club. I hope you will see Fuller before he leaves.

– Best of love & good luck to you

> Yr loving old Mother
>> M H Broome Witts

F.V. B. Witts
Major

[Anah]
May 31st 1920.

Dearest Mother.

...I am sorry letters have not been arriving regularly, but posts in these parts do not exist and it is merely a matter of chance how one gets a letter away. I try and write regularly but I know there have been some long intervals owing to moves and work.

Interesting to hear Capt. Savory should come to Slaughter – it shows how small the world is.

Things have been quieter lately up this side as we have frightened them over to the Tigris where they find raiding more profitable, as they are at present less prepared for them.

If things remain quiet we hope to move back to Ramadi in a week or ten days and settle down there for the hot weather, though personally I much doubt if there will be much settling down about it: I think this unrest will go on the whole summer.

There was some trouble in Baghdad last week, but nothing serious.[33]

I was delighted to get a letter from Edward by the aeroplane this morning too. He seems to be doing very well, and the price of his land appears to have gone up extraordinarily.

It is beginning to get hot, but we have a delightful billet on the edge of the river which gets all the wind, and we shall be sorry to lose it though we get fans, ice and other luxuries when we get back to Ramadi. But the billet there is in the town away from the river. Our present house here is however alongside an old Turkish ammunition dump which was blown up by us in 1918, there are thousands of dud shells lying about in every direction: one of them exploded yesterday afternoon without any damage being done luckily.

Very best love,
Your ever loving Son,
Fred.V. B. Witts.

THE MANOR,
UPPER SLAUGHTER,
GLOS.
June 2. 1920

Dearest Fred

Yours of April 23 came last week. No you have done very well & Father & Uncle George would be proud of you – Aunt Sybil writes & 'so is his old Aunt' –! Low of India but I hope they would make it worth your while?[34] & pay you well, for it would

---

[33] The arrest of a minor clerical agitator in Baghdad had provoked public riots which took a number of armoured cars to disperse.

[34] Mrs Witts is referring to India's efforts to entice F.V.B.W. to spend his leave there, giving bridging advice (April 23rd 1920, p. 356).

be no holyday. I think by the papers you must have moved – I see the Shah of Persia has been ill by heat in Bagdad – so hope you missed it. We have had very hot suns here for May. Sorry about teeth all are the same trouble to everyone.

I am so glad you are learning to drive a motor, you will find it so useful in England. Jack & Elma are here for 3 nights busy looking for a small house in London as he hopes for a job, something to earn a little. I am a bit stronger & hope to get well in time but I shall stay quiet here for the summer. I never saw the place look prettier. You will be welcome when ever you come. They say Wyck Hill is sold[35] – all big places are going or shutting up. No news of Edward he is busy with his Tobacco crop which is worth £1000 if he can get it in without frost.

Sorry for the General's bad luck [on having his leave cancelled].

I only get out for a drive most days so have no news & seen no one –

dearest love God bless you

    Yr loving Mother

      MH Broome Witts

Although tensions in the Upper Euphrates region had lulled in recent weeks, the wider situation in Mesopotamia was deteriorating rapidly beyond British control. The Islamic fasting month of Ramadan had initiated a dangerous reconciliation between Sunnis and Shi'ites in Baghdad and throughout the country.[36] Mosques were thus converted into political platforms for nationalist speeches. With the priesthoods of Karbala and Najaf rising to the trumpet calls of the nationalists, moderates were finding it increasingly difficult to divert the population from becoming consumed by revolutionary doctrine. Meanwhile, between Churchill's retrenchment plan and Teheran's demands for reinforcements to counter Bolshevik aggression in Persia, British military resources in Mesopotamia were being stretched to the limit. In the midst of these troubles, the first signs of a coordinated revolt began to appear on the Syrian border.

On 26th May, the Civil Administration received reports that a Sharifian force of some 1000 mounted tribesmen had crossed the Khabur River and were converging on Tel Afar, a British outpost some 35 miles west of Mosul. With striking sanguinity, comparable to that of General Nixon in the run up to the disaster at Ctesiphon, General Haldane dismissed pleas for

---

[35] Wyck Hill (see Illustration 8 in Colour Section) was sold to F.V.B.W.'s future father-in-law, Major Arthur Wrigley.

[36] Three months later in September 1920, Churchill reflected, 'It is an extraordinary thing that the British civil administration should have succeeded in such a short time in alienating the whole country to such an extent that the Arabs have laid aside the blood feuds that they have nursed for centuries and that the Suni and Shiah tribes are working together' (Catherwood, C., *Winston's Folly*, p. 88).

132. Tel Afar.

military support from Tel Afar's political staff. Later, however, and after a considerable delay, he agreed to send two armoured cars to discourage any violence. On that same day, the entire British political staff at Tel Afar were murdered by townsmen and Sharifian tribesmen alike, along with the crews of the two armoured cars despatched from Mosul. Haldane had made a grave misjudgement of the situation, and yet, remarkably, he still refused to recognise that Mesopotamia was on the verge of an outright rebellion. On the 6th June, just two days after the incident at Tel Afar, Haldane left Mesopotamia to go on a scheduled inspection of the British position in Persia. Meantime, on the Upper Euphrates, hostile tribesmen resumed their vigorous harassment of the 51st Brigade.

F.V. B. Witts
   Major.

[Anah]
June 12th 1920

Dearest Mother.

I am not quite certain when I last wrote though I know it is time I wrote again.

I have had a very busy week, as they attacked our advanced post at Al Qaim [10 miles below Albu Kemal] the day before we had intended to withdraw it. This meant altering all our plans and having to arrange to punish the people responsible. We had quite an anxious time, but things went off excellently and we punished them severely on the 10th, burning all their crops which had just been harvested and stacked. Everything is quiet again at the moment, but there is a lot of unrest in the land.

The same day as they attacked here, there was an outbreak up near Mosul [at Tel Afar].

We hope to spend the rest of the hot weather at Ramadi: our heavy kit and stuff left at Baghdad have already come out there.

I hear the Quetta Staff College list is out, my name is not on it and from what I hear only much more elderly gentlemen than myself, which is as it should be I suppose, though I should have liked to have got there without having to work for it though perhaps it would do me good!!!

I have been bathing the last few days; I find it very refreshing to body and brain these hot anxious days. The water is beautifully warm, and there are some charming islands where one can be in perfect peace – unless they started shooting from the opposite bank!

There has been no mail for ages owing to difficulty of getting it up the ninety miles above Hit where it is no longer safe for cars to move without strong escort.

We are getting some fruit and vegetables now: excellent cucumbers, tomatoes, apricots and figs, though they are rather tasteless.

No more news now.

> Very best love,
> Your ever loving Son,
> Fred.V. B.Witts

The following letter is from Major Witts' brother, Frank.

> KING'S GUARD
> ST. JAMES'S PALACE
> S.W.
> June 15ᵗʰ 1920

My dear Fred

I owe you a letter and the comparative leisure of King's Guard will be well employed in writing to you. I gather there is not much chance of your coming back to England this year but I hope you will be able to come next year, though I suppose your career is in the East, and you will have to follow it. Ruth & I have just been down to Slaughter for the week end, and I want to tell you about our visit. We had not been there since December last so it was extraordinary & very depressing to see the great change in Mother. At present she is supposed to be better than she has been lately, but she is still a cripple, has to be carried about the house, and she still suffers a good deal of pain. If she stays on at Slaughter I don't think she will live much longer, but it is very difficult to know whether it is wise or even possible to move her. I felt that more might yet be done for her but George & Agnes who alone know all the circumstances are satisfied that everything has been done. I am going to try and find a London specialist to see her, as I think London & the excellent treatment she could get here are the best things for her, if she can be persuaded to leave Slaughter. But it is very hard to know what is best to do. She realises that she cannot face another winter at Slaughter; she is very weak and depressed, and kept on asking me whether I thought she would ever get better again – in itself a bad frame of mind, which I think another doctor might counteract. She does not want to be separated from George & she feels that he might not follow her to London. Agnes is busy painting & longs to get away I think. The whole atmosphere at Slaughter is very depressing: it seems as if the light of the place had gone out and decay has set in. So I do hope Edward will soon be home. Don't think I am an alarmist but I do want you to realise – if you have not already, that Mother is very bad and cannot go on much longer unless she really gets better again and loses her pain. We are moving into our new house this week and it is all very exciting – but it is distinctly bad luck that we go to Aldershot in October, as we shall have to let it. There is much talk of the future of the Guards and of abolishing us but I don't think they will do it. Full uniforms are much more serious, as their cost is likely to be enormous, and nobody wants to spend money on them. Today is the first day of Ascot, but we are not going – it is very expensive & very tiring and neither of us are awfully well. I am the real crock – the doctor says it is the result of the war, but it is certainly taking me a long time to feel strong again.

The world is still upside down and nothing seems to be going straight; your country of Mesopotamia seems to be one of the difficulties. Don't for goodness sake start another war out there! We might be drawn in and my taste for blood has entirely evaporated!

    Best of luck
        Yours
        Frank

Frank Witts was not alone in his sense of weariness; the British public as a whole were tired of war and all in its train. Economic retrenchment, social upheaval and lingering grief from 4 years of fighting had extinguished the last remnants of romantic imperialism from the British psyche. The thought, therefore, of becoming embroiled in another prolonged conflict in the Middle East was, generally speaking, anathema to the entire population. However, events in Mesopotamia had already moved beyond the control of the Civil Administration; by June 1920, a costly uprising was almost inevitable.

On a personal level, Frank's distressing reports of their mother's ailing health heightened Major Witts' need to be granted leave, but the news came just as personal desires had to be discarded once again for military duty. With war in Mesopotamia looming on the horizon, the British, at home and abroad, found themselves unprepared and lacking any appetite.

CHAPTER XI

MASS INSURRECTION

Letters: June 22ⁿᵈ – Oct. 24ᵗʰ 1920

Since the beginning of 1920, a rift had emerged between the Civil Administration and the British military command regarding security. The Civil Commissioner, A. T. Wilson, relying on the advice of his political officers stationed throughout the country, was well aware of the gathering threat, but was unable to convince General Haldane to share his concern. Haldane, meanwhile, was under enormous pressure to meet Churchill's retrenchment plan, forcing him to run the occupation on what he called

133. General Sir J. Aylmer Haldane.

'rigid economy, not to say frugality'.[1] His obstinacy in rejecting Wilson's advice was derived both from his commitment to economise, and from his habitual optimism; he was more inclined to believe what he wanted to hear. He thus allowed himself to be swayed by those less disposed to agree with Wilson's unappealing predictions.[2]

By mid-June, Wilson's fears of a violent climax to mounting unrest were on the verge of becoming reality. The tribal propensity for violence and looting, suppressed arduously over the last two years by British political officers, was resurfacing with alacrity in the name of Allah and an Arab-ruled Mesopotamia. Further encouragement was given to insurgents by the strategically weak arrangement of Haldane's visibly depleted force, spread thinly across the country, exposing garrisons to the dangers of isolation. In short, the opportunity was gleaming for malcontents to drive the British forcibly from Mesopotamia.

---

[1] Haldane, A., *The Insurrection in Mesopotamia*, p. 66. In spring 1920, General Haldane had only 4200 British and 30,000 Indian troops stationed within the country – a hopelessly inadequate force considering the size of the country and the length of the necessary lines of communication.

[2] In explaining the reasons for his optimism on the state of the country, Haldane cites a letter from Miss Gertrude Bell, Oriental Secretary to the Civil Commissioner, which expressed strong doubts that an outright rebellion would ever materialise (*The Insurrection in Mesopotamia*, p. 46). In response, A. T. Wilson later wrote: 'it was, to say the least, imprudent of him [Haldane] to prefer her [Bell's] private miscalculations to the measured misgivings, amply supported by reports from all centres, of her official superior' (*A Clash of Loyalties*, p. 275).

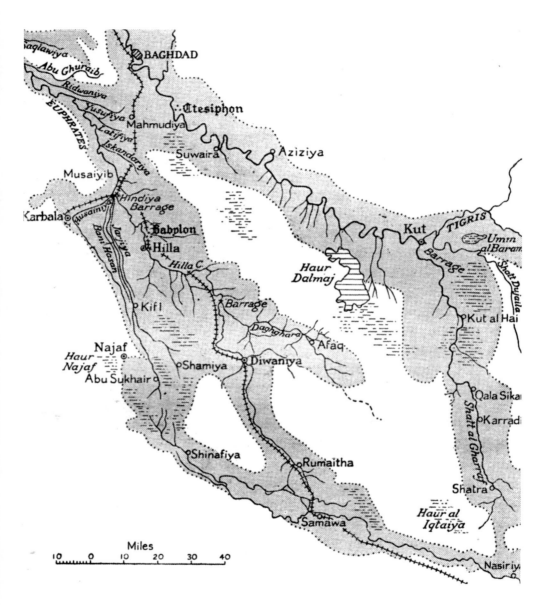

Map 14. The Tigris and mid-Euphrates

Back in England, the security of the British administration in Mesopotamia had taken a prominent role in parliamentary debate, escalating Mrs Witts' fears of growing British commitments there. Detailed information on the Middle East was hard to come by in the Cotswolds, but the impression gleaned from sporadic news reports was hardly encouraging, much like the tone of Major Witts' letters. Some good news, however, was forthcoming; Edward's reports of his promising mealie (maize) and tobacco plantations in Rhodesia were especially pleasing at a time of economic hardship.

> THE MANOR,
> UPPER SLAUGHTER,
> GLOS.
> June 22. 1920

Dearest Fred

No letter for ages – well I expect you are all over the place! Edward says his mealies are doing well & the 'Baccy' so he wants the heating & electric light & Bulbs done – it is a big job – but I am inclined to do it in Oct & Nov: & go away for those months I am getting better. My pains have gone & it is now to get up my strength

…Wyck Hill is up for Auction sale whole or in lots & most of Wyck Village.

Col Butter's only son was killed. Mervyn Wingfield is selling some office property in Gt Rissington & Taynton & fishing with it. I don't think you will know the country side soon! I shall add a line in the morning. They are using the Tennis ground now & it looks very nice, strawberries growing strong & Jim & Ben Day wonderful.

June 23. Yours of May 13th and 20 from Anah have just come so glad you have the books, they are very good. You have had a worrying time & your poor teeth – I rather wish you were out of the country – the Arabs will never have done; they understand nothing but force – the Gov: is getting worried about Mespot: I shall look out for the carpet it is very good of you to send it & it will do for your own house some day… Molly Nisbet is here but we cannot have many guests so short of servants… I do love getting your letters God bless you dear love

> Yr loving old Mother
> MHB Witts

Jack has not got a flat yet I wish they had as Elma expects a baby in Oct:

F.V. B. Witts
    Major

Ramadi
June 26th 1920.

Dearest Mother.

I am afraid a letter is long overdue, but I find it very hard to write regularly when on the move and getting no mails for ages.

We finally left Anah on the 18th in armoured cars. There was a bit of a scrap the previous day. That day we stopped at Haditha [30 miles down the Euphrates] where a very large mail with three weeks of letters from you met us. Many thanks for your letters of May 3rd, 12th and 19th.

The Major Daniel you mention as having been at Slaughter was on the Staff out here and went home on leave at beginning of January.

I am so sorry to hear you have had to go into a nursing home at Cheltenham, but am very glad you went and that you really benefited by it.

We stopped again at Hit and finally got here on the 20th. We hope to spend the hot weather here in peace and comfort. We are living in quite a good billet with electric light and fans – Unlimited ice and soda water. It is very nice getting back to all these home comforts, but it makes one think of the troops still out who are having a pretty rotten time of it. We share the billet with a small hospital.

But it remains to be seen how much peace we get: the country is seething with unrest, and all the troops have been called out in Baghdad where it is not safe to go about after dark. It remains to be seen if the declaration of our mandate will quieten things down or bring them to a head. At the moment we seem to be in about the quietest spot there is. There has been a lot of trouble up Mosul way.[3]

They look upon our little war up here [on the Upper Euphrates] as closed down and have sent most complimentary telegrams on the way it was run. 'It was excellently commanded, and the Staff work could not have been better.' etc, etc. The General has put me in for a Brevet Lieut Colonelcy which is very pleasing though I have not got a hope of getting it. It is also very nice to know that the powers that be in Baghdad appreciate our efforts.

The General has gone off this morning on a week or ten days leave to Baghdad to meet his wife, who has been there all this time. It is no place for a woman, though they live in a sort of fort with a strong guard.

Very best love,
Your ever loving Son,
    Fred. V. B. Witts

---

[3] F.V.B.W. is referring to the incident at Tel Afar in early June.

F.V.B.Witts.

Major

Ramadi.

July 4th 1920.

Dearest Mother.

Very many thanks for your letter of May 26th and congratulations. I was very pleased to get a mention: it was for our little trip in the mountains behind Aqra when I went up to Mosul a second time.

I am sorry to hear you are so weak; you must feel the heat tremendously, though the actual temperature recorded in the papers makes one smile out here, though it makes a great difference not adapting ones clothes and customs to the heat.

I don't think I shall know any of Apphie's family when I meet them!

With any luck I shall be home about Christmas, but this country is very disturbed and it is quite likely it will not be possible to get away. There has now been trouble between Baghdad and Basra, where they have been trying to interfere with the railway.[4]

The General has been in Baghdad on ten days leave, leaving me in charge. There has been some scrapping round Anah, but luckily nothing serious. He comes back tomorrow morning.

There is not much to do here. I go for a ride before breakfast each morning: it is a great improvement on Anah in that respect as one can get a good gallop in any direction, but there is nowhere nice to bathe, though I bathed last night for the first time here from a launch.

There is a tennis court but it is not a good one and is laid out the wrong way so that the sun is very bad in the evening. Later on we hope to get some polo, though here again the ground is very indifferent.

Our Society here consists of one Regt, one Battery and an Ambulance with three or four political officers.

No more news,

    Very best love,

    Your ever loving Son,

      Fred.V. B.Witts

A week before Major Witts wrote the above letter, a murmur of rebellion had arisen in the Diwaniyah district of the Mid-Euphrates. The forced liberation

---

[4] With lines of communication in Mesopotamia stretching for over 2,000 miles and insufficient troops to defend them, railway tracks were often torn up by insurgents. As a result, mobile columns which relied on trains for transport were slowed down enormously (*see* F.V.B.W.'s letter of 15th Aug 1920 for his description of the retreat from Diwaniyah) and it became difficult to keep isolated outposts supplied with food and ammunition.

134. Rumaitha – buildings defended are within white line.

of a local Sheikh, arrested by British authorities on account of an overdue agricultural loan, marked the beginning of three months of insurgency, costing over 8,500 Arab and 2,300 British and Indian casualties, and the British Treasury around £40,000,000.[5]

The British garrison at Rumaitha, a small town on the Shatt-al-Hilla branch of the Euphrates, was the first to encounter concentrated Arab aggression, worked up to a fury by religious hatred. The garrison was invested in a determined siege by townsmen and tribesmen alike, far outnumbering the defenders who, thus incapable of breaking out, were in alarming straits due to a lack of provisions. If starvation or massacre was to be avoided, and the germ of the insurrection stifled before it could spread further afield, the British response had to be quick and resolute. However, with his force deficient in numbers and dispersed sparingly across the breadth of the country, General Haldane could only find two infantry battalions and a cavalry squadron at hand at such short notice. The small column marched on Rumaitha on the 7th July, only to be repulsed immediately outside the town by a gathering of around 5000 insurgents.

The situation was becoming critical. Whilst each new day under siege exacerbated the plight of the Rumaitha garrison, the failure of the relief column struck another blow to British prestige, encouraging other tribes to join the revolt. In Britain, the papers reported an ominous outlook.

---

[5] Casualty numbers are rounded estimates taken from Haldane, A., *The Insurrection in Mesopotamia*, p. 334. The estimated financial cost is taken from Antonius, G., *The Arab Awakening*, p. 315.

The Manor,
Upper Slaughter,
Glos.
July 13. 1920

Dearest Fred

No letter from you since I last wrote and I gather from the Papers much disturbance out your way. Weather better & I have been sitting out all day. My pains are gone if I can only recover the use of my legs & get strong but I expect I shall have to use a stick now for ever – but still that does not matter if I can get about –

…Jack writes you offered him 2 arm chairs, but as prices go now he thinks one will be nearer the mark. Everything is just double[6] – he hopes to get into his abode in 3 weeks as they are doing it up… Frank & Ruth were having their first dinner party! & find their house all they could wish. Agnes is busy with her oil painting & I should not wonder if she goes for more lessons in the winter. I expect I shall have to move out when it gets cold – London or abroad to the sun if I have the strength. I think Edward & Edith better not return at Xmas, things are frightful & if we wait another year it might cost less to warm the house. George & Agnes have been picking fruit, Jim is bad & everyone has to turn a hand to anything – they went for tennis to the Barrows at Farmington[7] & Col B said he picked all his, – wages are so enormous now. Edwin Brassey has bought a house near Chippenham as Col of the Lifeguards his time was up – Sophie & her old man seem very happy you shall join us in her present Dickens' works – no end of volumes – she wants them…Annie comes on the 19th for 3 days but as I don't get up to breakfast I am a poor hostess. Good night a line in the morning.

July 14. Post has brought nothing but I know you always write. I am going for electric treatment today & hope to finish this week.

Bourton Flower Show August 11th things are resuming their usual course now. All papers & Blackwood went as usual.

    dearest love
      Yr loving Mother
      MHB Witts

In Rumaitha, a world apart from the Bourton Flower Show, aeroplane drops of food and ammunition were keeping the beleaguered garrison alive while General Haldane hurried to assemble a second relief force. He was acutely aware that the lives of the garrison depended absolutely on the success of this relief attempt. He thus selected a formidable force of twelve

---

[6] To meet heavy expenditure, a legacy of the war, the Government increased national debt, creating inflation.

[7] The Barrows at Farmington were old friends of the Witts family.

135. Diwaniyah and camp.

infantry battalions for the task, under the command of Brigadier-General F. E. Coningham. Attached to Coningham's staff was Major Witts; he would have been conscious of the risks Haldane was taking in committing almost his entire mobile force to a composite column, draining other districts of troops and thus exposing them to attack. The die, however, was cast. Coningham's force reached the outskirts of Rumaitha on the 19th July, encountering a strong Arab resistance at the same point as their previous victory twelve days before. This time, however, British efforts paid off; on the 20th July Rumaitha was re-occupied and the garrison, emaciated and exhausted, was delivered from their ordeal.

By this stage, the insurrection had spread across most of the Mid-Euphrates region. It was evident to General Haldane that a consolidation of strength was going to be the only hope of British survival before reinforcements could be mustered from abroad. Coningham was thus ordered immediately to abandon Rumaitha and march his enlarged force 35 miles up the Shatt-al-Hilla to Diwaniyah. Five exhausting days later, Major Witts was finally at leisure to update his mother on recent events.

F.V.B. Witts.
   Major

H.Q. 34th Inf: Bde Diwaniyah
Mes: Ex: Force.Lower Euphrates
July 28th 1920.

Dearest Mother.

It is ages since I wrote – over three weeks ago from Ramadi; – but things are moving out here and one never knows what the morning will bring forth.

The expected outbreak occurred on July 1st at Rumaitha. A small garrison got cut off there and the first relief column met with no success. A Column of half a Division was organised and my General given command and he asked for me to go with him. We relieved Rumaitha on July 20th after a stiff fight and withdrew here.

In the meantime the rising had spread, and another Battalion is cut off in Kufa. On the 24th a small column met with a reverse near Hillah and those tribes joined in.[8] Result is railway is cut behind us and we are isolated. However we are strong enough to look after ourselves and fight our way out. But it is very hot for fighting and there is not much water about.

If reinforcements are not pushed out very quick, I am afraid it will be a sad tale to tell.[9] Unlike India every Arab is armed with a modern rifle, and are marvellous at collecting and lying up for a small detachment and then dispersing when a decent force arrives.[10] However we live in hopes that the Govt will not let us down.

They have played the very devil with the Basra – Baghdad railway and we are now dependent on the river [Tigris] again.[11]

[8] F.V.B.W. is referring to the 'Manchester Disaster' – the worst single defeat of British forces in Mesopotamia in 1920. On 23rd July, a small column of Manchesters and Sind cavalry, acting as vanguard to a stronger force, was sent from Hillah on the road towards Kufa in response to its seizure by insurgents. The column had been instructed to avoid serious conflict and to make an initial march of only 6 miles from Hillah, but, having set out in the summer heat without adequate water arrangements, the column's commander was forced to advance a further 9 miles beyond his original objective. This second, unplanned march not only led the column into hostile territory, but also exhausted the new recruits who were fresh from England and unaccustomed to the perilous climate. Rest, however, was out of the question as gathering numbers of insurgents precipitated an immediate retreat back to Hillah. During the withdrawal, the column, in no condition to defend itself properly, suffered repeated assaults from mobile bands of Arab horsemen. There were 240 British and Indian casualties and 160 men taken prisoner. Although this was an intolerable loss of troops at a time when manpower was so limited, the real cost to the British came in the resulting encouragement and support the disaster generated for the nationalists.

[9] Having requested, on 7th July, an infantry brigade and field battery to be made ready for dispatch from India, Haldane informed the War Office a fortnight later that he actually required one, if not two, whole extra divisions. Because many of the reinforcements had to be recalled from leave, Haldane was told not to expect any arrivals in Mesopotamia for a month.

[10] The insurgents were often led by Arabs who had been officers in the Ottoman army. They were thus often accomplished in Turkish military tactics such as the tactical withdrawal, used to great effect against the British during the war.

[11] The safety of the River Tigris as a line of communication was paramount to the survival of the British. To their good fortune, the rebellion was, for the moment, confined to the Mid-Euphrates. Haldane was well aware, however, that should the influential Muntafiq confederation in the Baghdad wilayat join the insurgents, the Tigris tribes of Bani Lam and Bani Rabia were bound to follow, with disastrous results for the British.

I wonder if you have heard a word of it all at home, or if they have kept it quiet; but I suppose they can't have this time much as they would like to.

The latest papers full of economy and reduction of troops out here make us smile. They will have to double the present army out here to pull us out of the fire.

However enough of our troubles. I wonder how you all are at home. I have not had a mail since I left Ramadi.

> Very best love,
>> Your ever loving Son,
>>> Fred.V. B. Witts

I hope to get this away by aeroplane.

> THE MANOR,
>> UPPER SLAUGHTER,
>>> GLOS.
>>>> July 28ᵗʰ 1920.

Dearest Fred

Yours of June 12 came 2 or 3 days ago & was most welcome as there has been great stir in the papers & H of C. about Mesopotamia & rightly so – why should we keep you all out there?[12] No news here – weather bad rain every day but I am glad to say I am much better if I can only keep so. No news yet of Fuller & my Rug but it is a long journey. Edith says Edward is still out looking at land! Jack & Elma have got into their flat. Frank has been in for his Major exam & passed so far. Is it safe to bathe?[13] Are there no crocodiles about or sharks[14] one is so afraid say nothing of snipers! The year seems going very fast. I am sorry about Quetta – old duffers should be put on one side!! We should have won the war before but for their blunders. Your Godson Peter, really John Edward goes to school in Sept either to St Leonards or Eastbourne I forget which – he & Apphie come here on the 4ᵗʰ for a week or two I hope... Our extended reading room is nearly ready for opening – I hope to get over in my wheeled chair to see it soon... Best of love take care of yourself

> Yr loving Mother
>> MHB Witts

This is a dull letter but I have to keep quiet ...I have never missed a mail & I know you do the same.

---

[12] With expenditure and the British death toll rising dramatically, pressure was mounting on the Government to pull out of Mesopotamia. Various newspaper articles suggesting the causes of and the solutions to the Arab rebellion were also appearing with added frequency. Colonel T. E. Lawrence, a staunch critic of the Civil Administration, published his own highly influential views in *The Times* of July 23ʳᵈ 1920 (see Appendix XIII).

[13] See F.V.B.W.'s letter of June 12ᵗʰ 1920, p. 364-5.

[14] Sharks were quite common in the Shatt-al-Arab and the lower reaches of the Tigris and Euphrates. A number of men from Force 'D' had been bitten whilst bathing.

The letter below is from Apphia Woodroffe, Major Witts' eldest sister.

The Manor,
Upper Slaughter,
Glos.
August 10th 1920.

My dear Fred

You will be glad to hear that Mother saw Dr. Shaw yesterday. He is staying at Farmington, & we asked him to come & see her. He hopes to be able to get her strength up a bit. His visit has done Mother a great deal of good & cheered her up. He says that it would be madness to think of taking her abroad for the winter & strongly advises us to let her remain at home – I agree with him, as I think that she will be so much more comfortable here than anywhere else. She has a very good lady's maid, but I am afraid is not very strong.

I came down with Peter last Wednesday & am staying another week, as Agnes is away with the Nisbets. Peter goes to school on Sept 20th to Eastbourne. He has done very well at the little morning school he has been at for the last two years & I have had a charming letter about him from the lady who keeps it. He has been working with boys a year to 2 years older than himself. He tumbled into the stream yesterday while playing on its banks in the field.

Geoffrey comes on Friday for 10 days – He is working in an accountant's office.

> Yours affectionately
> Apphie

The Manor,
Upper Slaughter,
Glos.
August 11th 1920.

Dearest Fred

Yours from Ramadi June 26 came August 10th. I am glad you have some letters at last. I am glad you have some comforts as they say the heat is very great out there now. Churchill seems to have made a mess of everything as usual & spends so much money.[15] I wish you may get your step for you deserve it. Dr Shaw, who has been here on a holyday came to see me yesterday & his report is good – but he does not advise my going abroad for the winter, travelling uncomfortably & such unrest.

Dr Shaw lives at St Leonards & cured me of the Flue & gout 2 years ago so it was better to have him than a specialist who Frank wanted. Edward & Edith are asking

---

[15] The accusation against Churchill for being a spendthrift in Mesopotamia was a little harsh considering that he had been the chief proponent of a ruthless retrenchment plan. Ironically, however, his efforts to save money weakened Haldane's force to such a degree that considerable reinforcements were now needed at great expense.

for news of you the papers are so distracting & get no real news. We are hoping for some summer weather. Apphie is here with Peter a nice little lad & he seems to be clever. They are going with George to the Bourton Flower Show & Miss Morris' tea party! Do you remember it. Sophie comes over often to play tennis she likes our new ground – hers is not in order. Agnes is away for a change – I hope she may go abroad with her friends for painting. Emily is going to Switzerland for Xmas. I wonder if she will leave as we are raising the rent ...

Hope you will get leave next year. Edward too will be home till then I expect. Best of love take care of yourself

Yr loving Mother

MHB Witts

Jack has gone back & says his flat is beginning to look nice. Elma's Baby is due in Oct.

While in Parliament, as Mrs Witts attests, the Government was beginning to sweat under the weight of its Mesopotamian failures, along the Mid-Euphrates, British forces were fighting for their very survival. Since the Manchester Disaster the entire region had succumbed to the nationalist cause and, with the clerics of Najaf and Karbala churning inflammatory doctrine out across the country, the rot was bound to spread.

With reinforcements yet to arrive, consolidation was more vital to the British than ever. On 30th July, Coningham's column, accompanied by Major Witts, abandoned Diwaniyah for Hillah, some 55 miles further up the Shatt-al-Hillah, where the British garrison and remnants of the Manchester column had been put under siege by the local population. Before the march, all non-essential stocks were abandoned in Diwaniyah apart from surplus ammunition, food, water and medical supplies. To carry these provisions and the numerous casualties, a freight train was selected for transport. This was despite the fact that it would undoubtedly slow the retreat and restrict the march to the line of railway track. General Coningham was unaware at this point, however, that a substantial portion of the track between Diwaniyah and Hillah had been destroyed.

In *The Insurrection*, Haldane writes, 'our tenure in Mesopotamia and with it our position in North-West Persia hung...on the retreat from Diwaniyah.'[16] The Herculean effort demanded for the success of this operation suggests that the men involved shared Haldane's views.

---

[16] Haldane, A., *The Insurrection in Mesopotamia*, p. 128

F.V.B.Witts
   Major

H.Q. 34th Bde.
Hillah
August 15th 1920.

Dearest Mother.

It is over a fortnight since I last wrote but I have lived through one of the 'events' of my life.

We started on our withdrawal from Diwaniyah on July 30th, leaving hundreds of thousands of pounds worth of stuff behind, and eventually arrived here on August 9th – just eleven days to do the 55 miles. After the first fifteen miles the railway was pulled up in places all the way along. In all a length of twelve miles of broken railway with all sleepers missing had to be passed by our train on which were our sick and wounded, supplies and ammunition. We had to pull up the line behind us, lay it in front move on and pull it up again behind. As our train was a mile long it meant some carrying. And all the time hundreds of Arabs all round, continually sniping and waiting for any opportunity offered to close with us. Worst of all we struck the hottest spell of the year – 120° in the shade – and in many places were short of water.[17] The hardship to the men has to be experienced to be realized. They stuck it wonderfully and we killed quite a lot of Arabs and burnt all their villages within reach.[18]

At intervals all the way along we picked up small posts left for the protection of the railway which had all been cut off and attacked once or twice and were very pleased to see us. One had drunk its last drop of water, another had eaten its last ounce of food.

However we roped them all in and got them all and everything we started with back to Hillah where we arrived on the 9th, and have since been having a rest, writing up history etc.

We are cut off from the outer world here, no trains since end of last month, though railway has not been so very badly damaged. Our only means of communication are aeroplanes and wireless.

The other Brigade – some of whom were with us, – are now out opening the railway. The whole immediate cause of the general rising was the disaster to the Manchester Regt.

Goodness knows what is going to happen and where it will all end. It will take months of time, thousands of troops, and millions of pounds to re-establish order and

---

[17] Food supplies were also wanting as rations for only 6 days march had been loaded at Diwaniyah. Fortunately, however, this misjudgement was recognised early on and rations were decreased accordingly.

[18] The sluggish progress of the march allowed punitive expeditions to branch out and 'strafe' outlying villages, the inhabitants of which were thought to have been guilty of tearing up the railway tracks.

136. Mesopotamian scenery.

reopen the railway through to Basra. Will the British public face it or shall we be told to quit?[19]

Reinforcements are arriving in Baghdad, which may stop things spreading, but the outlook is still black.[20]

It will of course upset all plans for leave or getting back to England; though I think it is up to them to relieve any one who has been five years out here!

However as an ambitious soldier, I ought to be pleased at being mixed up in another war and at having had two good opportunities already, having played a prominent part in both the relief of Rumaitha and the withdrawal from Diwaniyah.

At present 17 Divn HQ are here, but they are probably going back to Baghdad leaving us in charge.

I paid Hillah a flying visit just over a year ago when I was with 17 Divn.[21] The ruins of Babylon are just outside, but it is not safe to wander about there now without about two battalions.

I was delighted on arrival here to get your letter of June 16th – nearly two months old! There must be at least another months mail waiting for me in Baghdad.

The Times may well cut up about Mesopotamia. I have always said we have bitten off more than we can chew; and there doesn't seem much doubt about it now.

We have got a very comfortable billet here, fans, electric light, ice etc. Most acceptable after our eleven days trek in the scorching desert. But it will make it all the harder when we have to move out again. However the worst of the hot weather must be over with any luck.

I hope you are keeping well and strong and looking after yourself. No need to

---

[19] Public disillusion about Mesopotamia had swayed the Government into considering evacuating the country entirely, or perhaps abandoning the Mosul wilayat and consolidating around Baghdad and Basra. The future of British involvement in Mesopotamia hung in the balance.

[20] Three infantry battalions and a Howitzer battery had arrived from India by 15th August.

[21] See F.V.B.W.'s letters of 29th June & 6th July 1919, p. 293-7.

worry about absence of news from me. No news on these occasions is always good news. I have had two great friends killed here so far: it always seems to be the best in the land who stop them.

My horse fell and rolled on my leg the other day, and my ankle has not yet quite recovered, but it is nothing serious. It doesn't stop me getting about, but it gets tired quickly.

Very best love

Your ever loving Son

Fred. V. B. Witts.

This I hope will go by aeroplane tomorrow.

THE MANOR,
UPPER SLAUGHTER,
GLOS.
August 18th 1920.

Dearest Fred

No letter to acknowledge but I trust all is well at Ramardi[22]...

...Mr Walter Scott has died somewhat suddenly, also Frank Cambray in this village – he went to Canada & came over with the Canadians to fight. Mr Eales has been over & administered the H.C to me with Apphie & George I had not been to church since Easter – do you ever get a service. Jack is busy settling in I have 'lent him' an old oak table for his dining room – he seems to find furnishing a big job and I fear has never saved I only wish he was earning money it is a worry – dearest love

Yr loving Mother

MHB Witts

The letter below is from Frank

7, CHESTER SQUARE,
S.W.1.
Aug.19th 1920

My dear Fred.

I feel it is ages since I wrote you a line but somehow the weeks pass so quickly by and seem all so fully occupied. However Ruth is away for a couple of nights so I have an opportunity which I will try & make good use of. Mesopotamia is again very much to the fore in the papers and one feels that things are not going very well out there. It is difficult to know the rights and wrongs of the policy being carried out, but it does seem strange that we should still have to support such a huge army out

---

[22] This comment by Mrs Witts illustrates the shortcomings of postal communications during the insurrection. F.V.B.W. had left Ramadi in early July and had had many adventures since then, but his mother was still ignorant of any of his activities.

there, when the country is in a very dicky financial state, and any return on the outlay must be in a very distant future. What is extraordinary is that our beloved Labour Party who make trouble over most things don't seem to bother their heads about it. Perhaps they are clever enough to see that the country continues to be weakened by the Mesopotamian war, and that is an object they seem to have set before themselves! Such a fuss they made with their council of Action when there was a chance of having to send help to Poland![23] However, the Poles seem to be doing well again and anyhow the Labour Party are not the only people in England who are determined to avoid another war! Everything points to a coal strike next month: what will be the result goodness knows, but revolution is a word on everyone's lips just at present. If it does come to a fight I think the extremists of the Labour Party who are only Bolshevists and in Bolshevist pay will be got rid of.[24] But the prospect of any sort of row of this kind is not exactly pleasant. I suppose that a great war necessarily produces alarums & excursions of this kind. Then Ireland – no one knows what is to be done and no one has any practical solution in spite of numerous letters to the papers which profess to have found a cure. You can imagine the size of the English army of occupation over there when I tell you that there is only one infantry battalion left at Aldershot.[25] An interesting side light is a letter I read today from one of our officers on leave over there in which he requested that official letters to him might be enclosed in unofficial envelopes, otherwise they were invariably opened & considerably delayed before he got them by the 'republicans'! In the meantime we here are gradually and somewhat painfully learning to be peace time soldiers and are busy getting ready for full uniform. I have not ordered mine yet, as I think we shall be about the last to have

[23] In May 1920, the Government proposed lending military support to Polish forces for their attack on the Soviet Ukraine. In response, the strong arm of the trade unions, with the determined backing of the Labour party, swung into action with revolutionary fervour, encouraging London dock-workers to refuse to coal ships suspected of containing munitions bound for Poland. Three months later, in early August, a Russian counter-attack into Poland recharged the Government's policy for intervention. The secretary of the Labour party formed a reactionary 'Council of Action' which threatened, with the support of the trade unions, to bring Britain's industrial engine to a standstill. The Polish victory at Vistula on August 14th relaxed the tension in Parliament but it was recognised that, if the issue had come to a head, the Government would have been forced to back down.

[24] Britain's budding Bolshevik party, formed on 31 July 1920, was a testament to the growing unrest and division over the established system of industrial organisation. Bolshevik ties with the Labour party were close from the start, but the parties were never officially affiliated, despite the repeated efforts of the Bolsheviks. The feeling amongst Conservatives, however, as Frank Witts attests, was that elements of Bolshevism existed on the fringes of the Labour party and would continue to do so until purged by a revolution – a very real possibility in the social climate of 1920.

[25] In 1920 the British were supporting a force of around 40,000 men in Ireland. Amid the highly disruptive guerrilla tactics employed by both the I.R.A. and the Black and Tans, Whitehall, itself divided over policy in Ireland, was beginning to lose authority to the growing influence of the Republicans.

it as we are by way of going to Aldershot and with councils of Action & coal strikes we may yet never require it! I am going in for the promotion exam in October: I have passed the practical part and am feeling fairly confident about the written so long as I am not stumped by too many unknown Army Forms. We have made ourselves very comfy here and feel very annoyed at having to leave London in October – however I hope we shall let the house well and on the proceeds we are planning a tour abroad in the winter. I am putting in for three or four months leave, as I have not been well all the summer. I am much better again now but the doctor says I want a really long rest. I have had a letter recently from Edward who seems very busy: Rhodesia is going well and he is investing more money out there. Jack is in London but we hardly see him or Elma. He came & dined with me on Guard last week and enjoyed himself thoroughly. They have got a sort of maisonette – two floors of a converted house, and have just finished getting into it. Agnes came & spent two nights here a fortnight ago on her way to the Nisbets. I think she is thoroughly miserable at Slaughter and will not stay there much longer. Mother does not seem to get any better from all accounts and therefore I fear it will go hard with her during the winter. It is very difficult to know what is best for her to do and I suppose in the end she will stay at Slaughter, but it is not fit for her. She is completely dependent on George and I don't think he will make much effort to move from Slaughter. Ruth and I are going to Grizedale at the end of the month for a fortnight and I do hope the weather will be kind. July has been a dreadful month but August has improved. Well I look forward to hearing from you again but I expect you are kept pretty busy, and I do hope you will soon establish peace out there. We have had enough war and rumours of war.

    Best of luck

        Your affect Brother

          Frank

War, however, was in full swing on the Mid-Euphrates. For the majority of troops who had endured the gruelling march from Diwaniyah, the comforts of a rest and a good billet, such as had fortunately befallen Major Witts, were out of the question. The railway to Baghdad was in urgent need of repair to re-establish efficient communications with the capital. At the same time, to the north of Hillah along the Euphrates proper, the Hindiyah Barrage[26] and the town of Musayib held valuable strategic advantages. Musayib was a major river crossing for insurgents; its capture would hamper severely enemy movements on the eastern side of the Euphrates. The capture of the Hindiyiah Barrage, meanwhile, was part of a grander scheme for the suppression of recalcitrant tribes of the Mid-Euphrates basin. Positioned on the bifurcation

[26] F.V.B.W. had visited the Hindiyah Barrage a year before, describing it, in his letter of 6th July 1919, as 'the one bit of enterprise the Turks [had] showed.' (p. 295)

that splits the Euphrates into the Shatt-al-Hillah to the east and the Shatt-al-Hindiyah to the west, the Barrage was designed to regulate water flow down each branch of the river to control irrigation and to optimise cultivation. Conversely, Haldane could use the Barrage as a weapon to dry out the precious crops of the rebellious tribes lying in the basin below.

Both positions were captured without much opposition and railway communications to Baghdad were also soon restored, precipitating the end of Major Witts' recuperation.

F.V.B.Witts.
Major

> H.Q. 34th Inf Bde
> [Hillah]
> Mesopotamia.
> August 22nd 1920.

Dearest Mother.

Railway communication was reestablished with Baghdad on the 19th, when the first train brought a truck load of mails including a fortnight's for me with your two letters of June 22nd and 30th.

I am very glad to hear Edward feels he can afford the heating etc, but I wonder where you will go while it is being done. So very glad to hear you are feeling better and that the pain is less. I hope the improvement has been maintained.

I am glad to hear Jack has fixed up a home.

We have had an almost complete rest since we came here, although the place was attacked three nights ago and again all day yesterday; but nothing suits us better than for the Arab to attack, he invariably gets it in the neck and suffers heavily at small expense to ourselves.

We go out again in three days time to strafe certain villages and bring in a battalion at present guarding a bridge,[27] which is to be left to its fate, as the general situation in the country has got much worse and concentration is essential. The tribes are up round Feluja, and Ramadi is cut off with H.Q. 51st Bde. I am wondering if I shall ever see the kit I left there again. Col Leachman – a byeword in this country – the Political Officer at Ramadi, who lived with us for three months at Albu Kemal and Anah has been treacherously murdered, and Mesopotamia has suffered an irreplaceable loss, and

---

[27] Having been essential to the retreat from Diwaniyah, the Jarbuiyah railway bridge over the Shatt-al-Hillah was rendered superfluous after Coningham's force had made its crossing. Haldane, nevertheless, had ordered a small garrison to remain at the bridge to preserve it for future operations and to give the impression that Diwaniyah had not been abandoned permanently. With the spread of insurgency, however, and the subsequent increase in demands on manpower and transport, the Jarbuiyah position became untenable.

myself another friend, who gave me tremendous help on the Upper Euphrates.[28]

The Situation develops quickly and it is impossible to foretell what it will be by the time you get this. Troops are coming from India but it will take a lot to clear things up.[29]

It has been very hot, and it is a relief to think August is nearly over, though September will not be pleasant for trekking about.

Very best love

    Your ever loving Son

        Fred. V. B. Witts

As A. T. Wilson inferred in his eulogy, Colonel Leachman's fearsome reputation and personal acquaintance with prominent Sheikhs had been major factors in keeping the Arab tribes of the Mosul wilayat at bay. Naturally, therefore, it followed that, after Leachman's death, the tribes of the Shammar confederacy, based around Tel Afar, took courage and began raiding British communications, spreading disturbances southwards towards Samarrah. Further east in Kurdistan, the notion of Arab nationalism was reviled by the Aghawat. In certain areas, however, the turbulence sweeping through Mesopotamia had invigorated the bellicose instincts of the Kurds, prompting them to drive out the flailing British. When a marauding band of the Central Kurdish Surchi tribe crossed the Greater Zab into the Erbil district, claiming to be the vanguard for a Turkish army, the Erbil tribes broke their bonds with the Civil Administration and joined the Surchi in their rampage. The region was only brought back under British control in mid-September when the Surchi made the fateful mistake of attacking an Assyrian refugee camp, unaware that its warlike inhabitants had been armed, trained and officered by the British.

Back in the Hillah district, punitive measures were starting to have some effect against insurgents; rifles were no match against modern British artillery. In the

[28] Brevet Lieutenant-Colonel Gerard Leachman, first mentioned by F.V.B.W. in his letter of 2nd Oct. 1919, was an extraordinary character, erudite and forceful with a legendary career in Mesopotamia. His mysterious murder by the son of his friend, Sheikh Dari, on the 12th August 1920 in the Falluja district, sent a wave of shock and grief throughout the country, testament to Leachman's unequalled fame. In the *Basra and Baghdad Times*, A. T. Wilson wrote the following eulogy: 'Distinguished alike by his soldierly qualities and his strong sense of duty and discipline, his courage, enterprise and ability earned him both amongst his countrymen and amongst Arabs a reputation enjoyed by no other political officer and his death is a serious blow to our position on the Upper Euphrates.'

[29] Since the outbreak of the insurrection, a total of 7,410 combatants had arrived from India by the end of August 1920; they were followed by a further 8,024 in September (Haldane, A., *The Insurrection in Mesopotamia*, p. 344).

chaos surrounding them, and with bitter resolve, the British were finally clawing back some advantage. In England, meanwhile, the holiday season had started.

THE MANOR,
UPPER SLAUGHTER,
GLOS.
August 25th 1920.

Dearest Fred

No letters but from the papers you are still shut in – the Gov: ought to be ashamed away on holyday & no thought of our soldiers or money![30] Weather still treacherous no summer – no shooting yet corn so late. Jack is coming for a week end later to try for birds – he & Elma have settled in & the Baby is due end of Oct

Edward & Edith are enjoying themselves. Apphie has just left me but promises to come in Oct: Agnes is home after paying visits. My old Dr reports well of me, strength better but I must stay quietly at home, have no fatigue & no excitement, in fact I do little but read & sleep! & I have a maid. Frank & Ruth are going to her people for 10 days shooting in Cumberland. I wonder when you will ever get a 'good long' holyday. They say the Tennis lawn here is very good – it is very pretty as I get round it sometimes in my wheel chair. This is a dull letter but I have no news – Best of love & may God take care of you

Yr loving old Mother
MHB Witts

Copies of the original telegraph and adjoining letter below are in appendix XIV.

POST OFFICE TELEGRAPHS.   **25 AU**

This Form must accompany any inquiry respecting this Telegram.   **20**

Office of Origin and Service Instructions.

Hillah 23 6 P M   *Handed in at} 2.40*   *Received here at} 3.30*

TO{ *P C O 6 P M*
Witts Upper Slaughter

Very fit Busy killing Arabs

Fred

---

[30] Despite the frantic political atmosphere in Britain, Mr. Lloyd George and several members of cabinet had repaired to Lucerne, at the foot of the Swiss Alps, for a two week break.

The Manor,
Upper Slaughter,
Glos.
August 25th 1920.

Dearest Fred

I wrote this morning but at 3.30 today comes your telegram – how good of you – but Arabs can kill back so look out! Agnes birthday – I don't know how the wire has come not as usual but so welcome

Yr loving old Mother

MHB Witts

I send this in case it may catch the mail.

F.V.B. Witts.
Major

H.Q. 34th Bde.
Hillah.
August 31st 1920.

Dearest Mother.

We got back on the evening of the 29th after a very successful week. The first day we met a large mob of Arabs with banners flying, who intended to give us a fight, but when we got down to it their spirits failed them and they fled, without our having a single casualty.

However they had flooded the road for a mile and our progress was very slow. We had to get on to the railway embankment, which also had been badly knocked about.

On the 28th we attacked Imam Hamza the head village of the particular tribe we were out to strafe, and here again their spirits failed them and they fled before our attack. We burnt up and blew up the place.[31]

On the 29th we started back to Hillah following the river and burnt up every village along the bank. Considerable opposition had been expected, but hardly an Arab was seen.

There is no doubt the spirit of the rebellion is broken in this particular area, and it is a thousand pities that we have not got time to see it through.

As it is we are entraining for Baghdad tomorrow with our whole brigade and are wondering where we shall go then. Most probably Persia way to open the road to Karind where all the ladies and children are.

The rebellion is still spreading. Samarrah where I spent seven months in 1917 is

---

[31] Imam Hamza lay in territory belonging to the Albu Sultan tribe whom Haldane asserted 'have some reputation as warriors' (*The Insurrection in Mesopotamia*, p. 151). Their courage, however, was of little worth against British guns.

137. Maude Bridge looking
     East.

now 'up' and the railway to Mosul has been cut.

I keep extraordinarily fit, though I should like a chance of getting my teeth seen to. I have been 'on operations' for six months now – it was Feb 27th we left Baghdad for Albu Kemal.

It is much cooler, and quite cold at night. So I think the heat won't worry us again. No mails, as I suppose they are trying to get to Ramadi.

Very best love,

Your ever loving Son,

Fred.V.B.Witts.

THE MANOR,
UPPER SLAUGHTER,
GLOS.
Sept. 1th 1920

Dearest Fred

I hope things are better than the Times tells us – no mail through but I hope you are in safe quarters. Weather quite autumn. Edward still talks of returning the end of this year & letting Bee rent his Farm for 3 years but nothing is settled…[32]

Best of love Yr loving Mother

MHB Witts

THE MANOR,
UPPER SLAUGHTER,
GLOS.
Sept 8th 1920.

Dearest Fred

Still fighting when will it all end – & we are going to open the New Reading Room today & there is a fete at Copse Hill at least Edwin has lent the grounds next mail you shall have full particulars – I am to open the room at 2.30- but I am not strong enough to go to Copse Hill & give the medals away – they are handsome

---

[32] Ted Bee was a farmer from Lower Slaughter who helped Edward Witts with his farming out in Rhodesia for many years.

138. Copse Hill Fete 8th August 1920: presentation of medals by Lieutenant-
Colonel Edwin Brassey.

bronze ones and you will have one!! There is not much doing now the weather is a
little better. Frank has to go to Aldershot the end of this month so they have let their
town house I wish I could have seen it first. Jack & Elma seem settled in comfortably.
Edward & Edith very gay in Rhodesia. Apphie comes here next month when I hope
George will go away for a change he is so good & devoted to me – helps to carry me
up to bed every night – Agnes is absorbed in her painting & goes abroad next month
with her friends the Wrights.

    Best of love God protect you
        Yr loving Mother
           MHB Witts

From September 1920 onwards, Major Witts' brother, George, who was caring
for their mother at home, frequently enclosed his own letter to his brother, to
go with that of his mother. Both letters always came in a single envelope.

THE MANOR,
UPPER SLAUGHTER,
GLOS.
Sept 14th 1920.

Dearest Fred

    Yours of the 28 July arrived on Sept 10th very little news from the War Office I see
Gen Cunningham is yours.

    I had the misfortune to fall down in my bedroom on Friday my leg slipt from
under me & I broke my thigh bone above the knee so I am laid up with 2 nurses &
useless.

Sept 15. yours of August 15 just come. I am so glad you have managed so well but the

Arabs are sly enough & the pay always is of a back hander! I am going on very well I am thankful to say & have 2 good nurses – everyone is very kind in inquiries & co

It is a matter of time –

dearest love Your letters were interesting and welcome

yr loving Mother

MHB Witts

139. *Cheltenham Chronicle* 11th September 1920: 'Opening of Parish Hall and Fete at Upper Slaughter'.

Sept 14th 1920

My dear Fred

It is ages since I wrote but I must tell you more of Mother's accident. As you know she has been very seedy for some months & then while standing in her bedroom last Friday, her left leg suddenly gave way & she fell: we could not get a Doctor for three hours & then he said it was a spontaneous fracture of the thigh bone due to water on the bone. She has been quite conscious all the time & was so pleased with your letter of the 15th Aug: which came this morning. The Dr. from Bourton has been attending her: we have tried to get Sir Alfred Pearce Gould down but he is away on holiday but his Son is coming down this evening. The bone is not yet set & it is doubtful if it can be owing to Mother's weak state of health.

However Dr Pearce Gould has suggested some new special form of splint: if he comes in time to catch this weeks mail I will write again to you.

Mother opened the Hall here splendidly: a local paper with the pictures & account have been sent to you.

What a devil of a time you seem to be having. It seems now that the Government are not going to let you down tho' they seem more engaged making a mess of things in Ireland.

The Doctor hopes to be able to put a splint on Mother which will enable her to sit up in bed as her back is already getting sore.

Best love & best of good luck

Yr affect.ate Brother

George B . Witts

It would be another six weeks before Major Witts would receive news of his mother's broken leg; a blessing in disguise as any request for leave would have faced immediate rejection given the situation in Mesopotamia. By the end of August, the focus of the crisis had shifted momentarily to the region along the Diyala River, to the north-east of Baghdad, where rumours of a British withdrawal had permeated the local tribes, convincing them to join the growing ranks of insurgents. Railway and telegraph communications in the area had been cut, precipitating the evacuation of the British garrison at Baquba, the region's principle town, to escape an impending siege. The fate, meanwhile, of a small pocket of British political and development officers based at Shahraban, twenty miles upriver, was tragically overlooked. They were left to the mercies of the impassioned Arabs who stormed their compound and killed them. With these murders and the absence of any further British resistance, the entire region gave way to anarchy, directly threatening the safety of British families stationed at Karind, just over the Persian border.

Urgent action was required and, as Major Witts had predicted, the ubiquitous General Coningham and his 'flying column' were summoned to the Diyala to carve a safe route through hostile territory to Karind.

F.V.B.Witts

Major

P. S. 55

Near Shaikh Saad

September 19th 1920.

Dearest Mother.

I am ashamed to say I don't remember when I last wrote. I have been so much on the move. I think it was immediately before leaving Hillah.

We had three nights in Baghdad – the first I had spent there since February when we left for Albu Kemal! I dined out each night and met many friends, but one evening was wasted by having to dine with my General at the Commander-in-Chief's. Perhaps it wasn't altogether wasted! He seemed very pleased with our relief of Rumaitha and withdrawal from Diwaniyah.

I collected one mail with your letter of July 28th and persuaded the authorities to open the mailbags for Ramadi to recover another fortnight's, which I finally got on my return to Baghdad three days ago with the latest mail as well – that is your letters of July 13th July 21st and August 4th.

On Sept 4th we moved on from Baghdad to Baqubah, and on the 6th marched out with a column to open up the railway to Persia, this was done by the 15th. We met with very little opposition.[33] Several prisoners were released including an English woman who, after seeing her husband murdered at her side, had been in Arab hands for nearly a month, but had been comparatively well treated.[34]

You can imagine our surprise when the General, myself and Staff Captain (Kingsberry) got orders to leave our Brigade and column and proceed to Basrah immediately en route to Nasiriyah. We got back to Baghdad on the 16th, spent 17th there at G.H.Q. etc and came down by train to Kut yesterday. Here we found a special fast boat waiting to take us to Basrah, and here we are now passing our old haunts of 1916.

We are to take over the command of the Samawah relief column [Samcol],

---

[33] The uprisings of the Diyala tribes had not been driven by political motives, but by an innate love for violence and plunder. An irresistible opportunity to loot with impunity had arisen from the British evacuation of Baquba, but upon the emergence of an armed column, the tribes quickly dispersed fearing harsh reprisals.

[34] Mrs Buchanan, wife of Capt. Buchanan, the British Irrigation officer in Shahraban, had been taken captive by hostile tribesmen on 13th August when the political officer's compound was attacked and overrun by insurgents. In the short fight, five Englishmen were killed, including Mrs. Buchanan's husband, who, as F.V.B.W. mentions, was shot dead before her eyes. At the time, the Civil Administration had no idea that she was even in Shahraban as her name had never appeared on any records. As a result, nothing had been done to rescue her or even find out if she was alive or dead. It was quite a surprise, therefore, when she was discovered by British forces a month later. She later recorded her experiences in her book *In the Hands of the Arabs* (Hodder & Stoughton, London 1921).

140. Baghdad skyline.

consisting entirely of new troops from India for whom it was considered desirable to have a General and Staff of experience. It is a great compliment to the General and throws some reflected glory on his Staff, from whom he refuses to be separated. But we are all getting a bit tired of having to do all the work! We have been at it since February now.

We are up against a pretty stiff proposition this time as in addition to heavy opposition there are very serious transport and water difficulties. I hope we shall see it through as if Samawah falls, it is difficult to foresee the effect on the country. It is a possibility that must be faced and all women and children have been ordered out of Baghdad to Basrah.[35]

My kit is still shut up in Ramadi. I wonder if I shall ever see it again!

I keep extraordinarily fit, though we don't have to rough it like the troops. On our last column we had our headquarters in a first class saloon with electric light and fans and bath – a train accompanied the column which was primarily opening up the railway.

No more news now.

> With very best love,
> Your ever loving Son,
> Fred. V. B. Witts.

In early September, British resistance to repeated assaults on river and rail communications out of Samawah had finally succumbed to overwhelming numbers of insurgents. As a result, the town's garrison was invested in a determined siege.

The implications of losing Samawah to the rebels could hardly be exaggerated. Located at the confluence of the Shatt-al-Hindiyah and the Shatt-al-Hillah, Samawah's capture would pose a direct threat to the entire British position on the Lower Euphrates. Even more significant, however, was the likelihood that it would convince the powerful Muntafiq Confederation to join the revolt. If such an event occurred, the River Tigris, Haldane's only

---

[35] By the 22nd September families were being safely evacuated from Karind to Baghdad, whence they were sent immediately on to Basra and out of the country on the first available transport.

remaining line of communication to Baghdad, would fall into the hands of the insurgents, forcing the British to abandon all parts of the country north of Basra. Every measure to ensure the success of the relief attempt had to be made. Inexperienced troops were all that was available but, in the capable hands of General Coningham, Haldane hoped that the situation could be saved.

Back in Slaughter, Mrs Witts' own battle with her health was showing slight cause for encouragement. However, the shambles that had befallen the Mesopotamian postal service meant that Major Witts would remain ignorant of her tribulations for some time yet.

THE MANOR,
UPPER SLAUGHTER,
GLOS.
Sept 22th 1920.

Dearest Fred

I am getting along alright but it will be slow work & I have 2 good Nurses. How are you in the heat – here it is cold – Frank has been to see me for the day they have let their house & go to Aldershot on the 25 Jack came for 2 nights but Elma's Baby may come any day he has sent you a Chelt paper with the opening of our room – glad I could do it – a cross at LS & I hear Edwin made a good speech –

dear love, yr loving Mother
MHB Witts

Sept 22th 1920

Dear Fred,

Mother has had a good week.

Last Wednesday afternoon, too late to catch last week's mail, Sir Alfred Pearce Gould's Son a surgeon with many degrees etc came down from Town & saw Mother: he said the accident was merely an incident in her illness a growth having eaten thro the thigh bone: that there would be no more trouble on that account & consequently much less pain: that she was likely to live another six months but not more than nine months as her heart was getting bad: that she would not be able to use her left leg for walking again: he put a new form of splint on her leg which enables her to sit up in bed & she now reads a little each day & very much enjoyed your last letter. I have told you exactly what the Dr. told me but of course Mother does not know & still thinks her pain was neuritis. She has now far less pain than she had before the accident so it may be a blessing in disguise. She likes her two nurses very much. Everyone is very kind in inquiring & sending Mother grapes. Apphie Jack & Frank were down last week for a few days.

Walter Whitmore comes next week.[36] Jack & I shot 4 brace of partridges one day but all the corn was not cut & now we are having drenching rain so it is a bad look out for the rest of the harvest.

Can you apply for special leave about Christmas with any hope of it being granted? According to the Papers things are better out your way.

The Bourton Dr. now only comes every other day.

Best love.

> Yr affect.[ate] Brother
> George B. Witts

In the run-up to the crucial Samawah relief attempt, news in Britain on Mesopotamia had mostly returned to paltry snippets, with 'situation improved' being the consistent gist. The following extract from *The Times* of September 21st illustrates the general character of current reports: '…From Mesopotamia some minor actions are reported in which our forces have inflicted casualties upon the Arabs. Kufa, which has been besieged since the end of July, has asked our airmen for supplies of tobacco and cigarettes.'

> THE MANOR,
> UPPER SLAUGHTER,
> GLOS.
> Sept 29th 1920

Dearest Fred

I am getting on well so don't worry about me I was lifted onto the sofa yesterday – it is quite autumnal. I wonder how you are getting on roasted with heat I expect! I hope the Strike will not come off now.[37] Aunt Sybil is enjoying Leith & Edinburgh with Bay & has rooms close to her hospital[38]

> dearest love
> Yr loving Mother
> MHB Witts

[36] The Whitmore family had lived at the Manor Lower Slaughter since the seventeenth century.

[37] The coal miners had associated themselves with the railwaymen and transport workers unions to form the 'Triple Alliance'. Negotiations over higher wages for miners between the Alliance and the Government had been going on for weeks. Just as strike action had seemed imminent, the miners agreed to postpone strike notices, allowing more time to reach a settlement. However, after much protracted negotiation, a coal strike did eventually start on October 17th.

[38] Bay Witts was F.V.B.W.'s first cousin; she was the daughter of his uncle George and aunt Sybil. (*see also* Chapter VII, p. 236, note 16)

Sept 29th 1920

Dear Fred,

Mother is making quite good progress & the Dr. only comes now twice a week. Yesterday for the first time we moved her from her bed to the sofa & we soon hope to get her into the South Room.

Your wire dated Basra 21st arrived on the 27th & pleased Mother enormously.

From the meagre accounts in the Times it seems as if things were not quite as bad as they were with you but one never knows the truth over here.

The Harvest is nearly all in now having had some glorious weather lately.

Elma's baby is expected in a few weeks now.

Edward talks of getting back soon after Christmas. When will you have leave to come & see Mother?

I have not seen you since June 1915.

Walter Whitmore comes today.

Best love,

Yr affect.ate Brother,

George B. Witts

THE MANOR,
UPPER SLAUGHTER,
GLOS.
Oct 5th 1920.

Dearest Fred

Yours of August 21 came on S – glad all is well but you have had some skirmishes according to the paper I am going on well of course it is a slow job & wearying tho not so painful as one would think. Elma's Baby has not come yet but may do any hour!...

dear love Yr loving Mother

MHB Witts

THE MANOR,
UPPER SLAUGHTER,
GLOS.
Oct 13th 1920.

Dearest Fred

Your letters are very welcome & Frank says he has had one – Edward says he feels the heat I wonder if he will soon come home. I should not wonder. Apphie comes today & Agnes is going for a change it will do her good – George manages to get on, tho he has not left me this year. I have been such a cripple – my leg is mending & I hope by Xmas I may be able to move crutches! I shall go into the South room as a sitting room when I can – what do you think of my taking your room? ...I have a hospital bed! It all seems so strange. Edwin is at home mostly looking after his animals. Frank & Ruth flourishing Jack & Elma also. Baby not come yet! dearest love

> Yr loving Mother
> Mrs MH Witts

The Times gives us very little news except killing Arabs!

Oct 13th 1920

Dear Fred

Mother is going on first rate & we hope soon to move her into the South Room tho' she says what will you say when you come on leave! I tell her you will prefer the Ivy Room.

Apphie & I are going to Oswald Bazeley's[39] wedding at Charlton Kings on Saturday. Agnes is going to the Wrights on the Riviera while Apphie is here.

I am reading Colonal Repington's book the First World War & it is most awfully interesting.[40]

Emily sat with Mother a short time yesterday & she enjoyed it.

Best of good luck

> Yr affect.^{ate} Brother
> George B. Witts

Although *The Times* showed little awareness, the entire British position in Mesopotamia was dependant on the success of the Samawah Relief Column. Haldane's faith in General Coningham, however, was soon vindicated. Having set out from Nasiriyah on the 30th September, Coningham's force marched victoriously into Samawah exactly a fortnight later, having defeated the horde of insurgents gathered four miles outside the city the previous day. Major Witts, with the column throughout, describes the experience in his letter below.

---

[39] F.V.B.W. mentions Oswald Bazely as serving in Mesopotamia in his letter of 8th March 1916. Oswald's father, Canon Bazely, was a close friend of Mrs Witts. He helped to officiate at her funeral (Feb 18th 1921, p. 424-5).

[40] Repington, Col., *The First World War 1914-1918*: 2 Volumes, Constable, London 1920.

F.V.B.Witts

 Major

H.Q. Samawah Relief Column

Samawah

October 16th 1920.

Dearest Mother.

 We accomplished our task and got in here on the 14th after a very stiff fight outside the day before [at Habdah, 4 ½ miles south of Samawah].

 Some 5000 insurgents met us and put up a very good fight until the late afternoon when they broke and a regular sauve qui peut followed across the river when many were drowned.[41]

 We had three other smaller scraps on the way up from Nasiriyah – in each case a fight for water. We followed the railway which runs across the desert with not a drop of water anywhere. All our water had to come up by train behind us. Often it was not enough to go round and animals had to go 48 hours without a drop. So whenever we came within a mile or two of the river we went down to water there which meant a fight.

 The railway was terribly damaged; every sleeper removed, rails bent, points and crossings damaged. One day we only advanced two miles.

 The garrison were very pleased to see us. They have been involved in the rising since it started on July 1st, and have been completely besieged for two months. They had enough food to last out ten days more when we got in.

 I don't know what we are going to do now, probably strafe every village within reach and possibly move on to Rumaitha later, but there are several big railway bridges burnt ahead.

 Three mails have reached me with your letters of Sept 8th, August 18th and July 6th which shows how disorganised things are out here. They last got into Ramadi just before the place was cut off, and has only just been forwarded on reestablishment of communications.

 The hot weather is really over at last and it is very cold in the early morning.

 No more news now.

 Very best love,

  Your ever loving Son,

   Fred.V. B.Witts.

---

[41] Haldane is generally more conservative in his estimates, reporting a mass of only 2500-3000 insurgents and just 20 drowned in the Euphrates (*The Insurrection in Mesopotamia*, p. 227).

Telegrams: Upper Slaughter.

Station: Bourton-on-the-Water G.W.R

THE MANOR,
UPPER SLAUGHTER,
GLOS.
Oct 19th1920

Dearest Fred –

Here I am in the South Room, which George & Apphie have fitted up as a sitting room! I get carried in & put in a chair for 2 hours each morning. I wonder where you are? Things are bad enough in England with all the strikes.[42] Sophie has been to see me but I am not up to many visitors

The hounds ran across the lawn last week full cry but lost the fox there are plenty about! Cub hunting is on. Stow Fair on the 23 & Edwards horses are to be sold as they have turned out a small lot & not worth keeping. No news – George is going to shoot on Thursday with Major Warner I am glad for him to go out while Apphie is here, for he hardly ever leaves me-

Agnes has got as far as Paris & by now on the Riviera, she wanted a change & finds it dull here after her exciting life during the war.[43] I hope you are keeping fit the Gov: does not tell us much & every place is in riot. I hope you get the papers & Blackwood alright:

Edward & Edith seem busy & happy. Frank was hastily sent to Wimbledon from Aldershot on Sat in consequence of the strike it is lucky they were only at an Hotel…

Best of love God bless you, Yr loving mother

MHB Witts

Oct 19. 1920

Dear Fred,

Mother is making good progress & enjoys sitting in the South Room very much. She is wondering when you will get leave & come to see her. Is there any chance of your doing in the Spring?

Harvest almost finished except one or two fields not worth getting in.

We hope Edward & Edith will soon be back.

I hear the mob broke into the Rag on Monday & collared everything in the Hall etc! things seem pretty bad.[44]

Repington's book most interesting.

Best love

Yr affect.^{ate} Brother

George B. Witts

---

[42] As well as the coal miners, the cotton workers of Oldham and the firemen and seamen of Dublin had also gone on strike, the latter stalling trade across the Irish Channel.

[43] Agnes had been in the 52nd Glos Voluntary Aid Detachment (V.A.D.), serving as Commandant of the Copse Hill Auxiliary Hospital (May 1915 – March 1916) and as an ambulance driver in Salonika (Aug 1916 – Sept 1917) and France (Dec 1917 – Dec 1918).

[44] The Army and Navy Club in Pall Mall, known as The Rag. F.V.B.W. was a member.

For a change, the news from Mesopotamia was encouraging. The relief of Samawah had re-established Britain as the superior military power in Mesopotamia, taking the wind out of the sails of the insurrection and restoring some degree of stability to the country. With ample reinforcements and the hot season well and truly over, light mobile columns were dispersed to the heartlands of the rebellion and throughout the rest of the country. They imposed British dominance on the minds of malefactors and enforced rigorous fines on the possession of arms and ammunition. Resistance still endured in certain areas, but more out of desperation than conviction.

With the encouraging turn of events, Major Witts' prospects of leave were becoming brighter. At the same time, the arrival of news of his mother's broken leg made the issue all the more urgent to him.

F.V.B. Witts
Major

H.Q. Samawah Relief Column
Samawah.
October 24th 1920.

Dearest Mother.

I was very distressed to get your letter of Sept 14th and hear of your most unfortunate accident. At your age it must be a very slow and weary process getting strong again. Please thank George for sending me full details.

I was delighted to get the Cheltenham Chronicle with all the pictures and description of the most successful manner in which you opened the Parish Hall. I am sure it is the most suitable thankoffering that could be thought of.

Since last writing I have also received your letters of June 2nd, June 9th and August 11th including one from Apphie. It shows how chaotic things have been out here. They have all been chasing me round the country and got besieged in one of the many places out here that have suffered that fate.

We have been having a more or less peaceful time confined to three quite local strafes burning villages. They put up a bit of a fight the third day, but nothing serious. We are all wondering what is going to happen now. Kufah has been relieved and the prisoners in Nejf released:[45] both Nejf and Kerbela, the heart and brains of the rising, have made formal submission. The tribes within our immediate reach are trying to come in but are rather frightened of our intentions. As we don't know ourselves it is rather hard to convince them.

---

[45] The Kufa garrison had been under siege since 20th July and had only survived thanks to the timely measures taken by its commander to stock up on provisions. At Najaf, 170 prisoners had been held, most of whom were captured at the fateful 'Manchester Disaster' of 24th July. They had been relatively well treated with only one man dying in captivity.

Samawah town is a filthy spot, and has been ransacked by the troops,[46] as we have not yet allowed the inhabitants back[47] – they behaved so treacherously during the siege. All sorts of souvenirs have been collected, but there was little of value from that point of view. Most people have collected a rug of sorts but they are all of the cheap variety.

The hot weather is really over – and my warm clothes are all up at Ramadi, I wonder if I shall ever get them – we had quite a heavy storm the other night and it has been very cold at nights since.

I am anxiously waiting for the next mail to hear how you are getting on, but I am afraid it will be a long business, and my heart goes out to you, Mother, in all your troubles: I wish I were at home to cheer you up.

With very best love,

> Your ever loving Son,
>
> Fred. V. B. Witts.

The insurrection in Mesopotamia had been caused by imprudent promises and insensitive administration by the British, and on the other side, by the belligerent character of tribal society and the rousing clamour of nationalist and religious propaganda. As mentioned before, the financial and human costs to both Britain and India were intolerable at a time of economic recession in a social climate sick to death of war. The Mesopotamian population, meantime, had suffered far worse, with around four times as many casualties as the British, and a devastating setback to the country's development. Pockets of resistance still existed, but British forces had regained control. The real challenges had now returned to the political sphere, and to addressing the root causes of the revolt.

For Major Witts, only time would tell when he would be permitted to go to his dying mother.

---

[46] The Manual of Indian Law of 1911, still valid in 1920, describes 'looting in time of war' as a capital offence. The theft of civilian possessions naturally sometimes occurred (for example see Fieldhouse, D. K. *Arabs, Kurds and Britons* p. 74 for Wallace Lyon's account of the theft by an Indian Sepoy of a tribesman's woollen sock containing £1,000 of Turkish sovereigns) but what makes F.V.B.W.'s description of the ransacking of Samawah particularly interesting is his apparent acceptance of it, suggesting that it may even have been sanctioned as a form of punishment to the town's inhabitants.

[47] When Coningham's force entered Samawah on 14th October, the whole population had fled, bar only 25 Arabs and 25 Jews.

CHAPTER XII

FINALE

Letters: Oct 26ᵗʰ 1920 – Jan 15ᵗʰ 1921

141. F.V.B.W. in *War Illustrated*, June 9th 1917.

The five years that Major Witts spent in Mesopotamia were arguably the most pivotal in the country's modern history. The final phase of change that he would witness was the inauguration of a provisional Arab Government, the first step towards an independent Iraq.

In October 1920, the beleaguered A. T. Wilson was finally relieved from his post as Acting Civil Commissioner by his predecessor, Sir Percy Cox, who returned to Mesopotamia as High Commissioner. In the aftermath of the insurrection, a clear path towards independence was vitally important. The country's racial, religious and tribal issues had to be taken into account, and the reservations of the British Treasury had to be heeded.

Upon arrival, Cox immediately set about establishing a provisional 'Council of State', the basis of which had been proposed four months earlier during Wilson's administration, but was postponed on the outbreak of hostilities. The idea was to establish a provisional Arab Government with Arab Ministers under the leadership of the Naqib of Baghdad, the senior Sunni cleric. Each Minister was obliged to follow the guidance given by an assigned British adviser, while Sir Percy Cox, in his capacity as High Commissioner, retained the right to veto any proposal without debate, even if it had the full backing of the Naqib. In this way, and in its domination by Arabs of the Sunni minority, the Council of State fell far short of nationalist aspirations, especially within the Kurdish and Shi'ite communities. However, 'a bridge,' as George Antonius asserts, 'between British authority and the disaffected population [had been constructed], paving the way to a series of developments which, in course of time, were to lead to the abolition of the mandate and to grant Mesopotamia its political independence.'[1]

In Britain, the Government was promising a new start in Mesopotamia; an age of peace, stability and diminishing British obligation.

142. Sir Percy Cox.

THE MANOR,
UPPER SLAUGHTER,
GLOS.
Oct 26th 1920.

Dearest Fred

No news of you later than Sept 19 when the letter came last week – you seem to have traveled down comfortably on the whole! The only startling news here is that Heythrop is for sale & Brassey giving up the hounds and clearing out! Everyone wonders who will be the new Master.

I am mending slowly & get into your room for 2 or 3 hours daily – Jack & Elma are very pleased with their Baby boy born Oct 21st – no news of Edward or Edith, the young horses sold Oct Stow Fair £60 for them, as things go not so bad I am told.

It will be a great nuisance if you lose your kit – I wonder when you will get leave? Sir P. Cox is supposed to settle everything up for Mespot! according to Parliament! If you get your Times you will see Jack's announcement on Oct 25th & 26th as the wrong address was first given. There are no big shoots about so little game & harvest so late the partridges are so wild. Jim Paterson is I fear not able to do much more work.

Walter Sellick[2] is in a big music shop in Manchester & getting on at last I believe, dear love.

Yr loving old Mother
MHB Witts

---

[1] Antonius, G., *The Arab Awakening*, p. 316

[2] George Sellick (died 1910) had worked for the Hole and Witts families for many years, and there is a plaque in his memory in Upper Slaughter church; it can be assumed that Walter was related.

Oct 26 1920

Dear Fred

Mother wrote to you yesterday while she was up in the South Room & this morning your letter of the 26th Sept. from Rivers Front Hotel Basrah comes which she asks me to thank you for.

The last few days the broken leg has given her a great deal of pain & it has shrunk a lot but the Dr. is satisfied & she still keeps up her strength & eats well. Apphie is remaining on a bit.

Mother is very much relieved that you say now the situation with you is well

Coal strike still on & railway strike threatened.[3]

Best love,

      Yr affect.ate Brother

      George B. Witts

The military situation in Mesopotamia was certainly much improved, but elements of restiveness still existed in some enclaves of the Mid-Euphrates region. Remaining on General Coningham's staff, Major Witts was transferred from Samawah relief column to a light, mobile force, designed to stamp out the last remnants of the insurrection.

F.V.B. Witts
    Major.

Samawah.
Nov 3rd 1920.

Dearest Mother.

Very many thanks for your letters of September 22nd and 29th. It is awfully good of you to write as I know it must be a great effort to you, confined to your bed and sofa. Please also thank George for his weekly letters, which I hope he will continue. I will write and thank him personally when things get a bit quieter, and I have a bit more leisure.

Samawah Relief Column, or Samcol as we were known for short, was broken up on October 31st, when another Brigadier came up and took over. General Coningham has gone off to Basra on a week's leave to see his wife, who is leaving the country as are all other women out here. When he returns another column is being formed for us to command. I am off to Nasiriyah tomorrow morning to go into details in connection with this next column.

We had four strenuous days to finish up with – Oct 27th 28th 29th and 30th. On both the 27th and 29th we had quite a good scrap and killed off a few more inhabitants of the country. The 28th and 30th were comparatively quiet as a result of the punishment

---

[3] The railwaymen were threatening to strike out of sympathy to the miners' cause.

inflicted the previous day.

This next show should take us again to Rumaitha, which we relieved from the other side when the rising first started in July. It will complete my tour of the Euphrates from Basra to Albu Kemal, 500 miles from the sea.

But it is a bad country; having got the difficulties incidental to the extreme heat and lack of water behind us, we are now faced with the rain and the mud which it brings in its train and which holds up all forms of locomotion from walking upwards.

I am trying to work for the Staff College, but it is rather impossible under present conditions – very little time available and absolutely no facilities in the way of library or books.

Have you read Kermit Roosevelt's 'The War in the Garden of Eden'[4] or Callwell's 'Sir Stanley Maude'.[5] I want to see them both, but have not yet. If you would like to present them to me, they would be a most acceptable Christmas present!! They would probably interest you too, so read them yourself first.

It is getting really cold now at nights, and I wish I had my winter clothes. The road to Ramadi, where everything is, is open again, so I am hoping to get them down sometime.

No more news today. Very best of love. I do hope your leg is not troubling you too much.

> Your ever loving Son
> Fred. V. B. Witts

Back in Slaughter, however, Mrs Witts' condition was quickly deteriorating.

Telegraph & station,
Bourton-on-the-Water.

Upper Slaughter
The Manor,,
R.S.O. Glos.
3rd Nov. 1920.

Dear Fred,

When poor old Mother was raising herself this morning by the pulley affixed to her bed her left arm snapped above the elbow & when we got the Dr. he could only say it was broken.

He has set it in a splint & intends to put it in plaster of Paris tomorrow if possible.

It has very much upset Mother but she keeps fairly well tho' it is no use disguising the fact that she is very ill & the Dr. now hardly expects her to live many more weeks.

I am thankful to say that Edward in this week's letter says he is starting home last

---

[4] F.V.B.W. met Kermit Roosevelt in Samarrah during the war, mentioning him to his mother in his letter of September 23rd 1917, p. 188-9.

[5] See Appendix XV for *The Times* book review of Callwell's *Life of Lieutenant-General Sir Stanley Maude* (Constable, 1920).

week so should be here in about a fortnight.

Mother was able to direct your letter this morning while the Dr. was attending to her arm but tells me to say she is not able to write till next week.

Mother is now taking Morphia as we are at any rate determined to save her pain.

Yr affect.^ate Brother

George B. Witts

Frank, meanwhile, wrote to his brother pressing home the fact that unless he managed to get leave soon, he would miss the chance to see his mother alive.

Telegraphic Address,
Telephone 4500 Kensington (6 lines).
Knightalla, Ken, London

KNIGHTSBRIDGE HOTEL,
LONDON, S.W.1.
Nov 7th 1920

My dear Fred.

I think I must be owing you a letter, but we have been so disturbed that I have lost count. The battalion was moved to London as soon as the coal strike began, and Ruth & I have been living here as of course our own house is let. We go back to Aldershot this week as soon as Armistice day is over; on that day we shall be lining the streets in order to keep us warm! It has been bitterly cold and London has been enveloped in fog of varying degrees of density for a fortnight or more. So we shall be glad to get out of it again. You will have heard ere this reaches you the last news of Mother, and how her arm broke a few days ago. I went down to see her yesterday. She was wonderfully well considering but certainly weaker than when I saw her six weeks ago. There is no doubt but that she is gradually dying and at any moment the end may come, though it may be delayed for a month or two yet if no vital part is affected by the disease. I do hope you realise this and that if you want to see her alive you ought to get home soon. I told George yesterday he ought to cable to you at once so that you can decide whether to come or not.[6] After all you have your own life to live! Edward & Edith will I hope be home at the end of the month and that will be something. It is very very sad to see Mother laid low like this but fortunately she does not know what is killing her and still expects to get well. So she is wonderfully cheerful. She is so helpless now that three nurses are necessary: she can't move at all without them. I have been busy with individual winter training and have been trying hard to teach the men something. The cancelling of all leave of course gave us a great

---

[6] This cable, if sent, seems not to have reached F.V.B.W. as he only hears of his mother's broken arm in mid-December, sending his commiserations in his final surviving letter of December 17th 1920.

opportunity to get all the men clear of other duties. I expect you know the endless difficulty of keeping the company together. Then we hope to go off on leave for about three months. Though I hope Mother will not think us very heartless going off, but we can do nothing and as it appears difficult for both of us to stay at Slaughter I shall only get down for the day occasionally.

Best of luck.

Yours

Frank

F.V.B.Witts

Major

H.Q. 34 Bde.

Samawah

Nov 10th 1920.

Dearest Mother

You will see we have changed our name again – Samawah having been relieved – and are now being called by our original brigade name.

The General [Coningham] returned from Basrah two days ago after seeing his wife off to India.

Our long halt here comes to an end tomorrow – Armistice day – when we move on a few miles to cover the repairs of another damaged bridge [Imam Abdullah], the bridge here [Barbuti] having been repaired. It will probably mean a scrap – a suitable celebration of Armistice day. But we were wondering how we were to observe the 2 minutes silence tomorrow!

I went down to Divn H.Q. at Nasiriyah on the fourth. The 60 odd miles took me 22 hours owing to blocks on the line: but it wasn't so bad as it sounds as I was travelling with the head of the railways with every convenience for this sort of emergency. I spent one day there discussing details of this next advance and came back on the sixth with the Divisional Commander [Major-General Cory of the 6th Division] by Railway Armoured Car. It took four hours only! It doesn't sound much to boast about for 60 miles: but it is for Mesopotamia railways as the earlier 22 hour journey exemplifies.

I was very pleased to get your letter and George's of Oct 5th – not so very long getting here –

I can well realize how very wearying it must be for you, and am thankful to hear it is not as painful as it might be.

I am so glad to hear Jack is so happy and must make an effort to write to him. But life has been so full and strenuous for me since February.

Frank is lucky to get four months long leave in England? It is more really than the six months one can get here – but for the war. I hope to be home about March, so hope Edward and Frank may be there too.

General Leslie – a sapper commanding the 17th Divn – has just gone home. He tried to pay us a farewell visit by air yesterday, but was prevented by weather. We are now in 6th Indian Divn. General Leslie is a great loss to me! He was my C.R.E. in France, and you met him at Waterloo one day when I was returning from leave.

Very best love,

Your ever loving Son,

Fred. V. B. Witts

THE MANOR,
UPPER SLAUGHTER,
GLOS.
Nov 11th 1920.

Dearest Fred

No news of you! Not even in the Times. We heard from Edith they were leaving on Oct 28 in the Harrison Rennie line but as that boat is 10 days late they will not come before the end of Nov: I fancy Edward wants a change – too much society out there now!

The boat is Ingoma[7] so you see it in the Times much cheaper than the U. Castle – a wonderful open Nov: & mild. Frank is lining the London streets today in Whitehall all the Guards called up today

I hope you will be the next to come home – Jack & I have suggested 'Anthony' for the Baby but I am not sure if Elma likes it. No particular news. Edwin Brassey is suggested as the new Master for the Heythrop. All the people round here are new so Edward will not be worried. I have only one arm so excuse a scrawl.

Best of love   Yr loving bed Mother MHBW

Nov 10th 1920.

Dear Fred,

Mother has made another marvelous recovery after breaking her arm & she was moved yesterday for the first time from her bed to a chair for an hour & in future will be moved each day.

She has dated her letter a day too soon: the Guards are lining the streets on Armistice Day tomorrow.

The name of the boat Edward is coming back on is the Ingoma of the Harrison Rennie line: we saw in yesterday's Times she had left East London [South Africa] on the 6th for Algra Bay en route to the Cape & then it takes 22 days to London so they will not be back till about the second week in December.

---

[7] Built in 1913 by D & W Henderson & Co. of Glasgow, *Ingoma* served as a troopship from 1915-17. She then returned to passenger duties until 1937 when she was sold to an Italian shipping company and renamed *Giovanni Battista*. She was finally scuttled off Tripoli in 1943.

When are you coming?

I am afraid now there is no doubt that Mother has cancer of the bones but of course she knows nothing of it: you will have had my letter some time ago telling you the London Dr. said he thought she would live for six months from Sept. & not more than nine but her condition is worse now she has the disease in her arm.

She has no pain or very little & has sleeping draughts when she cannot sleep at night.

      Your affect.[ate] Brother

      G. B. Witts

Major Witts was powerless to influence a concession for special leave, but as the strategic situation improved, so did his chances of getting home. Despite widespread dissatisfaction with the Council of State, General Haldane's extensive disarmament programme guarded against any serious aftershocks to the rebellion. The Civil Administration, meantime, was under no illusion that it had the power to suppress the illicit trade of rifles from neighbouring countries.

Before Major Witts could be granted leave, the surviving hotspots of the rebellion had to be extinguished; unsurprisingly, it fell to General Coningham to deliver the final blow.

F.V.B. Witts

Major

                                  Imam Abdullah.

                        4 Miles North of Samawah.

                          November 16th 1920.

Dearest Mother.

…This must be the Christmas mail, so let me wish you and all at home very many happy returns of the day and best of wishes for the New Year. How I wish I were at home to keep it with you, as I might have been but for this new war out here.

We moved out from Samawah on Nov 11th – Armistice day – and had quite a good fight here and killed more Arabs than we have for a long time. It might have been a nasty show but we moved early and got across the river here before the Arab was properly awake.[8]

There is a big bridge here very badly burnt which it will take a fortnight to repair before we can start on again towards Rumaitha. And before then the tribes may come in, as they have done nearly everywhere further north. But I am none too sure as this is where the whole show started as you will remember.

The weather nearly spoilt our Nov 11th fight, as it rained a bit in the early morning,

[8] See note 11.

since then it has been very cold and my winter kit is still at Ramadi! However the cold is a very pleasant change to the heat.

General Leslie has left the 17th Divn, having apparently been held responsible for the Manchester disaster – a most unjust thing. He has done more to break the back of the show than any single man out here.[9]

I shall soon be one of the oldest inhabitants in the country.[10]

No more news today.

   Very best wishes, once more, for Christmas and the New Year.

    Your ever loving Son,

     Fred. V. B. Witts.

            THE MANOR,
          UPPER SLAUGHTER,
              GLOS.
         Nov. 17th 1920.

Dearest Fred

Yours of Oct 16 just come & the account of your doings in the Times 16th!!![11]

You seem still in the fighting bit. Edward & Edith are on their way home & should get to London on Dec 7th. Frank & Ruth are looking for a house to go to on their return from Algiers they start Dec 15 & he has 3 months leave. Elma is very proud of her boy – the name is the next thing.

Apphie has gone home & I shall not see her till after the Xmas holydays – your Godson is doing very well at school & I think has the family brains.

Mrs Collett is giving up the school in Dec: after nearly 30 years or more hard at it.[12]

I am getting along but slowly – weather lovely – no news –

dearest love Yr loving Mother

    MHB Witts

---

[9] A. T. Wilson also takes issue with the scapegoating of General Leslie for the Manchester Disaster. While a good deal of the blame lies with the Manchester column's commander, who was forced to go beyond Leslie's orders because of inadequate water supplies, Wilson also claims to have documentary proof of Haldane's approval of the column's original dispatch from Hillah (*A Clash of Loyalties*, p. 280). General Leslie, as F.V.B.W. asserts, played a very significant role in tackling the rebellion. As commander of the 17th Division, he was owed partial credit for Coningham's string of successes with his subsidiary 34th Bde.

[10] New recruits from England and India were mostly young and inexperienced in both war and in the climatic extremes of Mesopotamia, as was seen in the Manchester Disaster.

[11] See Appendix XVI for *The Times* cutting entitled *Arab Bayonet Charge*. F.V.B.W. writes his own description of the battle in his letter of November 16th.

[12] Mrs Collett's son, George, had served in Mesopotamia. F.V.B.W. had found his name on the books at hospital in Amara reporting him to have had sand-fly fever (Jan 3rd 1917, Chapter III, p. 128).

143. Upper Slaughter School, 1895. F.V.B.W. far right, Mrs Collett far left.

Nov 17th 1920.

Dear Fred

Mother forgot to thank you for your cable which pleased her enormously.

I replied 'gradually worse' which I am afraid is only too true but I hope you will have started back before you get this if of course you can be spared. We hope for a cable saying you have started.

Morphia & sleeping draughts are easing Mother's pain which is not often bad now.

Yr affect.ate Brother

George B. Witts

The Manor
Upper Slaughter
Glos.
24th Nov. 1920

Dear Fred

We hope you are on your way home if leave is at all practicable.

Mother is slowly getting weaker but is now quite free from pain & is really looking forward to Edward & Edith's arrival about the 7th Dec.

Ireland seems to go from bad to worse.[13]

---

[13] Sinn Fein's threat of germ-warfare was the latest addition to the catalogue of kidnappings, murders and brutality which regularly comprised the weekly news on Ireland. Whilst the Labour Party launched a commission into the character of reprisals being carried out by the infamous 'Black & Tans', Churchill, with his mind on expenditure, wrote to the influential Bishop of Tuam, 'I need scarcely tell you how intensely I feel the desire and need for a truce and appeasement in Ireland' (Catherwood, C., *Winston's Folly*, p. 98).

Mabel & Jack have only one hunter between them & Sophie one which is now lame. They think Daly will take the hounds if subscriptions are about doubled.

No news.

> Yr affect.ate Brother
>> George B. Witts

F.V.B. Witts
Major

> H.Q. 34th Bde.
> Imam Abdullah
> Nov 29th 1920

Dearest Mother.

…It is keeping fine here inspite of several threats of rain, and has turned extraordinarily cold. Ice at night and a piercing wind by day. And my warm clothes are still at Ramadi inspite of my efforts to get them. Luckily the General has lent me some warm pyjamas!

The repair of the railway bridge was finished on the 26th and we move on again tomorrow. But I expect without fighting, as nearly all the hostile Sheikhs have accepted our terms. But they are a treacherous crowd. However I think Christmas should see a normal state of affairs in sight again with possibilities of early leave. But I don't want to start too early, as it would mean getting back before the hot weather was over[14] – if I had to come back which I do not at all want to, except that it means losing a good job with little prospect of getting another.

With little else to do I have been putting in quite a lot of reading the last ten days, but books are hard to get. I wish I had all the nice ones I had accumulated and left in India. One misses a library too. A cold draughty tent is not the best of places to work in!

There is no more news today,

> With very best love,
>> Your ever loving Son,
>>> Fred. V. B. Witts.

> THE MANOR,
> UPPER SLAUGHTER,
> GLOS.
> Dec 1st 1920.

Dearest Fred – no news of you for ages but I hope all is well. I am getting on well now but shall not be fit to do much more work! Jack has been down to look at

---

[14] Due to a postal strike in Bombay, F.V.B.W. was not yet fully aware of the severity of his mother's condition.

Edwin's shorthorns and the Sherborne lot — he is working for Sir Francis Barber as Agent for a few months — a rich London man connected with Vickers & has a farm just outside London.

No news of Edward's boat but it should be at London docks next week. Frank & Ruth start Dec 11th for his long leave Apphie & co are flourishing — Joan a grown up young lady! & Geoffrey waiting to go abroad in some office .. Peter is doing well at school.

Best of love Yr loving Mother

MHB Witts

My letters are dull but I am in a four walls only!!

Dec 1st 1920

Dear Fred,

Mother keeps wonderfully well — is of course much looking forward to next week when we expect Edward & Edith back. She has had a certain amount of pain in some other bone so it makes one anxious especially as the pain comes from somewhere near the thigh.

Very mild still & today brilliant sun.

Best love.

Yr affect.^{ate} Brother

George B. Witts

THE MANOR,
UPPER SLAUGHTER,
GLOS.
Dec 8th 1920.

Dearest Fred

Two letters from you Nov 4 & 18 quite quick — I hope you have your warm kit? The Cheddar scarf you gave me is so useful & warm a great comfort. Capt. Fuller has written and is sending the Rug to me I long for it. Edward & Edith are here both well Edith looks the best I think Edward is glad to be back as he has not been too well. Frank will be back at Aldershot in March & all the family in England if you have the good luck to get home & I hope it will be a long leave. My arm is nearly well & I shall soon use it again my leg also satisfactory only I have to be so long in one position…

dearest love

Yr loving Mother

MHB Witts

Dec 8th 1920.

Dear Fred,

Your cable came on the 6th having been sent off on the 30th.

We replied in Edward's name he having arrived back on the 4th.

Mother is much about the same but gets gradually weaker so we hope you have started ere this. She is so looking forward to seeing you. Edward & Edith say they would have hardly recognized her as she has changed so much.

Edward & Edith are both very fit & glad to be back again.

Best love,

    Yr. affect.^{ate} Brother

      George B. Witts

              H.Q. 34 Bde Column

                  Rumaitha.

              December 11th 1920.

Dearest Mother.

I was delighted to get your letter of Oct 26th yesterday. There has been a long break owing to a postal strike at Bombay I believe.

But I am very distressed to hear your leg has been giving you a great deal of pain. How I wish I were at home to help look after you. You are always in my thoughts, my letters seem so cold and give very little indication of my thoughts and feelings. At your age is must be a tremendous trial which you have now been called on to bear, and it hurts me to think of it.

Fancy Heythrop being for sale, and the Brasseys giving up the hounds! What is the old country coming to. Has he gone smash or what?

I am so glad to hear of the arrival of Jack's baby boy.

My kit has at last started from Ramadi on its way round. I am now wondering how much will be lost on the way. However the coldest weather we shall get this year is probably already passed. We had fifteen degrees of frost on Nov 30th and but seven weeks earlier it was 115° in the shade! What a country of rapid extremes it is.

I hope to get leave very soon, as things are really settling down. All the tribes have now made submission though an occasional shot is still fired. We left Imam Abdullah on Dec 1st and walked through here without a shot being fired, arriving here on the 6th. We had to take six days over it, as we had to repair the railway as we came.

I say without a shot being fired, but we had some very good partridge and snipe shooting on the way. One day we got 247 head. Another day over a hundred snipe. And we are living on game now. Another instance of the wonderful extremes you meet in this country. One day you can't go anywhere without being shot at, next day you can go shooting anywhere!

It is curious being back here in the place we relieved in July. I never expected to see it again.

Tomorrow we are going on half way to Diwaniyah – another old friend. A column [53rd Brigade] is coming from there to meet us. We shall be passing over our battlefields of July last. But I am afraid it is bound to rain. Our luck in this respect so far has been too good to last.

My next letter will be when I get back.

With very best love,

Your ever loving Son,

Fred. V. B. Witts.

The Manor,

Upper Slaughter,

Glos.

Dec. 15th 1920.

Dearest Fred

Your beautiful Rug came yesterday, it is lovely the colours are so rich & the birds & flowers quite wonderful[15] – it is a work of art & has been hanging on my sofa for the admiration of everyone – thank you so much – it must have cost you a lot. I am slowly getting on: weather very cold but I do not feel it. The books you name shall be sent unless we hear you are coming which the boys think is likely but I do not expect you before March which would also be nicer for you. Stow ball last night! Jack is very busy with his work. Frank came on Sunday to say good bye; they leave England today till the middle of March – & hope to find St George's Hotel Algiers comfortable they mean to stay there – best of birthday wishes

God bless you & the New Year

Yr loving Mother

MHBW

Dec 15th 1920

Dear Fred

Many happy returns of your birthday.

Vile weather – very cold with East wind but no skating owing to a little snow.

Mother keeps about the same but is no stronger & has pain in her back. We are hoping to hear you have started back.

Edward seems very glad to be back again. We shot at Eyford yesterday getting 11 pheasants 2 hares & 4 rabbits: we were round Cress Coppice way and the cold was intense.

Best of good luck.

Yr affect.ate Brother

George B. Witts

---

[15] See Illustration 18 in the Colour Section.

H.Q. 34th Brigade.
Rumaitha.
Dec 17th 1920.

Dearest Mother.

I was delighted to get your letters of Nov 3rd and 10th, but very sorry to hear about your poor old arm. What very bad luck you are having.

I am so very glad to hear Edward and Edith are on their way home and have probably arrived by this time. How I wish I was home too; but it is of course impossible to get leave while there is a war on. I wonder if you all realize we have been having a war since July?

However it is nearly over now, though already other warclouds are collecting on the horizon.[16] We joined up with the column from Diwaniyah and Hillah on Dec 12th and this may be taken as the real end of the show. On the 13th I motored through with the General [Coningham] and revisited Diwaniyah, which we had to evacuate on July 30th. We celebrated our meeting on the 12th with a champagne luncheon in the blue. We got back here on the 15th. The 14th was very wet – the first really heavy rain we have had and it was very miserable marching as the roads were very heavy.

Yesterday I put in for eight months leave, the General is very loathe to let me go before the end of January, when the whole show is expected to be over and he has himself been promised leave. It is one of the occasions it doesn't pay to be considered of value. However he has very kindly forwarded the application, and it now remains to be seen if I get away at once or at the end of January.

I wonder if Edwin will be the new Master; it would be nice for it to remain in the Brassey family.

Very many thanks for all the papers. It is so good of you to address them all yourself.

I am trying to read for the Staff College, but do not get much time and in fact have little inclination under present conditions.

I enclose a snapshot of myself taken during the Samawah Relief Column operations. It is the nearest approach to a Christmas Card, but I am afraid rather late for one.

No more news,

    With very best love,

        Your ever loving Son,

           Fred. V. B. Witts

---

[16] Bolshevik troops amassing at Baku had reignited fears for India's security. On December 19th, *The Times* described the move as the manifestation of 'Moscow's plans for undermining existing governments in the Near and Middle East with the object of obtaining 'corridors' for Bolshevist activity in India.'

This is the last surviving letter written by Major Witts to his mother. As he asserted, peace had been generally restored to Mesopotamia by mid-December, opening up the prospects for leave. Mrs Witts' condition, meanwhile, was clearly critical enough for the matter of a month's wait to make possibly all the difference. Thankfully, General Coningham was sensitive to this, and Major Witts did not have to wait long before he was heading home.

THE MANOR,
UPPER SLAUGHTER,
GLOS.
Dec 22th 1920.

Dearest Fred.

Yours of Nov 14 came yesterday. I wish you could get your kit as I am sure you want the things. You seem still killing whereas the Times says all is finished the War Office run very dark & tell us little – Weather wonderful no severe frosts. I have managed to sit up for lunch & stay in the chair several hours so it shows I am stronger.

Aunt Annie fell down & hurt her spine but is recovering she is 89–! We see nothing of our next door neighbour he is so disagreeable I hear & she is very nice. Jim is coming in for Xmas dinner which he has done for 46 years. No news of Jack & Elma so all is well & Jack busy on the Farm about 4 miles from Kingston one station below Wimbledon

Best birthday & New Year greetings may you be in England next time. I have the books for you. dearest love God bless you

Yr loving Mother

MHB Witts

Dec 22th 1920

Dear Fred,

We have been hoping for a cable announcing your return.

Mother keeps much the same but has had attacks of severe pain in her thigh.

We had one day's skating last Friday & had a good game of hockey with the Cheethams, two Moor boys & the people at the Bridges. We carried on till the ice gave & on the Monday hunting was in full swing.

Best of good luck,

Yr affect.^{ate} Brother

G.B. Witts

Major F.V.B. Witts
D.S.O. M.C.
Royal Engineers
Passenger
P. & O. 'Caledonia'
Marseilles
France

THE MANOR,
UPPER SLAUGHTER,
GLOS.
Jan 13th 1921.

Dearest Fred

Welcome back – your cable came yesterday 6 days from Bombay! So I hope this will catch you at Marseilles – Edward says you will feel the cold after Suez but we trust you have warm clothes. It is really warm wet & damp here! I sat up for tea as well as lunch yesterday so I am getting on –

Our express is running now so the 1.40 is due at 3.20 at Bourton but we meet the 4.45 from Paddington at Kingham no connection on. If you come by that don't forget to wrap up your head as you caught a most dreadful cold last time – I was with you & remember what you said. Edward has been very careful & stayed in doors often & escaped cold

Au revoir We shall all welcome you

Yr loving old Mother

MHB Witts

Jan 13th 1921.

Dear Fred,

We were delighted to get your wire. I have not seen you since June 1915!

Mother is about the same: she seems very poorly one day but better the next.

Edward & Edith are very fit.

Yr affect.ate Brother

George B.. Witts

The 4.45 down gets to Adelstrop 7.2 quicker than Kingham.

Major F.V.B. Witts
DSO. OBE. MC
Royal Engineers
P.& O Boat 'Caledonia'
Marseilles
France

THE MANOR,
UPPER SLAUGHTER,
GLOS.
Jan 15th 1921.

Dearest Fred

Best congratulations on O B E. The news has just come in a wire to you from Mesopotamia from your Brigade – I am sure you well deserve it – Edward is godfather to Jack's boy 'Stephen Travell' Christened today he returns tonight .

No news so looking forward to seeing you

My final letter in ink

Yr loving Mother

MHB Witts

Mercifully, Major Witts arrived back in Slaughter in time to spend a final few weeks with his mother before she died on 6th February 1921. It was undoubtedly a hard blow considering their close relationship, but some solace could be gathered from their timely reunion.

After his mother's death, Major Witts never set foot in Mesopotamia again. The country slowly gained its independence from the British, and British influence in the region waned. In 1932, Iraq was awarded full membership of the League of Nations and with it her full independence and the dissolution of the mandate. But the country failed to settle comfortably into the post-Ottoman era; stability seemed beyond her grasp. After independence came a series of military coups and the Hashemite monarchy, installed by the British in 1921, was finally ousted in 1958. The country's present troubles derive from many different and complicated influences, but it was the departure of the Turks, leaving a power vacuum that the British were unwilling, and the Iraqis unready, to fill, which allowed the problems to develop.

The part played by Major Witts in the Ottoman defeat was not insignificant. Never again, in his long military career, would he be given the same opportunities to shine as in Mesopotamia, where, in five years, he gained three medals for bravery, five mentions in Despatches and an O.B.E. The crossing of the Shumran bend on 23rd February 1917 was the defining moment of his career and would go down in the annals of the Royal Engineers as one of its brilliant successes. Mesopotamia, as Major Witts often told his mother, had been good to him.

EPILOGUE

Letters: Jan 28th– Feb 18th 1921

When Major Witts arrived back in England, his brother Frank was on holiday touring Algeria with his new wife Ruth, neé Brocklebank. The following are the surviving letters sent by Frank from Algeria to Major Witts in Upper Slaughter.

HOTEL ST – GEORGE

MUSTAPHA-SUPERIEUR
ALGER
Jan 28th 1921.

My dear Fred

This brings our belated good wishes for your birthday which I hope you are spending at home where you will remain for some months at least I expect. I am afraid you will not get the letter or post card I sent to you in Mesopotamia but neither of them contained much of interest. You will have heard all our news from home: we have had a delightful six weeks here and are now moving on to see something of the rest of the country. I only hope we shall like it as much as we have this. If only the sun shines all is well, because it is then quite easy to do nothing! We have had some good tennis and I have been trying hard to play golf; I think I have made some good progress. Then I have been reading about war in general and the war in particular laying a ground work for a possible staff college exam next year. But I expect the competition will be pretty severe. Anyhow I shall be interested to see the papers set next month. Many congratulations on your O.B.E. which I saw gazetted in the Times last week. I am quite certain you have richly deserved it. I am afraid you will find a great change in Mother. But she seems to be doing wonderfully and writes me the most cheering letters. Anyhow it will have done her a lot of good to have you there.

Ruth is very well and enjoying the sunshine. It is of course the first time she has been out of Europe. But this place is not in the least eastern: the French have worked hard and made the whole district thoroughly European. The country is theoretically part of France and all the natives are French citizens with equal rights. They have had a pretty bad famine last year and this has caused a good deal of trouble I think with the natives. It is not really safe to be out after dark outside the town without a revolver, as the natives will try and rob you. We have had gruesome stories told us but we have run no risks ourselves! But they attacked a motor bus the other day and made off with all the money and valuables of the passengers. There is a wonderful system of motor bus and motor charabancs all over the country: enormous affairs and all with pneumatic tyres. but the roads are excruciating so it is not much fun driving in them. We tried once and it was quite enough!

Well we do look forward to seeing you when we return to England: we shall get to London about March 30th and as soon as we have a house at Aldershot you must come and stop with us.

    Best of luck

        Yours

            Frank

ROYAL – HOTEL
BISKRA

Telephone 0.29

BISKRA, le 5 Feb 1921

My dear Fred

    Very many thanks for your letter from home and I do indeed rejoice that you are staying in England till the end of May as there will be plenty of time for us to see something of you when we get back. I am so looking forward to your meeting Ruth: it is about time!

    We are leaving here tomorrow after an excellent week: the weather has broken this evening and it is pouring at this moment with rain and hail. Very unusual for Biskra but as long as it is fine again tomorrow all will be well. This is a curious country for weather. You get perfect spells of sunshine and you think it [will] last for ever and then the wind gets up and you have very bad storms. It is the mountains that does it and as we are going to sleep the night in the centre of the mountains about 3500 feet up I am afraid it will be rather cold. It is the only way of seeing the Roman town of Timgad[1] which is I believe wonderful. However my next letter home will tell you how we fare. We may not go if the weather is too bad. I am so interested to hear that you are going in for the staff college exam and I hope you will be successful. I shone in my promotion exam getting over eighty per cent but it was not exactly difficult or a severe test. Everyone I know of who went in for it passed. I expect they will do away with it soon as they have already the one for Lt. Col. The Astors arrived here yesterday. She is a most remarkable woman and keeps you in fits of laughter.[2] She never stops talking to someone and I gather she is not very popular in the House of Commons. He is very nice but has a good job I should think looking after her. Otherwise there is no one very interesting about. Camille Clifford[3] that was has been here. She is very attractive but that is about all.

---

[1] Timgad, located on the northern slopes of the Aures Mountains in north-eastern Algeria, was founded in AD 100 by Emperor Trajan. It enjoyed a comparatively peaceful existence until the 5th century when it was sacked by Vandals. After a brief Christian reoccupation, the city was abandoned for good in the 7th century and disappeared into obscurity until, in 1881, European archaeologists began its excavation. As a ruin it has been well preserved by the dry climate.

[2] Lady (Nancy) Astor, neé Langhorne, originally from Virginia, was the first female MP in the House of Commons. Lord and Lady Astor lived at Cliveden and in St. James's Square.

[3] Camille Clifford was a Danish-American stage actress and archetypal 'Gibson Girl', a model of voluptuous but elegant proportions publicised by the American illustrator, Charles Dana Gibson, who, incidentally, was Nancy Astor's brother-in-law.

144. Ruth Witts riding a camel in Algeria on February 4th 1921
(Mrs Witts died two days later).

There are very few men traveling and those that are are middle aged or elderly. But there is nothing much to bring them out here. Everybody goes very much the round we are going and you keep on meeting the same people over & over again.

We have taken a lot of photographs and we shall have to get busy putting them into a book when we get home.

Give our love to everyone at home and I hope Mother is keeping fairly well.

Best of luck

　　Yours

　　　Frank

Keep your exam papers for me as I shall find them most interesting & instructive. Will you give the enclosed photograph of Ruth on camel to Mother: it is rather good we think.

GRAND HOTEL CIRTA

Constantine le 8 Feb 1921

CONSTANTINE

Curcio Morosini

Telephone 4.64

My dear Fred

We found the telegram from home when we arrived here last night about midnight. I do so long to know that the end when it came was peaceful and painless. Though we expected the news it was rather a shock to get it and it is somehow very difficult to realise out here. Of course one could not want her to go on living and it is sad to think that she had such a year of misery. But she was wonderful whenever I saw her and I don't think she ever realized that the end was coming. I am so pleased to think that you were there and got home in time to see her. She must have loved seeing you and having you there. I wish I had not been so far away but it was difficult to know what was best to do. However I don't think Mother wanted us to stay in England and it is the only chance I am likely to have of a long holiday. We are thinking so much of you all and I do hope we shall get plenty of letters as I want to know everything.

We had a lovely day at Timgad yesterday and it was really most wonderful to see a whole Roman town with streets and all complete of course only a few columns and walls are standing but you can see the outline of the whole thing. We had a very uncomfy night at a far from clean country inn but here we are in civilization again. The city here is built on a rock which is surrounded on two sides by a gorge about 1000 feet deep and from 50 to 200 feet wide, spanned by three bridges the highest in the world? It is a very old place but little that is old is left we shall be here till the 14th. Your letter of Feb 2nd arrived today enclosing one from Mother: I wonder if she wrote to me again but I am sure you have already written to me and I long for the letters.

Best of love to all from us both

Yours

Frank

GRAND HOTEL CIRTA

Constantine le 11 Feb 1921

CONSTANTINE

Curcio Morosini

Telephone 4.64

My dear Fred

I did so rejoice to get your letter of the 7th this afternoon. The worst of it all has been just the bare news in the telegram and nothing else. But now that I know that the end was natural and peaceful it does help a lot. It is strange what a shock it is even though we had been expecting it so long and it certainly does not make it easier being away. But there was nothing to be done by staying at home and it would probably have worried Mother more if we had not gone away. Still I should so like to have been with you all and to have been near in case she wanted me. However I have everything I want in Ruth and having her makes it all much easier to bear. I long for you to know her. I expect you have written again and send us any papers of interest as we see nothing now, not even the Times and we shan't till we get to Tunis at the beginning of March. The weather here is quite glorious but cold out of the sun. The country round is very pretty and this afternoon we have had a lovely walk through pine woods. The food is very thoroughly French but quite good.

The rooms are tiny but we have our own bathroom which serves as a dressing room & home for luggage. We move on again on Monday to Hammam Messkontine which is a sort of hot spring establishment and we are looking forward to good hot baths in the garden.

I thought so much of you all yesterday and do hope it was a fine day. I do wish I had been there. But it comforts me to think that you were at home. I think your arrival must have sort of fulfilled her last great wish and that after that the effort of living was too much.

Looking forward to your letters and with all our love to you all

Yours

Frank

ETABLISSEMENT THERMAL

ALGERIE

Climat Très Doux

D'HAMMAN – MESKOUTINE

HOTEL TRES CONFORTABLE

Service d'Automobiles

à tous les Trains

GARAGE POUR AUTOMOBILES

Location d'Automobiles

Telephone 0.01   le 18 Feb 1921

My dear Fred

I was so delighted to get your letter of 11th telling me all about the funeral. I am so glad that everything was done as Mother wished, but I think Longley is too hopeless for words and seems determined to make himself unpleasant whenever he can.[4] I wish I had been there but there was a good gathering of the family. I hope you are all beginning to feel more cheerful and I expect Canon Bazeley was excellent.[5] It was really nice & kind of the old man to come, as he was away from home.

Here we have struck quite a good spot provided the weather is kind. Yesterday it was as hot as anything and when we went to bed the thermometer was still over 50°. Today the wind has got up, the sun has disappeared and it is quite cold. We sit over our fire as there is really nowhere else and I am tired of public rooms, and making conversation to people you don't like! Mrs George Keppel[6] arrived here today but I don't expect for long. People break their journey here on the way to or from Tunis. She is still a very handsome woman, travels with a complete retinue including an oddest brother, and the vastest trunks, from which emerge at times wonderful costumes. We had great fun with Lady Astor at Constantine. She is as good as a play

---

[4] See Chapter II, p. 93, note 14.

[5] Canon Bazeley was an old friend of the Witts family. His son, Oswald, served in Mesopotamia. George and Apphie had recently gone to Oswald's wedding. *See* George Witts' letter of Oct 13th 1920, p. 397.

[6] Alice Frederica Keppel, née Edmonstone, wife of Lieutenant-Colonel George Keppel, son of William Keppel, 7th Earl of Albemarle, was most famous for her relationship with King Edward VII.

and never stops talking. They have gone back to England already. We had a great walk this afternoon and found fields full of mauve anemones. It is the first mass of flowers we have seen in this country. In fact flowers here are disappointing.

I am working away at Hamley's operations of war but it is difficult to read very seriously out here – however it serves to whet the appetite for military history. I have also read a history of the country: there is very little history really except a series of petty wars and murders & assassinations. We see no papers here but I suppose that nothing very alarming has occurred.

Poor darling Mother it seems yet difficult to realise that she has gone but we could not want her to go on living once she had lost her health. She was so extraordinarily cheerful over it all and the letters she wrote to me would imply that there was really nothing seriously wrong. But I think she died happy because she had seen you again.

Best of love from us both

Yours

Frank

F.V.B.W. spent the next six years in England, and was then posted to China to join the Shanghai Defence Force in 1927 for two years, just three days after he became engaged to Alice Wrigley. They married in 1929 after his return to England, and had four children. He served in Egypt and Palestine in 1936, and was in India from 1937 to 1939. In 1940 he was Deputy Chief of the General Staff of the British Expeditionary Force in France. From 1941 to 1943 he returned to India again as General Officer Commanding Southern Command, based in Bombay. From 1944 to 1948 he was Lieutenant Governor of the Royal Hospital, Chelsea.

145. F.V.B.W.

On retirement, he returned to Gloucestershire to live in Cirencester. He was active locally as a County Councillor, as Chairman of the Cirencester School, as Chairman of the local British Legion, just to name a few roles.

His eldest brother Edward, who had inherited the Upper Slaughter estate on the death of their father in 1913, settled down to live at the Manor, with his youngest sister Agnes, but retained some of his farming interests in Rhodesia. He too was active in local affairs, as a County Councillor and a JP, and in many other positions.

George went to live at Hillesley near Wotton-under-Edge with his sister Edith. He too was a County Councillor. (It would be interesting to know of any other examples of three brothers all serving as County Councillors in the same county).

Jack was slightly the black sheep of the family, and sadly his son Stephen suffered for many years from mental illness.

Frank died on active service in 1941, when he was commanding Glasgow district in World War II. He and Ruth had no children. Her huge family home Grizedale in the Lake District, which had been built in 1905, was demolished in 1955. It was a prisoner of war camp for German officers during World War II.

Of the sisters, Agnes was a distinguished artist, and some of her pictures are illustrated in this book. Apphie, the eldest of the siblings, was the last to die in 1969, shortly after F.V.B.W., the youngest.

F.V.B.W.'s son Francis inherited the Upper Slaughter estate on F.V.B.W.'s death in 1969. He converted the Manor into Lords of the Manor Hotel in 1972 and ran it for some years before selling it. He now lives at the Dingle, the house built as a dower house for Mrs Witts, but never actually used as such until F.V.B.W.'s death when his own widow moved there.

The old order changeth, and there are pleasant footnotes to our tale. Guy's cottage in Upper Slaughter, mentioned once or twice in these letters, is now owned by a distinguished Iraqi family. And three years ago, the second hand book stall at the Upper Slaughter church fete was manned by the granddaughter of a 1930s Iraqi Prime Minister, who started World War I fighting for the Ottomans, and ended it on the Allied side. It is probable that neither F.V.B.W. nor his mother would have foreseen any of this, but, after their initial shock, they would have been charmed by the Iraqis in question.

146. Family group in the Manor back garden December 1919: Frank, Ruth, Mrs Witts, Elma, Jack and Edith. (Photo taken by Agnes).

APPENDICES

APPENDIX I.

Reprinted from THE ROYAL ENGINEERS JOURNAL
XXXVII, pp.627-639 *December, 1923*
LIGHT FLOATING BRIDGES IN MESOPOTAMIA.
A Lecture delivered at the S.M.E., Chatham, on 11ᵗʰ October, 1923.
By MAJOR F. V. B. WITTS, C.B.E., D.S.O., M.C., R.E.

Introduction

In my lecture to-night, I am going to try to give you some idea of what was involved in bridging large rivers like the Tigris and Euphrates. The whole campaign in Mesopotamia was inseparably bound up with them, whether as lines of communication, as sources of water supply, or as obstacles. They were consequently always with us and equally always had to be bridged. And yet in the *Bridging* volume of the *Work of R.E. in the European War*, 1914-19, there is no reference whatever to the campaign in that country.

My lecture is based chiefly on my personal experiences, and, before going further, I wish to apologize for its inevitably personal character.

I arrived in Basra from France on 1ˢᵗ January 1916, and was left with my half-company of No. 4 Company Bengal Sappers and Miners to assist in building landing stages.

In the middle of March I was given the command of a newly raised Bridging Train, which was arriving from India. Its basic strength was 80 Indian sappers, afterwards increased to 100, and it arrived without any sort of equipment whatever, so I had a hectic week collecting tools and stores. Pontoons were arriving from India, of the Indian pattern made of sheet iron; in those days stores, etc., were still unloaded from the transports in midstream, and the embarkation authorities thought they had at last got something easy to handle, which needed only to be lowered into the river and floated ashore. However, they soon discovered their mistake – the pontoons were of such an inferior workmanship that they could not stand the knocking about of transit, and sank as soon as they reached the water. It was a bright beginning.

Orah. – We got up to the front at Orah at the end of March, 1916, when preparations were being completed for the final attempt to relieve Kut, and immediately took over the boat bridge there. This had been constructed by the Madras Sappers and Miners and was still being maintained by one of their field companies.

This bridge was some 400 yards long, and consisted of country boats known as *bellums* and *mahelas*. Those in use varied from 4 to 7 ft. beam, 25 to 40 ft. in length and 5 to 7 tons carrying capacity. The roadway, consisting of extemporized pontoon equipment superstructure, was carried on small trestles built up on the keel and supported on the gunwales. Like all the other bridges I refer to to-night, unless specially excepted, it was a light bridge, *i.e.*, for infantry in fours and vehicles of 2-ton axle-loads.

The river was then in full flood, running at 6 or 7 knots in the fastest places, and very stormy weather had been experienced. As a result, the bridge was, more often than not, quite impassable. It had consequently been decided to introduce larger boats in the most exposed portions. These were of the same design but much bigger, 13 to 17 ft. beam, 50 to 60 ft. in length and 40 to 70 tons carrying capacity. In their case the roadway had to rest on the gunwales, which required no special strengthening, but to keep them on an even keel, as a load passed over, their masts were utilized. These were spars of 50 to 60 ft. in length with a 12-in. base diameter, and they were firmly lashed right across the gunwales of every two neighbouring *bellums* on both sides of the roadway.

The bridge was anchored by every description of cable, from 4-in. manila and 3-in. steel downwards. The anchors used were the grapnel anchors belonging to the *bellums* themselves, varying between one hundred and two hundred pounds in weight.

The work of changing the boats had hardly been finished when a gale of wind blew up from the south-east against the current and I had my first experience of what a storm on the Tigris meant. Waves were anything up to 6 ft. in height and the bridge was frequently clean swept by them. All my sappers were continually on duty keeping it from breaking up or sinking. It was impossible to walk on it without serious risk of being thrown or blown into the river, and crawling on all fours was the only safe method of progression. Road-bearers were wrenched off their saddlebeams, and chesses* were thrown into the river. Some of the sappers even suffered from sea-sickness. It soon became obvious that the rigidity necessary to save the superstructure from being broken up, and achieved by diagonal bracing between boats, would only lead to the smaller boats being swamped. The superstructure was therefore dismantled and the boats left to ride out the storm. Later on, life-belts were issued at the rate of one per sapper for use on similar occasions and, at any rate, greatly reduced the anxiety of mind of the Bridging Train commander.

Sandy Ridge Bridge. – To accompany the relief force, in its attempt to reach Kut, material for a second bridge had been collected, consisting of Indian pattern pontoons and light bellums, to be towed up river by tugs. Our disappointment was great in being left behind to look after the Orah bridge, but my men were all recruits and entirely inexperienced in bridging, and the mobile bridge was therefore entrusted to two field companies of the Madras Sappers and Miners. It was erected at Sandy Ridge, where it remained until after Kut had fallen : it was put across at the top of the flood in another appalling storm, and the work took 24 hours; it was only kept afloat by a liberal use of tarpaulins, of which, fortunately, a large supply had been arranged for.

Orah Bridge. – Although deprived for the moment of the interest and excitement of accompanying the relief force, our life on the bridge at Orah was full of incidents, of which I propose to relate a few.

On one occasion a motor-launch came across the river too close above the bridge and was carried by the current down on to one of the bigger *bellums*. The launch sank immediately and was never seen again. The occupants managed to catch hold of various ropes and lashings and were soon pulled out by my sappers, who were very astonished to recognize in the dripping party the Commander-in-Chief of the Expeditionary Force, his C.G.S. and two or three other highly-placed G.H.Q. officers. They had a very narrow escape.

On another occasion a small steam-tug fouled the bridge in the dark and remained broadside on, resting on the bows of the boats: the crew, perhaps wisely, leapt onto the bridge, and got clear. However, nothing happened for the moment, and something had to be done to try to rescue the launch and the bridge, both of which were in imminent danger. Fortunately the Mejhidieh – the largest river boat in the country – was anchored just below, and the commander agreed to proceed above the bridge, anchor, let down a boat and cable to the tug and try and haul it off. He succeeded on his second attempt. This was Lieut.-Commander Cowley, who, a few days later, lost his life in a gallant attempt to run a shipload of provisions through to Kut and was awarded a posthumous V.C.

About this time, two of my sappers lost their lives in a most unfortunate way. Firewood was very short, and my men had orders to catch any driftwood floating down. Two of them saw a harmless looking piece of wood coming along, and jumped down into the boat and pulled it out; they had the surprise of their lives; it was the float of a small home-made Turkish mine, which partially detonated, killing them both, but without doing any serious damage to the bridge. The Turks were sending a number of mines down about this time, but I do not remember hearing of any other damage resulting.

It was shortly after Kut fell that the bridge finally received its *coup de grace*; the skipper of a large river steamer, with the usual barges lashed alongside, was caught napping by the current, and was carried broadside on to the centre of the bridge, where the bigger boats were; for a few seconds the bridge held and its boats seemed almost to climb on to the barges lashed to the steamer; then, with reports like guns, the bridge gave, the 3-in. steel cables either breaking or

---

* Chesses are the parallel planks of a pontoon bridge.

pulling clean away from their boats, and the steamer drifted down-stream surrounded by more than a hundred yards of the bridge. The skipper of this ship had come from the Yukon: he was relieved of his command and consigned to a much warmer climate. Material was not available to rebuild it, and, with the fall of Kut, there seemed no necessity for it: so permission was asked to dismantle it completely. This was shortly afterwards given, and the bridge was moved down to Shaikh Saad, which now became the advanced base, and re-erected at a much narrower and more sheltered site.

Shaikh Saad. – The summer of 1916 was spent at Shaikh Saad, and I propose at this point to describe how river traffic was dealt with.

Definite hours were published in orders during which the bridge would be open for road traffic and for river traffic. In this connection, the expression "the bridge will be open" is by itself entirely ambiguous, and in the early days caused frequent misunderstandings. Another cause of confusion, which took a long time to be appreciated, was the fact that it took a considerable time to open and close the bridge. Dealing with a large cut in a bridge of boats of local materials is a very different matter to forming double cut with pontoon equipment.

Cuts. – This leads me on the question of cuts. Their position in the bridge depended on the requirements of navigation, the ruling point usually being the channel and course of traffic coming down with the stream. Their width was governed by that of a large river steamer with a barge lashed on each side, which amounted to 120 ft., and cuts of 300 ft. were often made. This was either done by breaking the portion concerned into rafts of two or three boats or by swinging the entire cut. In a strong current, breaking up into rafts was found to be the only practicable method, though swinging was adopted whenever the conditions permitted. On two occasions I have seen the swung portion break away when opened, and depart downstream. To enable the swung portion to be closed rapidly by one cable from the end, it had to be very strongly braced between boats. In the absence of submarine cable, signal wires were often laid over a bridge, when special contact arrangements had to be made at the cut.

Signalling. – Another most important point is an efficient method of signaling to shipping coming downstream , to show whether they may proceed or not. The rule was that, unless shipping could see the "all clear" signal, they must anchor well above the bridge; the "all clear" signal consisted of a large cone by day and four lamps by night hoisted on a tall mast; this arrangement is much safer than any danger signals which, in a storm, are liable o be blown down or blown out. The ends of the cut were, of course, also well lighted at night with red lamps. Shipping coming downstream had right of way over any shipping coming up, though I have known two large river steamers actually pass in the cut. On another occasion I saw a naval gunboat drift through broadside on!

Anchors. – When we left Orah it was found impossible to recover the anchors, though a river steamer with a steam anchor winch was used. To prevent a recurrence of their loss, should the bridge again shortly be moved, they were periodically raised. It was difficult to judge how often to lift them to ensure that they were not irrevocably imbedded in the alluvial mud, and yet retained sufficient holding power to meet possible floods or collisions.

Mobile Bridging Train. – I now turn to an entirely new phase. One of the many preparations, which were initiated in the summer of 1916 with a view to turning the Turks out of the Sannaiyat position and recapturing Kut, was the formation of a mobile bridging train. Hitherto no land transport had been provided and a bridging train had depended for mobility on tugs, supplied as required.

Pontoons and Superstructure. – It was decided that pontoons and superstructure should be of English pattern and they were accordingly ordered from home. So far pontoons and superstructure had been of the Indian pattern, and I propose, before going on, to describe them generally and point out where they failed. The original pre war Indian pontoon was a bipartite pontoon made of copper, and was a thoroughly serviceable article, its only drawback being its weight and its cumbersome method of joining up sections. The same may be said of the original superstructure; the road-bearers, for instance, were not tapered and were not hollowed out, and were consequently much heavier than the British pattern. But when Indian factories were asked to turn out large numbers, copper for the pontoons had to be given up and sheet-iron substituted, and the workmanship and quality of both pontoons and superstructure reached a very low ebb. Bow and stern sections of pontoons were not interchangeable; as soon as one leak was patched they started another; and leaks were extraordinarily troublesome to mend. Road-bearers and chesses were made of inferior wood, and often broke under very small loads or warped to such an extent as to be unusable in bridge.

Transport. – The next point considered was the method of transport. It was thought that the English pattern pontoon wagon would be too heavy for the roadless plains of the country, often feet deep in dust or mud: the Indian pattern wagon was thrice the weight and intended for bullock draught, the slowest known form of transport. Experiments were therefore carried out with the Indian A.T. cart – a very light two wheeled cart with pole draught for two small mules: a longer axle was fitted, which enabled one section of a pontoon to fit down between the wheels, and a longer pole was necessary to keep the haunches of the mules clear of the front end of the pontoon section. With these alternations, and a few minor fittings, a thoroughly serviceable cart was evolved, which could go practically anywhere that the ordinary A.T. cart could go, and that is quite the most handy form of wheeled transport. Its unusually wide track and length of pole were its only drawbacks. The cart was equally serviceable for carrying loads of supplies when required, and, in a country like Mesopotamia, that was a really serious consideration. The superstructure, anchors and cables were to be carried on ordinary G.S. wagons. Transport was arranged for 500 yards of bridge, *i.e.*, 200 pontoon carts and 56 G.S. wagons involving 900 animals and 600 driver personnel.

Arab Village. – The bridging train I commanded had the good fortune to be selected for conversion into the Mobile Bridging Train, as it was officially called, and we were moved up to Arab Village.

Wadi Bridge. – Soon after this move the arrival of the rainy season was ushered in by a very heavy storm in the Pusht-i-Kuh range, clearly visible to us sixty miles away in the plains below. There was a bridge of boats and Weldon trestles across the Wadi which comes down from these hills. My successor at Shaikh Saad realized that this bridge might be in danger, and he wired to the O.C. battalion posted there asking "if the bridge was causing him no anxiety"; the reply he received was very much to the point: it ran, "Bridge causing no anxiety whatever, it was completely washed away half an hour ago." The spate apparently came down in a 10ft. wall of water, and swept everything before it.

I was told to do something about it. A floating bridge was obviously out of the question, but we had available a large amount of 3-in. steel cable, intended for use with anchors. The span was 105 or 120 ft. and I rigged up a tension bridge, using pontoon superstructure for the roadway. Material for the piers and anchorages was obtained by breaking up a wrecked *mahela*. It was calculated to carry a 12-pdr. man-handled across: a year or so later I was asked by wire how it could best be strengthened to take lorries. I was gratified to hear it was still standing but felt perfectly justified in replying, "pull it down and build another."

Secrecy. – Sir Stanley Maude had, in the meantime, taken over command, and he was a great man for surprise. Amongst other things he wanted the formation of this mobile bridging train to come as a surprise to the Turks. The pontoons, therefore, came up by river, either towed or on barges: the transport marched all the way by road, carrying supplies, and looking to the casual observer every bit like the ordinary A.T. cart. On arrival at Arab Village the carts were not allowed near the pontoons. My men, therefore, had no practice in packing and unpacking. It was only the day operations started that we were permitted to load up. The full number of carts had not then arrived, and a few pontoons had to be carried on G.S. wagons, a most unwieldy load. A G.S. wagon, on the other hand, is a surprisingly suitable form of transport for a couple of bays of superstructure of light bridge.

A general description of the operations which followed, with particular reference to bridging work, can be seen in the August number of the *R.U.S.I. Journal*, and I propose to-night to touch on certain details, technical and otherwise, not there mentioned.

Operations Round Kut. – Bridging the Hai was a very simple matter at the start: in fact, no bridge was essential, as it consisted of a succession of deep pools alternating with dry stretches. However, the water-level in the Tigris rose soon after and converted the Hai into a respectable river 150 to 200 yards wide, which gave us plenty of opportunity to practice for the major operation of forcing the passage of the Tigris, which one realized was in store.

The first attempt to get across some 15 miles above Kut depended for success entirely on surprise and the complete absence of opposition. When these conditions were found to be lacking, the attempt was soon abandoned, but not before all concerned had received very valuable experience.

General Maude then conceived the idea of imitating the River Clyde episode at the Dardanelles. His intention was to send up motor lighters, of which a number had come out from Gallipoli: they were to run the gauntlet of Sannaiyat and the back defences, as far as Kut, where they were to turn into the Hai. Here they were to pick up landing parties and then dash out, cross the river and beach themselves on the other bank. It is characteristic of the man that he took extraordinary precautions to keep this idea to himself. Soundings were necessary round the mouth of the Hai to see if the scheme was practicable, so he summoned the Bridging Train commander to a private interview. I was much surprised at being sent for, and still more so at being sworn to absolute secrecy, being particularly warned against whispering a word of what he was going to say to even the most senior members of staff. He told me what he wanted and added that my reports were to be private letters addressed to him personally by name. Paddling about in a pontoon for two or three nights with the Turks on one bank and our own troops on the other was no joke, and though the river was 400 to 600 yards wide, I was not sorry when I was in a position to report the scheme impracticable. He then told me to take every opportunity of reconnoitering the river for a bridge.

Pontoons for Live-Stock. – Pontoons had other uses than mere bridging. On one occasion I had to send a dozen out with the Cavalry Division on a raid: they came back filled with a couple of dozen sheep. It was not for a fortnight that any enquiries were made for these sheep, when I had to confess we had eaten half of them. However, it was about Christmas time, so no serious notice was taken of it. One pontoon section I had fitted with a movable wire-covering and used as a mobile hen-coop: consequently I was never short of fresh eggs, but I always dreaded this pontoon being launched, in the hurry of the moment, complete with hens.

Shumran. – When the Turks were finally cleared from the right bank, I was told to reconnoiter the Shumran bend. It was possible to get up to the river bund without difficulty at any hour, but it was not so easy to measure the width with any accuracy, particularly as special orders had been given not to attract undue attention to the locality. The 3-in. to 1-mile map, based on aeroplane photographs, gave one a good idea, but it was very desirable to check it, and particularly to note the effect of a possible flood. I took very good care that my estimates, based on prismatic compass readings, were on the right side. The site of the old Turkish boat bridge was finally abandoned in favour of the apex of the bend, which was by far the most suitable place tactically and also the narrowest. I made it out to be 340 yards. A pocket sextant is invaluable for accurate measurements of this sort.

The ferrying arrangements were kept quite separate from the bridging and were worked out to the last detail and carefully rehearsed by night on the Hai. Only pontoons were used.

Turning to the technicalities of the bridge, it was made by forming up. Unlimited labour was available, overcoming the objection of having to carry baulks and chesses two or three hundred yards; and it was also considered safer, in view of the strong flood running and of the inevitable interference from hostile artillery. For anchor work two motor launches, carried on Indian bullock-drawn pontoon wagons, had been provided; these were successfully got up and launched and proved invaluable. The rate of construction was entirely controlled by the time required to get out the anchors. The current was between five and six knots and the handling of the launches was a very delicate matter: one launch did foul the bridge, and complete disaster was narrowly averted. In view of the flood running, all the downstream anchors were sacrificed, the anchors themselves were used in kedge upstream and the cables to lengthen the upstream ones. Every second pontoon thus had a 1-cwt. anchor with a ½-cwt. anchor in kedge at the end of 400 ft. of 3-in. cable. As a result of these precautions no anchors seriously dragged, in spite of a tendency to do so when first cast.

Further details of these operations can, as I have said, be found in the August number of the *R.U.S.I. Journal*, and I will therefore now pass on.

Dialah. – I was not personally present at the crossing of the Dialah, but I cannot pass it by without notice, as it was quite one of the most heroic episodes in the whole campaign in Mesopotamia. The Turks were in retreat, and it was therefore decided to act boldly and try to rush the crossing without any adequate preparations, which meant loss of time. The first night pontoons appear to have been launched successively at more or less the same spot and each met the same fate – every man in them being shot down; the river was only 100 to 120 yards broad and no proper covering fire could be arranged in the time. The second night, under cover of a local barrage on the opposite bank, the first pontoons got across, but when the barrage had to lift, succeeding pontoons met the same fate as on the previous night and their occupants exterminated. But some sixty men of the Loyals were established, and held out under heroic conditions for 24 hours until the crossing was finally effected. This was largely due to the threat of the Cavalry Division and 1st Corps, which had been moved over to the right bank at Bawi, partly by steamer ferry and partly by a pontoon bridge which had been towed upriver from Arab Village. On this third night General Maude put into practice the River Clyde stunt he had considered before. Two armed motor lighters carrying 500 men started off to run ashore half a mile above the mouth of the Dialah. They grounded on the sandbanks in the Tigris, but in any case they would have been too late. The threat on the right bank had made the Turks move. The actual bridge then built over the Dialah near its mouth was an ordinary pontoon bridge and needs no comment.

Baghdad. – The Turks destroyed their bridge of boats in Baghdad before evacuating the place. The pontoon bridge from Bawi was towed up and put across at the old bridge site – the narrowest point of the river. My mobile bridging train marched up from Shumran and we put a bridge across at the new advanced base just below Baghdad.

The bridges were later replaced by two, known as the North and South Bridges. The North Bridge was made of large open iron pontoons sent out from India. The South Bridge was formed of dredger pontoons supplemented by a few locally made bridge boats. These dredger pontoons had previously been used in a bridge over the Euphrates at Gurmut Ali, where they were anchored end on right across the current, violating all the rules for floating bridges; this was done in the absence of sufficient material for any other method, and proved satisfactory. A 60-pdr. could be man-handled across the South Bridge. It sank once during construction and was completely destroyed later, when it was replaced by the Maude bridge, which met a similar fate in the floods this spring. Full details of this fine bridge can be found in the volume *With the Inland Water Transport in Mesopotamia.*

We stayed at Baghdad for a fortnight or three weeks, and were then ordered forward to take part in the operations for the capture of Samarrah.

Two incidents in connection with this move are, I think, of interest. Our orders came by clear line telegram one morning about ten o'clock to march that night at ten o'clock to a place some 20 miles ahead. The bridge was across the river and in use. I arranged my time-table for dismantling the bridge and loading up so as to allow my men three hours for rest and food before marching. About six o'clock in the evening I received another wire telling me not to dismantle the bridge until a certain brigade of artillery had crossed. By this time the bridge was completely dismantled, and loading up was nearly completed. When I telephoned to point this out I was informed that ten o'clock was the time ordered for my march. The time required to dismantle 300 yards of pontoon and load it on to transport, not to mention the fatigue caused to the men, had once again been overlooked entirely.

During the day I had taken the precaution to ask for the latest map. It seemed from it that if we stuck to the railway during the night we should find ourselves near the river in the morning. Instead, however, there was no sign of the river or of any other water; we therefore struck north and had some five miles to march to the river, making 25 miles in all. The map was all wrong. It was the same map which had led to our turning the Turkish position at Mushaidieh three weeks earlier; the

Turks did not anticipate such a wide detour from the river, and, in fact, there was no intention of making it.

After a halt for a day or two at Fort Kermea, we marched on to Beled. On the way we were caught by very heavy rain, the ground was completely flooded and we were able to water the mules as they stood. The only way we could get on again was by temporarily abandoning our carts and wagons and double-teaming the other half the remaining four miles to camp, and then sending back the double teams.

Sinijah. – From Beled we moved down to the Tigris at Sinijah and put a bridge across there. This place practically marks the limit of the alluvial deposit, and, from here on, the bed of the river consists of shingle with occasional rocks. I particularly remember the bridge for two reasons. To start with, every road-bearer and chess was in use, and there was literally not a single one spare; wagons were, therefore, particularly carefully scrutinized before crossing, and I recall bitter complaints from gunners at being told to throw off tents and grain from their ammunition wagons. Then the night it was done we got warning that the Turks had set fire to two ammunition barges which they could not take away upstream; that they were adrift and floating down towards the bridge. We opened a cut and sent a tug up. The latter piled itself up on the shingle almost at once. Fortunately the barges too soon stranded.

Samarrah. – As soon as Samarrah was occupied at the end of April, 1917, the bridge was moved up and put across there, and there it remained in peace for the next eight months. The site chosen was the most suitable during the low-water season, but it was evident that it would have to be abandoned during the floods, for when the floods finally came, it was found impossible to keep a pontoon bridge afloat, and it was replaced by a steamer ferry.

At Samarrah there was a difference of 23ft. between low and high-water marks. Floods were due either to heavy rain or to melting snow in Asia Minor; the former caused possibly the more sudden flood, but the latter was responsible for the highest floods. The water occasionally rose 8 ft. in the 24 hours. Elaborate flood-warning arrangements were initiated, but were of little value to the bridge furthest upstream, as our enemies the Turks would not co-operate!

During this summer, in addition to the main pontoon bridge, a flying bridge was maintained at another point. The raft was of the ordinary four-pontoon type and worked on a 3-in. steel rope, suspended between a tripod on the higher bank and a length of the Baghdad railway up-ended on the other bank, which was practically water-level.

This flying bridge was later replaced by a bridge of half-pontoons some 200 yards long. It did useful work, but is not a satisfactory form of bridge.

A handrail was made of oars fitting into hoops on the kelson and held by the rack-lashing and carrying spare anchor cable fixed by clove hitches. It was of considerable moral value, and its flimsiness was an advantage, as it did not complicate cutting a wagon clear, if the bridge itself was in danger after an accident, as often happened in a strong current.

The 60-pdr. guns and 6-in. howitzers had also to be moved across occasionally. This was done on a standard pattern 60-pdr. raft, moved across below the main bridge by ropes, pulled by sappers walking across the bridge.

The number of baulks in bridge was brought up to nine per bay to enable armoured cars to cross freely, but transport was only provided for seven baulks per bay.

The powers that be were very worried about mines, and a buoyed 3-in. steel cable was therefore maintained, with considerable difficulty, across the river above the upper bridge. The Turks tried to send mines down on several occasions. They were contact mines of the latest type, but our protections lay in the windings of the river and the many banks in its course. None ever reached the so-called mine-boom; though I was sent out on two or three occasions to blow up mines stranded upstream.

During the summer, pontoon wagons arrived from England to replace G.S. wagons for carrying superstructure. All the time our sappers were kept hard at work keeping pontoons in repair. These were of the Mark II pattern and were never designed for continual use of this nature, and, though they lasted well if always in the water, if taken out after a long immersion and required again two or three days later, they were useless. Waterproof canvas, India-rubber solution and marine glue were in great demand: the planking, too, often warped seriously and had to be replaced. Various notes on the pontoon equipment based on experience in this country were published in the *R.E. Journal* for November, 1921.

By this time, arrangements and regulations for the control of traffic across the bridge had been elaborated in considerable detail. A detachment of 1 N.C.O. and 6 men of the Military Police were permanently attached to the Bridging Train, and two of their number were always on duty. A sapper maintenance detachment was also on permanent duty, consisting of 1 N.C.O, together with three sappers per hundred yards of bridge, thus allowing of one sapper always on duty for each hundred yards of bridge. When artillery crossed, an officer of the bridging train was always on duty, and extra sappers, to allow of one in every other pontoon: any breakages were therefore promptly detected: a breakdown gang with drag-ropes, knives, and hand-axes were kept in readiness on the bank. One pontoon was always ready to be manned as a lifeboat, and often one of the launches was also in immediate readiness. I was fortunate never to lose a gun, but one or two ammunition and ambulance wagons were lost, and A.T. carts on numerous occasions, owing to the innate foolishness of the mule. The one ambition of many mules seemed to be to push its pair off the bridge, and a regular pushing match would ensue.

There was very good fishing at Samarrah. One of my warrant officers caught a 98-pdr. Tigris salmon on a rod and line: it took 1 ½ hours to land. A 132-pdr. was pulled out by one of my men on a ground line. The Arabs used to catch them by throwing in a loose bait containing opium: they then swam out and caught the drugged fish which came to the surface with their hands. Some of those they missed were often picked out as they floated through the bridge by my men.

Euphrates. – In January, 1918, we were suddenly ordered to march back to Baghdad, leaving all our actual pontoon material behind. At Baghdad we drew an entirely new outfit from the Engineer Field Park at the Advanced Base, and then marched over to the Euphrates, where operations were in preparation to round up the Turkish force.

However, we did little beyond building bridges which were never used, and thoroughly frightening the Turks. On of their aeroplanes observed us on the march and mistook our column of more than two miles in length for substantial reinforcements of field artillery; the Turks withdrew their advanced posts next day.

The Euphrates was much like the Tigris up to Hit, where it emerged on the alluvial plain. Above Hit it ran in a wide rocky bed, much cut up by stone weirs built out for water-power purposes during the low-water season.

We spent the summer of 1918 just above Hit, and the only incident of note was the complete swamping of the bridge – some 300 yds. long in a sudden violent squall. It sank and was swept away *en bloc*. Pontoons were scattered miles down the river, but only about half-a-dozen were never recovered, though all were much damaged.

Life at Hit was dominated by the bitumen springs which belched out sulphuretted hydrogen and made things almost unbearable in certain winds.

Tigris. – We marched back to the Tigris in September in time for the final push just before the Armistice. For this we were reinforced by half the other mobile bridging train, which had been formed, some time before, giving me 750 yds. of light pontoon bridge on wheels to play with.

During these operations we had our hands full and bridged the Tigris at Baiji and Fathah, the Lesser Zab at its mouth, and finally a bridge of half pontoons at Hadraniyah, where the two cavalry brigades had previously forded the river, and cut off the Turks. All these bridges were in position at once.

Fording the river here was a wonderful feat: the 18-pdrs., with which the horse artillery were specially armed, completely disappeared from view in the middle of the ford, which was almost a rapid. A number of men and horses were drowned, and one gun washed away but recovered by a subaltern of mine some days later. However, the Turks thought the river absolutely unfordable and were completely surprised. It was a great "finale" to the campaign.

Conclusion. – In conclusion there are two things I should like to mention. The first is that one bridge over the Dialah was constructed of *gufas* – the circular boat, made of reeds and bitumen, dating from the days of the Ark. Each pier consisted of two *gufas* held in correct position by a wooden frame. The other is that the Grand Stand at the Baghdad Racecourse* was made throughout of Weldon trestles and pontoon superstructure, and is evidence that they, too, like pontoons themselves, have other uses than mere bridging.

*See illustration 102.

APPENDIX II.

Reprinted from JOURNAL OF ROYAL UNITED SERVICES
INSTITUTION LXVIII, pp.447-455 1923

THE PASSAGE OF THE TIGRIS AT SHUMRAN, 23rd FEBRUARY, 1917.

By BREVET MAJOR F. V. B. WITTS, C.B.E., D.S.O., M.C.,
Royal Engineers.

---

1. *Introduction.* – Schellendorf, on page 413, says: "To cross a river by throwing a bridge over it, under fire, is certainly one of the most desperate undertakings that a General could be called upon to execute."

As far as large rivers go, the passage of the Tigris at Shumran, on 23rd February 1917, was one of the few occasions in the Great War on which the British Army was faced with the problem. The crossing should further be of interest as it was the crux of Sir Stanley Maude's operations which led to the recapture of Kut and the occupation of Baghdad.

2. *General Situation.* – At the beginning of December, 1916, the situation was as follows: -

The 1st Corps, under General Cobbe, was facing the Sannaiyat position, with the Meerut Division on the left bank and the Lahore Division on the right.

The 3rd Corps, under General Marshall, was holding the Sinn position from Magasis to Dujailah with the 14th Indian Division and the 13th British Division.

A Cavalry Division of two brigades, under General Crocker, was at Arab Village.

Shaikh Saad was the advanced base and a 2 ft. 6 in. railway ran out from there to Sinn.

There was a bridge of country boats at Shaikh Saad and two pontoon bridges at Arab Village, where there was also a mobile bridging train which had just been formed.

The Turks held Sannaiyat, the left bank of the Tigris to Kut, and a bridgehead round the mouth of the Hai. They also held the line of the Hai by posts and Arab irregulars. Their advanced base was at Shumran, where they had a bridge of country boats. They also had one over the Hai. Their total numbers were estimated at 20,000, with 70 guns.

The peculiar strength of the Sannaiyat position is too well known to need remark. The Tigris varied in width from 200 to 800 yards and was 50 feet deep in places.

3. *Maude's Plan.* – Maude was a great man for mystifying and mis-leading, and he was determined to see how much he could accomplish by surprise. His idea was to appear to intend to attack Sannaiyat once again, and then make a surprise night march and seize the Hai; he then intended to try his luck with a surprise crossing of the Tigris.

It was, consequently, of vital importance to keep the formation of a mobile bridging train a complete secret. The steps taken to do this were effectual, but added considerably to the difficulties of the new unit, which had no opportunity of practising. All the transport, too, did not arrive in time, and some of the pontoons had to be carried on G.S. wagons; this was not an easy problem to solve for a night march across country, and the final result cannot be called satisfactory.

4. *Seizure of Hai.* – The night December 13th/14th was fixed for the night march to the Hai. On December 12th considerable artillery activity was developed on the Sannaiyat front, and one of the two bridges from Arab Village was moved up to Sandy Ridge to further distract attention in that direction.

The Hai was seized without any opposition, and, much to the disgust of the newly formed and enthusiastic bridging train, was found to consist of a succession of dry crossings and pools. However, the going was heavy for wheels, and a pool large enough and deep enough to float pontoons was found at Atab and two bridges built. Unfortunately, it was also deep enough to engulf a messcart, which went over the edge.

5. *Attempted crossing.* – During the next few days our position on the Hai was consolidated, the cavalry reconnoitred the country and river ahead, and the railway was continued to the Hai.

Eventually, in the early hours of 20th December, the cavalry Division moved out, accompanied by one Infantry Brigade and the bridging train, and made a night march across country to the Brick Kilns. This place had been previously reconnoitred, but the only information as to the width of the river was that it was "300 cubits." The night march passed off without incident, beyond the breaking down of three or four wagons on the rough ground.

On arrival at the site it was found that the Turks were expecting us, presumably as a result of the previous reconnaissance, and had a small force with machine guns and a couple of guns on the other bank. However, it was decided to push on.

The country was like the rest of Mesopotamia – absolutely flat on both banks; the only cover consisted of the usual low bund or bank near the river's edge. However, at the point selected, a wide and deep, but dry, irrigation canal led up to within 50 yards of the river, where it was closed by a large dam. A section of the bridging train was sent up this canal, which afforded complete cover from view and useful cover against fire. A pontoon was got into the river, but before it could leave the bank casualties were so heavy that orders were given for the attempt to be abandoned. The one pontoon was lost.

All this time a flanking squadron were quietly watering their horses about a mile upstream, and preparations to make another attempt at this point were in hand, when orders were received by wireless from G.H.Q. to give up the attempt altogether and return to Hai. The way back will long be remember by those present; the majority of the animals had not watered since the previous day and got none till the next.

The attempt had apparently been a dismal failure, but actually it was a blessing in disguise, and contributed in a very large degree to the success of the final effort. It confirmed the Turks in their belief that a crossing was impossible and also gave them false notions of what would be done if any further attempt were made; this will be seen later. It also gave us a very good idea of what not to do, and of what extensive preparations were necessary. We profited by the experience.

6. *Clearing Right Bank.* – It was now evident that a purely surprise crossing was out of the question, and that it could only be accomplished by an organized assault. In order to have a freer hand in selecting a point of passage, Sir Stanley Maude decided to clear the right bank as a first step. This was finally accomplished on the morning of 16th February after very heavy fighting, which there is not space to go into here.

Meantime Maude had kept his cavalry busy – no doubt, to give the Turks something to think about as to what he intended to do. These excursions included on to Hai Town, and reconnaissance of the Suwaicha marsh with a view to finding a way round or across. It only resulted in the Horse Artillery guns getting bogged, and they were only recovered with difficulty. However, no doubt, the Turks heard of the trip and had their attention distracted in that direction.

Elaborate preparations were put in hand in the First Corps area a little behind Sannaiyat for a crossing there, and no doubt the Turks heard of these too. Sannaiyat was continually bombarded and on one occasion raided.

The bridging train had not been idle, and had valuable opportunity for practice on the Hai, which was now a swift river 200 yards broad.

The commander of the bridging train had been busy reconnoitering the Tigris under the immediate orders of Sir Stanley Maude. The latter carried secrecy to such extremes that reports to him and his further instructions took the form of personal letters.

On 16th February, when the right bank had been cleared, the bridging train commander was ordered to reconnoitre the river in the Shumran bend, and was told to take another officer out with him who could lead the bridging train up when required. This was disquieting, as it seemed the show was again going to be rushed, which meant probable failure. However, it started to rain that day and rained as it had never rained before in Mesopotamia. The result was that the whole country was flooded, and movement became quite impossible for nearly a week. This undoubtedly played an important part in the success of the crossing, as the time was utilized to organize every detail and practise on the Hai.

7. *Immediate Preparations.* – During this pause several more reconnaissances of the Shumran bend were made on its eastern and southern faces.

The eastern face was at first considered, as it was here the Turks had originally had their bridge, but it was found to be wide and did not lend itself to covering fire from the right bank. The southern end of the bend was then considered and, after reconnaissance, selected. Here the river was made out to be 340 yards wide; on the further bank the cliff was vertical and would require considerable ramping before pontoons could be launched. Its configuration lent itself to concentrated and converging covering fire from our side.

It was, of course, necessary to get a covering party across before the construction of the bridge began. The opposite bank was entrenched and loopholed, and defended by machine guns. It was decided to ferry troops across at three distinct points, all downstream of the bridge, M. 32, M. 29, K. 55; the point of this was the danger of derelict pontoons floating down on the bridge during construction. It was hoped that at least one of the ferries would be successful. Tracks to the three ferry sites and the bridge site were carefully marked out so as to be easily distinguishable at night and yet invisible to enemy aircraft.

Meanwhile the actual crossing was being rehearsed and practised every night on the Hai. Volunteer rowers were obtained from the different British regiments, supplemented by sappers of the British field companies and the Madras Sappers and Miners, including their Burma Company, and the 128th Pioneers.

The bridging train handed over forty complete pontoons for ferrying purposes. Thirteen of these pontoons were allotted to each ferry; of these, three were kept in reserve. Crews of four rowers and coxswain were detailed per pontoon and the leading parties were organized into parties of ten and equivalent loads of ammunition, Lewis guns, etc. Four complete reliefs for the crews were organized, the idea being to keep the ferries running all out for twenty-four hours should there be any delay with the bridge, and also to make ample provision for the inevitable casualties. Altogether 825 rowers were provided.

As a result of the heavy rain the Tigris had now come down in flood and was running at at least six knots. This made the building of the bridge a slow and delicate matter, without considering any opposition; the ferries, too, would drift many hundred yards downstream in the round trip; to meet this, definite parties were told off to tow them back to their original starting places. Fortunately, two motor-boats, heavily armoured, had been given to the bridging train for getting out anchors, and gear for launching them was devised. They were carried on heavy bullock-drawn wagons.

One battalion was to be ferried across at each ferry. 1st Norfolks at No. 1, 2/9th Gurkha Rifles at No. 2, 1/2nd Gurkha Rifles at No. 3. To assist the bridging train, a British field company and two companies of British pioneers were allotted, and also a second doctor and twenty four stretcher bearers, which was not as encouraging as it might be.

It was at first intended that the crossing should be made at night, but it was thought that all advantages of position and covering fire would be lost, and that no one would be able to see what was going on. So it was decided to start with the first streak of dawn, after a night approach march.

The 14th Indian Division were responsible for making good the crossing; this was a guarantee of a good show.

8. *Diversions*. – Before describing the actual crossing, it seems the best opportunity to describe what further steps Maude took to mystify and mislead his enemy.

In the first place, on 17th February, he ordered a surprise assault on Sannaiyat. Our troops captured the front trenches, but were afterwards driven out by a counter-attack. This was the fourth failure to capture this redoubtable position, but it was not in vain. It diverted the attention of the Turks from the principal attack and alarmed them to the extent that they moved more troops towards Sannaiyat. On the following days barrages were put down at uncertain intervals to keep the Turks in continual suspense of another attack, and also to get them used to bombardments followed by no attack.

The crossing was finally fixed for 22nd February, but on the previous day was postponed twenty-four hours to give the river a chance of going down, as the current was still very strong although it had passed its highest.

Two or three days previous to this, elaborate make-believe preparations were started at the Liquorice Factory: each night the Turks must have heard the movement of carts accompanied by the sound of planks being unloaded; their aeroplanes must have discovered a number of pontoons being stealthily towed up the Hai in that direction. They showed their suspicions by the active use of a searchlight opposite. Their suspicions must have been confirmed on the morning of the 23rd when daylight revealed artillery observation ladders in position all round the Kut peninsula.

At the Magasis bend a very successful small raid was made across the river in pontoons, the Turks were surprised and a mortar was captured and brought back. This probably was correctly taken by the Turks as bluff, and confirmed them in their belief that, if any attempt was going to be made, it would be at the Liquorice Factory. This was on the night 22/23rd February. Next morning our aeroplanes saw guns and infantry marching in that direction away from Shumran, where the real crossing had already commenced.

On the morning of the 22nd yet another attack on Sannaiyat was made by the Meerut Division, and by nightfall, after very heavy fighting, the first two lines of trenches had been captured.

9. *Night Approach*. – Returning again to the crossing, an hour before dark on the evening of 22nd February, the troops detailed to cover the crossing and to seize the far bank moved out to the rendezvous, including the bridging train well over a mile in length. At this moment an enemy aeroplane passed over – very high, it is true, but they must have observed the troops on the move. Luckily the first part of the march might equally well lead to the Liquorice Factory, where, no doubt, it was thought to be going. In any case the Turks were quite certain that an attempt to cross the river was most unlikely, for they considered it doomed to failure, and possibly thought attempts were being made to divert their attention from Sannaiyat.

The night march passed off without incident. The three ferry parties reached their positions, unloading their pontoons and carrying them the last quarter of a mile; before midnight all preparations for launching them had been made and the troops lay down to rest.

The bridging train moved up to within one mile of the bank and parked till such time as their services would be required – that is, when our troops had established themselves on the opposite bank. Ramps were dug at the bridge site for the bridge itself, for launching pontoons, and for launching the motor-boats. The rest of the night passed quietly, the Turks opposite showing no signs of suspicion.

During the night, too, our hold of the right bank was extended from the Nahr al Massig up to K66c, and all the artillery of the Corps was moved into position all round the bend to cover the crossing, as, also, were 10 trench howitzers and 45 machine guns.

10. *Ferries*. – It was about five–thirty, just as the first signs of dawn were visible, that the first journey of the thirty pontoons, which had been previously quietly launched, commenced. The surprise was complete. At No. 1 Ferry, nearest the bridge site and immediately down-stream of it, the surprise was so complete that the Norfolks captured 300 Turks and five machine guns. The Gurkhas at Nos. 2 and 3 Ferries were not so fortunate, being seen just as they were making the

bank. However, it was too late to stop them landing, though heavy casualties were suffered both in the pontoons and in the subsequent hand-to-hand fighting on the bank.

By No. 1 Ferry the work of ferrying proceeded throughout the day, but at the other two the casualties to troops, rowers and pontoons were so heavy that work had to be stopped, and the remaining men were moved up to No. 1 Ferry to cross there. Before 7 a.m., out of 230 rowers supplied by the Hampshire Regiment, 110 had been hit.

By 7.30 a.m., about three companies of the Norfolks and 150 Gurkhas were on the left bank. By 3 p.m. all three battalions were established on an east and west line one mile north of the bridge, and a fourth battalion was being ferried across. Two counter-attacks down the centre and west side of the peninsula were beaten off, largely by artillery and machine-gun fire from the right bank.

11. *Bridge*. – It was about 7.30 a.m. that it was suggested that work on the bridge should start. At this time, however, the Norfolks from No. 1 Ferry had not yet had time to work up the bank to the bridge site, and a considerable amount of sniping was going on. It was suggested that it would be better to wait a bit; it was then pointed out that the two lower ferries were out of action and that it was very necessary to give moral support by starting work on the bridge.

Orders were then given for the bridging train material to come up – the *personnel* had moved up earlier in the day. As previously arranged, the wagons and carts came up at full gallop at three hundred yards interval; they were rapidly unloaded and galloped off again. There was a deep dry canal at M32, two hundred yards or so below the bridge, similar to the one used by the bridging train at the Brick Kilns in December, and evidently the Turks thought we were going to use this one this time, as they kept up a steady stream of 5.9's on it all day. The bridging wagons had, therefore, only to run the gauntlet of the overs and none of them were hit. This is the more remarkable as the country was as flat as the rest of Mesopotamia, and devoid of cover except for the small river bund about three feet high, which, of course, gave no cover whatever to the wagons. The only assumption is that their arrangements for artillery observation were completely upset in the first few minutes.

The shore transom was placed in position and land anchorage fixed, while experiments were made as to rowing pontoons against the current; this was found impracticable. The first motor-boat was, therefore, ordered up, and it was a wonderful sight; towering as it did quite eleven feet in the air and visible for miles around, and drawn by sedate siege train bullocks, who ambled along as if nothing out of the ordinary was happening; it was a marvel to everyone present that they were never hit. The British field company undertook the launching and did it most successfully, though they had never had an opportunity of practising. As soon as the first motor-boat was in the water the second was ordered up and launched equally successfully. All this time accurate sniping was kept up from the other bank and a number of casualties to man and mule suffered. But from now onwards the far bank was sufficiently cleared, and no more sniping occurred. The construction of the bridge went on in earnest.

The rate of construction was entirely controlled by the time required to get out the anchors. The current was still running at at least five knots, and the handling of the launches was a delicate matter to prevent them fouling the cables of the portion of the bridge already constructed and the bridge itself. This did happen once when the bridge was half-built and nearly ended in disaster both to the launch and the bridge.

All this time the Turks kept up a steady fire with 5.9's on the nullah near by and frequently searched the river in the hope of finding ferry and bridge. H.E. shells fell in the water on either side of the bridge, covering it with spray, but neither the bridge itself nor any of the cables were touched. The motor-boats, too, had many narrow escapes.

The Turks had two other means of destroying the bridge. One was by sending down floating mines, and the other by steaming a ship down on to it.

Floating mines were known to be inevitable. A portable mineboom had been prepared, but, owing to the flood, was regarded as a serious danger to the bridge and not used. Machine guns were told off to sink or fire them, but several passed the bridge, fortunately without hitting any pontoons.

Any ship sent down it was hoped to deal with by gunfire. However, they did not attempt it, though a definite aeroplane report, which fortunately proved to be false, that one was coming, added considerably to the anxiety of the work.

About three o'clock the required notice was given that the bridge would be ready in one and a half hours' time. A party was now sent across to start work on the far bank. Little was required here beyond cutting a passage through the river bund; but, as soon as work was started on this, it was apparently observed by the Turkish gunners, who, for the first time, tried to reach the bridge with shrapnel. Luckily, they were apparently too far back for their fuzes, and could not get the range. They now had the exact line for their H.E., and redoubled their efforts to get a direct hit, which was the only thing that mattered. Fortunately, our luck held and no damage was done.

By four-thirty the bridge was completely ready for traffic, 295 yards long, after 8 hours' actual work. The first to cross were some 500 Turkish prisoners, who had been captured early in the day, and had been sitting, sheltering under the bund on the far bank, watching the construction of the bridge and hoping to see it hit. Shortly afterwards the other two Brigades of the 14th Division, which had supplied the Brigade for ferrying, crossed without incident, and the Division held the line one mile north of the bridge for the night.

12. *24th February*. – Next morning, 24th February, the Cavalry Division crossed the bridge, followed by the artillery of the 14th Division, and the whole of the 13th Division. Traffic crossed the bridge in a continuous stream. Anything in difficulties was at once thrown clear. The Turks, however, put up a very stubborn fight in the broken ground at the northern end of the Shumran peninsula, in order to secure the retreat of their troops retiring from Sannaiyat, where three more lines of trenches had been captured on the 23rd before the crossing at Shumran had sealed its fate.

13. *Pursuit*. – During the night, 24th/25th February, the Turks withdrew and the pursuit to Baghdad began. Here the story must be left, but before doing so it should be emphasized that this one bridge was, for a time, the sole means of communication for three divisions. And later the Lahore Division also crossed.

14. *Lessons*. – In conclusion, it is desirable to draw attention to certain points which experience in these operations on the Tigris, and again later on the Dialah, proved must be remembered if the operation is to be a success. These are: -

(1) An operation of this sort cannot be rushed. Accurate reconnaissance, elaborate detailed arrangements and, if possible, actual rehearsals are essential.

(2) The success of the first landing, on which everything depends, is entirely a question of surprise.

(3) Landings should be attempted in at least three places.

(4) The bridging train should not be committed until a definite footing has been obtained.

(5) The ferrying must be kept entirely separate from the bridging and cannot be looked after by the same individual.

(6) A liberal supply of men must be available, as, apart from casualties, pontooning is very heavy and tiring work.

(7) Traffic over the bridge must be controlled by a staff officer of the senior formation concerned.

(8) All units must have had thorough practice in crossing pontoon bridges, and be thoroughly trained in what may be called bridge discipline.

(9) Lastly, a word of warning against the expression 'throwing a bridge.' It tends to give the idea that there is nothing more in it than throwing a cricket ball, whereas actually, as it is hoped has been pointed out, it is a very complicated and delicate process.

APPENDIX III.

Telegram from F.V.B.W. to his mother from hospital in Amara
(sent 2nd Jan 1917, received 9th Jan 1917)

APPENDIX IV.

Telegram from the Secretary of the War Office detailing F.V.B.W.'s
discharge from hospital (sent 14 Jan, received 19 Jan 1917)

APPENDIX V.

Letter from H. D. Sweet-Escott to Mrs Witts, dated Jan 18th 1917

Redholme,

Stevenage,

Herts.

18th Jan. 17.

Dear Mrs. Witts

Thank you very much for your letter. I was delighted to hear that Freddy had only got a 'cushy one', & he is really to be congratulated on getting a little rest in Hospital.

No. I am not a proud Father. I expect it must have been some other member of the family, though I don't know who. I did not see the announcement; but I only see the 'Morning Post' I have written to Freddy, & trust he may get it eventually. Posts seem to take a longish time, as a rule.

I still go on getting a bit stronger; but my legs are no use to me yet.

I am going to see a man in town twice a week at present, who says he can cure me; but he may be a fraud.★

Kindest regards & best wishes for 1917

Yrs Sincerely.

   H. D. S-Escott

★ F.V.B.W.'s friend, Sweet Escott, had been crippled in a riding accident in 1911.

APPENDIX VI.

Secret correspondence between General Maude and F.V.B.W.
(5th-7th February 1917) re reconnaissance at the mouth of the Shatt-al-Hai

I reconnoitred the TIGRIS last night from the mouth of the HAI down to below N 12, sounding the channel swimming near the right bank. The sandbank opposite the ruin was shewing above water in patches. The channel here is very narrow and it is not safe to count on more than 3 ft of water with the TIGRIS gauge at 106, which is the same level as when I made my first reconnaissance of the HAI. The channel gradually improves and below N 14 there is ample depth and width. If the river rises another 2' 6", there should be no peculiar difficulty in navigating this channel upstream, as all you have to do is to keep near the bank as the depth admits. Coming down stream would be less reliable, as a slight mistake and you might be carried round broadside across the channel and jam across it. It is quite possible that further floods may shift the sandbank & alter the channel. I think there is very little chance of navigating round the north of this sandbank, because it is impossible to mark the channel and there would be nothing to steer by, and when taking the two sharp turns to make the mouth of the HAI there is very grave risk of being carried by the stream broadside on to the bank. I did not attempt to find a round this channel. Although dark a single sniper apparently heard us and fired a few shots in our direction near the RUIN: otherwise it was absolutely quiet.

S E C R E T .

General Headquarters,

I. E. F. "D".

6th February, 1917.

My dear *Witts*

     Many thanks for your report received late last night.

     I have been busy with many other things this morning, and so have not had time to answer it before this.

     I shall be glad if you will go on with the soundings of the HAI between the points mentioned.

     The river has gone up 2½-feet during the last 24 hours and this will materially affect the plans which I have in mind. As long as I know the date on which you carry out your reconnaissance I can always add on the extra rise of the river in making calculations later. As regards the portion of the TIGRIS where I want you to take soundings, it is between the mouth of the HAI and, say, N.12. This will be easier possibly in a day or two when we have further developed our positions west of the HAI, and I can let you know further about this when I receive your notes as regards the HAI.

                     yrs sincerely,

                     F. S. Maude

To:

  Captain F. V. B. Witts, M.C.,

     O.C., No.2 Bridging Train.

I went out yesterday afternoon on receipt of your instructions. I had hoped to be able to work by daylight, but found that with the rise in the river level, the banks no longer afforded cover from view to a boat moving about in midstream but that we could be easily seen by an observer either in the liquorice Factory and Bazaar alongside, or from the palm trees N.W. of KUT; so I judged it was desirable to wait till dark. While waiting at P.14.B during our intense bombardment at 6 p.m. a Turkish shell scored a direct hit on my pontoon; luckily we were all under cover at the time and only one half of the pontoon was smashed up. Half a pontoon is awkward and to work with and this subsequently greatly delayed my work, and I did not get back till 1 a.m. this morning. The pontoon was the shell, but I think it probable that it was meant for neighbouring batteries, though several more shells fell within 50ᵡ of the pontoon.

After consulting the local regimental head quarters I eventually got up to a point midway between N 21 B and N 21 d and sounded the channel down to P.10.f. the minimum depth of water found in this reach was 9 feet out about 10 p.m. It follows the channel as shown in T.C. 75 (A) from N 21 B to N 23 a, but between N 23 a and P.10.f. it is a little further towards the centre of the river.

General Headquarters,

I. E. F. "D".

7th February, 1917.

My dear Witts

Many thanks for your letter dated 7th.

I am very sorry to hear of your unpleasant

experience, but pleased that the results were no worse.

I do not want you to run any unnecessary risks in

carrying out the further reconnaissance, and so do not

hurry about it till you are quite satisfied that the

conditions locally render your movements in that area

tolerably safe.

If any doubtful point arises, drop me a line.

Yr sincerely,

F. S. Maude

To:

Captain F. V. B. Witts, M.C.,

No.2 Bridging Train.

APPENDIX VII.

Secret correspondence between General Maude and F.V.B.W.
(18th-21st February 1917) re a possible bridging site at Shumran

MESSAGES, SIGNALS AND FIELD TELEGRAPHS.

Army Form C. 2121. *Modified for India.*

Received	Sent	Prefix	Code	m.	No. of words.
At_____ m.	At_____ m.	Office of Origin and Service Instructions.			
From_____	To_____				
By_____	By_____				Station Call_____ Date_____

No. of Message_____

By telephone

To — 3rd Corps

See instructions on cover.

Sender's Number	Day of month	In reply to number
765	18	G 516/318

AAA	Suitable	site	exists
about	two	hundred	yards
downstream	of	point	mentioned
AAA	Work	on	ramps
and	immediate	approaches	about
average	AAA	Road	marked
out	to	vicinity	but
at	present	very	heavy
going	AAA	from	Q 13
to	N 47a	road	requires
remarking in places	as	some	original
nullah	crossings	are	impassable
AAA	S 13 direct	road to Q 13	runs

From
Place
Time

Through lake for half a mile.

No 2 Bridging Train   2.45 p.m.

May be forwarded as now corrected.   Class of message.

Censor.   Signature of Addressee.

How received.   How sent. *By telephone*

Lal Chand & Sons, Calcutta—No. 19 Army C.—25-9-15—80,000 Pads.

MESSAGES, SIGNALS AND FIELD TELEGRAPHS.

Army Form C. 2121. Modified for India.   No. of Message

Received	Sent	Prefix	Code	m.	No. of words.
At _____ m.	At _____ m.				
From _____	To _____				
By _____	By _____				

Office of Origin and Service Instructions.

SECRET

Station Call _____
Date _____

To
See instructions
on cover.

No 2 Bridging Train

Sender's Number	Day of month	In reply to number
514/318	18	T C. 62 (R)

AAA   Please report early today whether M34 is suitable as site for Bridge aaa please reconnoitre without attracting as little attention as possible aaa The river bank is held by us up to M39 and thence our line follows NAHR-AL-MASSA G aaa acknowledge and in/mm opportunate earliest hour report way to expected today

From
Place   3 Corps
Time   6-22 a.m.

May be forwarded as now corrected.
Censor. _____   Signature of Addressor. _____   Class of message. _____

How received. _____   By special DRLS.   How sent. _____

Lal Chand & Sons, Calcutta—No. 19 Army C.—5-1-16—80,000 Pads.

MESSAGES, SIGNALS AND FIELD TELEGRAPHS.

Army Form C. 2121. *Modified for India.*

No. of Message _____

Received	Sent	Prefix	Code	m.	No. of words.
At_____ m.	At_____ m.	Office of Origin and Service Instructions.			
From_____	To_____				
By_____	By			Station Call_____ / Date_____	

To — *See instructions on cover.* : 3rd Corps

Sender's Number	Day of month	In reply to number
774 W	21	

AAA | Reconnaissance report | AAA
Road to bridge site in good
condition and well marked AAA
Position of bridge fixed as reported
in my 765 of 18th AAA With present
river level very little work on ramps
AAA Arrangements for Launching
Motor boats decided on and may be
successful AAA River running very strong
making bridge work slow and ~~unreliable~~
AAA Turks heard talking on bank
opposite . By telephone

From — **Place** — **Time** : No 2 Bridging Train

8.30 a.m.

May be forwarded as now corrected.
Censor. _____ Signature of Addressor _____

Class of message

How received. _____ How sent. _____

Lal Chand & Sons, Calcutta—No. 19 Army C.—25-9-15—80,000 Pads.

APPENDIX VIII.

Congratulatory telegrams from Generals Marshall and Maude
on the successful crossing at Shumran

"C" Form (Original).
Army Form C. 2123.

MESSAGES AND SIGNALS.

No. of Message

Prefix M	Code 345	Words 5	Received	Sent, or sent out	Office Stamp.
		£ s. d.	From CCO	At m.	
Charges to collect		By		To	
Service Instructions.				By	

Handed in at **CCO** Office **9 42** m. Received **9.57** m.

TO No 2 Bridging Train

*Sender's Number	Day of Month	In reply to Number	**A A A**
Ms 35	23rd		

Following wire from General Maude
to General Marshall begins
Tell Your Corps how much
I admire + thank them
for their splendid work today
aaa to cross River in
flood in face of Enemy
in position is feat to
be really proud of ends

FROM 3rd Corps

PLACE & TIME 9.40 pm

* This line should be erased if not required.
(B 5004) Wt. w. 12550—4108 37,500 Pads 12/15 H & S Forms/C.2123.

APPENDIX IX.

Letter from C. E. Williams, Headmaster of Summerfields School,
to Mrs Witts, dated March 11th 1917

Telegrams,
Summertown.

SUMMER FIELDS,
NEAR OXFORD.
March 11:

Dear Mrs. Witts,

It was touching that you should remember us & Fred's old School in your pride at his performance. –

It was splendid, and we are delighted to have his name to add to our War distinctions – which are growing in number, as alas! are the names of those we shall never see again in this world. I am sending you on our Summer Magazine in case you have time to look at it : you will see many of your boy's friends mentioned there. Frank, too, must have remembered his ancient teaching! I did not realize that their father had been taken from you, and I regard with a kind of jealousy those who "passed on" before they knew about this awful war – Both we & the Alingtons have lost a son in France but, though we mourn for them, we do not regret that they gave their lives bravely for King & Righteousness : we are looking forward to joining them again soon.

With our kindest & sincere regards,

I am yours most truly

C. E. Williams

APPENDIX X.

Letter from Christine Farley to Mrs Witts, dated April 20th 1917

6, Alkirstone Terr:

Glos: R^d. S.W.7.

20. 4. 17

Dear Mrs. Witts

On my return from Falmouth this evening I found a letter from my husband dated Feb: 29th & am so delighted to hear your son has the honour of having made THE bridge that led the way to the whole advance 8mls. above Kut. He says he is still in the forefront hustling the Turk so I feel that perhaps you may not have heard from him – my husband & the Company were far behind at the tale-end. Kut was filthy & picked clean & he says should be burnt before it becomes a plague pit –

I hope you have had some news – anyhow it's a grand honour you have to comfort you meanwhile & something to be very proud of.

Yrs. v. sincerely

H. Chistine Farley

APPENDIX XI.

Letter from Cynthia Graham to Mrs Witts, dated Sept 11th 1917

Longtown 3.

NETHERBY,

CUMBERLAND.

Sept: 11, 1917.

My dear Mrs. Witts,

This is but a word, to tell you the gladness I felt, to know of all your younger son's splendid work and manifold decorations! How more than proud you must be of him; and of our special "Twitts", whose new post seems to be so good a one, and likely to lead him far. I am so very glad he has now found congenial and worthy work, to his mind attuned.

Hoping you are keeping well, in spite of your many anxieties, and that you let pride outweigh the less good things of the moment,

Yours sincerely

Cynthia Graham

Please don't answer – & forgive type, used to save neuritis arm

APPENDIX XII.

The Times, Monday, Sept. 15ᵗʰ 1919; pg. 9; Issue 42205; col B

A LITTLE WAR IN KURDISTAN.

HARDSHIPS OF BRITISH TROOPS.
(FROM OUR CORRESPONDENT IN THE MIDDLE EAST.)

BAGHDAD, SEPT. 10 (delayed).

I have returned from Kurdistan, having visited Mosul, Zakko, Erbil, and the Rowanduz neighbourhood.

Since the fighting on August 22 at Bermuna, north-east of Zakko on the Khabur river, and 75 miles north-west of Mosul, the Kurds have offered practically no resistance. Our two columns operating from the neighbourhood of Zakko and Amadia converged, met on August 31, and occupied Shankhanakale, a Kurdish natural fortress near Bermuna, only to find it abandoned. The columns have now returned to their former areas.

I accompanied a bombing raid on the unfriendly village of Garawan, south of Rowanduz, on September 6. One aeroplane which had to make a forced landing crashed, but the occupants were unhurt. The R.E. 8 are the only aeroplanes employed, and very few of these are available. This is a great handicap, as the aeroplane has proved invaluable in these operations.

The country is extraordinarily difficult both for infantry and airmen, the villages being tucked away in narrow ravines or on the lower slopes of barren crags. The troops have undergone immense hardships in the blinding August heat. The operations, which were punitive measures for the murder of political British officers at Zakko in April and at Amadia in July, now appear to be drawing to a close.

APPENDIX XIII.

The Times, Friday, Jul 23, 1920; pg. 15; Issue 42470; col F

ARAB RIGHTS.

OUR POLICY IN MESOPOTAMIA

COLONEL LAWRENCE'S VIEWS.
TO THE EDITOR OF THE TIMES.

Sir,- In this week's debate in the Commons on the Middle East a veteran of the House expressed surprise that the Arabs of Mesopotamia were in arms against us despite our well-meant mandate. His surprise has been echoed here and there in the Press, and it seems to me based on such a misconception of the new Asia and the history of the last five years, that I would like to trespass at length on your space and give my interpretation of the situation.

The Arabs rebelled against the Turks during the war not because the Turk Government was notably bad, but because they wanted independence. They did not risk their lives in battle to change masters, to become British subjects or French citizens, but to win a show of their own.

Whether they are fit for independence or not remains to be tried. Merit is no qualification for freedom. Bulgars, Afghans, and Tahitans have it. Freedom is enjoyed when you are so well armed, or so turbulent, or inhabit a country so thorny that the expense of your neighbour's occupying you is greater than the profit. Feisal's Government in Syria has been completely independent for two years, and has maintained public security and public services in its area.

Mesopotamia has had less opportunity to prove its armament. It never fought the Turks, and only fought perfunctorily against us. Accordingly, we had to set up a war-time administration there. We had no choice; but that was two years ago, and we have not yet changed to peace conditions. Indeed, there are yet no signs of change. "Large reinforcements," according to the official statement, are now being sent there, and our garrison will run into six figures next month. The expense curve will go up to 50 million pounds for this financial year, and yet greater efforts will be called for from us as the Mesopotamian desire for independence grows.

It is not astonishing that their patience has been broken down after two years. The Government we have set up is English in fashion, and is conducted in the English language. So it has 450 British executive officers running it, and not a single responsible Mesopotamian. In Turkish days 70 per cent. of the executive civil service was local. Our 80,000 troops there are occupied in police duties, not in guarding the frontiers. They are holding down the people. In Turkish days the two army corps in Mesopotamia were 60 per cent. Arab in officers, 95 per cent. in other ranks. This deprivation of the privilege of sharing the defence and administration of the country is galling to the educated Mesopotamians. It is true we have increased prosperity – but who cares for that when liberty is in the other scale? They waited and welcomed the news of our mandate, because they thought it meant Dominion self-government for themselves. They are now losing hope in our good intentions.

A remedy? I can see a cure only in immediate change of policy. The whole logic of the present thing looks wrong. Why should Englishmen (or Indians) have to be killed to make the Arab Government in Mesopotamia, which is the considered intention of his Majesty's Government? I agree with the intention, but I would make the Arabs do the work. They can. My little experience in helping to set up Feisal showed me that the art of government wants more character than brains.

I would make Arabic the Government language. This would impose a reduction of the British staff, and a return to employment of the qualified Arabs. I would raise two divisions of local volunteer troops, all Arabs, from the senior divisional general to the junior private (Trained officers and trained N.C.O.'s exist in thousands.) I would entrust these new units with the maintenance of order, and I would cause to leave the country every single British soldier, every single Indian soldier. These changes would take 12 months, and we should then hold of Mesopotamia exactly as much (or as little) as we hold of South Africa or Canada. I believe the Arabs in these conditions would be as loyal as anyone in the Empire, and they would not cost us a cent.

I shall be told that the idea of brown Dominions in the British Empire is grotesque. Yet the Montagu scheme and the Milner scheme are approaches to it, and the only alternative seems to be conquest, which the ordinary Englishman does not want, and cannot afford.

Of course, there is oil in Mesopotamia, but we are no nearer that while the Middle East remains at war, and I think if it is so necessary for us, it could be made the subject of a bargain. The Arabs seem willing to shed their blood for freedom; how much more their oil!

T. E. LAWRENCE.

All Souls College, July 22.

APPENDIX XIV.

Telegram sent from F.V.B.W. in Hillah on the topic of Arabs
(23rd August 1920), and his mother's reply (25th August 1920)

APPENDIX XV.

The Times, Thursday, Jul 15, 1920; pg. 17; Issue 42463; col E

BOOKS OF THE WEEK.

MAUDE OF BAGHDAD.

The career and personality of the distinguished soldier who redeemed the name of British arms in Mesopotamia are set out fully and sympathetically by Major-General Sir C. E. Callwell in his "Life of Lieutenant-General Sir Stanley Maude, K.C.B." (Constable, 21s. net). It is a fine story of public service well and faithfully done, but it provokes rather sad and ironical reflections on the perverseness of human affairs. Amiable and modest in disposition, beloved by all who knew him, conscientious to a fault, widely recognized as a soldier of exceptional capacity and insight, Maude's advance in his profession was slow. Again and again circumstances conspired to deprive him of the rewards that his services had earned. One adverse in the earlier part of his career, a heavy financial loss, restricted his choice of employment. Thus in the last phase of the South African War, during which he served as brigade-major of the Guards, he was constrained to forgo his prospect of rapid promotion under Lord Kitchener and to go to Ottawa as military secretary to Lord Minto.

At the outbreak of the European War Maude was 50 years of age, and had only attained the rank of colonel. But in the great emergency his qualities were bound to assert themselves. He went to France as a General Staff Officer. By the end of October, 1914, he was appointed to a brigade command. Eight months later he became a divisional commander in the Dardanelles. His next move was as Commander of the 13th Division in Mesopotamia, and within seven months he took over command of the Army in Mesopotamia from Sir P. Lake. In view of what came to pass, it is curious to read that one of the reasons for Maude's selection was that "he was known to possess a strong constitution, and he never seemed to be sick or sorry." From this point General Callwell traces in detail the history of Maude's victorious campaign, culminating in the triumph of Baghdad. How Maude's unlucky fate, which seemed at last to have been conquered, asserted itself for its last malign effort is a matter of history. It may be mentioned that the wild rumours that Maude died of poison are definitely disposed of by Colonel Willcox's report of the course of the illness. The clinical diagnosis of cholera was confirmed by the bacteriological examination, which disclosed a most virulent infection.

APPENDIX XVI.

The Times, Tuesday, Nov 16, 1920; pg. 11; Issue 42569; col C

ARAB BAYONET CHARGE.

------

200 ROUTED BY SIKHS.

The following communiqué was issued by the War Office yesterday:-

LOWER EUPHRATES.- The 34th Brigade Column, advancing from Samawah northwards, seized the bridge over the Euphrates at Imam Abdulla on the 11th and repaired the railway up to the bridge. Insurgent bands ensconced in nullahs on the north bank offered considerable resistance; 200 of them attempted a counter-attack with fixed bayonets to recover their positions. The 3/23rd Sikhs made a counter-charge, defeated them, and drove them off the field. Our casualties amounted to between 40 and 50 men; the insurgents lost more heavily. Our aeroplanes rendered valuable assistance in the operations, and our machine-guns also did excellent work. On the 12th the advance was continued, little resistance being met with. Blockhouses have been constructed as far as Imam Abdulla. Sniping continues against our blockhouses on the Ur-Samawah railway near the latter town, and an attack on the 12th was beaten off by our fire.

APPENDIX XVII.

UPPER SLAUGHTER CHURCH
CHAPEL WINDOWS
See Illustrations 20 & 21 in the Colour Section

1. The stained-glass windows in the chapel were installed in August 1995 in memory of Major-General and Mrs F.V.B. Witts. They were designed by Thomas Denny, who was given two themes:- (i) the 23rd psalm and (ii) the view from the Manor, Upper Slaughter (where General Witts lived when young) to Wyck Hill (where Mrs Witts lived at the time she met her husband).

2. * The small trefoil window (above the F.E. Witts tomb) is about "The valley of the shadow of death". A figure is beginning to move across a bridge, or causeway – - shadowy rocks loom over him (with menacing shapes discernible in the rocks); and ahead of him appears a veil of anxiety through which he must pass; a distant glimpse of green landscape encourages him. ("Yea, though I walk through the valley of the shadow of death, I will fear no evil: for thou art with me; thy rod and thy staff they comfort me")

3. The main windows comprise Thomas Denny's interpretation of the view from Upper Slaughter to Wyck Hill, a landscape that, it is felt, embodies the theme of spiritual comfort and renewal expressed in the psalm. In the foreground the lake below the Manor (now the Lords of the Manor Hotel) can be seen and at the top Wyck Hill. Just above the lake on the right a shepherd leads his sheep beside the still waters. ("He maketh me to lie down in green pastures")

The central part of the left-hand light comprises various trees seen in the view, an ash, a lime, an oak and a beech, which could also suggest an Eden-like landscape where "the Lord God made to grow every tree that is pleasant to the sight".

The central part of the right hand light includes elements of a Cotswold scene – leaves, stones, lichen, old man's beard on old thorns, and ant-hills in rough grass, all seen at close quarters.

The small triangular window draws together cloud shapes at the top of the two lights.

4. The design can, perhaps, be enjoyed initially as rhythms of colour and light. Within this abstract aspect of the windows the viewer can, increasingly, discern elements of the theme and of the landscape.

* There is a 1st World-War village link in the trefoil. In February 1917 Captain Witts R. E. constructed a floating bridge over the river Tigris in Mesopotamia at the Shumran Bend. George Collett, from a very old Upper Slaughter family, was one of the first to cross the bridge with the Gloucestershire Regiment. For both of them it was a dark time of war, but with happier times ahead.

APPENDIX XVIII.

Letter from General Sir Clarence ('Chiriya') Bird to Mrs F.V.B.Witts re statue of the 'Winged Figure of Victory', commemorating the crossing of the Tigris at Shumran on February 23rd 1917.
See Illustration 19 in the Colour Section

See Illustration 19 in the Colour Section

Polesden Lacey
19th July 1982

My dear Alice,

Ever so many thanks for your very kind letter of July 14th. I am delighted to know that I was able to be helpful. – As a corollary I send you the following note in case it may be new to you. –

The Officers' Mess at Roorkee was an R.E. Mess as distinct from a Bengal S & M Mess, (i.e. not an Indian Army unit Mess); and it included in its membership R.E. Officers additional to those serving with the Bengal S & M. – The distinction is relevant to what follows. –

After "World War One" the Bengal Sappers wanted to present a commemorative piece of plate to the R.E. Mess. – By an extraordinary piece of good fortune Percy Hobart (Bengal Sapper and later Royal Tank Corps & Major General) heard from our Military Attaché in Italy, that a fine statue of the "Winged Figure of Victory" (which the Italians had intended to present to the American President but decided not to because they resented his shabby treatment of them in the drawing-up of the Peace Treaty) was going begging, and immediately asked the M.A. to buy it in, which fortunately he was able to do. – The Bengal Sappers then had silver plaques added round the plinth, illustrating several distinguished episodes, of which one was Freddie's bridge at the Shumran Bend. The statue, a beautiful piece of work was duly presented to the R.E. Mess Roorkee.

When partition of India took place as between India & Pakistan, Auchinleck gave strict orders about the distribution or retention of mess trophies. – So, initially the trophy remained with the Roorkee sappers; but as the Mess was an R.E. Mess, they were permitted as a gesture to hand over the trophy to the "R.E. Officers" in accordance with the situation I described above, and was duly presented to the R.E.H.Q. Mess at Chatham where it now is (since 1947).

By kind permission of the Chatham Mess Committee, we "Bengal S & M. Officers' Assoc." were allowed to bring the trophy to London for our annual dinner at the "Rag" (A & N. club) and Ernabel Sandeman was permitted to bring it up by car, on his way to London, and take it back and deliver it safely at Chatham on his way home. – Quite a ceremony –

On the occasion of my last attendance, as Chairman, and with Freddie sitting on my right, the trophy was placed opposite his place at dinner, with Shumran plaque facing him, a gesture which I know he greatly appreciated. – Soon after that the London dinners ceased, and have as you know been replaced by the annual lunch reunion at Minley. –
I am sure you will be glad to be reminded of this permanent memorial to Freddie in the Chatham Mess – Forgive this long scrawl. –

Affectionately "Chiriya"

APPENDIX XIX.

The Witts Family Pedigree

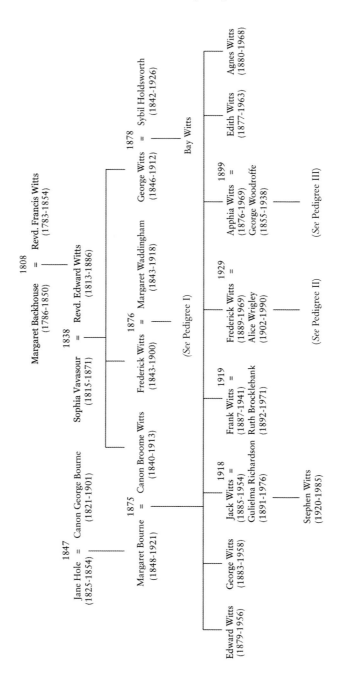

Pedigree I

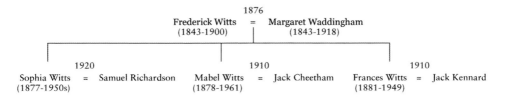

```
                              1876
              Frederick Witts    =    Margaret Waddingham
                (1843-1900)             (1843-1918)
      ┌───────────────────────────────┼───────────────────────────────┐
          1920                      1910                      1910
Sophia Witts = Samuel Richardson  Mabel Witts = Jack Cheetham  Frances Witts = Jack Kennard
(1877-1950s)                      (1878-1961)                  (1881-1949)
```

Pedigree II

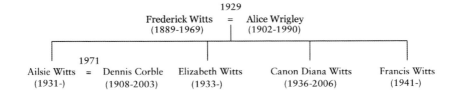

```
                              1929
              Frederick Witts    =    Alice Wrigley
                (1889-1969)             (1902-1990)
      ┌──────────────────────┬─────────┼──────────────────┬──────────────┐
          1971
Ailsie Witts = Dennis Corble  Elizabeth Witts    Canon Diana Witts    Francis Witts
(1931-)        (1908-2003)    (1933-)            (1936-2006)          (1941-)
```

Pedigree III

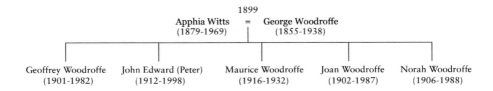

```
                              1899
              Apphia Witts    =    George Woodroffe
                (1879-1969)          (1855-1938)
      ┌──────────────┬──────────────┼──────────────┬──────────────┐
Geoffrey Woodroffe  John Edward (Peter)  Maurice Woodroffe  Joan Woodroffe  Norah Woodroffe
(1901-1982)         (1912-1998)          (1916-1932)        (1902-1987)     (1906-1988)
```

BIBLIOGRAPHY

Alexander, Major D. & Cooper, General Sir G., *The Bengal Sappers and Miners, 1803-2003* (Chatham: The Institution of Royal Engineers, 2003)

Anglesey, Marquess of, *A History of the British Cavalry 1816-1919, Volume 6: 1916-1918 Mesopotamia* (London: Leo Cooper, 1995)

Anonymous, *With a Highland Regiment in Mesopotamia* (Bombay: The Times Press, 1918)

Antonius, G., *The Arab Awakening* (Philadelphia: J. B. Lippencott, 1939)

Barker, A. J., *The Neglected War: Mesopotamia 1914-1918* (London: Faber & Faber, 1967)

Bidwell, R., *Dictionary of Modern Arab History* (London & New York: Keegan Paul, 1998)

Black Tab, *On the Road to Kut: A Soldier's Story of the Campaign in Mesopotamia* (London: Hutchinson, 1917)

Blackledge, W. J., *The Legion of Marching Madmen* (London: Sampson Low)

Burnell, A. & Yule, H., *Hobson-Jobson: The Anglo Indian Dictionary* (Ware: Wordsworth, 1996)

Callwell, Maj-Gen Sir C. E., *Life of Sir Stanley Maude* (London: Constable, 1920)

Candler, E., *The Long Road to Baghdad*, 2 vols (London: Cassell & Co., 1919)

Catherwood, C., *Winston's Folly: Imperialism and the Creation of Modern Iraq* (London: Constable, 2004)

Coogan, M., *The Oxford History of the Biblical World* (Oxford: University Press, 1998)

Corrigan, G., *Sepoys in the Trenches: The Indian Corps on the Western Front 1914-15* (Stroud: Spellmount, 2006)

Dane, E., *British Campaigns in the Near East 1914-1918* (London: Hodder & Stoughton, 1918)

Evans, Major R., *A Brief Outline of the Campaign in Mesopotamia 1914-1918* (London: Sifton Praed, 1926)

Fieldhouse, D. K., *Kurds, Arabs and Britons: The Memoir of Wallace Lyon in Iraq 1918-1944* (London: I.B.Taurus, 2002)

Fieldhouse, D. K., *Western Imperialism in the Middle East 1914-1958* (Oxford: University Press, 2006)

Fisk, R., *The Great War for Civilisation: The Conquest of the Middle East* (London: Fourth Estate, 2005)

Gilbert, M., *First World War* (London: Harper Collins, 1995)

Guyer, S., *My Journey Down the Tigris* (London: Fisher Unwin, 1925)

Haldane, Lt.-Gen Sir A., *The Insurrection in Mesopotamia, 1920* (London & Edinburgh: William Blackwood, 1922)

Hay, W., *Two Years in Kurdistan* (London: Sidgwick & Jackson, 1921)

Jackson, W., *The Pomp of Yesterday: The Defence of India and the Suez Canal 1798-1918* (London: Brassey's, 1995)

Kipling, R., *The Irish Guards in the Great War* (Staplehurst: Spellmount, 1997)

Kirk, G., *A Short History of the Middle East from the Rise of Islam to Modern Times* (London: Methuen, 1948)

Loch Mowat, C., *Britain Between the Wars 1918 – 1940* (Oxford University Press, 1955)

Loder, J. de V., *The Truth about Mesopotamia, Palestine & Syria* (London: George Allen & Unwin, 1923)

Longrigg, S., *Iraq, 1900 to 1950* (Oxford University Press, 1953)

Lyell, T., *The Ins and Outs of Mesopotamia* (London: A. M. Philpot, 1923)

McDowall, D., *A Modern History of the Kurds* (London: I.B.Tauris, 1996)

Polk, W., *Understanding Iraq* (London: I.B.Tauris, 2006)

Pope, S. & Wheal, E-A., *Dictionary of the First World War* (Barnsely: Pen & Sword, 2003)

Punch, *History of the Great War* (Stroud: Nonsuch, 2007)

Richards, D. S., *The Savage Frontier: A History of the Anglo-Afghan Wars* (London: Pan Books, 2003)

Sandes, Lt.-Col. E., *The Indian Sappers and Miners* (Chatham: Institution of Royal Engineers, 1948)

Sherson, E., *Townsend of Chitral and Kut* (London: Heinemann, 1928)

Tennant, Lt.-Col. J. E., *In the Clouds Above Baghdad* (London: Cecil Palmer, 1920)

Thesiger, W., *The Marsh Arabs* (London, Penguin, 1967)

Townshend, Maj.-Gen. Sir C., *My Campaign in Mesopotamia* (London: Thornton Butterworth, 1920)

Vowles, A., *Wanderings with a Camera in Mesopotamia* (London: Simpkin, Marshall, Hamilton, Kent & Co., 1920)

Wilcox, R., *Battles on the Tigris: The Mesopotamian Campaign of the First World War* (Barnsley: Pen & Sword, 2006)

Wilson, Lt.-Col. Sir A. T., *Loyalties 1914-1917* (Oxford: University Press, 1930)

Wilson, Lt.-Col. Sir A. T., *A Clash of Loyalties 1917-1920* (Oxford: University Press, 1931)

Winstone, H., *Gertrude Bell* (New York: Quartet Books, 1978)

Winstone, H., *Leachman: O.C. Desert* (New York: Quartet Books, 1982)

OFFICIAL PUBLICATIONS:

Moberly, Brig.-Gen. F. J., *The Mesopotamia Campaign 1914 – 1918*, 4 vols (London: H.M.'s Stationary Office, 1923-27)

Moberly, Brig.-Gen. F. J., *Operations in Persia 1914-1918* (London: H.M.'s Stationary Office, 1987)

Naval Intelligence Division, *Geographical Handbook: Syria* (Oxford: University Press, 1943)

Naval Intelligence Division, *Geographical Handbook: Iraq and the Persian Gulf* (Oxford: University Press, 1944)

JOURNALS:

Cohen, S., "Mesopotamia in British Strategy, 1903-1914", *International Journal of Middle Eastern Studies*, IX (1978), pp. 171-181

Rothwell, V. H., "Mesopotamia in British War Aims, 1914-1918", *The Historical Journal*, XIII (1970), pp. 273-294

Witts, F.V.B., "Light Floating Bridges in Mesopotamia", *The Royal Engineers Journal*, XXXVII (1923), pp. 627-639 [Re-printed in full in Appendix I]

Witts, F.V.B., "The Passage of the Tigris at Shumran, 23rd February 1917", *Journal of the Royal United Services Institution*, LXVIII, (1923), pp. 447-455 [Re-printed in full in Appendix II]

WEBSITES:

www.biship.com

www.merchantnavyofficers.com

www.theshiplist.com

The Times Digital Archive @ www.gloucestershire.gov.uk/libraries/vrl

INDEX